The Welsh Methodist Society

The Welsh Methodist Society
The Early Societies in South-west Wales 1737–1750

Eryn M. White

University of Wales Press
2020

© Eryn M. White, 2020

All rights reserved. No part of this book may be reproduced in any material form (including photocopying or storing it in any medium by electronic means and whether or not transiently or incidentally to some other use of this publication) without the written permission of the copyright owner except in accordance with the provisions of the Copyright, Designs and Patents Act 1988. Applications for the copyright owner's written permission to reproduce any part of this publication should be addressed to The University of Wales Press, University Registry, King Edward VII Avenue, Cardiff CF10 3NS
www.uwp.co.uk

British Library Cataloguing-in-Publication Data
A catalogue record for this book is available from the British Library.

ISBN   978-1-78683-579-6
e-ISBN   978-1-78683-580-2

The right of Eryn M. White to be identified as author of this work has been asserted by her in accordance with sections 77 and 79 of the Copyright, Designs and Patents Act 1988.

Typeset by Owain Hammonds, Ceredigion
Printed by CPI Antony Rowe, Melksham

Contents

List of illustrations	vii
Introduction	1
Chapter 1: 'No part of the Nation more inclin'd to be Religious'? The Religious Context	21
Chapter 2: 'The Young Striplings': Leaders and Exhorters	63
Chapter 3: 'The Lord's Peculiar Dwelling Place': The Location of the Societies	113
Chapter 4: 'The Great Shepherd's Little Flock': The Membership of the Societies	143
Chapter 5: 'Iron Sharpens Iron': The Appeal of the Societies	181
Chapter 6: 'The World, the Flesh and the Devil': Order and Discipline	225
Chapter 7: 'This Furnace of Affliction': Trials and Tribulations	265
Conclusion	303
Appendix: List of societies	309
Bibliography	313
Index	335

List of illustrations

1 A sketch drawn by Howel Harris to illustrate his 'Rounds', 13 April 1745
   (The National Library of Wales, Aberystwyth; Trevecca College/1 3189).   4
2 William John's report to the Association, 7 January 1747 (The National Library of Wales,
   Aberystwyth; Trevecca College/1 3037).   80
3 William Richard's report to the Association, May-August 1748 (The National Library of
   Wales, Aberystwyth; Trevecca College/1 3055).   205
4 William Williams's report to the Association, 14 October 1747 (The National Library of
   Wales, Aberystwyth; Trevecca College/1 3046).   279

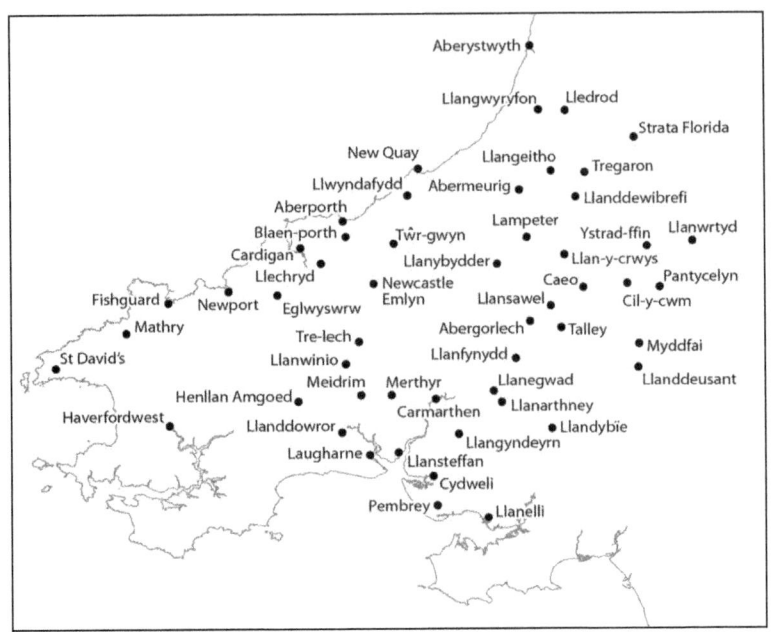

South-west Wales

Introduction

The year 1737 saw the founding of the first permanent Methodist *seiat* in Wales, an institution which became intrinsically important in Welsh history and culture. *Seiat* was a word derived from the English 'society', but developed in Welsh exclusively in a religious context and very specifically for the Methodist fellowship meeting, sometimes referred to as *seiat brofiad*, an experience meeting. Although the Welsh word for 'society', *cymdeithas*, was used on some occasions, it was the word *seiat* which came to be adopted within the movement and beyond as the specific term for this particular type of meeting. The *seiat* developed as an institution in order to meet the needs of its members and could easily be adapted as circumstances demanded. Since it required no consecrated building and was not fixed to any precise spot, it could be held in whatever venue was available and could move as suited its members. All that was needed to begin with was two or three converts who chose to meet regularly. The flexible nature of the society meant that it was ideally suited to cater for the scattered rural communities of south-west Wales. By 1750, over 400 had been established throughout Wales, a substantial proportion of them within the three counties of the south-west, an area which was home to several of the early leaders of Methodism, and in convenient proximity to Howel Harris's base in Breconshire. One of the reasons for focusing specifically on this region is that it was identified at the time as the main centre of the revival, referred to by Harris as 'the Lord's Peculiar Dwelling Place'.[1]

A good proportion of this 'Peculiar Dwelling Place' in the three counties of south-west Wales – Cardiganshire, Carmarthenshire and Pembrokeshire – comprises coastal lowland. As David J. V. Jones has pointed out, 'contrary to first impressions', much of the land is under 1,000 feet,[2] although the Pumlumon mountains in north Cardiganshire and the Black Mountain to the east form natural barriers. The rivers Teifi and Tywi, as well as the Cleddau in Pembrokeshire, fed fertile valleys and led to coastal ports. Several of these ports were centres for imports and exports, including the busy herring trade in south Cardiganshire, with Cardigan, Aberporth and Penbryn exporting herring mainly to Ireland.[3] A number of farmers along the coast became involved in some way with the sea trade, including owning shares in vessels, yet agriculture was the main source of livelihood for most of the inhabitants of the area, with many tenant farmers working small holdings of land.[4] Cardiganshire was jokingly referred to as 'the devil's grandmother's jointure' in the early modern period because of its poverty, but areas of Carmarthenshire were more agriculturally fertile and wealthy.[5] Despite economic hardship and crises of mortality in the first decades of the century, the area seems to have witnessed a steady growth in population from around the mid-1740s onwards, coinciding to some degree with the early impact of Methodism.[6] Population figures prior to the first census in 1801 are based on estimates which may not be wholly accurate, but suggest that at the start of the eighteenth century Cardiganshire had a population of around 27,000, Carmarthenshire 42,000 and Pembrokeshire 29,000.[7] The evangelical revival emerged in a Wales which had not yet experienced large-scale industrialisation. The south-west would escape many of the direct effects of that industrialisation when it developed, but that is not to say that the area was utterly without trace of industry in the mid-eighteenth century, since pockets of lead, copper and coal mining were to be found. Despite this, it was an overwhelmingly agricultural society, which fits the pattern of Methodist growth in a rural area with dispersed population where the traditional parishes of the Church of England increasingly strained to cope with a growing population.[8]

This is the area which would become known as 'Rebecca's Country', centre of resistance to state and church during the Rebecca Riots in the mid-nineteenth century. It was a region much of which was not always the most productive agricultural land, which mostly did not develop large-scale industry and was largely not well served by communication networks. The south-west was overwhelmingly Welsh-speaking in the mid-eighteenth century, save for a greater degree of anglicisation in the market towns and the long-established Englishry of south Pembrokeshire, where the landsker cut a stark boundary between Welsh- and English-speaking communities.[9] Travellers from outside the area were not always greatly impressed with a landscape that mainly lacked the rugged mountains which increasingly attracted admirers of the sublime but at the same time had all the frustrations of travel over poorly maintained roads. However, the region did benefit from a rustic rural charm which could be seen as natural and unspoilt.[10] Despite the disadvantages, the south-western counties contained within the sprawling diocese of St Davids proved to be of crucial importance for some of the key educational and religious developments of the eighteenth century.

One of those developments was the evangelical revival, the history of which in Wales is closely associated with the three main early leaders: Daniel Rowland, Howel Harris and William Williams. Their contribution has traditionally been compartmentalised, with Rowland regarded as the inspired preacher, Harris as the capable organiser and Williams as the gifted hymnwriter. Although there is considerable truth in this depiction of their predominant talents, they each made a broader contribution to the development of the movement. These three are hailed as the founding fathers of Calvinistic Methodism in Wales, but others such as Howel Davies and Peter Williams also played important supporting roles, especially in the south-west. There was thus a group of leaders who discussed the progress of the movement and also consulted with those of like mind across the border. In the initial heady days of revival, there seemed to be an eagerness to share experiences and pool resources, which later cooled as doctrinal differences overcame the urge to cooperate. One of the major differences in outcome of the Welsh and English revivals was the relative strength of Arminian and Calvinistic Methodism, with the Arminian Methodism associated with the Wesleys proving slow to gain ground in Wales. Since Calvinism was quickly adopted as the theological stance in Wales, it was George Whitefield who was the main ally in England. He was appointed official moderator of the Welsh Association and Harris helped maintain his Tabernacle in London while he was away in America. There was a close degree of cooperation, therefore, as there was with the Countess of Huntingdon's Connexion, also a Calvinistic branch of Methodism. Harris was the major contact with those other evangelical groups, maintaining links with the Wesleys and the Moravians as well as with the Calvinist wing of English-speaking Methodism. However, Welsh Methodism was not an offshoot of the English movement, but one of several streams of the evangelical revival which had emerged around the same time. One principle that united all of the Methodist groups in Wales and England was the commitment to remaining within the Church of England unless forced to leave. The

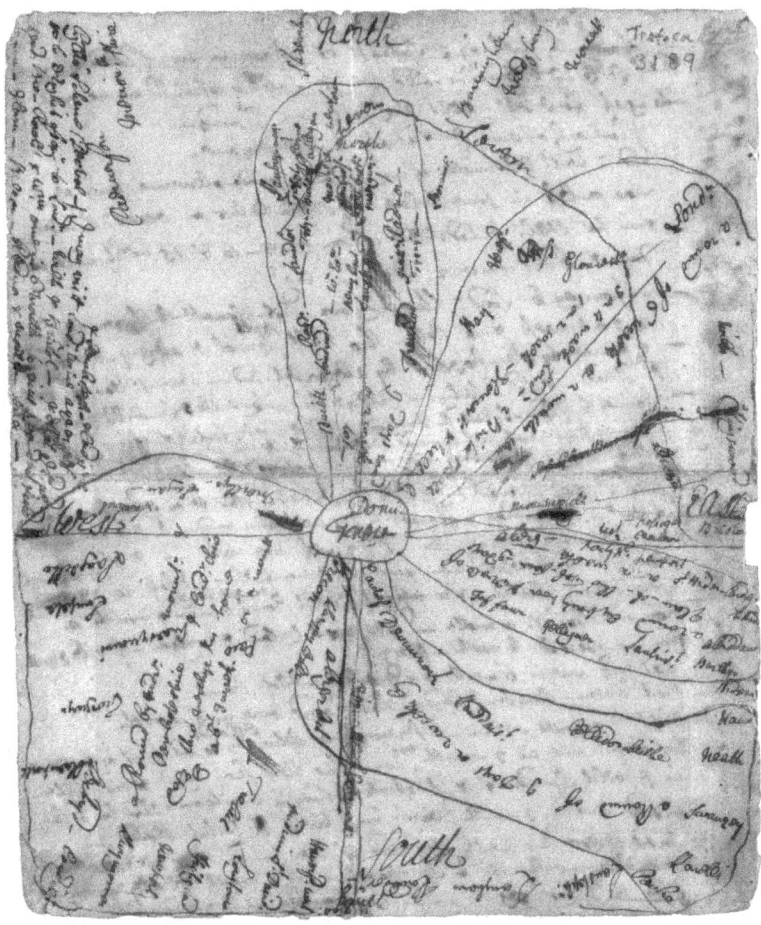

A sketch drawn by Howel Harris to illustrate his 'Rounds', 13 April 1745 (Trevecca College/1 3189).

Welsh Methodists were not forced to leave, but eventually chose to do so, forming the Calvinistic Methodist Church of Wales in 1811 and adopting the name 'Presbyterian Church of Wales' in the twentieth century. Another outcome of the movement which is sometimes overlooked was an evangelical element which remained within the Anglican Church when the majority of Methodists departed.

This study concentrates on the early Methodist societies set up during the 1740s in south-west Wales. The main focus is the county of Carmarthenshire, but the movement itself did not necessarily think and plan in terms of county boundaries. As Howel Harris's map of his 'rounds' reveals, the landscape was viewed according to where the centres of Methodist activity lay.[11] The key geographical units for the purpose of this study are really the superintendencies set up to oversee groups of societies, which often crossed over county borders. William Richard, for instance had the care of the societies in south Cardiganshire and north Pembrokeshire, as well as a few societies in nearby Carmarthenshire. The Cardiganshire societies developed as two distinct groups: one in the Llangeitho/Tregaron area under the influence of Daniel Rowland and the other along the coastline around New Quay and Aberporth. Both had close links to Carmarthenshire and Pembrokeshire and form a natural part of this study. The societies in Welsh-speaking north Pembrokeshire had a closer affinity to those of south Cardiganshire and Carmarthenshire than with the English-medium societies to the south. They are therefore included here, but the south Pembrokeshire societies are not, as they were under separate supervision and the records for them are not as full. In essence, the area under consideration fell under the jurisdiction of five men: William John, John Richard, William Richard, James Williams, and William Williams of Pantycelyn. Morgan John Lewis also features since he was responsible for the society of Llanddeusant in east Carmarthenshire.

Sources

The Calvinistic Methodist Archive preserved in the National Library of Wales, Aberystwyth, contains a wealth of sources on the movement from its earliest beginnings. The most essential for the history of the early movement is the Trevecka group of manuscripts, named after Howel Harris's home, where they were kept for many years. For much of the early material, the historian is indebted to the meticulous record-keeping of Harris as the chief administrator in effect of the Methodist Association. Harris preserved large numbers of letters he received, but also ensured the survival of drafts or copies of many of the letters he sent, securing a substantial archive of correspondence to be found in the Trevecka Letters collection.[12] He also maintained the minutes of the Association meetings, along with documents sent to the Association. In addition, he made copious entries in his diary from 1735 onwards, initially in Latin but from the end of 1736 in English, resulting in the 284 volumes listed in the archive.[13] This was in spite of his own doubts in 1739 that writing his thoughts in his diary was not right 'because I have great Delight in it'.[14] Unfortunately, Harris's handwriting is notoriously difficult to read as he wrote a close, cramped hand at best. His handwriting is usually at its worst in his diaries, where the effect is sometimes exacerbated by his occasional predilection for writing in patterns, so that, for instance, an entire page can be written in a diamond shape. From time to time he would quarter the page so as to write each quarter in a different direction, requiring the reader to rotate the diary. He was also prone to abbreviating words and adopting symbols to represent certain individuals, but subsequently using the same symbol for another person entirely. Harris was aware of his shortcomings, having been advised by a number of friends to try to write more clearly. His brother Joseph urged him to 'mend his hand-writing' as early as 1730 and suggested he practise round hand.[15] Complaints about Harris's handwriting would be a constant refrain thereafter. He confessed in one letter in 1742 that he had written so illegibly that he had to have the letter copied before it was sent[16] and at times he obtained the services of a secretary who copied his letters in a more legible hand, so there are a number of letter books in the collection which are rather more readable as a result. Although his diaries are a rich and fascinating source, they were written as introspective accounts of his spiritual condition and therefore do not always supply the basic details which would be immensely useful to historians. Harris usually records his location and activities but frustratingly often fails to name his hosts when he was staying at someone's home. He also often notes conversations and what he is told of the experiences of some members without naming the individuals, which is admirably discreet but, again, not as helpful for researchers. Moreover, despite the fact that he toyed with the notion of publishing his diaries, it cannot be said that they were written with an eye to the reader as the entries are often lengthy and repetitive, as well as difficult to decipher.

Despite these problems, Harris's practice of keeping so much paperwork has proven very useful to historians and his estrangement from the mainstream movement between 1750 and 1763 certainly had a detrimental effect on the preservation of its records, which peter out dramatically during the period of his absence. The records from the 1730s and 1740s were maintained in Harris's home, Trefeca near Talgarth in Breconshire, which served as a college for the Methodist Connexion in south Wales from 1844 after the religious community set up by Harris in the 1750s finally closed.[17] Concern for the safeguarding of the archive grew when the college's external examiner in the late nineteenth century, Sir Owen M. Edwards, spotted the woeful state in which the documents were stored. This prompted the creation of a catalogue, which proved immensely useful to researchers, and a tightening of access to the records, some of which were apparently lent out to some historians to study during the nineteenth century and subsequently lost. The Connexion set up a panel to examine the possibilities of cataloguing, transcribing and publishing the records which resulted in the formation of a History Committee to take responsibility for the archive, which remains the property of the Presbyterian Church of Wales, although deposited in the National Library of Wales at Aberystwyth.[18] From 1934, the National Library has provided a secure home for the Trevecka collection, combined with materials from Bala College, thus bringing together the archives of the two denominational theological colleges, previously located in the north and south of the country.

With the bulk of the sources for the history of eighteenth-century Methodism safely stored in the National Library, it became easier for researchers in the field to study the materials. This was further facilitated by efforts on behalf of the Historical Society of the Presbyterian Church to make some of the archives and their contents more accessible. Dr M. H. Jones spent years on the mammoth task of preparing the inventory of the Trevecka Letters which appeared in 1932 after his death and includes the published letters as well as those in manuscript form.[19]

A total of 2,787 letters in the archive were listed with, where possible, their dates, authors and recipients. This was followed by the *Calendar of the Trevecka Letters* in 2003, which includes items added to the collection since 1932 along with a brief summary of the contents of 3,344 items in total.

The most fundamentally important sources in the archive for a study of the early societies in the south-west are the society reports and the minutes of the Association. Superintendents who usually had oversight of some dozen or so societies were required to send regular reports on their progress to the Association from 1743 onwards. Many of these reports have been preserved, either in the original, often Welsh, document or in the translation provided by Howel Harris for the records. Another reason for concentrating on the south-west is that the material is fuller than for most other regions in Wales, thanks partly to the diligence of the superintendents and possibly also to a degree of happenstance with the survival of the records. In addition, Harris began to undertake preaching tours of the south-west fairly early on in his career in response to requests from the area, which means that his diaries and letters also provide useful snippets of evidence for the existence, location and progress of societies and their members. Sadly, none of the superintendents' own records have been preserved as they would have been likely to provide more detailed accounts of each society and its members than the summaries sent to the Association.

The crucial importance of the Trevecka manuscripts as a source for the history of the movement has inevitably meant a greater focus on Howel Harris and a tendency to view the history from his perspective, with fewer records available to trace the activities of other prominent figures, such as Daniel Rowland. However, there are some additional sources which help shed further light on the early movement. As might be expected, William Williams's published works provide extremely valuable insight into the nature and role of the societies. In addition there are some diaries and autobiographies by individuals who had links to the revival, including Richard Tibbott, an early superintendent of societies in the movement who was later ordained as a minister with the Welsh Independents, and Thomas Morgan, Henllan Amgoed, a student at Carmarthen Academy at the time of the revival. The spiritual autobiography of the Independent minister John Thomas, Rhaeadr, *Rhad Ras*

(Free Grace, 1810) refers back to his early association with the Methodist cause during this period. The diary of John Thomas, a schoolmaster from Tre-main in south Cardiganshire, provides useful insights into the situation in the 1750s but deals with a later period than that studied in this volume. The Methodist movement also published some of its own material, including its first rule book in 1742. A large proportion of the more administrative documents, including the Association records, are in English, but most of the published literature is in Welsh, as are many of the personal records. The better-educated sections of society tended to use English as the language of correspondence, and Howel Harris also used it for the bulk of his diary entries. However, this was a period when the vast majority of Welsh people were familiar only with the Welsh language, so the movement used that language to communicate with most of its followers, even if the Association meetings were held in English to cater for representatives from non-Welsh-speaking parts of Wales and the presence of English Methodists such as George Whitefield. It was also a time when literacy through the medium of Welsh was growing, but access to education in English remained limited. Several letters from the rank-and-file membership to Howel Harris or the Association were written in Welsh as a result, representing some of the earliest examples of correspondence in Welsh from individuals who did not belong to an educated elite. The movement provided them with a network of contacts and also the motivation to make use of their often newly acquired literary skills. Even most of the elite of the movement came from fairly modest backgrounds and represent the archetypal 'pious middling sorts' who would increasingly emerge as Gwyn Alf Williams's 'alternative' leaders of society by the end of the century.[20] Unfortunately, the fact that many key sources are in Welsh has hampered a number of historians from outside Wales, with a broader interest in revival, from including the Welsh experience in their research. There has sometimes been a reliance as a result on a limited number of secondary sources in order to gain an impression of developments in Wales which may not convey the full picture. At the same time, the research undertaken within Wales has not always been completely impartial. The result is that the significance of the revival in a Welsh context has been established, but a number of other questions have been left to a large extent unexplored.

Historiography

It must be said that objectivity has not always been a key element in much of the writing on the Welsh Methodist movement. Until well into the twentieth century most historical accounts of the eighteenth-century revival were written by ministers of the denomination which ultimately grew out of the revival: the Calvinistic Methodist Church of Wales, now primarily known as the Presbyterian Church of Wales. Their interest in tracing their roots is understandable, but their prominence in the historiography has inevitably had consequences. With the Calvinistic Methodists emerging from the 1851 Religious Census as the largest group of worshippers in Wales, the denomination's influential position in Welsh society seemed unassailable. The tendency of their histories was therefore to chronicle and map the growth rather than to analyse it in depth. John Roberts, in his study of the history of Welsh Calvinistic Methodism in 1931, acknowledged that the leaders of the movement would probably not have considered asking how and why it came about, since it would be attributed by them to God's work, which meant that no further inquiry was needed.[21]

Even so, the urge to record the history of the revival began in the 1740s. The leaders and those influenced were attuned to the significance of what they perceived as God's marvellous work in the world. Howel Harris was asked by the Revd William McCulloch, a correspondent from Scotland, to provide an account of the developments in Wales. McCulloch had recorded the spiritual experiences of those affected by the Cambuslang revival, near Glasgow, in 1742[22] and asked Harris to produce similar testimony from the Welsh revival. Harris demurred from preparing an account for publication,[23] although he sketched out his recollections of the beginnings of the movement periodically in his diary, a useful practice for the benefit of later historians. However, the first published historian of the revival was in effect William Williams, Pantycelyn, who did much to define the movement through his published works, both prose and poetry. His first prose work, *Llythyr Martha Philopur* (The Letter of Martha Philopur, 1762) and its sequel, *Atteb Philo-Evangelius* (The Reply of Philo-Evangelius, 1763), described the 1762 revival as the latest example of a cycle of renewal which had continued throughout Christian history and included the Reformation and the first stage of the Methodist revival in the 1730s and 1740s.[24]

According to his interpretation, outbreaks of intense religious enthusiasm were almost inevitably followed by periods when believers settled into a routine, before becoming perturbed that this was in fact a state of apathy, which they sought to rectify through a renewal of spiritual fervour. Thus, in Williams's account, Wales had been blessed in 1738 and had received a fresh visitation of the spirit in 1762. It was this new outbreak in 1762, referred to as the Llangeitho revival,[25] which demonstrated that the experience of revival could be repeated and the movement reinvigorated after a period of uncertainty and decline. It was from this point onwards that the influence of the fledgling movement spread more steadily to include greater numbers and wider areas, confirming its continued presence as a denomination in the making.

The renewal of the movement by subsequent recurring revivals reinforced the interest in producing a historical account of its growth, as evidence that it was divinely inspired. Thomas Charles urged Robert Jones, Rhoslan, to write such a history for publication in *Trysorfa Ysbrydol* (Spiritual Treasury), the journal modelled on the *Evangelical Magazine* which Charles edited with Thomas Jones, Denbigh.[26] Although that contribution was not forthcoming, between 1799 and 1813 the journal included accounts of the history of the movement in north Wales, based on the recollections of John Evans, a highly respected elder who had been a member of the cause at Bala since 1745.[27] Thomas Charles's request to Robert Jones may not have been wholly disregarded either, as Jones was to be the author of the first volume dedicated to recording the history of Welsh Methodism: *Drych yr Amseroedd* (A Mirror of the Times, 1820). Although never ordained, Jones was a busy lay preacher and author who was an influential figure in late eighteenth-century and early nineteenth-century Welsh Methodism with access to valuable sources of information. Despite having some usefulness as a historical source, like William Williams's works, this was never intended to be a dispassionate study. Jones continued in the same vein as Williams, depicting religious life prior to the revival as utterly moribund, in order to magnify 'the wondrous works of God' (... *rhyfedd weithredoedd Duw*) in bringing about such a remarkable transformation.[28] Jones's account has therefore been held partly responsible for the creation of the so-called 'Methodist view of history', which overstated the impact of the revival by painting a desperately bleak picture of pre-revival Wales.[29]

Like John Evans's contributions to *Trysorfa Ysbrydol*, the major concern of the book was the spread of influence to north Wales, although providing a general account of growth. The origins of the movement were in the south, but the fact that both these writers were north Walians prompted by Thomas Charles, who was based in Bala, indicated the extent to which north Wales had gained greater importance for the movement by the start of the nineteenth century.

Later nineteenth-century historians of the movement, such as the Revd John Hughes, were no less determined than their predecessors to portray the movement as an example of God's great work.[30] Studies focused on the Methodist leaders proved popular, as did biographies of a number of well-known ministers. The trend began with the publication of a brief account of Howel Harris's life soon after his death[31] and continued into the twenty-first century. As a prominent literary figure as well as a religious leader, William Williams has attracted considerable attention and has been the subject of a number of studies.[32] Daniel Rowland has suffered in comparison, chiefly because his papers were lost after having been sent following his death to the Countess of Huntingdon, who was planning to commission a biography. The likelihood is that the materials were unfortunately destroyed after the Countess's death, leaving a gap in the records of the early movement.[33] In addition to this fascination with individuals, there was also considerable interest in charting the progress of the Methodist cause in various different localities, so a number of regional histories were produced in the nineteenth and early twentieth centuries, including, for instance, for Caernarfonshire, Cardiganshire, Carmarthenshire, Flintshire, Glamorgan, Merionethshire and Montgomeryshire.[34] More recently, various county histories have included chapters on the growth of Nonconformity with particular emphasis on the Methodist revival and its local impact.[35] Individual chapels have also often produced booklets on their histories, particularly to coincide with special anniversaries such as centenaries or bicentenaries.

From the mid-nineteenth century onwards the Blue Books controversy and the findings of the Religious Census led to a response which meant trumpeting the success of Calvinistic Methodism and Nonconformity in general. The report of the 1846 Education Commission published in 1847 became known as 'the Treachery of the Blue Books' because of the scathing portrayal of the state not just of the country's education but also its women, its language, culture and morals.[36] It did not escape attention that the overwhelming majority of witnesses were Anglicans, approached for their evidence by Anglican commissioners, with the aid of assistants who were also chiefly Anglicans. The association of Nonconformity with ignorance and immorality gave rise to a sense of outrage which saw the Calvinistic Methodists unite with the other major Nonconformist groups in defending the good name of the Welsh language and people, unfairly traduced by both outsiders and traitors from within. One of the most methodical and effective critics of the report was Lewis Edwards, head of the Calvinistic Methodist Bala College, who analysed the weaknesses with the precision of a keen intellect bitterly enraged by the injustice suffered. The resulting desire to defend the reputation of Welsh Nonconformity doubtless influenced some of the representations of its history in the second half of the nineteenth century. This was encouraged further by the 1851 Religious Census, which, it must be said, was not statistically flawless as a number of individuals were inevitably counted more than once if they attended more than one service. However, the overall findings confirmed the assumption that Nonconformist worshippers together outnumbered the adherents of the Church of England, a conclusion which prompted the long campaign for disestablishment in Wales.[37] In this context, works like Thomas Rees's history of Protestant Nonconformity were by no means unbiased accounts of the growth of Protestant Dissent but bold, defensive declarations of success.[38] This confessional approach to history would be increasingly challenged by the rise of a more academic and secular approach to the history of Wales.

The emergence of Welsh history as an university subject in the early twentieth century had some effect, with increased research by those who were not ordained ministers, such as R. T. Jenkins in Bangor.[39] One of the most influential Welsh historians of the period, J. E. Lloyd, still considered the Methodist revival to have been of great significance in changing cultural and political life in Wales, so it was a subject which continued to engage historians.[40] There was a particularly productive period in the 1970s and 1980s with a flurry of publications, including the two first volumes of the official history of the Welsh Calvinistic Methodist Church in 1973 and 1978, both edited by the indefatigable researcher and prolific writer, the Revd Gomer M. Roberts.[41] By 1981, there emerged one of the first substantial works by an unordained university academic, *Y Diwygiad Mawr* by Derec Llwyd Morgan, an enduringly perceptive study of the origins, literature and ideas of the early revival.[42] At around the same time, further research into post-Reformation Wales by Glanmor Williams and Geraint H. Jenkins shed light on the context in which the revival emerged. Whilst the pioneering school system set up by Griffith Jones, Llanddowror, had long been identified as a vital element in enabling the Methodist revival to have the impact it did, other less heralded labours with less immediately obvious results were also revealed as having helped to pave the way. Glanmor Williams suggested that there was 'a much more receptive mental and emotional climate' by the eighteenth century as a result of improvements in literacy and religious knowledge.[43] The image presented by William Williams of Wales languishing in utter darkness before the dawn of revival in the 1730s was corrected by Geraint Jenkins's research into literary, religious and cultural activities in the preceding decades, which revealed the strenuous efforts of an educated elite among Anglicans and Dissenters to improve standards of religious knowledge.[44] A recent valuable addition to this historiography is D. Densil Morgan's *Theologia Cambrensis*, a comprehensive study which analyses many of the influences that helped shape the revival.[45]

It has become clear that the revival did not ignite suddenly and spontaneously from nothing in the 1730s, but instead was fuelled by an ongoing campaign to improve religious knowledge as part of a general growth in print and literacy in Wales. In essence, this campaign could be traced back to the translation of the Scriptures in the sixteenth century and the ensuing gradual increase in publications aimed at explaining the tenets of Protestantism through the medium of the Welsh language. Thomas Rees had argued strongly that the revival owed much to the printing and preaching of the previous hundred years, although in his desire to elevate Nonconformity, he emphasised the role of old Dissent far more than the Anglican Church, claiming that the rise of Methodism '... was much more the effect of the previous labours of the Nonconformists than it is generally represented to be'.[46] In recent years, historians of the Anglican Church have put forward a staunch defence of the early eighteenth-century Welsh Church, arguing that the health of its spiritual life, its bishops and its clergy has been underestimated.[47] There is a danger that attempts to defend the reputation of the pre-revival Church may lead to an imbalance in the opposite direction to the traditional 'Methodist view', with an account which admits few faults or ascribes the roots of revival entirely to the work of the Church and its clergy. An impartial, objective account of the revival, its origins and its impact remains difficult to achieve, therefore.

Much of the material produced on the history of Welsh Calvinistic Methodism has tended to be institutional histories of its leaders, ministers, causes and chapels, with less focus on what might be termed the social history of the movement. Considerable attention has also focused on the Methodist 'fathers': Howel Harris, Daniel Rowland and William Williams, each charismatic, talented and exercising a continued fascination for some historians. The early movement has often been viewed primarily from the aspect of the leadership, including their association with revival figures elsewhere in England, Scotland and North America.[48] The sources tend to sustain that approach, as many of the records centre on Harris's activities and connections in particular. To examine the internal life of the grass-roots movement represents something of a challenge. With the exception of W. G. Hughes-Edwards's MA thesis in 1966,[49] little has been written on the Methodist society, despite how crucial it was to the movement in the years before Methodism became a separate denomination in 1811.

The term 'Methodism' in Wales can invariably be taken as referring to Calvinistic Methodism, which was dominant from the eighteenth century onwards, in contrast to the situation in England, where it was the followers of the Wesley brothers who increasingly garnered support. The historiography of the Methodist movement in England has also had its challenges to negotiate and possibly a similar distinction between histories written by the Methodist community itself and by secular historians. Phyllis Mack suggests that Methodist historians labour in the shadow of the influence of E. P. Thompson, which has led to two separate streams in the history: a greater emphasis on theology and biography from within the Methodist community; and a focus on the connection with superstition and emotion, politics and industrialisation among secular writers.[50] Even so, a substantial historiography has emerged relating to Methodism in England, America and beyond, concentrating mainly on the Arminian Wesleyan branch rather than George Whitefield and his followers, despite the latter's early transatlantic influence. W. R. Ward's work has done much to develop the study of the evangelical revival within a much broader international context, as part of a global intellectual culture.[51] Studies of Methodism, heart religion and evangelicalism have burgeoned remarkably in recent years, with a greater variety of different approaches. As a result, David Hempton suggests that the highlighted themes have been transformed in the last few decades to include an acknowledgement of Methodism as an international movement, its capacity to adapt to modernity, and the predominance of women among the membership, whilst also noting that there remains further research to be done on Methodism as a 'lived religion'.[52]

There is inevitably still a tendency to dwell on the leaders of the movement, for whom there are far more sources than for the rank and file of the societies, although there have been some attempts to focus on the society and its subdivisions in the world of Wesleyan Methodism.[53] When writing about the situation in Wales, Howel Harris casts a long shadow which is difficult to avoid as he is the source of so much information. One of the most influential of Welsh historians of religion, Glanmor Williams, suggested that the success of the movement rested not primarily with the leaders, despite their 'outstanding gifts', but with those who became members. In his view, the fact that the people hearing the Methodist message were no longer as hampered by illiteracy and lack of knowledge of their faith as previous generations had been made an immense difference and allowed the Protestant Reformation in Wales at long last to come of age.[54] It is the experience of those people which is at the heart of this volume, although it remains hard to avoid viewing them through the eyes of their leaders. What was it about this generation that made them receptive to the Methodist message and what was the nature of their 'lived religion'? Since my first work on the subject was published in Welsh,[55] it is hoped that this revised and updated volume will allow access to a wider readership. This work does not purport in any way to be a study of the theology of the movement, which has received attention from those better qualified to examine it. The aim is rather a social history of the members and of their experience in the societies.

Notes

1. National Library of Wales, Aberystwyth (NLW), Calvinistic Methodist Archive (CMA), Trevecka MS 1392, Howel Harris to Thomas Adams, 10 January 1746.
2. D. J. V. Jones, *Rebecca's Children: A Study of Rural Society, Crime, and Protest* (Oxford: Clarendon Press, 1989), p. 3.
3. J. G. Jenkins, *Maritime Heritage: The Sailors and Seamen of South Cardiganshire* (Llandysul: Gomer Press, 1982), pp. 6–9.
4. D. W. Howell, 'The Agricultural Community of Cardiganshire in the Eighteenth Century', *Ceredigion*, VII/1 (1993), 64–6; D. W. Howell, *The Rural Poor in Eighteenth-century Wales* (Cardiff: University of Wales Press, 2000), p. 54.
5. W. Camden, *Britannia*, ed. R. Gough (3 vols, London: T. Payne and Son, 1789), II, p. 526.
6. B. Howells, 'Social and Agrarian Change in Early Modern Cardiganshire', *Ceredigion*, VII/3–4 (1974/5), 257–9; Howell, *The Rural Poor*, pp. 15–17.
7. D. W. Howell, *Patriarchs and Parasites: The Gentry of South-west Wales in the Eighteenth Century* (Cardiff: University of Wales Press, 1986), p. 2.
8. R. Currie, 'A Micro-theory of Methodist Growth', *Proceedings of the Wesley Historical Society*, 36 (1967), 69; D. Hempton, 'Evangelicalism and reform, c. 1780–1832' in J. Wolffe (ed.), *Evangelical Faith and Public Zeal: Evangelicalism and Society in Britain 1780–1820* (London: SPCK, 1995), p. 26.
9. See G. H. Jenkins, R. Suggett and E. M. White, 'The Welsh Language in Early Modern Wales', in G. H. Jenkins (ed.), *The Welsh Language before the Industrial Revolution* (Cardiff: University of Wales Press, 1997), pp. 51–5.
10. M. Benbough-Jackson, *Cardiganshire and the Cardi, c.1760–c.2000* (Cardiff: University of Wales Press, 2011), pp. 37–8.
11. See Fig. 1: A sketch drawn by Howel Harris to illustrate his 'Rounds', 13 April 1745 (Trevecca College/1 3189).
12. See B. S. Schlenther and E. M. White, *Calendar of the Trevecka Letters* (Aberystwyth: Llyfrgell Genedlaethol Cymru/National Library of Wales, 2003).
13. See National Library of Wales, Aberystwyth, website: *https://archives.library. wales/index.php/howell-harris-diaries-and-manuscripts*.
14. CMA, Diaries of Howel Harris (DHH) 45, 27 May 1739.
15. Trevecka MS 14, Joseph Harris to Howel and Susannah Harris, 7 March 1730; 15, Joseph Harris to Howel and Susannah Harris, 15 August 1730.
16. Trevecka MS 637, Howel Harris to William McCulloch, 11 September 1742.
17. One of the most intractable problems facing historians of eighteenth-century Welsh Methodism is the question of the appropriate spelling for Howel Harris's birthplace and lifelong home. The standard Welsh spelling is Trefeca, but various more anglicised spellings have been used over the years, including Trevecka, Trevecca and Trefecca. The documents deposited in NLW have long been known as the Trevecka group of manuscripts, but in recent years NLW's online catalogue has adopted 'Trevecka' for the bound volumes of letters (MS1-2787) and 'Trevecca College' for the remaining manuscripts, so for consistency this practice will have to be followed in the referencing, but 'Trefeca' will be used for the place itself.
18. O. M. Edwards, *Cartrefi Cymru* (Wrecsam: Hughes a'i Fab, 1896), p. 83; M. H. Jones, *The Trevecka Letters or the Unpublished MSS Correspondence of*

Howel Harris and his Contemporaries (Caernarfon: C. M. Bookroom, 1932), pp. 4–5; G. Tudur, 'Papurau Howel Harris' in *Cof Cenedl XVI*, ed. G. H. Jenkins (Llandysul: Gwasg Gomer, 2001), pp. 67–94; E. M. White, 'Addysg a'r Iaith Gymraeg', in *Hanes Methodistiaeth Galfinaidd Cymru, Cyfrol III: Y Twf a'r Cadarnhau (c.1814-1914)*, ed. J. G. Jones (Caernarfon: Gwasg Pantycelyn, 2011), pp. 263–4.

19 M. H. Jones, *The Trevecka Letters or the Unpublished MSS Correspondence of Howel Harris and his Contemporaries* (Caernarfon: C.M. Bookroom, 1932).

20 G. A. Williams, *When Was Wales? A History of the Welsh* (Harmondsworth: Penguin, 1985), pp. 150–2.

21 John Roberts, *Hanes Methodistiaeth Galfinaidd Cymru* (Llundain: Foyle, 1931), pp. 11–12.

22 See Keith Edward Beebe (ed.), *The McCulloch Examinations of the Cambuslang Revival (1742): A Critical Edition: Conversion Narratives from the Scottish Evangelical Awakening* (Woodbridge: The Boydell Press, 2013). See also A. Fawcett, *The Cambuslang Revival: The Scottish Evangelical Revival of the Eighteenth Century* (Edinburgh: Banner of Truth Trust, 1971); T. C. Smout, 'Born Again at Cambuslang: New Evidence on Popular Religion and Literacy in Eighteenth-century Scotland', *Past and Present*, 97 (1982), 114–27.

23 Trevecka Letters 854, Howel Harris to William McCulloch, 15 April 1743.

24 G. H. Hughes (ed.), *Gweithiau William Williams Pantycelyn, Volume II* (Cardiff: University of Wales Press, 1967), pp. 21-24.

25 See R. Geraint Gruffydd, 'Diwygiad 1762 a William Williams o Bantycelyn', *Cylchgrawn Cymdeithas Hanes y Methodistiaid Califinaidd/Journal of the Historical Society of the Presbyterian Church of Wales*, 54/3 (1969), 68–75; 55/3 (1970), 4–13; Eryn M. White, '"I will once more shake the heavens": The 1762 Revival in Wales', in *Revival and Resurgence in Christian History: Studies in Church History 44*, ed. Kate Cooper and Jeremy Gregory (Woodbridge: The Boydell Press, 2008), pp. 154–63; Eryn M. White, '"Yr Ysbryd Canu": Diwygiad Llangeitho, Williams Pantycelyn a'r Emyn', *Y Traethodydd*, CLXVIII (2013), 226–40.

26 Robert Jones, *Drych yr Amseroedd*, ed. G. M. Ashton (Cardiff: University of Wales Press, 1958), pp. xiv–xv.

27 Goronwy Prys Owen, *Atgofion John Evans y Bala* (Caernarfon: Gwasg Pantycelyn, 1997), pp. 30–2.

28 Jones, *Drych yr Amseroedd*, p. 1.

29 G. H. Jenkins, *Literature, Religion and Society in Wales 1660-1730* (Cardiff: University of Wales Press, 1978), pp. 305–7.

30 J. Hughes, *Methodistiaeth Cymru* (3 vols, Wrecsam: R. Hughes a'i Fab, 1851–6).

31 H. Harris, *A Brief Account of the Life of Howel Harris, Esq* (Trevecka: Trevecka Press, 1791).

32 For instance, G. M. Roberts, *Y Pêr Ganiedydd: (Pantycelyn), Cyfrol I: Trem ar ei Fywyd* (Aberystwyth: Gwasg Aberystwyth, 1949), *Cyfrol II: Arweiniad i'w Waith* (Llandysul: Gwasg Gomer, 1958); Derec Llwyd Morgan, *Williams Pantycelyn* (Caernarfon: Gwasg Pantycelyn, 1983); Glyn Tegai Hughes, *Williams Pantycelyn* (Cardiff: University of Wales Press, 1983); Eifion Evans, *Bread of Heaven: The Life and Work of William Williams, Pantycelyn* (Bridgend: Bryntirion Press, 2010); Saunders Lewis, *Williams Pantycelyn*, ed. D. Densil

Morgan (Caerdydd: Gwasg Prifysgol Cymru, 2016; Glyn Tegai Hughes, *Yr Hen Bant: Ysgrifau ar Williams Pantycelyn* (Talybont: Y Lolfa, 2017).

33 J. Owen, *Coffhad am y Parch. Daniel Rowlands* (Caerlleon: Edward Parry, 1839), pp. 4–5; D. J. Odwyn Jones, *Daniel Rowland Llangeitho (1713–1790)* (Llandysul: Gwasg Gomer, 1938), pp. 1–3.

34 Robert Owen, *Hanes Methodistiaeth Gorllewin Meirionydd: o'r dechreuad hyd y flwyddyn 1888* (Dolgellau: E. W. Evans, 1889–91); John Evans, *Hanes Methodistiaeth rhan ddeheuol sir Aberteifi o ddechreuad y 'Diwygiad Methodistaidd' yn 1735 hyd 1900* (Dolgellau: E. W. Evans, 1904); Griffith Owen, *Hanes Methodistiaeth Sir Fflint* (Dolgellau: E. W. Evans, 1914); James Morris, *Hanes Methodistiaeth Sir Gaerfyrddin* (Dolgellau: E. W. Evans, 1911); W. Samlet Williams, *Hanes Methodistiaeth Gorllewin Morgannwg: sef hanes Eglwysi y Methodistiaid Calfinaidd yng Ngorllewin Morgannwg, o ddechreuad Methodistiaeth hyd o gylch y flwyddyn 1870, Cyfrol 1* (Caernarfon: Cwmni y Cyhoeddwyr Cymreig, 1916); W. Hobley, *Hanes Methodistiaeth Arfon* (Cyfarfod Misol Arfon, 1924); Richard Bennett, *Methodistiaeth Trefaldwyn Uchaf, Cyfrol I: Hanes Cyfnod Howel Harris, 1738–1752* (Y Bala: R. Evans a'i Fab, 1929).

35 For instance, G. M. Roberts, 'Calvinistic Methodism in Glamorgan, 1737–73' in *Glamorgan County History, Volume 4: Early Modern Glamorgan*, ed. G. Williams (Cardiff: University of Wales Press, 1974), pp. 499–533; G. H. Jenkins, 'The Established Church and Dissent in Eighteenth-century Cardiganshire', in *Cardiganshire County History, Volume 3: Cardiganshire in Modern Times*, ed. G. H. Jenkins and I. Gwynedd Jones (Cardiff: University of Wales Press, 1998), pp. 453–77; J. Morgan-Guy, 'Religion and Belief, 1660–1780', in *The Gwent County History, Volume 3: The Making of Monmouthshire, 1536–1780*, ed. M. Gray and P.Morgan (Cardiff: University of Wales Press, 2009), pp. 146–73.

36 See P. Morgan (ed.), *Brad y Llyfrau Gleision* (Llandysul: Gwasg Gomer, 1991); I. Gwynedd Jones, '1848 and 1868: "Brad y Llyfrau Gleision" and Welsh Politics', in *Mid-Victorian Wales: The Observers and the Observed* (Cardiff: University of Wales Press, 1992), pp. 103–65; G. T. Roberts, *The Language of the Blue Books: The Perfect Instrument of Empire* (Cardiff: University of Wales Press, 1998).

37 I. Gwynedd Jones, *Explorations and Explanation: Essays in the Social History of Victorian Wales* (Llandysul, Gwasg Gomer, 1981), pp. 178–9; Frances Knight, 'The National Scene', in Glanmor Williams, William Jacob, Nigel Yates and Frances Knight, *The Welsh Church from Reformation to Disestablishment, 1603–1920* (Cardiff: University of Wales Press, 2007), pp. 310–15.

38 See P. Morgan, 'A Nation of Nonconformists: Thomas Rees (1815–85) and Nonconformist History', in N. Evans and H. Pryce (eds), *Writing a Small Nation's Past: Wales in Comparative Perspective, 1850-1950* (London: Routledge, 2013), pp. 97–109.

39 Methodism was the subject of a substantial section of Jenkins's volume on eighteenth-century Wales, *Hanes Cymru yn y Ddeunawfed Ganrif* (Caerdydd: Gwasg Prifysgol Cymru, 1928), pp. 70–103. He also published a number of articles on the subject, including a collection of essays, *Yng Nghysgod Trefeca* (Caernarfon: Llyfrfa'r Methodistiaid Calfinaidd, 1968).

40 H. Pryce, *J. E. Lloyd and the Creation of Welsh History: Renewing a Nation's Past* (Cardiff: University of Wales Press, 2011), pp. 86–7.

41. G. M. Roberts (ed.) *Hanes Methodistiaeth Galfinaidd Cymru, Cyfrol I: Y Deffroad Mawr* (Caernarfon: Llyfrfa'r Methodistiaid Calfinaidd, 1973; *Hanes Methodistiaeth Galfinaidd Cymru, Cyfrol II: Cynnydd y Corff* (Caernarfon: Llyfrfa'r Methodistiaid Calfinaidd, 1978).
42. D. Llwyd Morgan, *Y Diwygiad Mawr* (Llandysul: Gwasg Gomer, 1981), translated by Dyfnallt Morgan as *The Great Awakening in Wales* (London: Epworth Press, 1988).
43. G. Williams, *Grym Tafodau Tân:Ysgrifau Hanesyddol ar Grefydd a Diwylliant* (Llandysul: Gwasg Gomer, 1984), p. 101; G. Williams, *The Welsh and their Religion: Historical Essays* (Cardiff: University of Wales Press, 1991), p. 54.
44. G. H. Jenkins, *Literature, Religion and Society in Wales 1660–1730* (Cardiff: University of Wales Press, 1978); G. H. Jenkiins, *Cadw Tŷ mewn Cwmwl Tystion* (Llandysul: Gwasg Gomer, 1990).
45. D. Densil Morgan, *Theologia Cambrensis: Protestant Religion and Theology in Wales. 1 From Reformation to Revival 1588–1760* (Cardiff: University of Wales Press, 2018).
46. Thomas Rees, *A History of Protestant Nonconformity in Wales, from its Rise to the Present Time* (London: John Snow, 1861), p. 344.
47. See William Jacob and Nigel Yates in Williams, Jacob, Yates and Knight, *The Welsh Church from Reformation to Disestablishment*; W. Gibson, '"The most glorious enterprises have been achiev'd": The Restoration Diocese of St Davids 1660–1730', in *Religion and Society in the Diocese of St Davids 1485–2011*, ed. W. Gibson and J. Morgan-Guy (Farnham: Ashgate, 2015), pp. 91–128.
48. For example, D. C. Jones, '*A Glorious Work in the World*': Welsh Methodism and the International Evangelical Revival, 1735–1750 (Cardiff: University of Wales Press, 2004).
49. W. G. Hughes-Edwards, 'The development and organisation of the Methodist society in Wales, 1735–1750' (unpublished MA thesis, University of Wales, 1966).
50. P. Mack, *Heart Religion in the British Enlightenment* (Cambridge: Cambridge University Press, 2008), pp. 35.
51. W. R. Ward, *The Protestant Evangelical Awakening* (Cambridge: Cambridge University Press, 1992); *Early Evangelicalism: A Global Intellectual History, 1670–1789* (Cambridge: Cambridge University Press, 2006).
52. D. Hempton, 'The People Called Methodists: Transitions in Britain and North America', in W. J. Abraham and J. E. Kirby (eds), *The Oxford Handbook of Methodist Studies* (Oxford: Oxford University Press, 2009), pp. 67–84.
53. See D. L. Watson, *The Early Methodist Class Meeting: Its Origins and Significance* (Eugene, Oregon: Wipf & Stock, 2002); Andrew Goodhead, *A Crown and a Cross: The Rise, Development, and Decline of the Methodist Class Meeting in Eighteenth-Century England* (Eugene, Oregon: Wipf & Stock, 2010); Kevin M. Watson, *Pursuing Social Holiness: The Band Meeting in Wesley's Thought and Popular Methodist Practice* (Oxford: Oxford University Press, 2014).
54. Glanmor Williams, *Welsh Reformation Essays* (Cardiff: University of Wales Press, 1967), p. 30.
55. E. M. White, '*Praidd Bach y Bugail Mawr*': *Seiadau Methodistaidd De-orllewin Cymru, 1737-50* (Llandysul: Gwasg Gomer, 1995).

CHAPTER 1

'No part of the Nation more inclin'd to be Religious'?[1] The Religious Context in South-west Wales

The three counties of south-west Wales lay within the financially and administratively challenged diocese of St Davids. It was by far the largest of the four Welsh dioceses, comprising not just Cardiganshire, Carmarthenshire and Pembrokeshire, but also Breconshire and Radnorshire as well as part of west Glamorgan and a handful of parishes in Monmouthshire and Herefordshire. It therefore spread across the breadth of south Wales, yet its cathedral church was located on the west coast of Pembrokeshire in St David's itself, although the bishop's palace had been relocated to Abergwili, near Carmarthen. Despite its size, it was institutionally poor, as a result of alienation of property during the Reformation period and the lay impropriation of a substantial proportion of its tithes with the dissolution of the monasteries. The diocese and its benefices were impoverished as a result of the loss of 58 per cent of its income from tithe to lay impropriators, with the result that clerical incomes rose at a much slower rate than in England.[2] All the Welsh dioceses were amongst the poorest in the province of Canterbury, but the two southern dioceses of St Davids and Llandaff had historically suffered most from lay impropriation, so that clerical incomes there compared unfavourably with the northern sees of Bangor and St Asaph. It is estimated that the annual worth of St Davids was only £450 at the start of the eighteenth century, although this seems to have increased to around £900 by 1762.[3] At that time, Llandaff was reckoned to be worth £500 a year and Bangor and St Asaph both worth £1,400.[4]

Despite the abiding issue of poverty and its associated problems of pluralism and absenteeism, there is little sign of popular dissatisfaction with the Church in the early eighteenth century. The initial cool reception given in the sixteenth century to the imposition of a Protestant faith from outside the country had warmed over time with the introduction of Welsh services to correspond with the translation of the Bible and Book of Common Prayer. The Anglican Protestant Church was effectively rebranded as the 'British' or 'Welsh' faith, with an interpretation of history linking it to the nation and its language as a revived version of the old Celtic Church.[5] The Church had clearly succeeded in building on these developments to win public loyalty by the mid-seventeenth century, when the changes imposed under the Commonwealth regime were demonstrably not welcomed by the majority of people, who hankered after the liturgy and traditions of the Church.[6] There was little initial interest in the new Puritan movement which, like sixteenth-century Protestantism, struggled in its early stages to overcome the hurdle of language. Protestant Dissent remained very much a minority movement into the Restoration period and after Toleration was granted in 1689. The results of the Compton Census in 1676 for St Davids suggest there were 2,401 Nonconformists compared to 69,972 conforming Anglicans and 218 Catholics out of a total population of 72,591.[7] These figures may not be wholly accurate, and may understate the total number of Dissenters, but the overall picture is unlikely to be radically different. The vast majority of the population were at least nominally adherents of the Anglican Church by the early eighteenth century, even if they did not all by any means attend regularly. The local parish church was the focal point for the community where for generations they had baptised their children and buried their dead, as well as congregated to celebrate on holidays. Forces of tradition and loyalty predating the Reformation therefore bound them to the Church in large numbers. As the eighteenth century dawned, the Established Church seemed in a comfortable position of predominance with little to fear from any competition.

Welsh Methodism certainly did not set out to become that competition since it was by no means a protest against the Established Church. The fact that the movement did not officially separate from the Church until 1811 demonstrates the depth of abiding loyalty felt, especially by the leadership, the first generation of whom were mostly ordained Anglican clergy. Howel Harris remained a layman not out of choice but because he was refused ordination as a result of his Methodist activities. Harris constantly argued in favour of remaining within the Church whenever the subject arose. After a monthly association in 1745 he noted in his diary: 'I spoke home too of not giving offence to the clergy &c as much as possible as we are in the Established Church & as it bore with us more than any Church would.'[8] However, it must be said that there was at times a passive aggressive tone to his argument that the Methodists should not leave of their own volition, but should wait to see if they were turned out.[9] Discussions at Glanyrafonddu Association meeting in October 1743 apparently turned on the question of 'whether did the Christians leave the Jewish Church were they turned out & so the Protestants the Popish Church & we found they declared against that which was erroneous in the Church & for that were turned out but did not turn themselves out & we are guilty of none of the evils in our Church as having all born our Testimony against them'.[10] The Methodists often sought guidance from their perception of the early Christians and the sixteenth-century reformers and here they seemed to find precedents for remaining within a Church whilst conscientiously pointing to its failings. Yet there remained the implication that separation was the inevitable outcome even if not initiated by the Methodists themselves. Whilst Harris defended the Church on several occasions, he also described it as a 'poor, benighted Church' acutely in need of prayer for its renewal.[11] At times also he feared the clergy were 'blind guides' doing little to enlighten their most ignorant parishioners.[12] He was particularly moved in January 1742 by Bishop Nicholas Claggett's seeming opposition to Daniel Rowland and wondered whether God meant to 'utterly remove Thy Candlestick from this dark benighted Church of this Nation'. He felt inclined:

> to write for Brother Rowlands to the Bishop feeling Power to tell him home how he employs all the vilest men & is now against God's work how will this tear him in the last Day. Had Power in me to tell him & that though he should excommunicate me yet I must go though I should go to Death to feed the lambs that starve for want of food.[13]

The harshest contemporary attacks on the Church came not from the Methodists but from Anglican clergy unmoved by the revival. Ieuan

Gwynedd Jones perceptively commented that critics from within the Church attributed its problems to the bureaucratic failings arising from its poverty, whilst Methodist critics came to dwell on a lack of zeal and fervour.[14] Many of the criticisms of the Church at the time and subsequently have centred on two major themes: that the Church was too impoverished to provide adequate spiritual provision and that it was an anglicised institution with little respect for the Welsh language. By the nineteenth century the Church was considered by Nonconformist commentators to have failed in its spiritual duty to the Welsh people. The Nonconformists had become accustomed to a home-grown leadership who could communicate with them naturally through the medium of Welsh, which may have well have hardened their attitude to the very idea that non-Welsh-speaking spiritual leaders could adequately serve the people of Wales. The bishops in particular were frequently accused of being indifferent to their Welsh dioceses at best, and hostile to the language at worst. Jaundiced views of the pre-revival establishment and clergy have drawn on the remarks of one of the internal critics of the Church's bureaucratic failings, Erasmus Saunders in his *A View of the State of Religion in the Diocese of St. Davids* (1721). The Pembrokeshire-born Saunders was educated at Jesus College, Oxford, ultimately graduating as a Doctor in Divinity. Although initially appointed to a benefice in England, he was prebendary of Brecon from 1709 until his death in 1724, so maintained a connection with St Davids diocese.[15] It may be that his comments were aimed at provoking measures to improve the financial state of the diocese, in the same way that John Penry's barbed criticism in the sixteenth century had possibly prompted Archbishop John Whitgift to ensure funding for the printing of William Morgan's translation of the Bible.[16] It has also been suggested that he exaggerated the parlous conditions he described because he was disappointed not to have been promoted to a bishopric despite his qualifications.[17] It is important to bear this in mind when using his evidence, but his emphasis on the problems arising from the loss of tithe income means that he fits squarely into Ieuan Gwynedd Jones's first category of critics.

The most bitter contemporary critic was Evan Evans, or Ieuan Fardd, whose vehemently worded essay on the failings of the anglicised bishops of Wales was probably regarded as too sweeping to be published when written around 1764–5. Evans was in a position to compare conditions in Wales with those in parts of England, having served as a curate in Kent and several parishes in north Wales before returning as curate to his native parish of Lledrod in north Cardiganshire.[18] Acknowledged as one of the greatest Welsh scholars of the period,[19] he failed to distinguish himself in the Church and remained a curate throughout his career. This may well have been a factor leading to his condemnation of the *Esgyb Eingl* or 'Anglo-bishops' as utterly unsuited to their office. He was incensed by their inability to communicate with their flocks through the medium of the only language the majority of the Welsh people understood. He also bemoaned the fact that there was no hope for promotion for any Welsh-speaking clergy as their abilities went unnoticed and unappreciated. In doing so, he probably forfeited any remaining chance of preferment himself, but that would sadly have been a remote possibility in any case, given his lapses into drink and depression. By the time Evans was writing, Methodism was gaining ground sufficiently to be viewed as an increasing threat to the Church. Evans did not hesitate to attribute its growth to the bishops' neglect of the native tongue, which he claimed:

> *peri i'r gwerinos druain orphwyllo, a myned o'r Eglwys i ganlyn y goleuadau newyddion annaturiol ag y mae Methodyddion yn ymffrostio o'u plegid.*[20]

> caused the poor people to become distracted, and leave the Church to follow the unnatural new lights in which Methodists take pride.

Evans's anger was shared by other leading figures in Welsh culture, such as the Morris brothers. William Morris expressed his contempt in a letter to his brothers:

> *Wala, wfft i'r fath esgobion! O na bai Ddewi yn gwybod par fath gymdeithion sydd yn eistedd yn ei drŵn, ac yntau Elwy, a'i ddylynawr Rhisiart Davies yn gweled par fath goegyn sydd yn llenwi eu cadair!*[21]

> Well, fie on such bishops! O that David knew what sort of fellows sit on his throne, and that St Asaph, and his successor Richard Davies saw what a wretch fills their chair!

Such hostility was not voiced by contemporary Methodists, who showed little sign of inciting a rebellion against the Anglican Church. However, it is apparent that the Church faced a number of challenges in trying to minister effectively throughout Wales, a situation which is likely to have furthered the Methodist cause.

The Diocese of St Davids

During the first half of the eighteenth century, eight individuals served successively as bishop of St Davids. None proved anywhere near as controversial as their predecessor Thomas Watson, who was dismissed for simony in 1699, with the see left vacant until 1705 whilst Watson launched several unsuccessful appeals.[22] His Jacobite sympathies laid him open to suspicion, and he met with concerted opposition from within the diocese, particularly from the registrar, Robert Lucy, son of one of his predecessors as bishop, William Lucy. Archbishop Thomas Tenison oversaw the diocese in the meantime, but this was not a propitious start to the century, and it may have led to a tendency to play safe by selecting bishops whose political loyalties were regarded as more circumspect than Watson's. The fact that most of the bishops appointed were previously archdeacons, deans, canons or prebendaries in other dioceses confirms the suggestion that the diocese was regarded as most suitable for first or trial appointments to the episcopal bench.[23] In more affluent dioceses, bishops might be tempted from another see, but this did not happen in eighteenth-century St Davids. On the contrary, bishops tended to move on to a position higher up the ecclesiastical ladder, including Phillip Bisse (1710–13) to Hereford, Richard Smallbrooke (1723–31) to Lichfield and Coventry, Nicholas Claggett (1731–42) to Exeter and Richard Trevor (1743–52) to Durham. In some cases, this could happen extremely quickly if another, more attractive, prospect became available; Elias Sydall was translated to Gloucester within months of his installation in 1731, and Edward Willes translated to Bath and Wells having completed less than a year at St Davids between January and December 1743. Unusually, George Bull (1705–10) was already 71 years old when finally promoted to the episcopal bench as bishop of St Davids.[24] Despite his age and frailty, he was resident and active in his see until his death five years after his election. The other bishop to die in office during the first half of the eighteenth century was Adam Ottley, who was fifty-eight when elected in 1713 and served for ten years until his death.[25] Ottley and Claggett were the only two bishops in the first half of the century to fulfil ten years of service in the diocese. For most bishops, the diocese was not appealing for a protracted stay because the poor endowment meant a struggle to maintain a suitable lifestyle. Ottley, who was himself to die in debt, was warned upon his election by the widow of Bishop George Bull that her husband had never received more than £300 a year during his time and that the costs of his consecration year had amounted to £900.[26] Faced with such balance sheets, Welsh bishops often acquired additional livings in order to supplement the inadequate endowments of the dioceses.

During this period, bishops were chiefly selected for their political loyalties in order to support the government in the House of Lords. The ability to communicate with and offer spiritual leadership to the people in their diocese was therefore not a priority in their appointment. As a result of their political role they were expected to be on hand to vote in favour of the government in Parliament while it was in session. Failure to do so could have repercussions for their future careers. It was suspected that the rebellious Richard Watson was allowed to remain in Llandaff for thirty-four years, between 1782 and 1816, as a punishment for not complying with the wishes of his political masters.[27] This imperative to remain in London for much of the year meant that the bishops were generally only summer migrants to south Wales. Given the dreadful state of the roads, the journey could frequently be hazardous. Having arrived, travelling within the diocese by coach was also often fraught with difficulties. Bishop Claggett's coach came to grief during a journey from Brecon to the bishop's palace at Abergwili in 1733.[28] Even towards the close of the century, conditions remained so bad that it took Bishop Samuel Horsley five and a half hours to travel from Cardigan to Aberaeron in 1791, a distance of twenty-three miles.[29] There were exceptions to this pattern of absenteeism, including the elderly George Bull and also Adam Ottley, who resolved to be a resident bishop. Ottley took up residence at the bishop's palace at Abergwili, which was centrally placed for the diocese as a whole, and undertook its restoration.[30]

The selection of the bishops based on political expediency was one of the realities of a state-established church, but surely not the most desirable approach for a religious denomination. Between 1727 and 1870 no Welsh-speaking Welshman was appointed to any Welsh diocese, a remarkable record which has certainly fed the preconception that the Anglican Church was a highly anglicised and anglicising institution with little respect for the Welsh language. This dating is based on the assumption that John Wynne of St Asaph, who was born in Flintshire, had knowledge of Welsh, although there is no record of him speaking it.[31] It might therefore be more correct to date the period as beginning in 1716 when John Evans of Bangor was translated to Meath in Ireland.[32] It is in either event a lengthy period of over 140 years at least. The time span is even greater in the case of St Davids, where the last active Welsh-speaking bishop was William Thomas, who was translated to Worcester in 1683. He was a highly respected leader of the diocese who behaved reasonably towards Dissent and retained an interest in Wales even after departing for Worcester. The only other Welshman to be appointed in the post-Restoration period was John Lloyd, Principal of Jesus College, who died four months after consecration in 1686 without ever visiting his diocese as bishop. In effect, no Welsh-speaking Welshman took charge in St Davids between 1683 and the appointment two centuries later of Basil Jones in 1874, although his English predecessor, Connop Thirlwell probably learned to speak better Welsh than him.[33]

Welshmen appointed as bishops in Wales during the seventeenth century had therefore not been able to resist the attractions of crossing the border to better-paid positions. Many of the Englishmen appointed were decent churchmen and some, such as Thomas Burgess in the early nineteenth century, proved sympathetic and enlightened leaders of the diocese. Yet, it is impossible to believe that this situation was in the best interests of the majority of the population and it gave rise to a growing clamour for change during the nineteenth century.[34] It has been suggested that the criticism of the bishops for their unfamiliarity with the language dates from the nineteenth century rather than the eighteenth.[35] In fact a number of voices were raised in the eighteenth century but there was not in that period the kind of forum to facilitate the discussion that there existed by the nineteenth century with the growth of Welsh newspapers and journals. The fact that none of the bishops were Welsh or Welsh-speaking did not automatically ensure a negative attitude to the language on their part. In reality, there was considerable variation amongst the bishops of St Davids in the levels of support for the language of the majority of their flock. None of them expressed a desire that the language should be eradicated, as Bishop Robert Hay Drummond of St Asaph did,[36] although that is not setting the bar very high. Most seem to have accepted the principle that Welsh services should be available for the Welsh-speakers in the diocese, and some went further. Richard Smallbrooke apparently resolved to learn the language sufficiently to be able to officiate, which was commendable.[37] He was, of course, in post for a sufficient period of time for this to have been viable and worthwhile, whereas others would not have been in the diocese long enough to have much time to learn or opportunity to practise. Some, like Bull and Ottley, subscribed to Welsh religious publications, which might prove beneficial to those under their care. Yet Phillip Bisse refused to subscribe to a Welsh translation of Robert Nelson's *Feasts and Fasts* in October 1711. He claimed that this was not out of dislike for the author or the book, but on the grounds that such a publication would obstruct the spread of the English language, which he hoped to promote through establishing charity schools.[38] Bisse departed for Hereford in 1713, without having done much to develop schools in the area, although he was responsible for establishing a charity school at Hadley, Hertfordshire, in 1712.[39] Interestingly, as bishop of Hereford he appended his name, along with the bishops of Wales, to the 1714 SPCK proposals to reprint the Bible and Book of Common Prayer in Welsh, which led to the 1718 edition. The bishop of Hereford had been included in the terms of the 1563 Act for the Translating of the Bible and Divine Service because western areas of the diocese were Welsh-speaking. Welsh continued to be used in parishes in Herefordshire into the nineteenth century and Bisse seems here to have accepted this, despite his previous desire to promote English.[40]

Because St Davids covered such a large area, the patterns of language use were more diverse than in Bangor in the north-west, where Welsh was used throughout the counties of Anglesey, Caernarfon and Merioneth in the eighteenth century, with the town of Caernarfon the sole exception, holding services in English only.⁴¹ There was considerable variation across the diocese of St Davids, but with the use of Welsh paramount throughout most of the south-west, with the exclusion of south Pembrokeshire. Therefore, although the bishop of St Davids was faced with a more complex and varied situation than the bishop of Bangor, it would have been a dereliction of duty for any bishop of this diocese to have done other than to insist on the use of Welsh in the overwhelmingly Welsh-speaking parts of his diocese. All the evidence demonstrates clearly that the western part of the diocese was largely Welsh-speaking and received appropriate Welsh-medium services as a result. Visitation returns for the four Welsh dioceses regularly included a question on the language of service, to ascertain whether the Church was observing its legal duty to minister in the Welsh tongue in those areas where it was 'commonly used', as it was bound to do by the terms of the 1563 Act for the Translating of the Bible and the Divine Service.⁴² Unfortunately, the clergy's returns only survive for 1755 and 1799 for eighteenth-century St Davids, although there are also returns for 1807, 1813 and 1828, as well as the report of Archdeacon Edward Tenison on Carmarthen Archdeaconry in 1710, which help to reveal long-term trends. Despite the gaps in the surviving records and some ambiguous statements, it is possible to use these returns to discern the patterns of language use in churches and chapelries across the south-west.⁴³

Of the seventy-three Anglican places of worship returned for Cardiganshire, only the town of Cardigan operated bilingually in the eighteenth century, along with the parish of Llanbadarn Fawr, which still in that period contained the town of Aberystwyth. Lampeter may well have had a similar provision but the records do not survive before 1807. Apart from these market towns, English was not needed in any parish in Cardiganshire. English was more commonly used in Carmarthenshire, but remained a minority language there also. Of the eighty-seven places of worship listed in Carmarthenshire, an English service was conducted for the inhabitants of a cluster of parishes along the south coast, bordering south Pembrokeshire, including Eglwys Gymyn, Pendine, Llansadwrnen and Laugharne. There were some parishes where both Welsh and English services were conducted on a Sunday, including the town of Carmarthen, and others with a single, bilingual service, such as the parish of Abergwili, situated near Carmarthen itself and the location of the bishop's palace. Less specific and more flexible bilingual arrangements existed in other places, including Llanelli, where the balance between languages may have been more subject to fluctuation. However, 64 per cent of the county's worship was consistently conducted in Welsh only. The language of worship in Pembrokeshire reflected the distinctive and fixed pattern of linguistic geography in the county. There was a bilingual patch around the port of Fishguard and its vicinity. Otherwise, all the parishes in the north used Welsh only, as far south as (from west to east): St David's, Llanrhian, Mathry, Letterston, Little Newcastle, Castlebythe, Henry's Moat, Maenclochog, Llandeilo and Llangolman. This line of parishes formed a boundary with a slender band of bilingual parishes bisecting the county from Llanhowel and Brawdy in the west to Llanddewi Felffre and Llanbedr Felffre in the east, which bordered the Welsh-speaking areas of western Carmarthenshire. South of this line, all was in English. Unlike Carmarthenshire, there were hardly any adjustments to the arrangements in Pembrokeshire during the eighteenth and early nineteenth centuries, suggesting very little language shift in either direction, or much expansion of the narrow bilingual buffer zone between the Welsh- and English-speaking areas. Elsewhere in the diocese, the pattern in Breconshire was similar to Carmarthenshire, but with a slightly greater proportion of English and bilingual places of worship. In Radnorshire some Welsh lingered in parishes along the western border of the county, such as Saint Harmon, Rhaeadr, Llansanffraid Cwmteuddwr, Llansteffan and Boughrood but even here the use of English was increasing by the end of the century.[44] The Gower peninsula was also part of the St Davids diocese within the Archdeaconry of Carmarthen and, as another long-standing Englishry, most public worship there was in English.[45]

Parishes in traditionally English-speaking areas like Gower and south Pembrokeshire, as well as parishes in monoglot Welsh-speaking areas, were relatively simple to cater for properly. It was in areas where the two languages coexisted and had to be used in public worship that the local clergy could be faced with a dilemma. The difficulty for the Established Church was its responsibility to provide for all the residents of the parish. Dissenting causes and Methodist societies could be established in a particular language and would not usually recruit new members who did not speak that language. Separate causes could be established for those who had different linguistic needs. However, the Church was required to adapt to shifts in language, even if only for a small minority. Few instances are reported in the south-west of incumbents being required to conduct services in English to suit the wishes of leading gentry families, regardless of whether the rest of the congregation understood. This did happen in Llanfair Nant-y-gof in north Pembrokeshire by the early nineteenth century, with a regular congregation of around fifty hearing services in English whenever the Vaughan family of Trecŵn were present.[46] The seaside resorts in the south-west, Tenby and Aberystwyth, which were becoming popular by the late eighteenth century, were likely to already have English services, so that there was no need for any great change to accommodate visitors, as there was in places like Porthcawl.[47] By the early nineteenth century instances arose in the south-west of the language of service having to be altered because a few non-Welsh-speaking families had moved to certain parishes. In Tregaron, for example, by 1813 the arrival of two English families in a congregation varying between 200 and 300 meant that an element of English was introduced to church services.[48] Since it often depended whether or not a few individuals were present on a Sunday it could be difficult in such cases for the officiating clergyman to know beforehand whether he needed to include some English or not. Members of congregations facing such uncertainty may have been increasingly drawn by the absolute certainty of an intelligible service in the Dissenting churches.

Yet these were problems which did not seem to afflict the south-west very much before the nineteenth century. What the records of language of service for the eighteenth century demonstrate is that it was not likely to have been a lack of provision through the medium of Welsh which prompted parishioners in south-west Wales to turn to the Methodist societies, or indeed to Dissent. The majority of parishes in which societies were established in the 1740s had Welsh-medium provision in the churches, so there would have been no need to look elsewhere simply for the sake of spiritual provision in a language the people understood. All the Cardiganshire societies were located in parishes which made use of Welsh. Indeed, the services were conducted exclusively in Welsh in all save Lampeter. It is impossible to be sure what the situation was in Lampeter because records of language of service do not survive for the parish in the eighteenth century. However, in the early nineteenth century there was a bilingual service, which suggests that that was likely to have been the case earlier, given the similar tendency in the other main towns in the county. The situation in north Pembrokeshire was similar, with widespread use of Welsh only, except for the port of Fishguard, which had bilingual services. The vast majority of Carmarthenshire societies also developed in parishes where Welsh was the sole language of service, in Aber-nant, Cil-y-cwm, Cynwyl Elfed, Cynwyl Gaeo, Henllan Amgoed, Llanarthney, Llanddarog, Llanddeusant, Llandefaelog, Llanegwad, Llanfair-ar-y-bryn, Llanfihangel Aberbythych, Llanfynydd, Llangynnwr, Llangyndeyrn, Llanllwni, Llanpumsaint, Llansadwrn, Llansawel, Llanwinio, Llanwrda, Llanybydder, Meidrim, Merthyr, Myddfai, Pembrey, Talley and Tre-lech a'r Betws. Abergwili, Carmarthen, Llandeilo, Llanelli, Llangathen and Llan-non had bilingual services, which might not have been wholly satisfactory for those who only understood Welsh. Laugharne was said to have bilingual services by Archdeacon Edward Tenison in 1710, but by 1755 the services were reported to be English. A greater measure of Welsh was reintroduced later in the century, with Welsh sermons every fortnight, although the parish continued to conduct services largely in English.

An archdeacon's report, or the report of a rural dean, was an opportunity to correct any deficiency in the language provision and provided some check on what clergy wrote in their visitation returns, as did the returns of the churchwardens. Parish clergy reporting back to the bishop might have wished to gloss over any failings and might at times convey a more positive impression than was actually the case. However, most were native Welsh-speakers who should not have had any difficulty in conducting the services in Welsh, so it is unlikely that they were other than truthful in response to this question. In 1743 two churchwardens and thirteen parishioners from the parishes of Llandeilo, Llangolman and Maenclochog in Pembrokeshire wrote to Bishop Edward Willes to complain about the incumbent William Crowther. He was accused of neglecting his duty, of failing to observe the Sabbath and of keeping a woman 'of lewd immoral behaviour' in the vicarage. In addition to his lack of moral standards, the parishioners complained that 'he hath never performed divine service in either of his parishes in a known tongue, the parishioners being mostly illiterate, save in Welsh, and he an utter Stranger thereto'.[49] There are no surviving visitation returns for these parishes for the eighteenth century, so that it is impossible to know what Crowther had noted about the language of service. Certainly, each parish had Welsh services during the early nineteenth century as might be expected in the Welsh-speaking part of Pembrokeshire.

This does seem to have been an exception to the general rule. There was a tendency for wealthier benefices to attract a greater number of non-Welsh speakers, but there were far fewer of these to be found in the archdeaconries of Carmarthen, Cardigan and St Davids. Some of the clergy could at times show their annoyance at any sign that the linguistic needs of the local population were being disregarded by colleagues. Samuel Williams and his son, Moses Williams, both expressed anger at clergymen who insisted on inflicting English services on congregations who could not understand the language.[50] Griffith Jones expounded on the topic of appointing pastors unable to officiate in Welsh with some feeling:

> The Sheep could not know their Shepherd's Voice from first to last, and must therefore perish, or go astray, for want of Pasture ... We cannot help thinking, that English Sermons to Welsh Congregations are neither less absurd, nor more edifying than Welsh Preaching would be in the Centre of England ... It cannot justify English Preaching, that there may be one or two, or a small Number, who understand the Language, when all the rest of the Parish know nothing of it, nor excuse an Incumbent, to devolve the whole of the Work on his Curate, because he knows not the Tongue himself, which he is bound, by the Laws of God and Man, to study and minister in, or to disengage himself from the Obligation thereof.[51]

Jones here refers to the trend for non-Welsh-speaking incumbents to employ a curate who could officiate on their behalf. For instance, James Phillips, rector of Llangoedmor, Cardiganshire, and vicar of Nevern, Pembrokeshire in the 1740s, although a native of the area, employed a curate since he felt his own grasp of the Welsh language was insufficient to conduct services in his parishes.[52] This ensured Welsh-medium provision for the parishioners, but may still have been considered hard on the curate who undertook the bulk of the work without receiving the full income from the parish. Jones may also have felt that any clergyman unable to officiate in Welsh was basically unqualified for Welsh-speaking parishes, and to appoint them was to show a disregard for the local people. The fact that such strong opposition was voiced by some of the clergy in Carmarthenshire and Cardiganshire suggests that the services and sermons in English may have been more common than the visitation returns indicate. Possibly in some instances bilingual arrangements may have been introduced on the judgement of the incumbent before the majority of the congregation could understand English, leaving some parishioners feeling deprived and aggrieved. However, overall, it seems unlikely to have been the language of public worship in the Church that drove parishioners to join the Methodist societies, as it would appear that the majority had access to Welsh services, and in most cases nothing but Welsh services.

The Parish Clergy

If the language of the Church's provision was not likely to have been problematic, what of the quality of the provision? The state of the Church at a parish level is likely to have been a much more important consideration for most people than the character of the somewhat distant figure of the bishop. Restoration of the cathedral, which has been identified as a key sign of the vitality of the Church in the diocese, may well have been a positive development in general, a source of local pride and a boost to clerical morale, but it is difficult to know what impact, if any, it would have had on most of the inhabitants of the diocese.[53] The parish priest and parish church were probably of greatest significance to their lives and have traditionally been identified as frequently problematic. The stereotypical image of the overworked and underpaid Welsh curate is conveyed by Erasmus Saunders, who painted a vivid picture of the poor curate in 'a kind of perpetual motion', struggling to serve three or four benefices for around £10–£12 each a year, often ten to twelve miles apart, rushing between churches to recite his prayers breathlessly with not a moment to spare between services for a bite to eat.[54]

Pluralism caused by low clerical incomes was evidently a factor in St Davids. At the heart of the problem was the lay impropriation of the tithe in so many livings in the diocese. Sir John Philipps of Picton Castle, known for his philanthropic activities, in 1705 expressed a desire for an Act of Parliament to buy back impropriations. He had in mind in particular Charles Seymour, Duke of Somerset, who was impropriator to six livings in Carmarthenshire, receiving £900 a year but allowing less than £70 in total to the six curates.[55] Erasmus Saunders gave the example of Llanddewibrefi in Cardiganshire, where the incumbent was said to be allowed just £8 a year by the impropriator, despite the fact that the tithe was said to be worth £400 a year.[56] This kind of situation was not the product of Saunders's prejudice, and there are similar examples to be found in the church records. Bishop Nicholas Claggett commented after his primary visitation that the impropriators had 'almost exhausted the whole revenues of the Church' in Cardiganshire.[57] Edward Tenison rather pointedly remarked on the fact that the lay impropriator of Talley allowed £8 a year in salary out of a tithe income of £100.[58] The rights to the tithe were held by Mrs Jane Cornwallis of Abermarlais, a wealthy heiress in her own right as the daughter of Sir Sackville Crow of Westmead, Laugharne. The Abermarlais estate was considered amongst the wealthiest in the south-west, with an annual income of up to £1,000 from rent in the early eighteenth century.[59]

Archdeacon Edward Tenison was but one of the clergy to highlight the issue of low clerical incomes. Thomas Philipps, vicar of Laugharne and prebendary of St Davids, complained to Bishop Ottley in 1718 that most of the livings in the archdeaconry of Carmarthen had been appropriated, with so little provision made for the clergy that he claimed it was difficult to survive on the combined salary for serving three or four benefices. In his opinion, the situation forced every curate in the archdeaconry to become a pluralist in order to sustain himself and his family.[60] Philipps himself also held the parishes of Llansadwrnen and Pen-boyr, in addition to the chapelries of Cyffig and Marros, which were linked to the parish of Laugharne.[61] Although he voiced these complaints, he was far from the most beleaguered of clergymen. Laugharne had a relatively new parsonage provided by Bishop William Thomas, and the vicar also received 6s. 8d a year in lieu of glebe land, as well as letting the parsonage at Llansadwrnen for £4 a year. The tithe was worth £250 a year, but the vicar received £65, out of which he paid £20 to the curate serving Cyffig and Marros on his behalf. However, Phillipps also received around £25 a year from the hay and corn tithes in the parish, and Llansadwrnen and Pen-boyr were said to be worth £40 and £45 a year.[62] Philipps lived comfortably and was well connected, with his father John a former mayor of Carmarthen and his brother James a future MP for Carmarthen Borough.[63] This may have placed him in a stronger position to complain on behalf of others in a worse predicament.

Some of the clergy tried to augment their income by taking on additional employment outside the Church, such as keeping a school like John Thomas of Llandysul, Cardiganshire.[64] That was a respectable undertaking for a churchman, but others diversified further according to some accounts. Howel Harris was told in Llangadog, Carmarthenshire, that the local clergyman kept a dancing school.[65] The vicar at the time was Thomas Protheroe, who also held the livings of Llangathen and Llanddeusant, the latter being served by a curate. Another original idea was to keep a tavern in the churchyard, as one of the former incumbents of Llan-y-crwys was said to have done, according to Edward Tenison's report in 1710.[66] It is difficult to know if there is any truth behind these rumours, but they hint at the common perception of the clergy in hard straits financially. It could be a struggle for a clergyman to save for an old age in retirement or for the comfort of his widow after his death. The widow of Samuel Morris, Llan-gan, only had a roof over her head through the charity of a neighbour who allowed her the use of a cottage rent-free. Even so, she was in fear of having to resort to the parish for assistance to survive when John Lloyd, the vicar of Narberth, wrote to Bishop Richard Trevor requesting that she receive some benefit from a fund for the widows of clergy.[67]

Pluralists should not by definition automatically be considered negligent or uncaring clergymen. Griffith Jones was rector of Llanddowror, a benefice worth £38 a year, but also held Llandeilo Abercywyn, worth £16 8s. a year. Daniel Rowland had two curacies, Llangeitho and Nancwnlle, one worth £20 a year and the other £13, under his brother John Rowland, who was the vicar.[68] Howel Harris accompanied Rowland one Sunday as he officiated in both parishes, between 11 a.m. and midday at Llangeitho and between 1 p.m. And 2 p.m. at Nancwnlle.[69] Fortunately for Rowland and his parishioners, the two churches were close enough for him to be able to travel between them in the space of an hour; many other curates had a greater distance to travel on a Sunday. As Thomas Philipps, Laugharne, admitted to Bishop Ottley, pluralism was likely to affect the efficiency of the Church locally. Even with the best will in the world, travelling between livings could be something of an ordeal, especially in severe weather, as Thomas Rees stated in the visitation returns of 1755 when describing the journey of four miles between his two parishes of Llanfihangel Abercywyn and Meidrim: 'A long way my Lord; and the Roads from one church to the other, are so very bad, as must, of course, render travelling very irksome and tedious in the Winter.'[70] Erasmus Saunders suggested that the uncertainties of travel meant that many churches could not set a fixed time for the service, so that the congregation instead had to wait until the officiating clergyman managed to arrive.[71]

Hand in hand with pluralism inevitably went the problem of absenteeism. It was impossible for a pluralist to be resident in two or three parishes, so the best a diligent clergyman could do in such cases was to try to establish himself as centrally as possible for the area under his pastoral care. Where an incumbent was entirely absent, he would appoint a curate to undertake the responsibilities for his parish. In 1745, for instance, both the vicars of Llangadog and Llangathen, Owen Evans and Thomas Tenman, lived in England and left their parishes in the care of their curates.[72] Not all absentee clergy were non-resident entirely through choice, since several parishes lacked a parsonage in a suitable state of repair to house them. When William Williams was appointed to serve as curate to Theophilus Evans in Llanwrtyd, Llanddewi Abergwesyn and Llanfihangel Abergwesyn in Breconshire, he claimed he had to travel from his home in Llanfair-ar-y-bryn, some ten miles distant, as there was no house available in his new parishes. In the twenty-eight parishes listed by the rural dean of Carmarthen in 1745, sixteen were without any kind of accommodation for the clergy, five had a house in ruins and only seven were equipped with a habitable parsonage. It was also noted that sixteen churches were in need of some repairs, generally to the roof or the windows.[73] Poorly paid curates were unlikely to be able to afford to buy houses of their own, but might have to resort to renting locally where feasible. Erasmus Saunders confirmed the lack of suitable housing, adding that in many parishes there was not even any glebe land or ground on which to build a parsonage.⁷⁴ At Caeo, the vicar in the early years of the century, William Price, had two rooms built on the glebe land to provide a residence as the previous parsonage had fallen into decay about a century previously.⁷⁵ However, many of the necessary improvements were already under way during the 1740s, and there was an increase in the number of habitable parsonages noted in the visitation returns for 1755.

It may be that the gaps in provision created by pluralism and absenteeism did create space for Methodist societies to develop. For instance, three of the most successful societies in Carmarthenshire in 1744 were located in the deanery of Llandeilo and Llangadog: Talley with 60 members, Caeo with 55 members and Llansawel with 51 members.⁷⁶ These numbers may not seem very substantial, but they compare quite favourably with the communion figures for the churches in 1755: 100 at Easter in Talley, 180 at Easter in Cynwyl Gaeo but 100 more regularly, and 60 at Llansawel rising to 90 at Easter.⁷⁷ Lewis Evans, the vicar of Cynwyl Gaeo, was an absentee, living twenty miles away, and employed curates to take care of his livings in Cynwyl Gaeo and its chapelry, Llansawel.⁷⁸ Although there is some discrepancy about the value of Cynwyl Gaeo and Llansawel combined, they seem to have been worth around £55 a year, although Edward Tenison notes that they were reputedly worth £100 but let at £60.⁷⁹ Neither of the curates were likely to have seen much of that money. Evan Jones was curate of both Cynwyl Gaeo and Talley, the latter being worth only £8 a year.⁸⁰ He lived at Talley, despite there being no parsonage there.⁸¹ Llansawel was under the care of Nicholas Griffiths, who was also the curate of Llan-y-crwys, another curacy said to be worth £8 a year.⁸² For a small salary, therefore, they were expected to have the care of some 180 families in Talley, 240 in Cynwyl Gaeo and 100 in Llansawel.⁸³ Communion was administered monthly in these parishes, although the evidence of the consistory courts suggests that Nicholas Griffiths may have neglected his living in Llan-y-crwys in order to concentrate on Llansawel. Even after his departure, with Leyson Lewis officiating, communion was only celebrated three times a year in Llan-y-crwys in 1755.⁸⁴

There was no suggestion that Evan Jones was anything but a conscientious pastor, but the very fact that he lived in Talley was likely to cause some inconvenience to his parishioners in Cynwyl Gaeo. Talley and

Cynwyl Gaeo were amongst the most extensive parishes in Carmarthenshire and it was no easy task to ensure adequate oversight of every part. Evan Jones also served the parish of Llanfihangel Rhos-y-corn during the winter of 1732–3, at the request of the churchwardens, to substitute for the incumbent, James Thomas, who was in the process of being accused of neglecting his duties.[85] The fact that the wardens turned to Jones suggests that he had a good reputation and could be trusted to take his duties seriously. Jones also found venues to host the circulating schools in the neighbourhood, as well as catchising the pupils of the schools publicly and privately.[86] Despite his best endeavours, a thriving society continued to meet at Talley and Caeo.

St Davids also had the lowest proportion of graduates amongst its clergy of the four Welsh dioceses, another reflection of its financial condition. Only 32 per cent of its clergy in 1714 were graduates, compared with 61 pe cent in St Asaph and 72 per cent in Llandaff and an apparently high proportion of the clergy in Bangor.[87] Despite this, there were some distinguished scholars and authors to be found serving its parishes, including Theophilus Evans, Griffith Jones, Moses Williams and Samuel Williams. University education was a distant dream for many of the inhabitants of the south-west, but the grammar school at Carmarthen would have provided valuable education for those who could afford it. There were attempts to maintain some sort of standard of education amongst the clergy and to recruit 'literate persons', largely educated at grammar schools, as appropriate substitutes for graduates.[88] Certainly a number of competent clergy helped maintain the bureaucracy of the diocese, especially in the absence of its bishops. Edward Tenison in his report on his archdeaconry in 1710 singled out David Havard, the vicar of Abergwili, as 'a very good man' who 'would be of great use in Carmarthen'. He preached every Sunday and was striving to rebuild the chapel of ease in the parish in order to minister there also in the hope of thwarting the growth of Dissent in that part of the parish.[89] Havard came from a respectable farming family in the parish of Pen-boyr and went on to become a canon of St Davids and a linchpin in the administration of the diocese including deputising for the bishop in the examination of Griffith Jones.[90] Overall, the disreputable clergy were in a minority in the diocese and seem to have been disapproved of by their brethren, who were largely decent and diligent.

Deficiencies in parish clergy may well have fed the desire for some alternative such as the Methodist societies. Despite his innate loyalty to the Church, Howel Harris suggested that were 'every Minister in every Parish sent and owned of God – there would be no need of us'.[91] Harris's attitude towards the clergy was rather ambiguous, perhaps as a result of his own failure to gain holy orders. He respected the office, but saw failings in some individuals, suggesting that many 'put on black cloaths rather out of private views to grow rich and live easie than to study to promote the publick good, rich they grow but what good they do I know not'.[92] Harris may at times have been rather too credulous of the lurid tales he heard on his travels regarding the shocking misbehaviour of some of the clergy in south-west Wales. In St Kennox, Pembrokeshire, Harris heard of a clergyman who was so drunk that two men were required to carry him in and out of church.[93] He was told in 1739 that nobody was willing to take the sacrament at Llandybïe, Carmarthenshire, because the parishioners were so disgusted by the drunken behaviour of the vicar and his wife.[94] This is likely to have been inflated gossip, as the vicar of Llandybïe at the time was Thomas Rees, who served the parish for the best part of his life, as curate from 1724 and as vicar from 1736 until his death in 1756.[95] He was described in 1739 by his Methodist parishioner, Anthony Rees, as being too reluctant to offend and ended up 'like a shopkeeper or an Innkeeper which keeps every body willing' rather than preaching to them honestly of their faults.[96] Although Rees criticised the vicar, he made no mention of drunkenness, which one would certainly have expected to be added to the account if there were grounds to do so. It is difficult to accept some of the more scandalous aspects to the stories, including the tale of the clergyman in the Haverfordwest area who was said to have been imprisoned for six months for murdering his illegitimate child. According to local gossip, he kept a prostitute in the parsonage, and the garden of his house was full of the buried bodies of the illegitimate babies he had slaughtered, presumably in a futile attempt to preserve his reputation.[97] The subject of this particular gossip is likely to have been William Crowther of Maenclochog, Llangolman and Llandeilo in north Pembrokeshire, who was the subject of complaint to the bishop in 1743. He was said to keep an immoral woman in the vicarage, 'where he often frequents', who had two 'base children', although there is no mention of infanticide, nor any record of it in the secular courts.[98] There is no evidence to substantiate the more colourful rumours, but general concerns were being voiced about the standards of the clergy. Griffith Jones complained to Bishop Adam Ottley in 1715 that the immoral behaviour of some clergy was thoroughly undermining the worth of their sermons in the eyes of their parishioners:

> tis easier to hear a good sermon than see a good preacher for some there be strict in rules but loose in practice, preach as if they believed in earnest, but live as if they preached in jest, our lives either add much to or detract much from the Authority of our sermons, some profligates have owned that nothing promoted their prophaneness so much as the Immorality of Clergymen.[99]

The records of the consistory courts suggest that there may have been ample cause for complaint in some cases. One of the worst-afflicted parishes was Llan-y-crwys, which seemed to have endured a series of undesirable incumbents in the first half of the eighteenth century. In 1710, Edward Tenison listed a catalogue of complaints about the vicar, a Mr Jones who does not appear elsewhere in church records. He was non-resident, living about ten miles away, and was not always available when required to conduct services, to the point that the clerk of the parish read the burial service for a two-year-old child in the absence of the minister. Jones's predecessor had been removed for conducting clandestine marriages, which usually meant conducting services outside the prescribed hours, and was also said to interrupt divine service on a Sunday in order to serve customers in the alehouse he kept in the churchyard.[100] The situation was hardly helped by the fact that the incumbent was allowed a salary of just £4–£5 a year by the lay impropriator, Marmaduke Lloyd of Caeo.

By 1741 Nicholas Griffiths had been curate of Llan-y-crwys for five years, also serving Llansawel, with some eight miles to travel between the two churches. Griffiths was accused in the consistory court by a churchwarden, David Edwards, of neglecting his duty to Llan-y-crwys on Sundays in favour of conducting services at Llansawel.[101] In addition, on Christmas Day 1740 the parishioners had assembled in anticipation of a communion service but their curate had not appeared. Another witness explained that a service had been provided on Christmas Eve but in the failing light Griffiths proved too short-sighted to be able to read the liturgy without stumbling badly. His most heinous offence was regarded as the three-day delay in burying the deceased child of Rees Thomas David, a parishioner described as a husbandman. The parish clerk testified that Griffiths had refused because he had to tend to his corn but had promised to send another clergyman to take his place, a promise he had failed to keep. There were suggestions that the parishioners were attending Dissenting meetings in the absence of regular public worship in their parish church, and a hint that the underlying problem was financial with Griffiths doubling up as a farmer as well as a pluralist curate.

Griffiths was succeeded by around 1748 by Lewis Lewis, son of James Lewis, a member of the minor gentry, of Cefntrenfa, in Cil-y-cwm. Lewis had spent a few months at Jesus College, Oxford, in 1716 before being ordained. In 1721 he married Mary, the daughter of David Morgan of Rhosybedw, Llan-y-crwys, so had a connection to the parish. Their only daughter, Mary, married Marmaduke Bowen, a former army captain and younger son of the Bowen family of Gurrey, near Llandeilo.[102] Lewis was the clergyman who married Howel Harris and Anne Williams at Ystrad-ffin chapel on 18 June 1744, and it is likely that he is the Lewis Lewis who offered Harris hospitality overnight on one occasion in August 1744.[103] Even then, Harris had doubts about his character, as he noted in his diary: 'I met Mr Lewis Lewis a Clergyman who seemed to me to be full of Power & Life & yet falls abominably.'[104]

Lewis's time in the parish of Llan-y-crwys was marred by controversy, leading to a number of accusations before the consistory court. The records suggest that the trouble started with the churchwardens using benches to bar the door to prevent Lewis entering the church on two successive Sundays. On the second occasion, on 14 October 1750, Lewis apparently lost all patience and took an axe to the door, with the backing of a group of supporters, including his son-in-law, Marmaduke Bowen. Having broken through, Bowen entered armed with a drawn sword in one hand and an oak cudgel in the other, which suggests that Lewis's group had come prepared for a fight. Bowen was accused of repeated attempts to run through one William Thomas, ultimately resorting to using the cudgel to render Thomas unconscious. During this attack, he reportedly uttered a number of 'terrifying oaths' and threats to murder Thomas, 'not fitting nor becoming in the Holy Church'. The conflict led to a series of reciprocal accusations before the consistory court, with Thomas recovering to accuse Bowen of brawling and violence in church.[105] Lewis was accused by his churchwardens of breaking open the church door and of neglect of duty by getting so drunk after service on Easter Sunday that he managed to lose both his hat and his horse on his way home and was incapable of officiating on Easter Monday.[106] Lewis in turn accused two of his churchwardens, John Edwards and David Thomas, of obstructing him from performing divine service.[107] Quite a gang had apparently gathered to break the siege on the church, since two others, John Price and Thomas Price, were also accused of violence in church by Lewis's opponents.[108] The whole affair suggested a remarkable degree of tension in the parish and a breakdown in the normal relationship between incumbent, churchwardens and parishioners. Since both Griffiths and Lewis were accused by their churchwardens, in all fairness it must be acknowledged that it is possible that some of the prominent parishioners were difficult to manage and that the fault was not entirely with the clergy.

However, although the outcome of the consistory court cases is not documented, the Carmarthenshire Quarter Sessions records reveal that Lewis and his companions were found to be at fault. Lewis, along with Marmaduke Bowen and Rowland Evan, pleaded guilty to five counts of riot and assault. They received a 6d fine in each case, which was not the heaviest penalty the magistrates had at their disposal, and this did not seem to have been considered sufficiently serious for the Great Sessions.[109] It is no great surprise to see no further record of Lewis Lewis as curate at Llan-y-crwys or elsewhere in the archdeaconry. His combative son-in-law Marmaduke Bowen was to be in trouble with the law once again when, along with his son Lewis Lloyd Bowen and ten other co-defendents, he was accused in 1770 of being an accessory to the murder of his brother-in-law, William Powell of Glanareth. The case caused something of a sensation involving as it did a brutal murder, combined with the rumour that the instigator of the murder plot was having an affair with Powell's wife, Marmaduke Bowen's sister Catherine. However, Bowen and his son were amongst those acquitted at trial in Hereford, although six others were hanged for their part in the crime.[110]

A number of other clergy were accused of various offences before the consistory court, including James Thomas, vicar of Llanfihangel Rhos-y-corn, for drunkenness and neglect of duty in 1733; John James, vicar of Meidrim and William Price, curate of Llan-non, both for neglect of duty, in 1740 and 1741; John Jones, curate of Llan-gain, in 1745 for drunkenness; and William Thomas, vicar of Aber-nant for neglect of duty in 1747.[111] Only the witness statements survive in most cases and not the outcome, except for the case of James Thomas, who was found guilty of both charges. The testimony of seven witnesses survives to confirm that Thomas would spend entire nights drinking in various alehouses. He was reported to have thrown up three times during one of his drinking bouts, but to have carried on regardless. The accusation of neglect of duty stemmed from his refusal to visit Llanfihangel more than four times a year, and not at all during the winter months, since it was only a chapelry under Llanllwni. Thomas was vicar of Llanbydder and of Henllan in Cardiganshire, as well as curate of Pencarreg. The witnesses all agreed that there was a distance of nine to ten miles between Llanfihangel and Henllan, where it seems Thomas was resident. When he had been absent for six successive Sundays by September 1732 and declared that he had no intention of visiting for the rest of the winter, the churchwardens turned to the lay impropriator Erasmus Philipps for assistance. Philipps promised to consult the bishop and in the meantime was ready to pay for the services of a substitute clergyman. The churchwardens therefore requested Evan Jones, curate of the neighbouring parish of Talley, to conduct services, which he did regularly until Easter. However, on Easter Sunday, with the return of spring, Thomas arrived to resume his duties, threatening Jones and snatching the Book of Common Prayer from his hands to prevent him continuing with the service. The consistory court ruled that he was at fault and required him to pay the costs of £6 9s. Since he did not pay, he was suspended from all his offices.

In most of these cases there is no record of the judgement and therefore is no certainty that all or any of the other individuals were guilty of negligence. The fact that they reached the court suggests that it was felt there was a case to answer, since when Samuel Williams, vicar of Llandyfrïog, was accused of neglect of duty in 1719 it was decided not to pursue the case, as the accusations were too general with insufficient supporting evidence.[112] No consistory court records survive for the archdeaconries of St Davids and Cardigan during this period, so these complaints about clergy are drawn from the archdeaconry of Carmarthen alone. In the archdeaconry of Brecon, with the exception of accusations of conducting clandestine marriages, only one complaint relating to neglect of duty appears in the records for 1730–60, compared to the seventeen over the same period in the archdeaconry of Carmarthen.[113] It is worth noting that there were fewer livings worth under £20 a year and more worth over £50 a year in Brecon archdeaconry than in any of the other archdeaconries in the diocese.[114] In Llandaff between 1730 and 1760, there were thirteen complaints against members of the clergy. One related to a clandestine marriage and the remaining twelve to drunkenness and neglect of duty, although in the case of John Powell of Aberystruth and Philip Thomas of Wenvoe this arose mainly from absence arising from their activities with the Methodist movement.[115] There are unfortunately no consistory court records for St Asaph between 1730 and 1760 to provide a comparison. However, in the diocese of Bangor, no complaints against clergy appear in the consistory court records over the same period, although there are references to accusations in the surviving act books, but without any details. The evidence is rather too scarce to allow for firm conclusions, although it would broadly seem to confirm Evan Evans's suggestion that the better-paid clergy in the north were better placed to fulfil their duties to the satisfaction of all.

One of the potential causes of offence seems to have been the occasional unavailability of the clergy to bury the dead in what was considered a seemly and timely fashion. It was a theme in a number of complaints of neglect of duty and was sometimes caused by the pressures facing a pastor with several parishes calling out for various services. Edward Tenison noted in 1710 that, in the absence of the minister, the parish clerk of Llan-y-crwys read the burial service for a two-year-old child. In the same parish, the sexton's wife lay in the grave for three days before William Price, the minister of Cynwyl Gaeo, happened to be in the area and was prevailed upon to conduct the service.[116] In the parish of Meidrim in 1739 and 1740 there were several issues relating to the treatment of the dying and dead which led to accusations in the consistory court against the vicar, John James, and the parish clerk and sexton, Thomas Rees John. The sexton was said by the vicar to have refused to dig a grave for David Lewis, so that the vicar and the deceased's friends had to complete the task. During another burial service he was reported to have interrupted the vicar with 'Irreverent Noise and disturbance'.[117] The vicar in turn was accused by several witnesses of neglecting to visit parishioners on their deathbed to give communion, to their profound distress. He was also said to have twice refused to perform the burial service, so that corpses lay unburied in the church. The most painful experience was that of William Brown, a thirty-eight-year-old butcher, who testified that he had requested the vicar to visit his seriously ill wife on 7 May, but that she had died on 11 May without receiving the sacrament as requested. In August of the same year, James was said to have refused to bury Brown's dead child unless he was paid beforehand, with the result that the child was put in the grave without Christian burial.[118] James appeared at the court at St Peter's Church Carmarthen on 19 March 1741 before the Revd Joseph Hill, dean of St Davids, standing in for Edward Jones, the chancellor. James's defence was that he had been taken prisoner by David Morgan, the under-sheriff of Carmarthenshire, seemingly on some matter relating to financial offences, just as he was about to proceed to the churchyard. When he returned to the parish, he offered to open the grave to perform the burial service, but William Brown refused, since the child had been buried a week already. Giving evidence relating to another controversial incident, David Lewis, the vicar of Aber-nant testified that he had been asked by James to take the funeral of William Thomas on 3 April 1740, but on the day was interrupted by James, who snatched his surplice from him and refused to allow him to proceed.[119]

The consistory court records show no sign of general dissatisfaction with the Church, despite disquiet over some of those in its holy orders. There are no instances of refusal to pay tithe or church rate because of opposition to the Church or its clergy. Usually only Quakers refused to pay the tithe on religious grounds, and any occasions of failure to pay the church rate are usually explained by a complaint that the rate had been unfairly calculated or had been raised on land which had not previously been subject to payment. For instance, Alex Ferguson of Carmarthen complained in September 1742 that the wardens of St

Peter's Church had taxed him 1s. 1d for a field called Parc y Conduit, which he had never paid before.[120] The rate was levied on all inhabitants of the parish who owned land or were in receipt of income, and was assessed on the basis of estimates of the worth of dwellings in town and of the annual income of agricultural land in the countryside. Since it was normally seen as a fixed payment, any reassessment was very rare, so perceived unfairnesses could continue to grate. There might also be protests that land was being taxed in the wrong parish, which would then require an examination of the parish boundaries.[121]

Another member of the clergy in Carmarthenshire who fell foul of the usual rules of conduct was Griffith Jones. Having been ordained in 1708, he was curate of Laugharne for a period before advancing quickly to become rector of Llandeilo Abercywyn in 1711 and in 1716 rector of Llanddowror, the parish with which his name is inextricably linked. As a young clergyman, Jones caused a stir in south Carmarthenshire with his energetic, heartfelt preaching. He was in great demand beyond the confines of his own parish, attracting eager crowds, sometimes more than any church could contain, requiring him to preach outside. One of his sermons in Llanddewibrefi had a profound effect on Daniel Rowland, inspiring him to embark on a similar preaching career.[122] Jones was called before Bishop Ottley in 1714 to undergo 'a sort of trial' over accusations of neglecting his own duties, whilst intruding without permission in the churches of other ministers.[123] From the evidence of other clergy, it was established that Jones had only ever responded to express invitations from incumbents, or their curates or 'the best inhabitants' of the parishes concerned. The bishop was willing for him to preach anywhere in future, as long as he did so at the invitation of the minister and did not trespass on other parishes without consent. It was obvious that the support of Sir John Philipps of Picton Castle was an important element in protecting Jones from the displeasure of the Church, and it was his patronage which secured him the parish of Llanddowror. Philipps considered Jones 'one of the most sincerest Christians I ever had the happiness to converse with', and it is therefore no wonder that he was happy to see him wed to his sister Margaret in 1720.[124] Jones himself mounted a robust defence under pressure. His letter to Bishop Ottley was remarkably frank in its assessment of the prevailing ignorance of large sections of the population and the failure of the clergy to act to address the problem.¹²⁵ This concern with trying to improve basic standards of knowledge would impel him at a later date to take further actions beyond preaching.

Despite some evidence of inappropriate conduct by some of the clergy, there seems to be no clear correlation between parishes where clergy were accused of negligence and the location of societies. There was a fairly successful society in Llan-non, but Meidrim society varied considerably in number between twenty to forty and back to fifteen.¹²⁶ No society seems to have been established in Llanfihangel Rhos-y-corn or Llan-gain. It may be that matters improved quite quickly in Llanfihangel Rhos-y-corn once John Thomas became vicar there and at Llanllwni in 1741. Crucially perhaps, he did not also serve Llanybydder, Pencarreg and Henllan, so did not have such a wide area under his care. Henllan, Llanybydder, Pencarreg and Llanllwni were all relatively close together, but Llanfihangel Rhos-y-corn was something of an outlier, which was perhaps more than James Thomas had been able to manage in combination with his other responsibilities. In the case of Llan-y-crwys, it is conceivable that parishioners joined the nearby societies at Cwm-ann and Cwrtycadno, but there is no record of any Methodist society in the parish itself, although Howel Harris visited fairly regularly.

The Church did face a number of problems in the south-west, therefore, and the consistory courts did hear some extreme cases which could have caused relatives and parishioners in general considerable offence. There was an abiding fear apparent from the early eighteenth century that any such failure on behalf of the Anglican clergy could result in desertions to Dissent. In 1707 Captain Lewes of Llangoedmor wrote to the bishop to complain of the shortcomings of the rector of the parish, including storing malt in part of the church building which it was said:

> has given great offence to many of his Parishioners, & in these dissenting times lead some into an opinion that all places are alike to honour God in, & that a Barn or Beast house is as good as the Church for that purpose, & so several of them have gone from him over to the Conventicle.¹²⁷

Tenison expressed similar concerns over the situation in Llan-y-crwys in 1710, noting that parishioners drifted off to the newly established Presbyterian meeting house when there were no sermons preached in the church. He detected a similar problem in Tre-lech, and suspected that there would be fewer Dissenters in Henllan Amgoed if duty was done properly in the church.[128] It was said in 1741 that William Price's neglect of his duty as curate of Llan-non had driven parishioners to other churches. In the case of William Thomas, vicar of Aber-nant, the church-warden who accused him of drunkenness claimed that the 'best and sober part of the congregation' had gone to other, unspecified, places of worship because Thomas had neglected divine service and communion throughout his five years in the parish, and his curate was only in deacon's orders and could not therefore fulfil all the obligations of the role.[129] It may have been nearby parish churches or established Dissenting meeting houses that gained most when regular church services broke down completely, rather than the emerging Methodist groups, which may have seemed a less than adequate substitute for public worship. Methodist societies seemed to recruit more where they operated as additional spiritual provision in parishes where the clergy were not necessarily negligent but struggling to fulfil all the demands on their time.

Erasmus Saunders regarded the willingness of the people of the south-west to tolerate dilapidated churches and harassed curates as sure evidence of their religious inclinations.[130] Whereas Saunders has been castigated for prejudice in his comments on the Church, these observations have generally been accepted, although here again he may be somewhat biased as a native of Pembrokeshire. Saunders pointed to the delight in religious songs such as carols and *halsingod*, as well as the popular verses composed by Rees Prichard in the seventeenth century, as evidence. To this may be added the obvious enthusiastic response to the preaching of Griffith Jones, twenty years and more before the start of the revival. Yet the tradition of the travelling field preacher goes further back even than Griffith Jones to the itinerancy of the seventeenth-century Dissenters such as Vavasor Powell and Stephen Hughes.

The Influence of Dissent

Despite concerns that the Church might lose support, it must be said that Dissent was not a strong force in south-west Wales in the early eighteenth century. Figures from the Compton Census suggest 247 Nonconformists compared to 13,494 conformists in the Cardigan archdeaconry, 597 Nonconformists in the Carmarthen archdeaconry compared to 23,171 conformists, and 196 Nonconformists compared to 10,557 conformists in the archdeaconry of St Davids. Overall, for St Davids the results suggest a total of 2,401 Nonconformists across 353 returns compared to 69,972 conforming Anglicans and 218 Catholics.[131] Once the Toleration Act of 1689 granted freedom of worship to Protestant Dissenters, there was some gradual growth, but nothing to threaten the predominance of the Church. By *c.* 1715–18, Dissenters still amounted to less than 5 per cent of the population according to the figures collected by the Dissenting denominations themselves. There were said to be around 89 Dissenting congregations in total, with a total membership of 17,770, mainly located in the southern counties.[132] By 1742 Edmund Jones estimated that the two largest denominations, the Independents (or Congregationalists) and the Baptists, had 106 chapels in Wales, with 88 located in the south of the country.[133] Dissenters therefore remained a small proportion of the worshipping population, although they were often a significant and influential scattering. They probably had an influence in terms of publishing that was disproportionate to their levels of support in society. This was a result of the activities of a group of educated Dissenters who saw the printed word as an essential means of spreading religious knowledge. Some like Stephen Hughes and Charles Edwards, who had lost their parishes with the restoration of the monarchy and the passing of the Act of Uniformity in 1662, sought alternative means of making a contribution by writing, translating and editing suitably instructive works in Welsh.

During the period of persecution between the restoration and the advent of Toleration in 1689, Dissenting groups had been forced to adapt and to develop methods of continuing with their religious beliefs without attracting too much attention from the authorities. They were unable openly to ordain any new clergy during this period, so were reliant to a large extent on ministers ejected from their Anglican parishes and on lay pastors who emerged from amongst the congregations. The members were often spread over a considerable distance with a limited number of ministers to care for them. In many ways, their situation was similar to that of the early Methodist movement, and they developed similar solutions to the problem of maintaining small, scattered communities of adherents over a wide area. Their churches were often 'county churches' comprising a number of groups meeting at varying locations in order to avoid persecution. Gathered churches emerged like the Baptists of Rhydwilym who worshipped at different places on the Pembrokeshire–Carmarthenshire border and recruited members from all three counties in the south-west. It was not unusual to find such churches lurking on county boundaries where jurisdictions might be blurred and where there was a better chance to escape an irate magistrate who had no power across the county lines. By 1689, Rhydwilym already had 113 members located in thirty-eight different parishes in the three counties.[134] By 1723, the membership had almost doubled to 220.[135]

With this sort of geographical range, itinerant preachers were an essential element, as indeed they had been during the Commonwealth period, when there were not enough ministers of an appropriate Puritan persuasion to fill all the gaps left by clergy removed for their loyalty to King and Established Church. Stephen Hughes, a native of Carmarthenshire, had been ejected from his parish of Meidrim in the wake of the Restoration and had settled in Swansea with his wealthy and well-connected wife, Catherine Daniel.[136] Yet he continued to serve the Dissenting congregations of Carmarthenshire, travelling some eight or ten miles between different groups to visit them all, with a steadfast dedication which earned him the title 'the Apostle of Carmarthenshire'.[137] His death in 1688 deprived him of the opportunity to act as official minister to his flock in Carmarthenshire, but the Independent churches formed in the county after 1689 continued to honour him as their founder.[138] This sort of broad supervision over small groups of fluctuating size and location was by no means dissimilar to the circuits developed by the Methodist superintendents in the 1740s.

There were territorial similarities between Dissent and early Methodism, both gaining ground mainly in the south in their initial stages and both appealing largely in rural areas. Most Dissenting churches had a membership drawn from across a wide area, beyond the immediate locality, so that parishes without a meeting house could still contain Dissenting families. The report of Edward Tenison on the archdeaconry of Carmarthen suggests that Dissent was a real presence in many areas, even if only in relatively small numbers. The Baptists of Rhydwilym continued to meet in Llandysilio, although seemingly only attracting four families from the parish itself, most members travelling from other areas. The strongest centre of Dissent seemed to be the parish of Llanfair-ar-y-bryn, where half the 156 families were said to be Dissenters. This parish contained the Independent church of Cefnarthen, where William Williams's family were members, and that region of Carmarthenshire was later to respond positively to the evangelical revival. It was likely to be the cause at Pant-teg which caused concern in Tenison's report on Abergwili parish, although its members were dispersed across some five parishes in total. This Independent church was already associated with Christmas Samuel in 1710 and he would become their minister in 1711 until his death in 1764. As with the Methodists, the support for Dissent was much weaker in the towns, with no more than ten Dissenters listed for Carmarthen.[139] Some Dissenters saw common cause with the early Methodists and welcomed their activities. In its early years, when the revival remained somwhat fluid and not clearly defined, it seemed to transcend some of the traditional denominational allegiances. Howel Harris visited several areas on the express invitation of Dissenting ministers who extended a hand of friendship to the young movement. The Methodist leaders gained a great deal from the good will of experienced ministers such as Philip Pugh who, for over fifty years between 1709 and 1760, had the care of the churches of Cilgwyn, Llwyn Rhys, Caeronnen, Abermeurig and Crug-y-maen in Cardiganshire.[140] Pugh gave valuable advice to his young Anglican neighbour Daniel Rowland at the start of his career, but distanced himself from the movement in later years, as did a number of other previously well-intentioned Dissenters.

One area of the south-west which proved remarkably resistant to the forces of the evangelical revival was the area on the borders of Cardiganshire and Carmarthenshire along the river Teifi between Llandysul and Lampeter and inland towards Ciliau Aeron which became the stronghold of Arminianism. This was derided as 'the Black Spot' in the early nineteenth century by Calvinistic Methodists whose energy and enthusiasm failed to have any impact on the rational Dissent which developed there. The first Arminian chapel was founded at Llwynrhydowen, near Lampeter, in 1733 by Jenkin Jenkins, a former student at Carmarthen

Academy, whose ideas were regarded as too suspect for the Independents amongst whom he had been reared. The cause threw out several offshoots, so that a cluster of Arminian chapels developed in the surrounding area. After Jenkins's death in 1742, David Lloyd led them along a path towards Arianism, denying the divinity of Christ.[141] Some of Philip Pugh's Independent chapels also espoused similar theological ideas after his death in 1760, leading to the largest concentration of Unitarian chapels in Wales by the early nineteenth century.[142]

It is difficult to assess precisely the influence that Dissent had on the early Methodist movement, but both appealed to similar sections of society in similar geographical locations. Even more intangible is the influence of Dissenting publications which may well have played a part in preparing the way for the evangelical revival. Both original Welsh works and translations from the work of successful English authors were read by those affected by the revival. Howel Harris felt convinced that God had entrusted his gospel to the predecessors of the Dissenters and praised Morgan Llwyd's remarkable *Llyfr y Tri Aderyn* (The Book of the Three Birds).[143] Versions of John Bunyan's works proved highly successful, especially *Taith y Pererin*, the translation of *Pilgrim's Progress* overseen by Stephen Hughes, the conclusion of which proved a comfort to Richard Tibbott.[144] It was another of Bunyan's works, *Come and Welcome to Jesus Christ*, which helped David Jones, of Dygoed, Llanarthney, towards his conversion experience.[145] Seventeenth-century Puritan works were evidently still being read and appreciated, several of them being translated for the first time in the early eighteenth century. It is highly significant that the first printing press to be established in Wales in 1718 was situated in Adpar, on the Cardiganshire side of the border with Carmarthenshire near Newcastle Emlyn. It soon moved to Carmarthen, which became a major centre for print culture through the medium of Welsh. This location drew on and encouraged the works of authors from the south-west, both Anglican and Dissenter, whose chief focus was on instilling greater knowledge of the principles of the Protestant faith. Even William Williams, though he depicted Wales languishing in darkness prior to 1738, also stated that revival was the expectation of many ministers who were hoping and striving towards that end, so that there were 'a thousand sighs for the sun to rise' in revival.[146]

In the years after Toleration, Dissent was said to consolidate its support 'in large parishes and scattered rural communities where church discipline was at its weakest', a pattern similar to the early Methodist societies.[147] It was probably in such areas that the devout, increasingly literate middling sorts were becoming more open to the offer of some additional or more exciting spiritual provision than that which was available in the parish church. The problems of the diocese certainly contributed to the growth of the movement, and the Methodists offered attractions that the Church seemed to be lacking in some respects. William Morris denounced the eighteenth-century bishops as unfit to follow in the footsteps of St David. This suggests that in Wales itself the saint and his diocese retained a certain status, although this may not have had as much significance for those outside the country.[148] Morris also referred to Richard Davies, as an eminent former bishop of St Asaph and St Davids who would be horrified by the current crop of bishops. Not all of the early Anglican bishops of Wales were without fault by any means, but a substantial proportion of them were dedicated to their dioceses and concerned with ensuring spiritual guidance for those under their care. There was a policy under Elizabeth I of selecting Welshmen to serve Welsh dioceses, with thirteen Welshmen amongst the sixteen bishops appointed in the period. They tended as a result to be more aware of the local circumstances and were described by Glanmor Williams as 'a learned, resident, preaching clergy, familiar with their dioceses, and well-known to their parish priests'.[149] By the eighteenth century, Welsh remained the only language of the majority of the population, and knowledge of the language would still have been of use to any bishop who wished to communicate beyond the ranks of his own clergy. There may have been little expectation that any bishop would do so, however. It has been argued that to judge the bishops for their lack of knowledge of the Welsh language is to fail to appreciate their political role, which was generally the major consideration in their appointment, with a sense perhaps that it was for the clergy in the diocese to undertake pastoral care.[150] Yet that argument in essence confirms that they were never likely to be active spiritual leaders. Measured by the standards of the broader institution of the Established Church, the early eighteenth-century bishops of Wales were often conscientious enough, and the bishops of St Davids on the whole were far from the worst examples of their kind. In all fairness, the most fundamental problem of the poverty of the Church in the area was beyond the capacity of the episcopacy to remedy. The bishops generally regulated their clergy adequately, performed ordinations regularly and advocated suitable provision of services and sermons. Several of them could thus be considered effective, if absentee, managers of their dioceses. Yet how much more might have been achieved by resident bishops with an understanding of the needs of the people and a wholehearted commitment to developments such as the circulating schools? In order to uphold the rules and regulations of the Church and to maintain order and discipline among the clergy, Adam Ottley was undoubtedly right to question Griffith Jones's practice of preaching outside his parish. But Griffith Jones had a far deeper insight into the needs of the people than any of the bishops, and was prepared to take action on his own initiative to improve matters. His efforts, along with the dedicated work of both Anglicans and Dissenters, did much to help prepare the ground for Methodism, which was by no means a startlingly sudden phenomenon, but the outcome of decades of careful development.

Notes

1. E. Saunders, *A View of the State of Religion in the Diocese of St David's about the Beginning of the 18th Century* (reprint, Cardiff: University of Wales Press, 1949), p. 32.
2. W. Gibson, *Church, State and Society, 1760–1850* (London: Macmillan, 1994), p. 36.
3. NLW, Ottley (Pitchford Hall MSS and Documents)/30, 21 May 1707; William Jacob, 'Episcopal Administration' in G. Williams, W. Jacob, N. Yates and F. Knight, *The Welsh Church from Reformation to Disestablishment, 1603–1920* (Cardiff: University of Wales Press, 2007), p. 83.
4. Jacob, 'Episcopal Administration', p. 83.
5. G. Williams, 'Unity of Religion or Unity of Language? Protestants and Catholics and the Welsh Language 1536–1660', in G. H. Jenkins (ed.), *The Welsh Language Before the Industrial Revolution* (Cardiff: University of Wales Press, 1997), pp. 212–19; E. M. White, *The Welsh Bible* (Stroud: Tempus, 2007), pp. 24–37.
6. See G. H. Jenkins, *Protestant Dissenters in Wales 1639–1689* (Cardiff: University of Wales Press, 1992).
7. A. Whiteman (ed.), *The Compton Census of 1676: A Critical Edition* (Oxford: Oxford University Press, 1986), pp. 456–8.
8. DHH 118, 26 October 1745.

9   For instance, DHH 84, 8 January 1742; Trevecka MS 736, Howel Harris to William McCulloch, 23 November 1742.
10 DHH 103, 5 October 1743.
11 For instance, DHH 90, 9 May 1742; Trevecka MS 755, Harris to Anne Williams, 11 December 1742; Trevecka MS 916, Harris to Miss BeeBee, 9 July 1743; Trevecka MS 934, Harris to Richard Thomas Bateman, 25 July 1743; DHH 105, 2 December 1743.
12 For instance, DHH 121, 19 January 1746; Trevecka MS 343, Harris to David Lloyd, 14 June 1741.
13 DHH 84, 9 January 1742. Claggett had sent Rowland a copy of the *The New Weekly Miscellany* which contained an article condemning Rowland's activities, an action interpreted as a threat to Rowland's position in the Church and to the Methodist cause in the diocese. See E. Evans, *Daniel Rowland and the Great Evangelical Awakening in Wales* (Edinburgh: Banner of Truth Trust, 1985), pp. 155–63.
14 I. G. Jones, *Mid-Victorian Wales: The Observers and the Observed* (Cardiff: University of Wales Press, 1992), p. 63.
15 D. L. Thomas and D. F. Evans, 'Saunders, Erasmus (1670–1724)', *Oxford Dictionary of National Biography* (Oxford University Press, 23 September 2004). Accessed 30 September 2019, https://www.oxforddnb.com/view/10.1093/ref:odnb/9780198614128.001.0001/odnb-9780198614128-e-24693.
16 G. Williams, 'Bishop William Morgan and the First Welsh Bible', in *The Welsh in their Religion: Historical Essays* (Cardiff: University of Wales Press, 1991), pp. 208–9.
17 G. H. Jenkins, *Literature, Religion and Society in Wales 1660–1730* (Cardiff: University of Wales Press, 1978), p. 305.
18 A. Lewis, 'Edward Richard a Ieuan Fardd', *Ysgrifau Beirniadol*, 10 (1977), 270–7; G. H. Jenkins, 'Yr Eglwys "Wiwlwys Olau" a'u Beirniaid', *Ceredigion*, 10 (1985), 140–1; G. Morgan, *Ieuan Fardd* (Llandysul: Gwasg Gomer, 1988), pp. 8–16.
19 See Ff. Jones, 'Celticism and Pre-Romanticism: Evan Evans', in B. Jarvis (ed.), *A Guide to Welsh Literature c. 1700–1800* (Cardiff: University of Wales Press, 2000), pp. 104–25.
20 NLW (Panton) MS 2009B, 'The Grievances of the Church in Wales' (c. 1765), pp. 30–1.
21 J. H. Davies (ed.), *The Letters of Lewis, Richard, William and John Morris, of Anglesey, (Morrisiaid Môn), 1728–1765* (2 vols, Aberystwyth, 1907–9), I, p. 288.
22 The charge was related to the appointment of Watson's nephew, John Medley, as archdeacon of St Davids. Jacob, 'Episcopal Administration', pp. 94–5; W. Gibson, '"The most glorious enterprises have been achiev'd": The Restoration Diocese of St Davids 1660–1730', in W. Gibson and J. Morgan-Guy (eds), *Religion and Society in the Diocese of St Davids 1485–2011* (Farnham: Ashgate, 2015), pp. 97–102.
23 R. L. Brown, *In Pursuit of a Welsh Episcopate: Appointments to Welsh Sees 1840–1905* (Cardiff: University of Wales Press, 2005), p. 8.
24 R. D. Cornwall, 'George Bull (1634–1710)', *Oxford Dictionary of National Biography* (Oxford University Press, 23 September 2004). Accessed 30 Sep. 2019,

https://www.oxforddnb.com/view/10.1093/ref:odnb/9780198614128.001.0001/ odnb-9780198614128-e-3903.

25 J. D. Davies 'Adam Ottley (bap.1655, d.1723)', *Oxford Dictionary of National Biography* (Oxford University Press, 23 September 2004). Accessed 30 Sep. 2019, *https://www.oxforddnb.com/view/10.1093/ref:odnb/9780198614128.001.0001/ odnb-9780198614128-e-63755.*

26 Ottley (Pitchford Hall MSS and Documents)/3230, 10 October 1723; S. R. Thomas, 'The diocese of St David's in the eighteenth century' (unpublished MA, University of Wales, 1983), 237.

27 Gibson, *Church, State and Society*, p. 7; Brown, *In Pursuit of a Welsh Episcopate*, p. 8; R. Hole, 'Richard Watson (1737–1816)', *Oxford Dictionary of National Biography* (Oxford University Press, 23 September 2004). Accessed 30 September 2019, *https://www.oxforddnb.com/view/10.1093/ref:odnb/ 9780198614128.001.0001/odnb-9780198614128-e-28857*.

28 Thomas, 'The Diocese of St David's in the Eighteenth Century', p. 238.

29 NLW MS 6203E, Papers relating to Isaac Williams, c. 1764–1805, p. 34.

30 Davies, 'Adam Ottley'; Gibson, '"The most glorious enterprises have been achiev'd": The Restoration Diocese of St Davids 1660–1730', p. 104.

31 Brown, *In Pursuit of a Welsh Episcopate*, p. 7.

32 D. W. Hayton, 'John Evans (c.1652–1724)', *Oxford Dictionary of National Biography* (Oxford University Press, 23 September 2004). Accessed 30 September 2019, *https://www.oxforddnb.com/view/10.1093/ref:odnb/ 9780198614128.001.0001/odnb-9780198614128-e-8961.*

33 See R. L. Brown, 'Bishop William Basil Tickell Jones (1822–1897)', *Ceredigion*, XVI/4 (2012), 85–101.

34 Brown, *In Pursuit of a Welsh Episcopate*, p. 2.

35 O. W. Jones, 'The Welsh Church in the Eighteenth Century', in David Walker (ed.), *A History of the Church in Wales* (Penarth: Historical Society of the Church in Wales, 1976), p. 119.

36 Davies (ed.), *The Letters of Lewis, Richard, William and John Morris*, I, pp. 237, 288.

37 Thomas, 'The Diocese of St David's in the Eighteenth Century', p. 69.

38 M. Clement (ed.), *Correspondence and Minutes of the S.P.C.K. relating to Wales, 1699–1740* (Cardiff: University of Wales Press, 1952), p. 42.

39 Clement, *Correspondence and Minutes of the S.P.C.K.*, p. 276.

40 Clement, *Correspondence and Minutes of the S.P.C.K.*, p. 335.

41 NLW, Records of the Church in Wales, Bangor Diocesan Records B/QA/2-12. Two places of worship in Caernarfon and fourteen in Merioneth were part of St Asaph diocese, but these were also Welsh-medium.

42 I. Bowen (ed.), *The Statutes of Wales* (London: T. Fisher Unwin, 1908), p. 150.

43 NLW, Records of the Church in Wales, St Davids Diocesan Records, SD/QA/1–15, 61–72, 120–35. See also E. M. White, 'The Established Church, Dissent and the Welsh Language c.1660–1811', in G. H. Jenkins (ed.), *The Welsh Language Before the Industrial Revolution* (Cardiff: University of Wales Press, 1997), pp. 235–87.

44 SD/QA/180–200.

45 In 1755, of sixteen places of worship who submitted visitation returns, thirteen had English services, three had Welsh services and there was one bilingual service. SD/QA/61.

46 SD/QA129.
47 LL/QA/10.
48 SD/QA/7.
49 SD/MISC/1199, 3 September 1743.
50 S. Williams, *Amser a Diwedd Amser* (Llundain: Ebenezer Tracy, 1707), A2r–v; M. Williams, *Pregeth a Barablwyd yn Eglwys Crist yn Llundain* (Llundain: Printwyr y Brenin, 1718), p. 14.
51 *The Welch Piety* (London, 1740), pp. 41–2.
52 SD/QA/1. White, 'The Established Church, Dissent and the Welsh Language *c.*1660–1811', pp. 240–1.
53 Gibson, '"The most glorious enterprises have been achiev'd": The Restoration Diocese of St Davids 1660–1730', pp. 109–10.
54 Saunders, *A View of the State of Religion in the Diocese of St David's*, pp. 24–5.
55 M. Clement (ed.), *Correspondence and Minutes of the S.P.C.K. Relating to Wales 1699–1740* (Cardiff: University of Wales Press, 1952), p. 254.
56 Saunders, *A View of the State of Religion*, p. 15.
57 Quoted in Gibson, '"The most glorious enterprises have been achiev'd": The Restoration Diocese of St Davids 1660–1730', p. 109.
58 G. M. Griffiths (ed.), 'A Visitation of the Archdeaconry of Carmarthen, 1710', *National Library of Wales Journal*, 18 (1973), 321; Saunders, *A View of the State of Religion in the Diocese of St David's*, p. 128.
59 NLW, St Davids Probate Records, Jane Cornwallis, Westmead, Laugharne, 1731; D. Howell, *Patriarchs and Parasites: The Gentry of South-west Wales in the Eighteenth Century* (Cardiff: University of Wales Press, 1986), pp. 10, 231, 236.
60 Ottley (Pitchford Hall MSS and Documents)/89, Thomas Philipps, Laugharne, to Bishop Ottley, 29 October 1718.
61 NLW MS 9145F, List of clergy at Bishop's Visitation 1745, pp. 101, 103.
62 Ottley (Pitchford Hall MSS and Documents)/VI, *c.* 1708; Griffiths, 'A Visitation of the Archdeaconry of Carmarthen, 1710', 306–7, 312–13.
63 Clement (ed.), *Correspondence and Minutes of the S.P.C.K. Relating to Wales*, p. 14.
64 Thomas, 'The Diocese of St David's in the Eighteenth Century', p. 229.
65 DHH 36, 14 December 1738.
66 Griffiths, 'A Visitation of the Archdeaconry of Carmarthen, 1710', 319.
67 SD/Let/1183, 1744.
68 Ottley (Pitchford Hall MSS and Documents)/VI, *c.* 1708.
69 DHH 84, 10 January 1742.
70 SD/QA/61.
71 Saunders, *A View of the State of Religion in the Diocese of St David's about the Beginning of the 18th Century*, p. 25.
72 NLW MS 9145F, p. 103.
73 NLW MS 9145F, p. 103; SD/MISCB/39.
74 Saunders, *A View of the State of Religion in the Diocese of St David's*, p. 15.
75 Griffiths, 'A Visitation of the Archdeaconry of Carmarthen, 1710', 320.
76 Trevecca College 1/3021, 29 December 1744.
77 SD/QA/61.
78 NLW 9145F, p. 103.

79 Ottley (Pitchford Hall MSS and Documents)/VI, *c.* 1708; Saunders, *A View of the State of Religion in the Diocese of St David's*, p. 127; Griffiths, 'A Visitation of the Archdeaconry of Carmarthen, 1710', 319.
80 Saunders, *A View of the State of Religion in the Diocese of St David's*, p. 128; Griffiths, 'A Visitation of the Archdeaconry of Carmarthen, 1710', 321.
81 NLW MS 9145F, p. 103.
82 SD/MISC/B/39.
83 SD/QA/61; SD/MISC/B/39.
84 SD/QA/61.
85 SD/CCCm(G)/241.
86 *Welch Piety* (London, 1741), pp. 55–64.
87 G. H. Jenkins, *Literature, Religion and Society in Wales 1660–1730* (Cardiff: University of Wales Press, 1978), pp. 213–14; Jacob, 'The Welsh Clergy', p. 119,
88 O. W. Jones, 'The Mountain Clergyman: His Education and Training', in O. W. Jones and D. Walker (eds), *Links with the Past: Swansea and Brecon Historical Essays* (Llandybïe: Christopher Davies, 1974), pp. 165–84.
89 Griffiths, "A Visitation of the Archdeaconry of Carmarthen, 1710', 296–7. The chapel of ease was presumably Llanfihangel-uwch-Gwili, described as being in the part of the parish nearest Llanegwad. See N. Vousden, RCAHMW, 2013, http://www.coflein.gov.uk/en/site/403951/details/st-michael-and-all-angels-church-llanfihangel-uwch-gwili.
90 F. Jones, *Historic Carmarthenshire Homes and their Families* (Newport, Pembrokeshire: Brawdy Books, 2006), p. 83.
91 DHH 98, 21 March 1743.
92 DHH 12, 30 March 1736.
93 DHH 90, 11 May 1742.
94 DHH 49, 7 September 1739.
95 Gomer M. Roberts, *Hanes Plwyf Llandybïe* (Caerdydd: Gwasg Prifysgol Cymru, 1939), p. 67.
96 Trevecka MS 137, Anthony Rees to Howel Harris, 13 January 1739.
97 DHH 54, 13 March 1740.
98 SD/MISC/1199, 3 September 1743.
99 Ottley (Pitchford Hall MSS and Documents)/100, Griffith Jones, Laugharne, to Bishop Ottley in London, 11 July 1715.
100 Griffiths, 'A Visitation of the Archdeaconry of Carmarthen, 1710', p. 319.
101 SD/CCCm(G)/290, 19–20 March 1741.
102 Jones, *Historic Carmarthenshire Homes*, pp. 28, 88–9; R. Bidgood, 'The Lewis and Bowen families of Cefntrenfa, Cilycwm', *Carmarthenshire Antiquary*, 48 (2012), 38–50.
103 DHH 112, 15 August 1744.
104 DHH 109, 16 April 1744.
105 SD/CCCm(G)/348, 13 December 1750.
106 SD/CCCm(G/349, 13 December 1750.
107 SD/CCCm(G)/354, 28 February 1751.
108 SD/CCCm(G)/351–2, 10 January 1751.
109 Carmarthenshire Archive, QSI/1, p. 123.
110 NLW Great Sessions records, Wales 4/739/5, 8 January 1770; H. J. Lloyd-Johnes, 'The Glanareth Murder', *Transactions of the Honourable Society of*

Cymmrodorion 1948 (London, 1949), 271–8; Jones, *Historic Carmarthenshire Homes*, p. 73.
111 SD/CCCm(G)/241, 31 December 1733–31 December 1734; SD/CCCm(G)/289, 23 October 1740–25 August 1741; SD/CCCm(G)/296, 1741; SD/CCCm(G)/312, 31 May–26 June 1745; SD/CCCm(G)/326, 1747.
112 Ottley MS (Pitchford Hall MSS and Documents)/126–8, 18–21 February 1719.
113 SD/CCB/G.
114 Jacob, 'The Welsh Clergy', p. 108.
115 LL/CC/G/918; LL/CC/G/952.
116 Griffiths, 'A Visitation of the Archdeaconry of Carmarthen, 1710', p. 319.
117 SD/CCCm(G)/287-a, 20 May 1740, 5 July 1740.
118 SD/CCCm(G)/289, 289a–j, 23 October 1740–5 February 1740.
119 SD/CCCm(G)/289k–o, 19 March–25 August 1741.
120 SD/CCCm(G)/303.
121 W. T. Morgan, 'Cases of Subtraction of Church Rate before the Consistory Courts of St Davids', *Journal of the Historical Society of the Church in Wales*, 19 (1959), 70–91.
122 J. Owen, *Coffhad am y Parch. Daniel Rowlands* (Caerlleon: Edward Parry, 1839), pp. 17–18.
123 Clement, *Correspondence and Minutes of the S.P.C.K.*, pp. 71–2; G. H. Jenkins, 'Griffith Jones (bap. 1684, d.1761)', *Oxford Dictionary of National Biography* (Oxford University Press, 23 September 2004). Accessed 30 September 2019, https://www.oxforddnb.com/view/10.1093/ref:odnb/9780198614128.001.0001/odnb-9780198614128-e-15006.
124 Clement, *Correspondence and Minutes of the S.P.C.K.*, p. 55.
125 Ottley (Pitchford Hall MSS and Documents)/100, Griffith Jones, Laugharne, to Bishop Ottley in London, 11 July 1715.
126 Trevecca College 1/3012, 3023, p. 35.
127 Ottley (Pitchford Hall MSS and Documents)/24, Captain Lewes of Llangoedmor to Bishop Ottley, 1707.
128 Griffiths, 'A Visitation of the Archdeaconry of Carmarthen, 1710', pp. 302, 315, 319.
129 SD/CCCm(G)/326, 1747.
130 Saunders, *A View of the State of Religion in the Diocese of St David's*, p. 32,
131 Whiteman (ed.), *The Compton Census of 1676*, pp. 456–8.
132 Geraint H. Jenkins, *The Foundations of Modern Wales: Wales 1642–1780* (Cardiff: University of Wales Press, 1987), p. 195.
133 Jenkins, *The Foundations of Modern Wales*, p. 381.
134 NLW, NLW Deposit MS 127A.
135 Geraint H. Jenkins, 'The Established Church and Dissent in Eighteenth-Century Cardiganshire', in Geraint H. Jenkins and Ieuan Gwynedd Jones (eds), *Cardiganshire County History, Volume 3: Cardiganshire in Modern Times* (Cardiff: University of Wales Press, 1998), p. 470.
136 Edmund Calamy, *A Continuation of the Account of the Ministers ... who were Ejected and Silenced* (2 vols, London: R. Ford, R. Hett and J. Chandler, 1727), II, p. 718; Glanmor Williams, 'Stephen Hughes (1622–1688): "Apostol Sir Gâr", "the Apostle of Carmarthenshire"', *Carmarthenshire Antiquary*, 37 (2001), 22, 25; Non Evans, 'Stephen Hughes: The Family Man', *Carmarthenshire Antiquary*, 37 (2001), 31–40.

137 Calamy, *Account*, II, p. 718.
138 For instance, the Pant-teg Church register, NLW MS12388, pp. 129, 136; E. D. Jones, 'Llyfr Eglwys Pant-teg', *Y Cofiadur*, 23 (1953), 18–70.
139 Griffiths, 'A Visitation of the Archdeaconry of Carmarthen, 1710', pp. 292, 294, 300.
140 E. D. Jones, 'Phylip Pugh', *Diwinyddiaeth*, 15 (1964), 62–9.
141 Jenkins, 'The Established Church and Dissent in Eighteenth-Century Cardiganshire', pp. 472–4.
142 Euros Lloyd, 'Datblygiad Undodiaeth yn Ardal y Smotyn Du', *Ceredigion*, 15/4 (2008), 58–66; Euros Lloyd, 'Unitarianism', in R. C. Allen and D. C. Jones (eds), *The Religious History of Wales* (Cardiff: Welsh Academic Press, 2014), pp. 115–23.
143 DHH 54, 7 March 1740; 70, 5 March 1741; 72, 28 April 1741.
144 NLW MS 18435B, p. 15, 15 August 1741.
145 Trevecka MS 299, David Jones to Howel Harris, 20 December 1740.
146 Hughes (ed.), *Gweithiau William Williams Pantycelyn II*, p. 16.
147 Jenkins, *The Foundations of Modern Wales*, p. 195,
148 See G. Williams, 'The Tradition of St David in Wales', in *Religion, Language and Nationality in Wales* (Cardiff: University of Wales Press, 1979), pp. 118–26; J. W. Evans and J. M. Wooding (eds), *St David of Wales: Cult, Church and Nation* (Woodbridge: Boydell Press, 2007).
149 Glanmor Williams, *Wales and the Reformation* (Cardiff: University of Wales Press, 1997), p. 225.
150 N. Yates, 'The Welsh Church and the Welsh Language', in Williams, Jacob, Yates and Knight, *The Welsh Church from Reformation to Disestablishment, 1603–1920*, p. 267.

CHAPTER 2

'The Young Striplings': Leaders and Exhorters

The influence of the Methodist leaders was often the key factor in the founding of the early societies in the south-west. For instance, Howel Harris visited the area of Myddfai in Carmarthenshire in 1739 and was informed of a society meeting there which had come into being after hearing Harris exhort some time previously.[1] The success in the south-west may be attributed partly to regular visits by Harris to preach and to hold society meetings. Also important for inspiring and sustaining the Methodist movement in the area, however, was the continued presence there of several of the leading figures of the early movement: Daniel Rowland, William Williams, Howel Davies and Peter Williams. Despite the significance of their contribution, the movement would not have grown as it did if it had not also been able to rely on the support of a network of committed exhorters and stewards. The leaders themselves would not have been able to provide the constant supervision that was so fundamental to the movement's approach without the support of a number of willing assistants.

Harris referred to the exhorters as 'the young striplings who are sent to the highways and hedges'.[2] He himself had reached the ripe old age of twenty-nine when he described them thus, but was only twenty-one when he went through the experience of conversion in 1735. Although Daniel Rowland's birth date is not certain, he is likely to have been three years older than Harris, in order to have reached the required age of twenty-three so as to be ordained deacon in 1734.[3] Tradition maintains that Rowland walked to London with the Tregaron drovers in order to be ordained by Bishop Nicholas Claggett, who did not find it convenient to visit his diocese that summer. However, Claggett had reached Abergwili the following year when Rowland was ordained as priest.[4] William Williams was younger than either Harris or Rowland, born in the early weeks of 1717 and experiencing his conversion at around the age of twenty after hearing Harris preach in the churchyard at Talgarth. Howel Davies was likely to have been of an age with Williams, and was also converted after hearing Harris speak. Both went on to be ordained in 1740, suggesting that it was in that year that they both attained the minimum age of twenty-three. Most of the others recruited to assist in the work were of the same generation, so this was a movement of 'young striplings' who matured in the service of the societies. Birth dates are only known for a small minority of the early exhorters, generally those who went on to become Dissenting ministers and were the subjects of obituaries at their death. Richard Tibbott was born in 1719, began preaching before he reached the age of twenty and was appointed a superintendent in the Methodist movement by the time he was twenty-five; Christopher Mends was born in 1724 and was approved as a Methodist exhorter at the age of twenty-one; John Thomas, originally of Myddfai in Carmarthenshire but later associated with Rhaeadr, was baptised in 1730 and began exhorting in Carmarthenshire in 1750.[5] In addition, there is a surviving will or elegy to date the deaths of each of the individuals who acted as early superintendents in the south-west, making it possible to state that James Williams died in 1764, Milbourne Bloom in 1766, William Richard in 1771, John Richard in 1775, William John in 1776 and Morgan Hughes in 1792. All these dates tend to confirm that these were young men when they took on their responsibilities for the societies in the 1740s.

Harris and Rowland met for the first time in August 1737 and it was from that time onwards that the movement in Wales began to formulate a structure and a hierarchy of personnel. Each of the main leaders had close connections with the south-west, which helps account for the early crop of converts in the region. The earliest influence was Daniel Rowland, although the information on that period of his career is scarce. He went through a conversion experience the year after his ordination in 1734, having been shaken to the core by a sermon preached by Griffith Jones at Llanddewibrefi, near Llangeitho. Since he was already a curate, any change would first have been reflected in the tone of the public worship in his parish churches. His son suggested that he began preaching outside his own pulpits to some of his parishioners in Llangeitho whom he found playing games on a Sunday, a practice in which Rowland himself had indulged as a young man fond of sporting activities.[6] He soon began to preach beyond the boundaries of his own cures, including in Carmarthenshire, certainly by 1737, since Joshua Thomas recalled hearing him preach to a large congregation in the county in that year.[7] Those efforts obviously continued, since Harris took pleasure in the impact Rowland's preaching had in Carmarthenshire by 1740.[8] Rowland's earliest biographer, John Owen, was informed by Nathaniel Rowland that his father had first preached in Carmarthenshire at Ystrad-ffin, at the request of a woman from that area who used to visit Llangeitho regularly to hear 'the angry cleric', as she called him.[9] In his elegy to Rowland, William Williams also states that it was in Ystrad-ffin that Rowland first ventured to preach in Carmarthenshire. The date of that first visit is not recorded, but Harris said in May 1742 that the people of Ystrad-ffin had by then had the benefit of Rowland's presence for a long time, confirming that his mission to Carmarthenshire was likely to have begun by 1737.[10]

On his various preaching tours, Harris encountered a number of Methodists who claimed to have been converted through the influence of Daniel Rowland, and confessed he could not feel the same affection for them as he did those who owned him as their spiritual father.[11] The Llanwinio society wrote to Rowland in 1748, begging him to return to their midst, since his last visit had proved a great blessing and his sermon had convinced several of the hearers.[12] In one of the few letters of his that have survived, written to Harris in 1742, he outlines a busy schedule, with recent visits to Montgomeryshire, Breconshire, Carmarthenshire and Glamorgan, and a planned itinerary in the following week to Pembrokeshire and south Carmarthenshire.[13] This was not his first visit to Montgomeryshire, since Llanidloes Methodists reported that during Rowland's visit to the area in 1741 'our poor hungry souls were fed by his ministry as with marrow and fatness, he maketh the Devil's kingdom to shake wheresoever he Cometh'.[14] There are also references to him embarking on preaching tours to north Wales, including to Anglesey and Merionethshire in 1743.[15] Although Harris worried that Rowland did not itinerate enough,[16] he was not free to travel at will or far from his benefices. However, if he could not always go to the hearers, they instead came to him. Rowland quickly established himself as the foremost preacher of the revival, with Llangeitho emerging as the focus for Methodist pilgrims who flocked to hear him preach and receive communion from him. Harris called him 'a second Paul' in the pulpit, 'one of the most surprising men that ever I heard'.[17] The impact of Rowland's preaching is a constant theme in Harris's diary. For instance, Harris described the response to Rowland's preaching on one occasion in Nancwnlle Church; 'o what crying like little Children whipped was here up and down the Church! O glorious days.'[18] His fame as a preacher spread far and wide, with William Thomas, the diarist from the south-east of Glamorgan, who was no great lover of Methodism, describing him as 'one of the clearest, most experimental preachers in all Wales' and 'an extraordinary preacher'.[19] The Baptist Joshua Thomas reported the general consensus at the time that Rowland and Griffith Jones were unrivalled in the Established Church as preachers.[20]

Rowland's influence penetrated Carmarthenshire over the border from Cardiganshire into the north-eastern region of the county, whereas Harris initially approached the county from the east across the Breconshire border. In the first instance he came to seek counsel from Griffith Jones at Llanddowror in 1736, a journey which would be often repeated over the following years. By December 1736, he noted that he was 'going now as a peripatetick', so had begun exhorting locally and would increase his efforts in the coming year.[21] He visited Llanddowror again three times in 1737, usually travelling through Llandovery and Carmarthen. It was in 1737 that he first visited Cardiganshire, at the invitation of Daniel Rowland, recalling later that the response he witnessed to Rowland's preaching was evidence that this was God's work.[22] After these tentative first steps, Harris's circle of activity widened considerably during 1738. There is a marked difference in the surviving correspondence in the Trevecka collection between 1738 and the preceding years. The letters begin to multiply and include a much broader range of correspondents, as various individuals who had heard of Harris wrote to ask him to preach. This soon led to visits to places which would become significant centres for the movement, including Rhiwiau in Llanddeusant and Llwynyberllan in Llandingad. David Evan of Cwm-y-dŵr in Llanwrda, a faithful member throughout the 1740s, wrote to Harris in

1738 inviting him to preach in the area. His letter hints at the existence of some sort of nascent society, as he refers to a number of men and women having gathered on the previous night.[23] A similar invitation came from Griffith Jones of Pantyrhaidd, Cynwyl Elfed, who felt encouraged by Harris's reputation to ask him to come to exhort at his house.[24] Anthony Rees of Llandybïe wrote in January 1739 reporting on progress in the area since Harris's last visit.[25] Harris was obviously being drawn ever deeper into the south-west in response to requests to visit specific locations and by 1739 undertook his first preaching tour in Pembrokeshire.

These early invitations were from people who contacted Harris on the basis of his reputation, usually to preach not just to their own households but to networks of individuals who seemed to be forming. Interested parties invited their friends who they thought might share their inclination to hear more. In subsequent years, Harris was increasingly being asked to impose some sort of order over newly formed societies, some of which had evolved as a result of his previous preaching engagements. For instance, in November 1742, John Gibbon and John Morgan of Fishguard society asked Harris to write with an explanation of the usual pattern for 'godly' societies ('*pa fodd y mae cecesitis diwiol yn ymddwyn*').[26] Also in 1742 he received a letter from John Richard, Llansamlet, Glamorgan, who would become the superintendent for south Carmarthenshire. Richard explained that he and some five or seven of his friends wished to keep a private society and requested information on what order to follow. He fervently hoped that Harris would be able to spend an evening in their company to instruct them.[27] It was quite possibly this kind of request which convinced Harris of the need to develop a firm structure of pastoral care to ensure the supervision and survival of each society, so that there would be no such uncertainty in future.

The Association

The structure set up was the Association, designed to 'prevent Confusion & least wicked Persons should go out in our Names & do mischief'.[28] Howel Harris had already come up with a plan for the system of stewards and exhorters by 1740.[29] From 1740 onwards, he and the other leading figures in the movement had been holding various meetings to try to arrange the work of the exhorters and to discuss the possibility of formulating a more fixed framework and set of rules. One of these meetings took place on 2 October 1740 at Glyn in Defynnog parish, Breconshire, with around sixteen present, including eight clergymen, a gathering Harris referred to as a meeting of 'Associated Brethren' and which included some Dissenting ministers such as Edmund Jones, Pontypool, and David Williams, Pwll-y-pant, near Caerphilly. Further meetings took place throughout 1741, with a core of committed participants emerging during the course of the year, although with fewer Dissenters as that relationship became more difficult to negotiate successfully. The outcome was the first General Association of evangelical clergy and lay exhorters held on 7 January 1742 at Dugoedydd in Cil-y-cwm, home of William Lloyd, one of the members of the local society. The way forward was confirmed in the first General Association of Welsh and English Methodists at Watford on 1 January 1743. This confirmed that Welsh and English Calvinism should be regarded as a joint enterprise and George Whitefield was officially appointed moderator, even if not always able to be present at the meetings because of his other commitments. The connection to Whitefield was an important one and he was consulted by letter and provided with reports of progress. Harris operated as the main link with the other branches of Methodism and corresponded regularly with Whitefield as well as substituting for him in the Tabernacle in London during his absences. Harris's letters to Whitefield and Griffith Jones show a similar sense of deference and respect and it was apparent that Harris regarded both as his spiritual elders, although his friendship with Whitefield was to cool by the end of the decade.

It took further time and meetings to finalise the organisation of the movement and a number of key decisions were reached at the Assocation at Glanyrafonddu, 1 March 1743. The arrangement was for the General Association of the Welsh and English leaders to meet twice a year. The Welsh leaders and exhorters would meet separately in the Quarterly Association four times a year, and as many as possible of the clergy and superintendents would also meet in the Monthly Association.[30] The Association was installed as the governing body of the movement, with all exhorters reporting to it and carrying out its decisions locally. It was representative in that all those who held positions of responsibility in the movement were expected to participate, but there was no election to these roles, which were appointed by the Association. It gave some of the middling sorts who became involved with the movement a taste of committee membership, which there may have been fewer opportunities to experience in more secular fields.

Heading every list of attendees at any Association, however, were the names of the clergy who were involved in the movement. In October 1742 Howel Harris announced to George Whitefield that there were ten clergymen in Wales who supported the movement, five of them beneficed and five in curacies. The first five he listed were Griffith Jones, Thomas Jones of Cwm-iou, Breconshire, John Hodges of Wenvoe, Glamorgan, John Powell of Blaenau Gwent and John Davies of Llanddarog, Carmarthenshire. The five curates were Daniel Rowland, Howel Davies, William Williams, Thomas Lewis and Philip Thomas of Gelli-gaer, Glamorgan.[31] Whilst all of these might be considered evangelically inclined, not all of them by any means became fully fledged members of the Methodist movement, and certainly not Griffith Jones. Anyone in holy orders who was attracted to the movement was invariably afforded a place of respect. Foremost among them were Daniel Rowland and Howel Davies, who were ordained priests, ensconced in their parishes. William Williams had been ordained deacon in 1740, but was refused full priest's orders in 1743 because of his involvement with Methodism.[32] He had acted as curate to Theophilus Evans in Llanwrtyd, Llanddewi Abergwesyn and Llanfihangel Abergwesyn in Breconshire, but had been accused by the churchwardens of his parishes of neglect of duty, so it is little wonder that his career in the Church ground to a halt. Nonetheless, he remained in holy orders, to be referred to respectfully as 'the Reverend Mr Williams', with all the status that came with that distinction. It gave him a greater entitlement to preach than any of the lay exhorters, even if he might regret that, as a deacon, he lacked the right to conduct communion services. One of the other promising young clerical supporters was David Jenkins, also ordained in 1740 and licensed as curate of Cellan, near Lampeter, in Cardiganshire. He gained early prominence in the movement and was one of the first missionaries to north Wales. The geographical proximity of Jenkins and Rowland and the natural affinity between them led to a close degree of cooperation. After Jenkins's untimely death in April 1742, Rowland claimed to feel as bereft as if he had lost his right arm.[33] For Harris this represented the loss of one of the most eminent of the Church's ministers and 'one of the sweetest brightest of all the young methodists'.[34] The year 1742 proved a testing time for the evangelical clergy, who had already earlier faced the acute danger of losing another of their number when Williams was struck down by smallpox.[35] He survived and in 1743 left his curacies in order to act as Rowland's assistant, becoming his firm friend and ally.

By January 1746, Peter Williams's name appeared on the list of evangelical clergy attending Association meetings. Williams was a native of Carmarthenshire, educated at Carmarthen Grammar School. Hearing George Whitefield preach in Carmarthen in 1743 had a lasting effect on him, and he subsequently sought deacon's orders in the Church. He was licensed as curate to John Evans in Eglwys Gymyn, Carmarthenshire, but dismissed for preaching in an evangelical manner, a transgression which was reported to the absentee rector by his infuriated wife. By January 1747 Williams had abandoned the idea of a benefice in the Church and devoted himself to the Methodist cause. He was a busy itinerant preacher who experienced considerable persecution during his visits to north Wales. He also became one of the most important literary figures in the movement, responsible for one of the most popular versions of the Welsh Bible from its first publication in 1770, despite his ultimate expulsion in 1791 for supposedly deviating from orthodox views on the Trinity.[36] A few other evangelical clergy were to be found in the other counties of south Wales, including John Powell, curate of Aberystruth and later rector of Llanmartin, Monmouthshire, who was present at the early Association meetings, and Edward Phillips, rector of Maesmynys, Breconshire, whose name appears in the Association minutes from 1749.[37] There were several other sympathisers among the clergy, who showed differing levels of engagement with the movement, including another clergyman who was native to Carmarthenshire, Philip Thomas, curate of Gelligaer and later of Wenvoe, Glamorgan, along with his rector at Wenvoe, John Hodges.[38] However, the most deeply involved of the evangelical clergy were located in the south-west, which greatly encouraged the progress of the revival in that area.

Despite the respect afforded to any ordained Anglican clergy present, the driving force behind the Association seems to have been Howel Harris, who had a greater gift for administration and organisation than his colleagues. His position was ambiguous as he was not ordained by the Anglicans or the Dissenters. Dissenting ministers who supported the movement, such as Henry Davies of Cymer, were also given pride of place in the list of those present at Association meetings. Possibly to compensate, Harris was appointed the 'Superintendant over Wales', to go to England when called, at Watford Association in April 1743. This was an adjustment to the previous arrangement whereby Harris was one of six 'general visitors' who operated under the oversight of the ordained ministers. This ensured that Harris had a leading role in the revival, reserving the right to act on his own judgement rather than simply acting as subordinate to Rowland and the other ordained clergy. Through a combination of efficiency and force of character, he emerged as a key figure in Association discussions and on occasions when he was absent, such as Newcastle Emlyn Association in November 1749, decisions might be delayed in order to await his input.[39]

The Exhorters

One of the primary functions of the Association, in its various forms, was to regulate the activities of the lay preachers, or exhorters. The very term used was a sign of the caution exercised by the movement in order to avoid giving the impression that a new denomination was forming with its own ministry. Harris was careful to describe his own activities as 'exhorting' or 'discoursing' rather than preaching. The Welsh term which emerged was '*cynghori*' or 'to advise', although Richard Tibbott regularly used '*ymddiddan*', which is closer to 'converse'. The use of laymen was controversial and provoked frequent opposition. Harris cited the example of Apollos in the New Testament preaching to the people of Corinth despite never having been ordained, but it was a precedent which did not sway the bishop of St Davids when Harris raised it at an acrimonious meeting in August 1739 to discuss the possibility of ordination.[40] Harris was the first of the lay preachers, but others soon followed suit. By 1741, Harris knew of four exhorters going about their work in Carmarthenshire, as well as three apiece in the counties of Cardiganshire and Pembrokeshire.[41] One of those in Carmarthenshire was Richard Tibbott, whose diary for 1741–2 shows just how active the Methodists already were in the county, as he invariably spent several nights each week exhorting, attending societies and listening to other preachers.[42] Later that same year, Harris stated that there were a total of ten public exhorters and twenty private exhorters throughout Wales.[43] They were not necessarily selected on the basis of any academic qualifications and Thomas Morgan, a student at Carmarthen Academy, judged most Methodist exhorters he heard to be lacking in knowledge.[44] Some concerns were raised regarding the standards of education of some of the exhorters, including their knowledge of English, with George Whitefield apparently recommending some improvement. Howel Harris also favoured training them in the polite use of a knife and fork so that they could mix more easily in better circles of society and appear 'not like a fop nor like a fool'.[45] The Association in 1749 did discuss requiring the exhorters to attend school to improve their grammar or to receive tuition from some of their better-educated colleagues including John Sparks and George Gambold in Pembrokeshire. Those within reach of the Llansawel society house would receive lessons in grammar, divinity and philosophy from William Williams, who had been educated in these subjects at Llwyn-llwyd Academy.[46] However, the Welsh Methodist movement would maintain its tradition of favouring spiritual experience or 'heart religion' over formal education as a qualification to preach, being reluctant to establish formal training for its ministers until well into the nineteenth century.[47]

Since they were not entitled to use church pulpits, the exhorters used all manner of other available venues and soon adopted the practice of field preaching, as Griffith Jones had resorted to doing when his congregations proved too large to be contained within church walls. Harris carried out what he termed his 'highway commission' to preach by speaking from the top of a garden wall in Cardigan, by the castle walls at Carmarthen and perched on a stone in the street in Lampeter.[48] William Seward described Harris regularly using 'a place like a weighing post (at horse races) which they raise for him'.[49] Even some of the clergy also took to field preaching, with George Whitefield preaching by the walls of the graveyard at Prendergast in 1743 because the crowd was so great. Howel Davies was apparently refused access to the church at Llangyndeyrn and so was forced to deliver his sermon outside.[50] William Williams also had to preach outside 'to a large Auditory' when he was not able to use the church at Llanllwch.[51] There was talk of disciplinary action against Daniel Rowland in 1742 for preaching in an alehouse.[52]

This sort of behaviour would be regarded as extremely irregular in conventional opinion. When Bishop Nicholas Claggett refused to consider ordination for Harris in August 1739, one of the accusations he levelled against him was that he went about and preached on tabletops.[53] Despite Griffith Jones's own practice of preaching out-of-doors he was vehemently opposed when he heard of Methodist exhorters climbing on chairs to speak.[54] After the Watford Association in January 1743, Harris wrote to placate Jones with the news that the exhorters would now be kept under strict supervision in the hope of avoiding any irregularities in future.[55]

The structure put in place to organise the exhorters was developed during a series of Association meetings between January and April 1743. The Glanyrafonddu Association in March 1743 came up with a firm set of proposals which was to be approved at the next meeting, including the appointment of six general visitors or 'ministers' helps': John Cennick, Thomas Adams and Joseph Humphreys in England, and Howel Harris, James Beaumont and Herbert Jenkins for Wales. As their helpers, six exhorters were to be appointed with some twelve societies each and another six with some six societies each. The general visitors were not to be confined to a specific sphere and could range freely.[56] None of the three was based in the south-west, with Harris and Beaumont both living in Breconshire and Jenkins in Monmouthshire. Although it was proposed that the twelve exhorters should be given limited circuits to oversee, they should be allowed to exchange with each other and discourse in each other's areas. In addition, there should be a steward in every society to care for the poor and sick, collect money and be a messenger and 'peacemaker'. In larger societies, two stewards might be appointed to undertake these tasks. These proposals were then considered and refined further at Watford in the following month when Harris was designated general superintendent. At the same time, James Beaumont seemed to be relegated to acting as superintendent over Radnorshire and Herefordshire, rather than having the greater responsibility as one of the general visitors for Wales.[57] It was at this Association that the term 'superintendent' was first adopted to describe the most senior of the public exhorters who had oversight over a wide district of twelve societies or more. It was also decided that William Williams should leave his curacies to act as assistant to Daniel Rowland.

Monthly Association meetings in May and June led to the confirmation of some of these appointments, but also to some shifting of personnel to try to find the most appropriate arrangements. The General Association at Trefeca on 29–30 June 1743 was described as the first 'after the Brethren took their Places', with the implication that a settled order had been established after a few months of discussion and adaptation.[58] The first superintendents for the south-west were:

Morgan Hughes: north Cardiganshire and Montgomeryshire;
William Richard, Llanddewibrefi: from near New Quay in Cardiganshire along the coast to St David's in Pembrokeshire;
Milbourne Bloom, Abergwili: Carmarthenshire to the north of Carmarthen towards Cardiganshire and Pembrokeshire;
John Richard, Llansamlet: part of west Glamorgan and south Carmarthenshire as far as the river Tywi;
James Williams (or William), Llanddewbrefi: north-east Carmarthenshire as far as the river Cothi as well as part of Cardiganshire near his home;
Morgan John Lewis: Llanddeusant in Carmarthenshire, with other societies in Monmouthshire and Breconshire.
John Harris: south Pembrokeshire.

One of the major changes to this arrangement came with the resignation shortly afterwards of Milbourne Bloom as superintendent for west Carmarthenshire. He had emerged as a leading figure in the early movement, having been converted after hearing Harris preach. His home at Gelli Glyd, Abergwili, played host to a society as well as to a meeting of the Association on 1 May 1743 which was attended by George Whitefield.[59] Bloom had gained a good reputation as an exhorter prior to being appointed as a superintendent, and his loss was something of a blow. He turned instead to Dissent and was ordained as an Independent minister in September 1745.[60] He retained his evangelical fervour, however, according to Thomas Morgan, who continued to visit him in 1744 and commented favourably on his warmth and zeal.[61] His post as superintendent was given in the Watford Association, 4 January 1744, to his assistant, William John of Glancothi in Llanegwad parish.[62]

The other major alteration was the loss of Morgan Hughes, in circumstances which are not as clear. On the entry in the Association minutes of his appointment as superintendent over Montgomeryshire and north Cardiganshire was appended a note in Howel Harris's handwriting explaining: 'This was after a long Tryal changed & Richard Tibbott set in his place'.[63] It was on 1 May 1744 that Richard Tibbott recorded in his diary that he had been promoted to superintendent, but his name had already been included among the superintendents in the Association minutes from January onwards.[64] Tibbott was appointed to the Montgomeryshire societies, but, at the Trefeca Association in 1744, it was decided that William Williams should visit the societies in north Cardiganshire once every six weeks on trial and it was he who reported as superintendent of the district from 1745 onwards.[65] It would seem that there were by then some grave doubts about Hughes, since the Association in August discussed whether he should be allowed to exhort in private, but opinion was equally divided when the question was put to the vote, so no decision was made and the matter does not seem to have been raised subsequently.[66] Two months previously, members of two of his societies, Tan-yr-allt and Bron-y-mwyn, had written to Howel Harris to plead his case:

> Dear Sir if there is some Infirmities found in our Brother to which we are sure severall stories are added to his charge which we know not, his sin as far as we know may as Righteously Layd to our Charge as to him alas how apt we are to Idolize the Instruments by whom the Lord ministers to our souls ...[67]

It is difficult to know what the 'infirmities' might be, but they are unlikely to relate to his faith and commitment to the cause, since Harris judged him to be 'one of the sweetest and most full of Faith of liberty of any'.[68] Thomas William's remark to Harris in 1745 associating Hughes with gossip about adultery may have some bearing. Whatever his faults, they seem to have been too serious to be ignored and the fact that by January 1745 William Williams was referring to him as the former exhorter at Tan-yr-allt confirms his absence.[69] The resulting list of superintendents for the rest of the 1740s, and those most concerned in this study, was:

William Williams: north Cardiganshire;

William Richard, Llanddewibrefi: from near New Quay in Cardiganshire along the coast to St David's in Pembrokeshire;

William John, Glancothi: south-west Carmarthenshire;

John Richard, Llansamlet: part of west Glamorgan and south Carmarthenshire as far west as the river Tywi;

James Williams, Llanddewbrefi: north east Carmarthenshire as far as the river Cothi as well as Lampeter and Llangeitho in Cardiganshire;

Morgan John Lewis: Llanddeusant in Carmarthenshire, with other societies in Monmouthshire and Breconshire.

Increasingly the term 'private exhorter' seemed to be used to refer to those who operated in a more restricted sphere in two or three societies, answerable to the superintendent or public exhorter. The Haverfordwest Association in 1745 ruled that private exhorters should visit places outside their own societies 'only so that neither their charge nor their calling be neglected; and as directed by their Superintendants'.[70] Each superintendent was expected to visit each of the societies under his supervision twice a month and to report on their progress to the General Association. He should also meet the private exhorters and society stewards on a monthly basis. In these Monthly Meetings, the superintendent conveyed the decisions of the Monthly and Quarterly Associations to his assistants and received their reports on the members of each society. It was the responsibility of the private exhorters and stewards to inform the superintendent of matters such as applications for membership, the need for disciplinary measures and proposed marriages. The exhorters in Cardiganshire and Carmarthenshire met in a Monthly Association with Daniel Rowland as Moderator and those in Pembrokeshire were led by Howel Davies.

One of the developments that Howel Harris emphasised when explaining the new order to Griffith Jones was the decision that no exhorter would be allowed to speak without first having the approval of the Association. Although some individuals seemed to be regarded as established in their roles by the time the Association began to discuss these matters, certainly from 1743 onwards it was usual for any new recruits to be put on probation for a month or more under the supervision of one of the clergy or superintendents. This occurred at all levels. George Gambold was placed on trial as a public exhorter and potential superintendent in Pembrokeshire under the supervision of Howel Davies.[71] William John of Llanwrda assisted James Williams in the societies of Llanwrda, Llansadwrn, Caeo and Talley for several months in 1743 before being appointed private exhorter to Talley society.[72] John Meurig, one of two brothers from Llandafen, near Llanelli, who exhorted with the movement, was placed on trial in Pembrey under John Richard in March 1743, before he was accepted as a private exhorter in May.[73] John Meurig again appeared to be on trial in 1747, possibly to take on greater responsibility as a public exhorter, when the Association determined to ask the opinions of Howel Davies, with whom he took communion, and John Richard, in whose district he lived, on his candidacy.[74] John David, Llandyfaelog, was also put on probation in March 1743 in the societies of Llandyfaelog and Cilcarw in Llangyndeyrn. He was obviously successful, as his name appears on the list of private exhorters during the following year.[75] He may have been the John David whose preaching in February 1744 received a review from Thomas Morgan, Henllan Amgoed, which had something of a sting in its tail: 'his Zeal & warmth gave me occasion to reflect on my own lukewarmness; but I found him very ignorant in several things of importance'.[76] Quite often, the exhorter, if approved, would end up working in the circuit of the superintendent who mentored him, so to some extent their working relationship was also part of the test. Not all aspiring exhorters had an easy passage. William John, Glancothi, failed to attend the Association meeting at which he was due to be examined in February 1743, so could not be approved and was ordered to be present at the next meeting.[77] John David, along with Thomas Price of Llandeilo Abercywyn, had been silenced in February 1743 until opinions could be sought on their suitability. There was some uncertainty about William Edward, a carpenter from Rhydygele in Pembrokeshire, who discoursed with fire and feeling, but engendered a mixed reaction from his hearers, making it difficult to know how to proceed in his case.[78] He remained on trial in the St David's, Pen-rhos and Mounton societies in January 1745 and does not appear to have been approved as an exhorter.[79] A verse he composed about himself reveals his enthusiasm, but also the volatile disposition which caused misgivings:

Mae canon mawr yn Rhydygele
Wedi ei lodio hyd y gene
Y mae'n barod i fynd allan
Yn erbyn calon diawl ei hunan.[80]

[There is a great cannon in Rhydygele, loaded to its mouth. It is ready to go out against the heart of the devil himself.]

The selection of exhorters was often crucial for the development of societies, since they usually had great influence over the members. The members of Tan-yr-allt and Bron-y-mwyn, in the Tregaron area of Cardiganshire, felt deprived after losing Morgan Hughes as their exhorter. They argued that although Daniel Rowland and William Williams were often amongst them, they did not have the same time to spend discussing their personal problems.[81] It was evidently difficult to find private exhorters who were acceptable to the societies in north Cardiganshire, and Williams explained that the members were not happy with the exhorters allocated to them, but that those they would have preferred were unavailable.[82] The link was often especially strong with the private exhorters, who visited a small number of societies very frequently and could form a close bond with them. William Williams noticed in his visits to the north Cardiganshire societies that the private exhorters often set the tone for the societies under their care, so that if they were full of faith and zeal, the societies would be likewise. Conversely apathy on the part of the exhorter would lead to similar lukewarmness among the members.[83] The vital importance of the private exhorter was also noted by John Jones of Llys-y-frân, Pembrokeshire in 1743: 'Indeed Private Societies will be very beneficial if the Lord will be pleased to bestow wisdom from above on the Private Exhorters, for indeed 'tis a weighty & Important work and an high calling in the Church, to nurse up Dear Lambs.'[84] Jones feared that the Devil was seeking to undermine the movement by sending unworthy workers to the vineyard. He believed that it was of paramount importance to choose experienced and sensible exhorters who could offer wise guidance to the members under their care. Morgan John Lewis also worried that the private exhorters did not always fulfil their duties assiduously, and if that meant that the societies were not providing the expected degree of support, he feared this could lead to the loss of some members.[85] It proved difficult to provide an adequate supply of exhorters as the numbers increased. Even when new exhorters were recruited and appointed, they might not always forge a constructive relationship with the societies. As Daniel John of Llanfair Clydogau pointed out to Howel Harris, not all of Christ's ministers evoked the same response from different individuals.[86] There were instances where the Association was forced to intervene when relationships between societies and exhorters broke down. The superintendent William John requested that the Association send someone else to Carmarthen in January 1747 as the relationship with the society there had become so strained. The society was placed under the supervision of the brothers William and Christopher Mends as a result.[87] Yet, it seems the situation had not been resolved by April 1748, when Howel Harris noted that he had had to settle 'some Jars here among them' during a visit to Carmarthen.[88] It may have been the ongoing tension which prompted Howel Harris to deliver a rather stern rebuke in the town in September 1748, outlining the role of William John and John Richard as superintendents and, by his own account, strengthening 'Bro. Mend's Hands'. Harris hoped subsequently to be able to visit Carmarthen 'in love and meekness and never be obliged to bring a Rod for that grieves me', which suggests that he had come there with the intention of reproving the members locally.[89] Such situations did arise and there were times when Harris intervened to reinforce the position of superintendents who were facing a lack of respect from some members. In 1749, Harris met with members from the societies in James Williams's region and rebuked them for want of obedience and respect to their superintendent. Harris advocated the principle that the authority of the leaders, the superintendents and the private exhorters stemmed from God and therefore had to be respected equally. In James Williams's case, he argued with those under his authority that

> if he is not settled of the Lord why does he come over the Hills here & we have all judged that he is sent & expect you to submit to our Light att the same time you to use this Liberty that if you have any reasonable objection go to him & tell it & if that don't give you ease come to me as my Place is to overlook the Societies and Exhorters &c & if you are not

William John's report to the Association, 7 January 1747 (Trevecca College/1 3037).

there and come to the association & you shall be heard & if you are not satisfied you must leave us.[90]

The rules therefore allowed societies to complain about the exhorters set in authority over them, although the tendency seemed to be to uphold the authority of exhorters who were approved by the Association. If an exhorter was deemed unsatisfactory in some way, he could be disciplined by curtailing his actitivies or expelling him from the movement. In Caeo Assocation in April 1744, a number of exhorters were reproved for various shortcomings which are not listed in the minutes.[91] It was rare that serious misgivings arose, but one exception was John Harris of St Kennox, Pembrokeshire, who came into conflict with Howel Davies and was expelled by Howel Harris in 1747.[92] John Harris insisted that Davies did not preach the true gospel and rejected all offers of reconciliation, which would have required him to repent his attitude. John Harry, of Ambleston, was appointed in his place as superintendent for south Pembrokeshire from 1747 onwards. John Harris continued to exhort in the county, causing considerable friction and creating divisions among the local members, some of whom may have felt loyalty to him personally. In order to confirm Howel Davies's authority in the region, Howel Harris threatened to expel anyone who received John Harris to exhort in their house. By 1753 he had joined the Moravians in the county, with whom he had family links. His sister was married to George Gambold, the Methodist exhorter who was the son of William Gambold, the lexicographer from Cardigan, and brother of John Gambold, the Moravian bishop. It was George Gambold, along with another former Methodist exhorter, John Sparks, who was responsible for the first Moravian meetings in Haverfordwest which led to the founding of a Moravian society there in 1763, which John Harris also joined. It is believed that another of the Gambold brothers, William, continued to exhort with the Methodists in spite of the close family association with Moravianism.[93] John Harry, who replaced John Harris, was a forthright individual who tended not to mince his words in his reports to the Association. He was also a dependable figure, who at times towards the late 1740s seems to have helped ease William Richard's burden by visiting some of his societies in the lower reaches of his circuit in Pembrokeshire.

Despite the importance of the private exhorters, it was often the local superintendents who shouldered the heaviest burden, as they were ultimately responsible for both the exhorters and the members under their jurisdiction. At times they expressed a keen sense of the significance of their work, such as John Richard's declaration that 'I plainly felt that I had commission from God, to Efangelise, shewing to sinners their necessity of having a part in Jesus Christ …'.[94] Their reports frequently reveal this sense of mission and their joy at witnessing the success of the societies. They were expected to combine the ability to provide comfort with the need to discipline transgressions. William John was the subject of an elegy by his friend Thomas Dafydd which suggests that he possessed the necessary skills, offering support and reproach as required:

Fel brawd fe gydymdeimlai â mi mewn tlodi a pho'n,
Fe ddygodd ran o'm beichiau, fe'm hargyhoeddai'n llym,
Bendithiol fu'i gymdeithas flynyddau hirion im'.
Dichlynedd yn ei fywyd, diwyd a ffyddlon iawn,
A'i saeth yn erbyn pechod o foreu i brydnhawn.[95]

Like a brother he sympathised with me in poverty and pain,
He shouldered a share of my burdens, he admonished me severely,
Blessed was his society for long years to me.
Circumspect in his life, industrious and very faithful,
And his arrow aimed against sin from morning to afternoon.

The strain of fulfilling the duties required of the superintendents must have been considerable. The geographical extent of some superintendencies was enough to represent major logistical problems, even with the relative speed and luxury of travelling on horseback. Some superintendents noted the difficulty in covering the ground as often as was needed in order to report back on all the societies, usually more as a simple statement of fact rather than a complaint. As a result of the expectation that they would have sufficient time to visit the societies regularly and the requirement that they be literate, most of them tended to be drawn from the middling sorts of society or above. Without some measure of financial security, it would have been difficult to be able to afford to dedicate the time to the societies whilst also striving to make a living. The leaders were generally in a more secure position, with a regular income coming to those who held church benefices. Even though William Williams had forgone this when he left his curacies, he inherited the farms of Cefn-coed from his father and Pantycelyn from his mother, as well as gaining further wealth through his marriage to Mary or Mali Francis. He supplemented his income from the farms through the sale of his books, copies of which he regularly took with him on his preaching trips. The various bequests in his will amounted to over £800, as well as a number of annuities, which demonstrate that he was a man of considerable means.[96] Marrying well is a theme in the history of most of the Methodist leaders, with Daniel Rowland also making a match which bolstered his financial position, with his will demonstrating that he held lands in Llanbadarn Fawr and Llanddewi-brefi in Cardiganshire, and in Pencarreg in Carmarthenshire, as well as the mortgage on land in Llanbadarn Odwyn, Cardiganshire.[97] Howel Davies's first wife, Catherine Poyer, was the heiress of the estate of Parciau in Henllan Amgoed, and after her death he subsequently married Elizabeth White, another wealthy woman. Howel Harris's wife, Anne Williams, was a member of the gentry as the daughter of John Williams, Ynys-grin or Skreen in Breconshire. Her family was by no means overjoyed with the match, and Harris's financial position was somewhat more precarious than the other leaders'. His home at Trefeca had been inherited by his elder brother Joseph, and Harris needed the assistance of his father-in-law to obtain the £90 needed to buy it from his brother in 1747.[98]

Of the superintendents, Milbourne Bloom was one of the wealthiest, as a descendant of the gentry family of Penybanc Uchaf in Abergwili. He owned four farms in Abergwili parish – Pistyll-rhydd, Borth-ddu, Tyddyn-tir-hir and Gallt y Goitre – as well as his own home at Gelli Glyd.[99] Morgan Hughes was also financially secure, largely it seems as a result of his marriage to his wife Elizabeth, who inherited the farm Cwmhowni, also known as Dyffryn Howni and the place where the local society met in Blaen-porth, as well as the farm of Ffos-y-gaseg.[100] Although no will survives for Hughes, there is a record of probate administration being granted in 1792, which helps date his death.[101] He had considerable assets, as he had also in 1770 inherited Neuadd Fawr and other lands in Blaen-porth and Aberporth through his wife's aunt,

Catherine Lewis.[102] Although none of the other superintendents were quite as well off, the evidence suggests that they were mostly fairly comfortably placed and often living in sizeable farmhouses. In each case, the date of death can be traced in the surviving records or in elegies in their honour, so some idea of their economic situation can be gleaned from probate material for many of them. No probate material survives for William Richard, who died in 1770 of consumption according to William Williams's elegy.[103] There is no will or inventory either for William John, who died in 1776, but since he mentioned a debt of twelve pounds to his landlord in a letter in 1741, it is evident that he was not the owner of his home, Glancothi in Llanegwad.[104]

Although the date of James Williams's death does not appear in the records associated with the movement, it is highly likely that his is the will from Llanddewibrefi proved in 1764. He is described as coming from Cardiganshire, and his circle of activity suggests Llanddewibrefi as a likely base.[105] His fellow superintendent, William Richard, was one of the two assessors who drew up the inventory accompanying the 1764 will, as his signature is familiar from his reports to the Association. It is fairly certain, therefore, that James Williams lived at Llety'r Berws, also known as Berws, in Llanddewibrefi. His inventory demonstrates that his effects at his death in 1763 were worth £9 8s., including cattle worth £4 15s., horses worth 10s. and sheep worth 8s.[106] This does not indicate great wealth, although his will described him as a gentleman. He left Llety'r Berws to his wife, Catherine, for a year after his death, after which she was to have the use for the remainder of her lifetime of the parlour and the room above, the outside door, the stairs and the garden on the eastern side of the house, along with the land known as Talwrn Crach and the field called Cae Nant-y-ffin, with his son William as residual legatee. The level of detail here suggests a prudent farmer rather than a member of the gentry. Wills also survive for his widow, Catherine Williams, written in 1769 and proved in 1776, and his son William Williams, proved in 1785.[107] Both of these included fairly sizeable bequests of sums of £2 and £10 to relatives, as well as a horse left by Catherine to William, so they continue in the same vein as James's will suggesting a comfortable farming family of middle rank.

For some of the superintendents, the calls on their time obviously became a pressing matter, affecting their ability to carry on with their daily occupation and endangering their livelihood as a result. The superintendent who seems to have struggled most to combine his Methodist activities with his everyday occupation was John Richard of Llansamlet, who was a bookbinder by trade, although he turned to making and repairing clocks later in his life.[108] By 1750 he desired the Association not to send him on a preaching tour to north Wales as he had a debt of fifteen pounds and no means of paying it other than by focusing on his craft for a period in order to raise the money. Although it is not clear when he made the change of career, it was as a clockmaker that he described himself in the will written by him in July 1775 and proved in September 1776.[109] Gomer Roberts attempted to find a record of his death in the parish records of Llansamlet and located two possibilities: one who was buried on 12 November 1775 and the other on 26 December 1784.[110] The will confirms that the earlier date of 1775 was the correct one.

Some of the exhorters more generally were even less secure, as a number were young men who married during the 1740s and struggled to maintain growing families. One such was Richard William Dafydd of Llandyfaelog, whose efforts to provide for his wife and two children was a cause of great concern for Howel Harris, who obviously had a high opinion of him as a 'sweet soul, full of God, of love and of life'.[111] In 1742, Harris was trying to find exhorters from Glamorgan to cover the ten or twelve societies located between Margam and Neath, and Llanddowror and Carmarthen, since Richard William Dafydd was then the only exhorter available to them and his financial situation made it difficult for him to spare the time to visit them all regularly.[112] His straitened circumstances may have been a factor in the decision to restrict him to the care of six societies in March 1743, rather than giving him greater responsibilities as a superintendent.[113] The two brothers George and William Gambold were approved as exhorters in July 1744, but with the stipulation that George would itinerate as much as he was able whilst also taking care of his grandmother.[114] The brothers Edward and John Meurig were approved as private exhorters in 1743, provided they were not turned out of their parents' home.[115]

The Association therefore may have had to take various familiy and financial circumstances into account when allocating duties; it seemed to do so also in the case of John Jones of Caeo who assisted John

Richard in Llanddeusant, Cwmaman, Llan-non, Pembrey and Llandafen and was instructed to spend alternate weeks visiting the societies and concentrating on his work.[116] The Association on occasion took the further step of attempting to organise employment for exhorters in difficulties, including arranging for Richard Tibbott to work as a schoolteacher.[117] Tibbott had worked in the fields for Griffith Jones, Llanddowror, for a while when he first arrived in Carmarthenshire in around 1741.[118] The Association also dispatched him to learn the craft of bookbinding from John Richard in Llansamlet, despite Richard's own precarious financial position.[119] Despite these efforts, Howel Harris still marvelled that exhorters contrived to make a living, informing his hearers that 'no Cobler lives as poor as we your Preachers'.[120] In 1749–50, it seemed that a number of the most impoverished exhorters had to refrain from preaching in order to concentrate on earning their daily bread, leading Harris to complain that members often gave the evangelical clergy gifts of money, but ignored the more pressing needs of the lay exhorters.[121] Yet he also maintained that the exhorters would carry on preaching no matter how their circumstances were reduced, even if barefoot and without clothing.[122] Harris associated himself with the exhorters as one who was also without a clerical stipend to support his labours, insisting that he lived frugally, spending no more than £50–£60 a year prior to his marriage.[123] In March 1749 he complained that, hampered by a debt of £5, he was in a sorry state: 'all ye Cloaths I have about me not worth 10s. being all rags and a sore hack Horse & cant buy better – a Hat of 2/6 and old saddle and boots worth nothing – no whip'.[124] He hinted that he expected to be treated with honour when he made a comparison with Christ, who might not have had a place to lay his head but still 'went about as a Gent and not as a Beggar'. He maintained that he did not speak 'by the hour or for wages' and his self-respect was evidently offended by the condescension displayed by some of those who did offer him assistance, but did not see 'it as an Honour as giving to the Lord's ambassadors but seeing it Charity as thinking me in Want'.[125]

The pressure on exhorters increased as the number of societies and demands on their time grew ever greater. By 1744, William John claimed to be visiting a total of twenty parishes, and by July 1745 William Richard was reporting to the Association on the sixteen societies under his care.[126] The increase from the twelve societies originally allocated in 1743 would have entailed an appreciable increase in effort and travel. Richard was held in sufficient esteem to have been sent on missions to other districts such as north Wales, which meant that John Harry, the superintendent from south Pembrokeshire was increasingly tasked with helping out further north. By January 1749, Richard suggested that Harry might take over the societies 'below the mountain', that is south of the Preseli, including Fishguard, Longhouse and St David's, which would certainly reduce the distance Richard had to travel.[127] The Association realised the pressure placed on the superintendents by the extent of their circuits by April 1744 and decided that they should not be expected to visit the societies more often than once a fortnight, which was demanding enough.[128] John Richard was much troubled by his inability to visit the societies more frequently by 1750:

> *Yr wyf weithiau mewn part o flynder meddwl eisiau gallwn bod yn fwy cyfarwydd o gyflyrau a phrofiadau neulltuol bob un or brodur ar chwiorydd ag sydd dan fy ngofal ond nid wyf yn gallu bod mor fynych yn ei plyth ag y dymynwn ir pwrpas hynny.*[129]

> I am at times in a state of some anxiety wishing I could be more familiar with the particular conditions and experiences of every one of the brothers and sisters who are under my care but I am not able to be as often in their midst as I would wish for that purpose.

He concluded that it would be wiser for him to restrict the number of societies under his supervision, but at the same time could not bear the thought of parting with any of them. None of the other superintendents complained to the same degree, but John Richard's financial circumstances were more difficult and he was perhaps also rather more inclined to express his opinion. Both George Whitefield and Howel Harris felt obliged to write to admonish him in 1743 for his 'irregularity' in voicing his opposition to some of the arrangements made by the Association, including keeping lists of the members' names and allocating exhorters to specific areas.[130]

The exhorters therefore faced considerable burdens of work and financial pressure, in addition to the frustrations of their position as lay preachers and pastors. Several of them were evidently impressive in both aspects of their role and were buoyed up by a sense of purpose and vocation. It was not only the leaders who were responsible for recruiting members by the force of their preaching; Howel Harris remarked that William Richard preached 'most excellently well' and also found himself enlightened by hearing George Gambold discourse and strengthened by John Richard.[131] Yet their contribution was limited by their lack of ordination and would remain so as long as the movement remained within the Church. The prospect of dissenting from the Church was one which inevitably appealed to some of the exhorters as a result. The most significant early losses to the Dissenters were two of the first superintendents in the south-west. Milbourne Bloom resigned from his role as superintendent in west Carmarthenshire and was ordained by the Independents in September 1745. The other superintendent who left during the 1740s was Morgan Hughes, who also turned to Dissent, seeking to register his house as a meeting place in the Cardiganshire Quarter Sessions in May 1747.[132] He settled in Blaen-porth and married the heiress of the farm of Cwmhowni, where the local society met.[133] Thomas William of Eglwys Ilan, one of Harris's assistants, visited Hughes in 1751 and was told that Hughes had refused an invitation to be installed as minister to a group of Independents in Troed-yr-aur parish, but continued to preach in the small meeting house built at Cwmhowni.[134]

The prospect of serving as Dissenting ministers proved attractive to several of the private exhorters also, including the two brothers, William and Christopher Mends, sons of a clothier from Pembrokeshire. Harris described them as natives of Haverfordwest, but the obituary for Christopher in the *Evangelical Magazine* states that he was actually born slightly further south in Hasguard in 1724.[135] The obituary also notes Christopher's recollections of his conversion as a result of hearing George Whitefield and others connected with him speak. Christopher was appointed by the Association as private exhorter in the societies of East Walton and Studder in south Pembrokeshire in January 1745.[136] At least one of the brothers was living in Carmarthen by April 1748, since Harris directed letters to be sent to him there, care of 'Brother Mends', and Christopher was a student at the Carmarthen Academy under Evan Davies for a period in the 1740s.[137] By September 1748 they had apparently relocated to Laugharne, where they were establishing a house for the society although Harris fretted about the cost.[138] They had by then been placed in charge of the societies of Carmarthen, Laugharne and Llandeilo, reporting to the Association, instead of William John, who had experienced difficulties with the Carmarthen society in particular.[139] By 1749, however, William John had resumed his responsibilities, and in January 1750 the house in Laugharne was registered as a Dissenting meeting house, suggesting that they had cut their ties with the Methodists sometime around late 1748 or early 1749.[140] Christopher was ordained as a minister with the Congregationalists in Brinkworth, Wiltshire, and subsequently in Plymouth, but there is no further mention of his brother, William.[141] The Laugharne house became a centre for the Moravians in 1767.[142]

In addition to these individual defections, during Association discussions in the 1740s some of the exhorters argued in favour of separation from the Church in order to benefit from the possibility of ordination. It was not surprising that several exhorters felt that they could better care for their societies if they could act as ministers to them and conduct communion services. Registering as Dissenters would also protect them from accusations of vagrancy and the unwelcome attentions of the press gang, which was a concern for Richard Tibbott and John Richard. Morgan John Lewis, the superintendent for parts of Breconshire and Monmouthshire and Llanddeusant in Carmarthenshire, was one of the most vociferous on the subject of separation. At the Quarterly Association at Glanyrafonddu on 5 October 1743, he argued in favour of leaving the Church on the grounds that 'its foundations are Jewish – its Canons antiscriptural, its Ministers God's Enemies & its worship intermixt with much Popish Superstition & that he thought we should now leave it.'[143] Harris remained concerned that Lewis might join the Dissenters, which he eventually did after the New Inn society in Pant-teg, Monmouthshire, broke away to become an Independent Church with Lewis ordained as its pastor in 1756.[144] Each time the subject of separation was raised, the leaders were adamant in insisting on remaining in the Church, but it was perhaps inevitable that some exhorters would seek ordination with the Dissenters.

It would be fair to conclude that a strong sense of hierarchy prevailed in the early movement. Exhorters could be overruled by the will of the leaders in the Association, as they were on the issue of communion and separation. John Richard seemed to have gone too far in voicing his opinion and was reproved by both Howel Harris and George Whitefield as a result. As with early Dissenting groups, the organisation was largely devised by the immediate necessity of finding practical solutions to the problems of providing for scattered communities of followers. The result was perhaps something of a combination of the hierarchical structure of the Church – with its rural deans and archdeacons – and the broad territorial circuits of the 'county churches' of early Dissent.

Harris and Rowland

The dedication of the leaders of the movement would have provided the exhorters with an example to follow. Constant communication and regular meetings ensured that they were not isolated in their work, and could turn to the leaders for advice as and when needed, in person or by letter. Harris was perhaps the chief liaison with the exhorters and was himself a constant traveller. He was not alone in this, however, especially after William Williams yielded his curacies to act as a full-time Methodist exhorter and superintendent. Although his duties probably increased considerably after Harris distanced himself from the movement, even during the 1740s he became a familiar figure on the roads of south-west Wales. A few months before his death in January 1791 he calculated that he had travelled some 40 to 50 miles every week for 43 years, which would be 2,600 miles a year, and over 43 years would amount to 111,800 miles, or, as he defined it, more than four times around the world.[145] Yet it was Harris who was the chief itinerant in the 1740s, especially in the early years of the decade before he began to spend more of his time in England. He claimed to travel regularly in the region of a hundred miles a week, usually discoursing twice a day.[146] He would often record how far he travelled in a day, at times distinguishing between actual or 'Welsh' miles and 'computed' miles, indicating the difficulties in calculating distance. On 1 February 1743 he travelled '20 long miles' and on 25 May 1743 '40 computed miles'.[147] On 12 April 1746, he estimated that he travelled twenty-five or forty miles from the Swansea area through Llanelli, Cydweli, Llansteffan and Laugharne to

Llanddowror, a journey which took nine hours.[148] The distance is actually in the region of forty miles, but would then have included two ferry trips, across the Loughor to begin with and then over the Tywi between Ferryside and Llansteffan. He tried to inspire the exhorters to emulate his example of travelling 'when my body is fatigued and bruised to ruin' and, like him, to 'preach of Christ till to pieces I fall'.[149] The regular long journeys on horseback at least offered the opportunity to catch up with some reading, including George Whitefield's journal; Philip Doddridge's biography of Colonel James Gardiner, which proved a 'great blessing'; and Humphrey Prideaux's *History of the Jews*, which he found 'dry'.[150]

As a result of these lengthy journeys, combined with numerous meetings, his days were long and his habits at times became practically nocturnal. Marmaduke Gwynne expressed concern that one letter he had received from Harris had been written at 4 a.m. and feared for his health as a result.[151] On one occasion Harris arrived in Llanddowror, Carmarthenshire, so late that several people had to be roused from their beds to hear him speak.[152] In early March 1743, on a visit to the Cardigan area, he spent the night of 6 March and early morning of 7 March until 5 a.m. in the company of the Blaen-porth society. The following night he held a society at Cardigan until 5 a.m. and did not reach his bed to sleep until 6 a.m.[153] He was in Carmarthen on 5 January 1749 when news reached him of the death of his infant daughter. He continued with his engagements that evening, but set off at 3 a.m. to travel the distance of nearly sixty miles back to Trefeca, stopping on the way at Pontargothi, Troedyrhiw in Llanddeusant and Trecastle, arriving home at 2 a.m. the following day.[154] It was a lifestyle which over a period of time must surely have taken its toll. He often complained of being racked with pain and of suffering the consequences of sleepless nights and long hours on horseback, frequently soaked to the skin. In January 1742, he was struck with such pain in his jaw that he could not speak a word.[155] On a journey through Pembrokeshire in 1743, he woke to

> a very violent & acute Pain in my Neck – as if it had been Crackd so I cd not turn it witht ye greatest Pain ... my Pain ... wd go thro' my head to make it ake exceedingly & to my Heart too so to Suck up my spirits so that my Eyes & Ears &

Tongue cd not give attention each to their offices & I had much to do to forbear crying out.[156]

Although he claimed 'I am never better than when on full stretch',[157] Harris himself sometimes marvelled at his own capacity to persevere, convinced that this was through God's help, not through any strength of his own. Various incidents on his travels reinforced the conviction that he was doing God's work, and he saw evidence that providence was operating to smooth his path and lighten his way. On the very same day in 1742 that he was rendered speechless with pain, for instance, he found himself stranded on the banks of the river Loughor, with a lame horse he could not afford to shoe and without the means to pay for the ferry crossing. When financial assistance was provided by friends of the cause, he felt assured that this was the intervention of providence.[158]

A pattern was developing from 1740 onwards whereby Harris would embark on lengthy tours as far as Pembrokeshire, calling in several places in the other two counties en route. In addition, he would arrange brief visits of around a week in duration to Cardiganshire and Carmarthenshire, which were slightly closer to home. The focus of these shorter trips was usually a specific visit to Llanddowror or Llangeitho, but other meetings would be included in the travel plan in order to take advantage of his presence in the area. Harris deliberated very carefully over 'settling his rounds' as he called it. He always did so 'with great Prayer and circumspection', taking the advice of local contacts, exhorters and superintendents who would have a keener idea of where he was most needed.[159] In May 1742, for instance, William Richard helped arrange his itinerary for a visit to south Cardiganshire and north Pembrokeshire, being in a position to judge where Harris might stay the night and where he could meet with society members.[160] The fact that a number of Association meetings took place in the area also regularly attracted him. Harris's visits to the three counties were most common during the formative period between 1740 and 1743, and he spent around a third of the year 1743 in the area, a total of 124 days. This was the pinnacle of his mission to the south-west, as his visits dwindled thereafter, with only 51 days a year spent there during both 1744 and 1745 and just 26 during 1746. This was largely because of the other calls on his time, including periods in London overseeing the Tabernacle society in the absence of George Whitefield. It may also have been the result of the increased role of William Williams as Daniel Rowland's assistant from 1743 onwards, which meant that Harris's presence could more readily be spared.

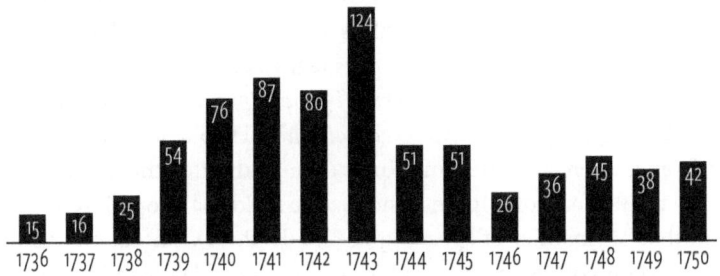

Number of days spent by Harris in the south-west 1736–50, on the evidence of his diaries

However, it was not just the demands of other commitments, or the development of William Williams's contribution, which caused a reduction in the frequency and duration of Harris's visits to the south-west. From 1746 onwards he avoided the area as a result of the deterioration in his relationship with Daniel Rowland. Whereas he had previously visited Llangeitho and the surrounding district fairly regularly, to meet with Rowland and to attend communion service, he was conspicuously absent for a period of three years. On his next visit on 5 March 1749, he acknowledged the root cause of his absence when he noted that he had not been there during the three years since 'the Confusion' had arisen.[161] Although he visited Llangeitho again in July for an Association meeting, that would be the last time for several years. By 1748, he appeared to be concentrating his efforts in the south-west on Carmarthenshire, spending 25 of the 45 days he spent in the south-west in that county, 14 in Pembrokeshire and only 6 in Cardiganshire. He probably felt that he had a greater number of allies in the other two counties and was in effect relinquishing Cardiganshire to Rowland.

This was a consequence of the stresses and strains in the movement which would lead to the separation of 1750. Methodist historians have at times found the division between the leaders to be an uncomfortable subject for discussion, perhaps especially in connection to Harris's friendship with Sidney Griffith. Some of the earliest accounts refer only somewhat obliquely to the causes of the dispute, several, including William Williams in his *Atteb Philo-Evangelius* (The Reply of Philo-Evangelius) in 1763, attributing it to the machinations of the Devil who sought to sow discord in order to undermine the success of the revival.[162] Robert Jones interpreted the events in a similar vein, describing the arrival of the Devil 'as a hellish bloodhound to the midst of the flock, to disturb the sheep, pursue them, and disperse them across the wilderness' (*'fel gwaedgi uffernol i ganol y praidd, i darfu y defaid, eu herlid, a'u gwasgaru ar hyd yr anialwch'*). Theological and personal differences were also cited and Robert Jones admitted that Harris was of a determined cast of mind not inclined to yield to the opinion of others and that his manner of speaking of 'the death of God' caused disquiet amongst his colleagues.[163] John Morgan Jones and William Morgan in *Y Tadau Methodistaidd* (The Methodist Fathers) launched one of the harshest attacks on Sidney Griffith's role in Harris's expulsion. They condemned her as a hypocrite and criticised Harris for being so credulous in his dealings with her, but cleared him of suspicions of heresy by attributing the problem to his inconsistent and clumsy choice of words rather than any fundamental fault.[164] Richard Bennett suggested that it was mental rather than moral decline which led Harris into trouble, emphasising the many references in his diaries to severe headaches as evidence.[165] His most recent biographer, Geraint Tudur, has proposed that the crux of the problem was the tension between Harris's enthusiasm and the more conservative tendencies represented by Rowland and the other evangelical clergy, suggesting that it was this enthusiasm which made him receptive to the idea of Sidney Griffith as a prophetess.[166] Derec Llwyd Morgan also regarded Harris's very nature as a fundamental element in the clash.[167] The division was certainly caused by a number of factors, which undoubtedly included tensions created by Harris's commanding personality, concern about his interpretation of doctrine and, as a final straw, unease about his relationship with Sidney Griffith.[168] The fatigue and stress caused by years of travelling, preaching and organising doubtless also contributed to Harris's failure of good judgement in his dealings with others.

Harris was quite correct to suggest that the problems, or 'Confusion', dated back to at least 1746. By 1750, he had come to regard the 'Confusion' as a 'war' that was being waged between him and the 'clergy party', as he termed Rowland, Davies, Williams and their followers.[169] Early signs of the trouble to come could be detected in the formative years of the Association, with relations sometimes strained and tempers flaring from time to time. Morgan Hughes, recalling his time in the movement in conversation with Thomas William in 1751, believed that the tensions had begun some ten years previously.[170] Harris drove himself without mercy and expected a similar commitment from others, as well as a similar striving for perfection. He was often severe in his self-searching and did not spare his colleagues the same level of criticism. Richard Tibbott confessed that he had felt quite ill (*'yn gryn dosd'*) when Harris denounced Dafydd William Rhys's faults at an Association meeting at Bryniau Bychain, Llansawel, in May 1744.[171] Thomas Price of Watford, Glamorgan, urged Harris to treat his colleagues with more respect having been grieved by his 'imperious spirit' towards the brethren and by his insistence on one occasion that he might as well have been listening to a ballad for all the good one of Rowland's sermons did him.[172]

Even when paying tribute to him in an elegy, William Williams spoke of Harris's desire to 'be head' (*'chwenychu bod yn ben'*).[173] Williams also claimed that it was Rowland who had first proclaimed the Methodist message, although Harris described himself as 'the first field Preacher in this work having gone out some years before Bro. Whitefield or Rowlands'.[174] It is still possible that both versions are truthful, however, in as much as Rowland may have been preaching in an increasingly Methodistical fashion in his own parishes before venturing forth to itinerate. That might coincide with or predate Harris's beginnings as a lay preacher, although Harris might technically have been the first to itinerate. Yet Harris obviously became determined from 1746 onwards to establish his 'place' in the movement by insisting that it was he who began the work and that he should not be regarded as inferior to Rowland or Whitefield, even if he was but a layman. Exhorting with the Methodists had led to him being refused holy orders, yet he could not refrain in order to appease the bishop of St Davids and gain ordination. He consoled himself with the fact that if ordained he could save the 'lost of one parish' whereas by retaining his lay status he could assist in the salvation of many.[175] Even so, he felt keenly that he was derided for his lack of status. His sensitivity about his position as a layman may have been behind the constant emphasis on his mission from God, since divine inspiration was the only justification he had for his activity. Even having been appointed to the role of chief superintendent of the societies, he still felt he was being undermined by Rowland and the other evangelical clergy. Issues of discipline were amongst the sore points, as Harris grew frustrated over Rowland's willingness to allow members who had been expelled by Harris to receive communion.[176] This, in Harris's view, was 'weakening his hands'. His assertion of his own authority could give the impression of arrogance. For instance, he explained that he was placed as a father in the movement and saw the brethren as children to be guided by him.[177] In 1749 he noted: '… seeing when I dye Wales shall suffer loss – God having made me faithfull and impartial & willing to go thro' all slavery to lead them to Xt'.[178] When angry with him, Griffith Jones frequently accused Harris of being overly fond of singing his own praises, calling him 'proud & haughty' and 'obstinately erroneous & conceited'.[179]

In addition to such tensions, the movement was also plagued by doctrinal differences. The decision to adhere to Calvinist theology rather than side with the Arminian Wesleyan camp was relatively straightforward, but other subtleties of doctrine caused disagreements. As early as 1742, Harris and Rowland were locked in dispute over the doctrine of assurance.[180] Further arguments would occur over elements of Harris's preaching which were regarded as potentially unorthodox, or at least unwisely expressed. It was felt that he was prone to adopt some of the language and teachings favoured by the Moravians, whose influence Harris had encountered during his visits to London. Their emphasis on personal experience and spiritual fellowship were in accord with Methodist principles, so some similarities were to be expected.[181] However, there were suspicions that the Moravians espoused sinless perfection and were also drawing Methodist converts and entire societies in England in particular to join them.[182] Harris certainly seemed to dwell on the blood and wounds of Christ in a way that was highly reminiscent of Moravian devotion, with numerous references to 'the mangled body' and the 'blood of the lamb' in his sermons.[183] He preached that the blood of Christ 'cures all our Evils', and of the need to 'prize the Blood of Christ because we need to wash all in that fountain'.[184] Harris insisted that he had not changed his style or beliefs since he began preaching, and it is certainly true that there are earlier references to the blood of Christ. In 1740, for instance, he reflected:

> admiring this Blood seeing more & more of ye amazing Riches in this Blood & seeing it shed for me … o amazing Blood o spring of all Happiness … saw this ffountain – o this Blood! that destroys guilt – sin – Satan &c – o that nothing was preachd but this![185]

However, it is apparent that it became an obvious theme in his preaching by the end of the 1740s, judging by his own summaries of sermons such as:

> I cryd Blood Blood Blood … if you don't drink it drink it drink it you are damnd – God wont look on any of the sons of Adam nor suffer them to look to Him but in Blood what vast Expence did He put the Jews to to keep Blood in his Temples & even in Egypt before He had a Temple He would have Blood.[186]

Theophilus Evans certainly became convinced that Methodism was an offshoot of Moravianism, and there were concerns within the movement that Harris might be straying too far in that direction and towards antinomianism.[187] These suspicions were heightened by Harris's defence of James Beaumont, the exhorter who became superintendent of the Radnorshire societies in 1743.[188] Although originally an Independent, he was drawn to the Moravians and wrote of stepping 'in to the Crimson Pool, the holy holy holy Blood of our Almighty GOD', whilst acknowledging that this was a doctrine viewed with suspicion by the Welsh Methodists.[189] Harris had reproved him for antinomianism, and relations between them had been strained as a result.[190] Beaumont complained that Harris and the other Welsh brethren had 'some Ifs and some Buts & Becauses, some legal fears'.[191] Yet, Harris believed that one of the root causes of the opposition to him was that he had supported Beaumont more generally, refusing to 'fetter' him and prevent him from preaching in the belief that God might have something to say through such a 'greatly blessed preacher'.[192] He would in later years suggest to the

Countess of Huntingdon that it was his attachment to the Moravians in general which had created the hostility towards him within the Welsh movement.[193]

The most serious accusation levelled against Harris, however, was the charge of Patripassianism, that he was teaching that it was God who had died on the cross and not the human Christ. There seemed little doubt that Harris's preaching was causing confusion on this point, as he freely confessed in April 1748 that:

> He was God everywhere on the Cross & in the Grave else how could He give us His fflesh & Blood … then I declard that He on the Cross is my God and however you old Professors may despise our dying God I shall have a Thief to Joyn with me in My Confession.[194]

Exhorting on other occasions during the same week, he also 'preached of God dying strong and home' and stated that 'we say tis ye Manhood dyd but ye man that dyd was ye Eternal God'.[195] Harris held that those who opposed him were Arians who denied the divinity of Christ, complaining that in Carmarthenshire, 'Arianism is strong every where they cant bear to hear of a dying God'.[196] A fierce debate arose with Thomas Morgan of Henllan Amgoed, one of Harris's converts who was a student at the Carmarthen Academy before being ordained as an Independent minister. Harris berated him as a heretic for daring to suggest that the man who died on the cross was not 'the Eternal God'.[197] Conflict over Harris's perceived heretical tendencies soured a number of Association meetings in 1746. Harris was forced to defend his position at the Trefeca Assocation in June 1746. He explained his conviction that it was the man-God who suffered and died and that he could not distinguish between the two persons, viewing the child in the manger and the corpse in the tomb both as God. On the suspicions of Moravianism, he stated that he worshipped the blood, as part of Christ, since all parts of his body were divine. In answer to accusations from the brethren that his convictions had changed over the years, he maintained that he had kept to the same truths as when he had begun exhorting without shifting in the slightest.[198] Despite suggestions that he should be removed from his post as general superintendent, some sort of reconciliation was achieved by October 1746, although the issues had not been truly resolved.

Grave misgivings also arose over the wisdom of Harris's choice of Mrs Sidney Griffith as spiritual companion. She was the wife of William Griffith, squire of Cefnamwlch in Caernarfonshire, and the daughter of the Wynne family of Foelas, Denbighshire, so well connected by birth and marriage and thus frequently respectfully dubbed 'Madam Griffith'. The lady had been converted to the cause in 1747 after one of Peter Williams's visits to the north, and made Harris's acquaintance in 1748. Harris became convinced of her spiritual insight and prophetic ability, believing that she was a gift from God who would prove to be a 'Pillar of Glory to Wales' and a 'Cherub wearing a Body'.[199] Although he had previously insisted that it was God's will that he marry his wife Anne, Harris became equally convinced by Sidney Griffith's prophecies that it was now God's intention for both Anne and William Griffith to die so that the widow and widower would then be free to unite.[200] He judged it 'not expedient' to share this revelation with everyone.[201] His reasoning was that he had been as a child when he married Anne, who had not matured with him in the time since, so was not a fit helpmeet for him in the work.[202] He had previously persuaded her that she was a Rebecca to his Isaac, but now believed Sidney Griffith was intended to be a Phoebe to his Paul and a Deborah to his Barak.[203] Griffith's feelings are rather more difficult to ascertain as her letters to Harris were largely destroyed, although it is impossible to know whether this was by Harris himself or by some of his associates after his death. However, if Harris reported her opinions with any degree of accuracy in his diary, then she was in agreement with Harris's views of their future together: '... she beyond all Delusion saw that she was to be with me & never freed because of the Union with me to m[arry] any one if Gr[iffith] dy'd.'[204]

Her continued presence at Trefeca and decision to accompany Harris on his travels, in the light of so much hostility and gossip, suggests that she was committed to their spiritual and personal relationship. That also meant being prepared to inflict considerable distress and embarrassment on Harris's wife. Anne Harris was in an invidious position, as any opposition to her rival's presence was censured by her husband as evidence of the Devil's possession of her. Harris proved immune to all suggestions that the relationship with Madam Griffith was imprudent and was causing damage both to his own reputation and that of the movement in general. Within his household, his wife, his mother and servants all remonstrated with him to no avail.[205] Colleagues who attempted to reason with him were condemned for aiding and abetting the Devil, including Morgan John Lewis who was turned out of Trefeca for defending Anne.[206] All doubt and resistance within the movement was seen as disobedience. Doubts were not confined to the Welsh movement, however, and Thomas Morgan received a letter from a former fellow student at the Carmarthen Academy, Noah Jones, now a minister at Cradley in Worcestershire. Of Harris, Jones had heard: "tis to be fear'd his moral Character is not good: I find the Carnarvonshire Esquire's Lady travels with him & as he declares is of vast use to him to enlighten his mind."[207] A visit to London in December 1749 took place without the usual rooms being reserved for Harris at the Tabernacle or the usual immediate invitation to preach. Harris was infuriated by Elizabeth Whitefield's hostility, but Whitefield was also adamant that the attachment to Madam Griffith was injurious to Harris and Methodism, expressing the common perception of the relationship: 'that many had been speaking to him of it, that it would hurt my Character and that to sit with her to 2 or 3 in ye Morning did not seem right'.[208] There is no evidence that his co-workers believed the worst aspects of the rumours about the liaison, but they did warn of the immeasurable harm it was doing to the good name of the cause. It is likely that the split would have come at some point in any case, on the grounds of doctrinal issues as well as Harris's insistence on predominance within the movement on the basis of his special calling from God. The reliance on Sidney Griffith certainly helped precipitate the separation and served to confirm Harris's impaired judgement, probably exacerbated by mental exhaustion.

Harris's presence in the south-west during these years was missed, with Daniel John of Llanfair Clydogau, Cardiganshire, urging him to return to the area where he had been instrumental in converting many, and was still needed even if they had the benefits of the ministry of Daniel Rowland close to hand.[209] Yet, it is debatable whether his preaching was as beneficial to his hearers as it had been in the past. The fear was that by not choosing his words sufficiently carefully when talking of the blood and death of Christ, he might be leading the members into error. Judging by what he recorded of the content of his sermons in his diary, many of his preaching engagements from 1748 onwards were also used as opportunities to attempt to reinforce his position in the movement and to undermine his opponents. That indication of internal tensions may have been unsettling for his hearers and did little to improve relations. Harris's choice of text or topic often reflected the issues which preoccupied him at any given time and his constant return to the story of Corah's defiance of Moses would seem to reveal his condemnation of those who resisted him as guilty of the sin of disobedience.[210] Tensions were often heightened by gossip related to Harris on his travels, including that the clergy in the movement called him 'Pope' behind his back.[211] In 1751, Richard Tibbott, one of the most perceptive commentators on the movement's internal difficulties, suggested to Harris that he had been too inclined to believe unfavourable stories recounted about Rowland and the others. Harris often gained the impression from tales he was told that Rowland and Howel Davies in particular were intent on 'weakening his hand' and conspiring against him. He had once compared his friendship with Davies to that of David and Jonathan, so it must have been extraordinarily painful to hear that Davies was plotting to remove him.[212] Harris was also being fed negative information by his assistant Thomas William, of Eglwys Ilan, Glamorgan, who was apparently regarded as something of a talebearer by other exhorters.[213] He was suggesting in 1749 that there were moves afoot to replace Harris and that the two sides in the debate, like the followers of Calvin and Luther, could not be brought together again.[214]

Although Harris is usually seen as the chief cause of the problems, Rowland was not completely without fault. Most contemporaries found him an easier person to deal with than Harris, and the diarist William Thomas proclaimed him to be by reputation 'a chearfull man and clear of understanding, without Bigotry'.[215] Yet, he was prone to levity, which caused Harris to fear that 'his dark witty cutting carnal way of speaking I could not see came from the spirit of God'.[216] Harris was not alone in finding Rowland's occasional lightness of spirit to be disturbing, as Richard Tibbott was also sometimes perturbed by it.[217] However, Rowland was a serious upholder of doctrine, who spent hours in his study researching and preparing his sermons.[218] As a leader of the Methodist movement and as an ordained cleric in the Anglican Church, he had to preserve what he held to be orthodox belief. Williams praised him for his defence of orthodoxy, as 'a strong pillar in the church of God, a means to keep the Welsh Methodists from many Errors your nei[gh]bours have fell to'.[219] This was a theme he returned to in his elegy to Rowland, where he praised his stance against all enemies of the Trinity.[220] Harris's own perception was that Rowland's 'wisdom' militated against the light and that he opposed the 'witness of the spirit'.[221] Harris was more of an enthusiast who held that he was guided by the spirit and was more open to the idea of revelation from a prophetess who was a medium to express God's will.[222] He marvelled that so many were opposed to the influences of Sidney Griffith and James Beaumont when he had received such enlightenment through them.[223] The difference in approach was confirmed in Rowland's pamphlet, *Ymddiddan rhwng Methodist uniawn-gred ac un camsyniol* (Discourse between an Orthodox Methodist and a Mistaken One), published in 1750, with its allusions to Harris clear. The mistaken Methodist insists on having received a revelation that the Father was made flesh to suffer and die with the Son and refutes the suggestion that this is contrary to the revealed word of God in the Bible. Harris's defence that he cannot distinguish between the two natures of Christ is repeated by the mistaken Methodist.[224] He also dismisses the value of book learning compared to the spirit, and desires all books to be burnt, which is a far more extreme attitude than Harris would espouse.[225] The analysis in essence finds Harris guilty of the accusations against him of Patripassianism, Sabellianism (confusing the persons of the Trinity with modes) and antinomianism (suggesting that the believer was not bound by moral convention).[226]

Although Harris feared Rowland was set on separation as early as April 1746,[227] the division was not to take place until 1750. Harris had confidently told Howel Davies in February 1750 that Rowland would not have the capacity to set up his own party, possibly referring to a lack of organisational skills as well as to levels of support among the exhorters.[228] However, the last united Association met at Llanidloes on 9 May 1750. On 23 June, Harris learnt that four clergymen and eleven exhorters had met at Llantrisant and expelled Harris in his absence.[229] Although Harris initially had a substantial amount of support from exhorters in certain areas – Breconshire, Radnorshire, Montgomeryshire and Glamorgan – several began to fall away. The names who immediately disappeared from Harris's diary and correspondence reveal those who were staunchly in Rowland's camp and include William Richard and James Williams. During the course of 1750 it became clear that neither William John in Carmarthenshire, nor John Harry in south Pembrokeshire, would join Harris's Association either.[230] Harris stated that he would go only where he was called, so his visits to the south-west were curtailed largely to specific districts associated with his supporters, including John Sparks in Haverfordwest. He also remained in close contact with some of the Llwynyberllan family, chiefly the younger John Williams and his maternal uncle, Nathaniel Williams, whom Harris visited at Hen Fynachlog farm at Strata Florida in Cardiganshire.[231] He also visited John Richard in Llansamlet and the area of south Carmarthenshire which was under his influence. Gradually, some of these colleagues also withdrew. John Richard was not wholly convinced about Sidney Griffith's role and wrote in January 1751 to explain that, although united with Harris in spirit, he could not join with him. He seemed to be trying to avoid inflicting too much pain by assuring Harris that he was merely acting in obedience to God's will:

Credwch fi Anwyl Dad yn yr Arglwydd yr ydwyf yn tebig mai nid fy meddylieu fy hun yw yr hyn ac yr wyf yn ei sgrifenni at ond gwirionedd pwysig yr wyf yn ei Llefary ger bron Duw yngrist.[232]

Believe me dear Father in the Lord I suppose that what I write to you are not my own thoughts but an important truth which I declare before God in Christ.

By October 1751, it must have been clear to Harris that he was losing all remaining support in the south-west. On 4 and 5 October he wrote a series of poignant letters to erstwhile friends and colleagues, including John Richard and John Sparks, entreating them not to forsake him and his cause, but to no avail.[233] For Harris, the way forward was to retreat to Trefeca to set up his religious community. Unsurprisingly, very few Methodists from the south-west were to join him there.

William Williams acknowledged later that the effects of Harris's withdrawal had been unfortunate for the movement.[234] Yet Rowland had already been a more consistent presence in Wales, whilst Harris had spent a good proportion of his time deputising for Whitefield in London. Although the division was unsettling for the membership in general, the south-west probably suffered less than other areas because the presence of Daniel Rowland, Howel Davis and William Williams provided a robust sense of continuity. Although information from the 1750s is scarce, one valuable source is the diary of John Thomas, of Tre-main in south Cardiganshire, one of Griffith Jones's teachers in the area, which shows that William Richard persisted in his efforts as superintendent of south Cardiganshire and north Pembrokeshire.[235] The area was also well served by regular visits from the evangelical clergy, who preached and, in the case of the ordained priests, provided communion services in the nearby chapels of ease. Methodist societies continued to function in the 1750s, therefore, although possibly without quite the same vigour or organisation as in the previous decade. A certain degree of cooling might have been foreseen, as it was difficult to maintain the early levels of recruitment and fervour of revival undiminished. However, a sufficiently solid foundation had been laid by Harris's capacity for organisation to ensure the movement's survival, even after his withdrawal.

Notes

1 DHH 50, 18 December 1739.
2 Trevecka MS 916, Howel Harris to Miss BeeBee, 9 July 1743. This sounds as if it may be an echo of Josiah Woodward's description of the members of the earliest religious society in London as 'these young Striplings, who stand up with a generous Courage to assert the Honour of God, and stop the Mouth of Blasphemy'. J. Woodward, *An Account of the Rise and Progress of the Religious Societies in the City of London, &c, And of the Endeavours for Reformation of Manners Which have been made therein* (London: JD for the author, 1698), p. 26.
3 R. Jones, *Drych yr Amseroedd*, ed. G. M. Ashton (Caerdydd: Gwasg Prifysgol Cymru, 1958), p. 43; D. J. Odwyn Jones, *Daniel Rowland Llangeitho (1713–1790)* (Llandysul: Gwasg Gomer, 1938), p. 76; E. Evans, *Daniel Rowland* (Edinburgh: Banner of Truth Trust, 1985), p. 29.
4 Evans, *Daniel Rowland*, pp. 29–35.
5 *The Evangelical Magazine* (1802), 161–2; *The Evangelical Magazine* (1799), 397; R. Tudur Jones, 'John Thomas (bap. 1730, d. in or before 1806)' (Oxford University Press, 23 September 2004). Accessed 30 September 2019, https://www.oxforddnb.com/view/10.1093/ref:odnb/9780198614128.001.0001/odnb-9780198614128-e-62918 .

6   J. Owen *Coffhad am y Parch. Daniel Rowlands* (Caerlleon: Edward Parry, 1839), pp. 8–9, 21–2.
7   J. Thomas, *Hanes y Bedyddwyr, ymhlith y Cymry* (Caerfyrddin: John Ross, 1778), p. 53.
8   DHH 63a, 11 November 1740.
9   'Yr offeiriad crac'. Owen, *Coffhad am y Parch. Daniel Rowlands*, pp. 17–18; E. Evans, *Daniel Rowland and the Great Evangelical Awakening in Wales* (Edinburgh: Banner of Truth Trust, 1985), pp. 41–2.
10 DHH 90, 31 May 1742.
11 DHH 39, 30 January 1739.
12 Trevecca College/1 3110, Llanwinio Society, Carmarthenshire, to Daniel Rowland, n.d. 1748.
13 Trevecka MS 705, Daniel Rowland to Howel Harris, 20 October 1742. Printed in *Account of Progress of the Gospel*, 2/i (1743), 3–7.
14 Trevecka MS 356, Richard Jenkins and Benjamin Cadman to Howel Harris, 21 July 1741.
15 Trevecka MS 939, Howel Harris to George Whitefield, 31 July 1743.
16 DHH 113, 4 October 1744; 115b, 22 January 1745.
17 Trevecka MS 1295, Howel Harris to James Erskine, 19 February 1745.
18 DHH 98, 27 March 1743.
19 *The Diary of William Thomas of Michaelston-super-Ely, near St Fagans Glamorgan 1762–1795*, ed. R. T. W. Denning (Cardiff: South Wales Record Society, 1995), pp. 235, 393.
20 Thomas, *Hanes y Bedyddwyr*, p. 54.
21 DHH 18, 28 December 1736.
22 Trevecka MS 338, Howel Harris to Griffith Jones, 15 May 1741.
23 Trevecka MS 108, David Evan to Howel Harris, 6 April 1738.
24 Trevecka MS 123, Griffith Jones to Howel Harris, 8 October 1738.
25 Trevecka MS 137, Anthony Rees to Howel Harris, 13 January 1739.
26 Trevecka MS 732, John Morgan and John Gibbon to Howel Harris, 20 November 1742.
27 Trevecka MS 454, John Richard to Howel Harris, 3 January 1742.
28 Trevecca College/1 2945, p. 50, 4 January 1744.
29 DHH 59, 9 July 1740.
30 Trevecca College/1 2945, pp. 10–11, 1 March 1743.
31 Trevecka MS 694, Howel Harris to George Whitefield, 15 October 1742.
32 SD/MISC/1279, a list of candidates for orders with names of alleged Methodists on dorse, c. 1744.
33 Jones, *Drych yr Amseroedd*, p. 40; Evans, *Daniel Rowland*, p. 209.
34 Trevecka MS 545, Howel Harris to Marmaduke Gwynne, 29 April 1742; 546, Howel Harris to George Whitefield, 30 April 1742.
35 DHH 85, 14–15 February 1742.
36 See G. M. Roberts, *Bywyd a Gwaith Peter Williams* (Caerdydd: Gwasg Prifysgol Cymru, 1943); E. M. White, 'Peter Williams a'r Beibl Cymraeg', *Transactions of the Honourable Society of Cymmrodorion*, new series, 14 (2008), 58–72.
37 Trevecca College/1 2945, pp. 15, 6–7 April 1743; p. 19, 29–30 June 1743; p. 91, 27 June 1744; Trevecca College 1/2991, 1 February 1749.

38 G. Roberts, 'Y Llafurwyr Cynnar', in Roberts (ed.), *Hanes Methodistiaeth Galfinaidd Cymru, Cyfrol I: Y Deffroad Mawr* (Caernarfon, Llyfrfa'r Methodistiaid Calfinaidd, 1973), pp. 206–9; Roger L. Brown, *Evangelicals in the Church in Wales* (Welshpool: Tair Eglwys Press, 2007), pp. 49–59.
39 Trevecca College/1 2994, 18 November 1749.
40 DHH 48, 18 August 1739.
41 DHH 83a, 6 September 1741.
42 See Richard Tibbott's diary, NLW MS 18435B.
43 DHH 82, 12 December 1741.
44 For instance, his comments on Dafydd William Rees and on John Morgan, whom he considered to be 'more knowing than most of ye Methodists'. NLW MS 5456A, p. 13, 10 February 1744; p. 54b, 19 June 1744.
45 DHH 134, 14 March 1749.
46 DHH 133, 1 February 1749; Trevecca College/1 2991.
47 See E. M. White, 'Education and the Welsh Language', in J. G. Jones (ed.), *The History of Welsh Calvinistic Methodism, III: Growth and Consolidation (c.1814–1914)* (Historical Society on behalf of the Presbyterian Church of Wales, 2013), pp. 116–17.
48 DHH 72, 29 April 1741; 96, 20 December 1742; 112, 13 August 1744; 132, 16 September 1748.
49 Trevecka MS 148, William Seward to Daniel Abbott, 10 March 1739.
50 NLW MS 5456A, 22 January 1744.
51 NLW MS 5456A, 7 May 1744.
52 Trevecka MS 705, Daniel Rowland to Howel Harris, 20 October 1742; printed in *Account of the Most Remarkable Particulars relating to the Present Progress of the Gospel*, 2/i (1743), 3–7.
53 DHH 48, 18 August 1739.
54 DHH 54, 23 March 1740.
55 Trevecka MS 776, Howel Harris to Griffith Jones, 10 January 1743.
56 Trevecca College/1 2945, pp. 10–12, 1 March 1743.
57 Trevecca College/1 2945, p. 13, 6–7 April 1743.
58 Trevecca College/1 2945, p. 19, 29–30 June 1743.
59 Trevecca College/1 2945, p. 15, 1 May 1743.
60 Trevecka MS 973, William John to Howel Harris, 10 September 1743; Roberts, 'Y Llafurwyr Cynnar', pp. 264–5,
61 NLW MS 5456A, pp. 29a, 44b.
62 Trevecca College/1 2959, 4 January 1744.
63 Trevecca College/1 2945, p. 13, 6–7 April 1743.
64 Trevecca College/1 3187, p. 76.
65 Trevecca College/1 2945, p. 92, 27 June 1744.
66 Trevecca College/1 2945, p. 110, 12 August 1744.
67 Trevecka MS 1197, William Jones and eleven others from Tan-yr-allt and Bron-y-mwyn societies to Howel Harris, 25 June 1744.
68 Trevecka MS 821, Howel Harris to John Lewis, 7 March 1743.
69 Trevecca College/1 3025, January 1745.
70 Trevecca College/1 2945, p. 143, 28 January 1745.
71 Trevecca College/1 2945, p. 144, 28 January 1745; p. 147, 3 July 1745.

72 Trevecca College/1 2945, p. 6, 3 February 1743; p. 9, 1 March 1743; Trevecca College/1 3005, 30 September 1743.
73 Trevecca College/1 2945, p. 8, 1 March 1743; p. 17, 19 May 1743.
74 Trevecca College/1 2982, 21 July 1747.
75 Trevecca College/1 2945, p. 9, 1 March 1743; p. 89, 15 April 1744.
76 NLW MS 5456A, 11 February 1744, p. 13b.
77 Trevecca College/1 2945, p. 6, 3 February 1743; p. 9, 1 March 1743.
78 DHH 72, 28 April 1741.
79 Trevecca College/1 2945, p. 143, 22 January 1745.
80 J. Hughes, *Methodistiaeth Cymru*, II, pp. 299–301; G. M. Roberts, 'Y Llafurwyr Cynnar', in *Y Deffroad Mawr*, pp. 264–5.
81 Trevecka MS 1197, William Jones and eleven others from Tan-yr-allt and Bron-y-mwyn societies to Howel Harris, 25 June 1744.
82 Trevecca College/1 3026, 29 June 1745.
83 Trevecca College/1 3025, January 1745.
84 Trevecka MS 897, John Jones to Howel Harris, 26 June 1743.
85 Trevecka MS 1207, *c.* 1 October 1744.
86 Trevecka MS 1765, Daniel John to Howel Harris, 4 February 1748.
87 Trevecca College/1 3037, 7 January 1747.
88 DHH 130, 29 April 1748.
89 DHH 132, 19 September 1748.
90 DHH 133, 3 January 1749.
91 Trevecca College/1 3023, p. 15, 14 April 1746.
92 DHH 127, 8 August 1747; 129, 12 February 1748.
93 G. M. Roberts, 'William Gambold a'i Deulu', *Y Genhinen*, 22 (1972), 15–16; G. M. Roberts, *Cynnydd y Corff* (1978), p. 16; G. H. Jenkins, 'Bywiogrwydd Crefyddol a Llenyddol Dyffryn Teifi, 1689–1740', in *Cadw Tŷ Mewn Cwmwl Tystion* (Llandysul: Gwasg Gomer, 1990), pp. 110-11.
94 Trevecca College/1 3023, pp. 10–11, October 1745.
95 T. Dafydd, *Coffadwriaeth am y Cyfiawn mewn hanes byrr o fywyd dichlynedd a dedwydd farwolaeth William Sion, ym mhlwyf Llanegwad, yn Sir Gaerfyrddin* ... (Caerfyrddin: John Ross, 1776), p. 1; G. H. Hughes, 'Thomas Dafydd, Un o Emynwyr Sir Gaerfyrddin', *Journal of the Welsh Bibliographical Society*, 7 (1950), 89–90.
96 SD/1791/107: William Williams, Llanfair-ar-y-bryn, Carmarthen, clerk, 1791.
97 SD/1790/107: Daniel Rowland, Llangeitho, Cardigan, clerk, 1790.
98 DHH 127a, 17 October 1747.
99 Jones, *Historic Carmarthenshire Homes*, p. 70.
100 NLW, St Davids Probate, SD/1770/220: Jenkin Lewis, Fareham, Hampshire (Blaen-porth), 1770.
101 SD/1792/9: Morgan Hughes, Blaen-porth, Cardigan, 1792.
102 SD/1770/6: Catherine Lewis, Blaen-porth, Cardigan, 1770.
103 W. Williams, *Marwnad William Richard o Abercarfan* (Caerfyrddin: John Ross, 1771), p. 3.
104 Trevecka MS 308, William John to Howel Harris, 14 January 1741; see also G. M. Roberts, 'William John, Glancothi', *Cylchgrawn Cymdeithas Hanes y Methodistiaid Calfinaidd/Journal of the Historical Society of the Presbyterian Church of Wales*, 36 (1951), 32. By the early nineteenth century Glancothi

was owned by a Captain William Hughes and was regarded more as a mansion than the farm it had been in the eighteenth century. Coflein, RCHAMW, 9 January 2008, *http://www.coflein.gov.uk/en/site/407240/details/glancothi-glan-cothi-mansion*.
105   DHH 98, 2 March 1743.
106   SD/1764/132: James Williams, Llanddewibrefi, Cardigan, gentleman, 1764.
107   SD/1769/109: Catherine Williams, Llanddewibrefi, Cardigan, widow, 1769; SD/1785/117: William Wiliams, Berws, Llanddewibrefi, Cardigan, 1785.
108   I. C. Peate, *Clock and Watch Makers in Wales* (Cardiff: National Museum of Wales, second edn 1960), p, 69.
109   SD/1776/138: John Richard, Llansamlet, Glamorgan, 1776.
110   G. M. Roberts, 'John Richard, Llansamlet', *Cylchgrawn Cymdeithas Hanes y Methodistiaid Calfinaidd/Journal of the Historical Society of the Presbyterian Church of Wales*, 27 (1942), 145.
111   DHH 89, 2 May 1742. His brother, Dafydd William Dafydd, also known as David Williams, was also an active exhorter in the 1740s, chiefly in Glamorgan.
112   Trevecka MS 556, 15 May 1742.
113   Trevecca College/1 2945, p. 11, 1 March 1743.
114   Trevecca College/1 2945, p. 109, 16 July 1744.
115   Trevecca College/1 2945, p. 17, 19 May 1743.
116   Trevecca College/1 2945, p. 8, 1 March 1743.
117   Trevecca College/1 2945, p. 9, 1 March 1743; p. 15, 1 May 1743.
118   NLW MS 18435B, p. 19, 25 August 1741; *The Evangelical Magazine* (1802), 162.
119   Trevecca College/1 2945, p. 127, 18 October 1744; E. Rees, 'Bookbinding in Eighteenth-Century Wales', *Journal of the Welsh Bibliographical Society*, 12 (1984), 61.
120   DHH 132, 7 September 1748.
121   DHH 144, 22 April 1750.
122   DHH 138, 20 October 1749; 134, 15 March 1749.
123   DHH 105, 14 December 1743.
124   DHH 134, 10 March 1749.
125   DHH 105, 15 December 1743; 132, 5 September 1748.
126   Trevecca College/1 2945, p. 103, 16 July 1744; Trevecca College/1 3027, 2 July 1745.
127   Trevecca College/1 3042, 3044, 3048, William Richard to the Association, 14 July 1747, 10 October 1744, 26 January 1749.
128   Trevecca College/1 2945, p. 84, 24 April 1744.
129   Trevecca College/1 3081, 1750.
130   Trevecka MS 901, George Whitefield to John Richard, 30 June 1743; 908, Howel Harris to John Richard, 8 July 1743; 919, Howel Harris to George Whitefield, 13 July 1743.
131   DHH 123, 27 June 1746; 115b, 1 February 1745; 97, 2 February 1743.
132   NLW, Cardiganshire Quarter Sessions, QS/OB/1, 20 May 1747.
133   NLW, Cwrt Mawr MS 182B.
134   Trevecka MS 2013, Thomas William to Howel Harris, 19 October 1751.
135   DHH 105, 16 December 1743; *Evangelical Magazine* (1799), 397.
136   Trevecca College/1 2945, p. 143, January 1745.

137 Trevecka MS 1782, Howel Harris to Charles Wesley, 18 April 1748; *Evangelical Magazine* (1799), 398–9.
138 DHH 131a, 5 May 1748; 132, 17 September 1748.
139 Trevecca College/1 3067, 25 October 1748.
140 Trevecca College/1 3073, 24 May 1749; Carmarthenshire Archive, Quarter Session Records, QS1/1, p. 57.
141 Christopher Mends's call to Plymouth became the subject of a case before the Court of King's Bench in January 1762, as the trustees refused him access to the meeting house, despite his being approved as minister by the majority of the congregation. *Evangelical Magazine* (1799), 399–400.
142 R. T. Jenkins, 'The Moravian Brethren in Carmarthenshire', *Cylchgrawn Cymdeithas Hanes y Methodistiaid Calfinaidd/Journal of the Historical Society of the Presbyterian Church of Wales*, 21 (1936), 1–2.
143 DHH 103, 5 October 1743.
144 DHH 113, 3 October 1744; Morgan John Lewis, *Cynhwysiad Byr o Feddyliau'r Eglwys a Ymgrpholodd dan y Drefn hon yn Sir Fonwy: Pa un sy'n ymgyfarfod yn bennaf, yn y Neuad yn y Pant-teg, gerllaw Pont-y-pool: yn agos ir modd y Proffesswyd hwynt ar Ddydd ein Hordeinassiwn, sef Dydd y llun y Sulgwyn, 1756* (Bala: John Rowlands, *c.* 1761); Roberts, 'Y Llafurwyr Cynnar', pp. 368–9.
145 G. M. Roberts, *Y Pêr Ganiedydd: (Pantycelyn), Cyfrol I: Trem ar ei Fywyd* (Aberystwyth: Gwasg Aberystwyth, 1949), p. 164.
146 DHH 132, 19 September 1748; 134, 7 March 1749, 16 March 1749.
147 DHH 97, 1 February 1743; 99, 25 May 1743.
148 DHH 122, 12 April 1746.
149 DHH 136, 31 July 1749; 95, 24 October 1742.
150 DHH 98, 1 April 1743; 102, 4 August 1743; 134, 18–19 March 1749; H. Prideaux, *The Old and New Testament Connected in the History of the Jews and Neighbouring Nations* (1716); P. Doddridge, *The Life of Colonel James Gardiner* (1747). William Williams owned a copy of Prideaux's book. G. T. Hughes 'Llyfrgell Pantycelyn', in '*Yr Hen Bant': Ysgrifau ar William Pantycelyn* (Talybont: Y Lolfa, 2017), p. 91.
151 Trevecka MS 823, Marmaduke Gwynne to Howel Harris, 21 March 1743.
152 DHH 141, 10 February 1750.
153 DHH 98, 6–8 March 1743.
154 DHH 133, 5–7 January 1749.
155 DHH 84, 18 January 1742.
156 DHH 100, 10 June 1743.
157 DHH 46, 15 July 1739.
158 DHH 84, 18 January 1742.
159 DHH 103, 6 October 1743.
160 Trevecka MS 550, William Richard to Howel Harris, 7 May 1742.
161 DHH 134, 5 March 1749.
162 G. H. Hughes, *Gweithiau William Williams Pantycelyn, Cyfrol II: Rhyddiaith* (Caerdydd: Gwasg Prifysgol Cymru, 1967), p. 24.
163 R. Jones, *Drych yr Amseroedd*, ed. G. M. Ashton (Caerdydd: Gwasg Prifysgol Cymru, 1958), pp. 79–81.
164 J. M. Jones and W. Morgan, *Y Tadau Methodistaidd*, Cyfrol I (Lewis Evans: Abertawe, 1895), pp. 379–85.

165 R. Bennett, *Methodistiaeth Trefaldwyn Uchaf, 1738-52* (Y Bala: R. Evans a'i Fab, 1929), pp. 101-2.
166 G. Tudur, *Howell Harris* (Cardiff: University of Wales Press, 2000), p. 193.
167 D. Ll. Morgan, *The Great Awakening in Wales*, trans. Dyfnallt Morgan (London: Epworth Press, 1988), pp. 68-71, 79-85.
168 A. W. Owen, 'Yr Ymraniad', in Roberts (ed.), *Y Deffroad Mawr*, pp. 314-55; E. M. White, '"A Breach in God's House": The Division in Welsh Calvinistic Methodism 1750-63', in Nigel Yates (ed.), *Bishop Burgess and his World: Culture, Religion and Society in Britain, Europe and North America in the Eighteenth and Nineteenth Centuries* (Cardiff: University of Wales Press, 2007), pp. 85-92.
169 DHH 145, 23 June 1750.
170 Trevecka MS 2013, Thomas William to Howel Harris, 19 Occtober 1751.
171 Trevecca College/1 3187, p. 89, 19 May 1744.
172 Trevecka MS 544, Thomas Price to Howel Harris, 27 April 1742.
173 W. Williams, *Marwnad Er Coffadwriaeth am Mr. Howel Harries, yr hwn oedd un o'r rhai cyntaf a ddechreuodd y Diwygiad mawr yng Nghymru: ac a ymdawodd a'r byd hwn, Gorphenhaf yr 21, yn y Flwyddyn, 1773* (Aberhonddu: E. Evans, 1773), p. 12.
174 DHH 122, 18 June 1746.
175 DHH 12, 30 March 1736.
176 DHH 131a, 17 May 1748; Evans, *Daniel Rowland*, p. 271.
177 DHH 129, 13 February 1748.
178 DHH 138, 22 November 1749.
179 DHH 54. 9 March 1740; 70, 8 March 1741; 72, 9 May 1741; NLW MS 6137D, p. 416, Griffith Jones to Bridget Bevan, 29 April 1741.
180 DHH 86, 18 March 1742.
181 D. W. Bebbington, *Evangelicalism in Modern Britain: A History from the 1730s to the 1980s* (London: Routledge, 1989), pp. 39-40.
182 C. Podmore, *The Moravian Church in England 1728-1760* (Oxford: Clarendon Press, 1998), pp. 80-96.
183 For instance, DHH 141, 16 February 1750; 144, 26 February 1750. See also Tudur, *Howell Harris*, pp. 170-2; C. D. Atwood, *Community of the Cross: Moravian Piety in Colonial Bethlehem* (University Park, Pennsylvania: Pennsylvania University Press, 2004), pp. 203-22.
184 DHH 130, 28 April 1748; 131a, 5 May 1748.
185 DHH 63a, 11 November 1740.
186 DHH 144, 30 May 1750.
187 T. Evans, *A History of Modern Enthusiasm* (London: W. Owen and W. Clarke, 1752), p. 70; D. Densil Morgan, *Theologia Cambrensis: Protestant Religion and Theology in Wales, I: From Reformation to Revival 1588-1760* (Cardiff: University of Wales Press, 2018), pp. 373-4.
188 Trevecca College/1 2945, p. 13, 6-7 April 1743.
189 Trevecka MS 1876, James Beaumont to Lady Gertrude Hotham, 4 August 1749.
190 Trevecka MS 1571, Thomas Dale to Howel Harris, 27 November 1746; 1572, Howel Harris to John Jones, 28 November 1746; 1575, Howel Harris to Thomas Dale, 6 December 1746.
191 Trevecka MS 1940, James Beaumont to John [Burnill?], 12 June 1750.

192 DHH 133, 1 February 1749; 135a, 25 May 1749; 141, 31 January 1750; Trevecka MS 1744, Howel Harris to Mr Crowley, 11 December 1747; Tudur, *Howell Harris*, pp. 193–4.
193 DHH 241, 4 November 1763.
194 DHH 130, 30 April 1748.
195 DHH 130, 28 April 1748, 3 May 1748.
196 DHH 130, 29 April 1748.
197 DHH 132, 17 September 1748.
198 DHH 123, 17 September 1746
199 DHH 144, 21 April 1750.
200 For instance, D144, 19–21 April 1750. At this point Harris foresaw that they would die within the month.
201 DHH 144, 21 April 1750.
202 DHH 144, 19 April 1750.
203 Trevecka MS 439, Howel Harris to Anne Williams, 9 December 1741; Trevecka MS 946, Anne Williams to Howel Harris, 11 August 1743; DHH 145, 21 June 1750.
204 DHH 146, 17 October 1750.
205 DHH 141, 3 February 1750, 22 February 1750; 144, 17 May 1750.
206 DHH 144, 31 May 1750.
207 NLW MS 5459D, 14 December 1750.
208 DHH 140, 20 December 1749.
209 Trevecka MS 1765, Daniel John to Howel Harris, 4 February 1748.
210 For instance, DHH 141, 11 February 1750, 19 February 1750; 144, 19 April 1750.
211 DHH 144, 12 May 1750.
212 DHH 134, 20 March 1749.
213 Denning (ed.), *Diary of William Thomas*, p. 152.
214 Trevecka MS 1877, Thomas William to Howel Harris, 10 August 1749.
215 Denning (ed.), *Diary of William Thomas*, p. 235.
216 DHH 123, 27 June 1746.
217 Trevecka MS 1241, Richard Tibbott to the Association, October 1744
218 D. J. Odwyn Jones, *Daniel Rowland, Llangeitho*, pp. 114–15; D. Ll. Morgan, 'Daniel Rowland (?1711–1790): Pregethwr Diwygiadol', *Ceredigion*, XI/3 (1991), 218–37; E. M. White, '"Gwnaeth ei Farwnad yn ei Fywyd": Cofio Daniel Rowland Llangeitho (1711?–1790)', *Y Traethodydd* (2011), 263–4.
219 Trevecka MS 1381, William Williams to Howel Harris, 7 December 1745.
220 N. Cynhafal Jones (ed.), *Gweithiau Williams Pantycelyn, Cyfrol I* (Treffynnon: P. M. Evans & Son, 1887), p. 586.
221 DHH 131a, 5 May 1748; 141, 18 February 1750. See also Geoffrey Nuttall's exploration of Harris's 'enthusiasm' in *Howell Harris: The Last Enthusiast* (Cardiff: University of Wales Press, 1965).
222 Morgan, *The Great Awakening*, pp. 65–85; Tudur, *Howell Harris*, pp. 190–4; Morgan, *Theologia Cambrensis*, pp. 373–4.
223 DHH 141, 1 February 1750.
224 D. Rowland, *Ymddiddan rhwng Methodist uniawn-gred ac un camsyniol* (Bristol: Felix Farley, 1750), p. 8.
225 Rowland, *Ymddiddan rhwng Methodist uniawn-gred ac un camsyniol*, pp. 5–6, 9.

226 Morgan, *Theologia Cambrensis*, pp. 375–6.
227 DHH 122, 21 April 1746.
228 DHH 141, 18 February 1750.
229 DHH 145, 24 June 1750.
230 DHH 145, 20 July 1750; 146, 7 October 1750.
231 A. H. Williams (ed.), *John Wesley in Wales 1739-1790* (Cardiff: University of Wales Press, 1971), p. 69; D. E. Williams, 'Rice Williams: The Contact between Thomas Percy and Evan Evans', *Journal of the National Library of Wales*, 7 (1972), 289.
232 Trevecka MS 1968, 7 January 1751.
233 Trevecka MS 2006, Howel Harris to John Sparks junior, 4 October 1751; Trevecka MS 2009, Howel Harris to John Richard, 5 October 1751.
234 Williams, *Marwnad*, p. 7.
235 See NLW MS 20,515C; R. G. Gruffydd, 'John Thomas, Tre-main: Pererin Methodistaidd', *Cylchgrawn Cymdeithas Hanes y Methodistiaid Calfinaidd/ Journal of the Historical Society of the Presbyterian Church of Wales*, 9 (1986), 55.

CHAPTER 3

'The Lord's Peculiar Dwelling Place': The Location of the Societies

'Three counties especially – Pembrokeshire, Caermarthen and Cardiganshire seem to be the Lord's Peculiar dwelling Place and to be as it were the center of the Work.'[1] This was Howel Harris's assessment in 1746, and he was not the only commentator to point to the pious tendencies of the people of the region. Erasmus Saunders famously declared of the people within the diocese of St Davids: 'There is, I believe, no part of the Nation more inclin'd to be Religious, and to be delighted with it than the poor Inhabitants of these Mountains.'[2] Overall, there were a number of religious, social, geographical and cultural factors which may have contributed to making this western peninsula fruitful ground for the early movement.

There were also challenges arising from the nature of the landscape and the methods of travel. The problems which bedevilled bishops in south-west Wales also faced itinerant preachers, although they may have been more inured to them as residents of the region. Being considerably younger too, they may have had more reserves of energy to cope with the obstacles. Local knowledge was often crucial as a guide to where to cross rivers without risk of drowning, or which treacherous paths to avoid in harsh weather. Difficulties ranged from trying to find a suitable place to ford the river Cothi in Carmarthenshire to encountering hay wains in narrow places.[3] Roads in the south-west were largely based on old Roman roads and on well-worn drover paths, such as from Llanddovery past Ystrad-ffin in the north-eastern tip of Carmarthenshire towards Tregaron in Cardiganshire.[4] The economic importance of local markets and the drover trade meant that places which may seem more remote in modern-day terms were important centres in the eighteenth century. Common routes also ran alongside the rivers Tywi and Teifi, as well as along the southern coast of Carmarthenshire from the Loughor estuary via Llanelli and Cydweli. Bridges over rivers such as the Loughor were often only constructed with the advent of the railways, prior to which travellers had to negotiate the additional hazard of ferries across the Loughor and the Tywi rivers. On one visit to the area, John Wesley was forced to go miles out of his way because heavy rain meant crossing the Tywi via the Llansteffan ferry was impossible.[5] There was also a fee to be paid, which could present problems. On one occasion, Howel Harris feared he would be stranded because he lacked the penny needed to cross the Tywi, when one of the members of Pembrey society chanced to give him sixpence, an action Harris believed to be inspired by providence.[6] Wesley encountered problems travelling in August, and the autumn and winter months usually offered even greater frustrations, with the roads quickly becoming treacherous in bad weather. Richard Tibbott set out with William Christopher and Dorothy Jones of Llangyndeyrn society for Llangeitho in September, only to have to turn back to Carmarthen because of the unrelenting rain.[7] Daniel Rowland had to admit defeat in his efforts to reach the Association at Watford in Glamorgan in January 1744, since the road was so hard, his horse so slow and he himself so tired.[8]

Although the first known permanent society was established by Howel Harris in 1737 at Wernos in Breconshire, there are very few references to societies in the south-west before the 1740s, although several of those listed when the Association first set up the circuits for the superintendents of societies in 1743 may well have been in existence for some years. Llanddeusant and Llanfair-ar-y-bryn are the first societies in Carmarthenshire to be named, in an entry in Howel Harris's diary for November 1738.[9] It is worth mentioning in passing that Llanfair-ar-y-bryn was home to William Williams of Pantycelyn, who by November 1738 had been drawn to the Methodist cause by hearing Howel Harris preach and might have been involved in this society. These societies on the eastern edge of Carmarthenshire were closer to Harris's home in Breconshire, and he was likely to have been more aware of them at this stage than any societies further west. Not surprisingly, Harris was less specific about societies in Cardiganshire, although noted that a number had been formed as a result of Daniel Rowland's efforts, but there was no mention of such early progress in Pembrokeshire.[10] By August 1740, Harris recorded that there were forty societies in total in south Wales across Breconshire, Carmarthenshire, Glamorgan and Monmouthshire.[11] In December of the same year, he added that there were five or six societies around Llandovery in Carmarthenshire, five in the vicinity of Carmarthen town and five in Pembrokeshire. He did not note the number of societies in Cardiganshire, but suggested that they had 'the most Power though not so good order'.[12] By 1743 the newly formed Association, as the governing body of the movement, arranged superintendents to oversee groups of societies. William Richard was allocated the area where the three counties meet at the river Teifi. His circuit stretched along the coast from New Quay in Cardiganshire to St David's in Pembrokeshire and inland along the Teifi towards Newcastle Emlyn and Llangeler in Carmarthenshire.[13] James Williams was responsible for the societies in eastern Carmarthenshire, along with a few societies over the border in Cardiganshire, including Lampeter.[14] Since it was convenient for John Richard to oversee the societies in south Carmarthenshire that were close to his home in Llansamlet, these were attached to the societies he cared for in the Swansea area of Glamorgan.[15] Llanddeusant on the eastern edge of Carmarthenshire was attached to Morgan John Lewis's societies in Breconshire for similar reasons. The rest of Carmarthenshire fell under the supervision of Milbourne Bloom, of Abergwili, until he left to be ordained as a minister with the Independents. William John of Glancothi, Llanegwad, was appointed in his place in 1744.[16] The list was complete with the appointment of William Williams in June 1744 to oversee the societies of north Cardiganshire instead of Morgan Hughes.[17]

There are many difficulties in trying to determine the precise number and location of societies established in south-west Wales in this period. Not all societies were consistently listed by the same name. A society could be referred to at times by the name of the house in which it met and at other times by the name of the area or parish. Thus the society which met in Bryniau Bychain in Llansawel is sometimes listed as Bryniau Bychain but at other times as Llansawel.[18] Since Bryniau Bychain and Llansawel never appear together on a list as separate societies it seems most likely that there was just a single society in the area, although it is difficult to be completely sure. To confuse matters further, some societies met in different locations and therefore appeared under different names, such as Ystrad-ffin, which sometimes met in Galltybere.[19] There were a cluster of societies meeting in various farmhouses in the Cil-y-cwm area making it difficult to be sure to what extent they were fixed as separate societies or were simply the same group of people using different locations. However, the fact that some society reports include a number of separate societies for Cil-y-cwm makes it clear that there were at least three societies meeting regularly in the area.

Reports by superintendents are naturally the major source for identifying societies, but not all societies appear, especially as the reports became rather more general with increased pressure of work during the 1740s. Nor do the Association records necessarily refer to all societies, particularly those formed after the system of pastoral care was first laid out in the early Association meetings in 1742–3. Howel Harris's diary is unfortunately not as helpful as might be expected. Although he quite often refers to society meetings in houses where he was offered hospitality, those meetings were often arranged especially to take advantage of his presence and these might not have been the regular venues or the usual members. For instance, when Harris visited Llwynygorras in Pembrokeshire in March 1743 he held a private society with members drawn from four separate local societies.[20] There are a few named societies which it is impossible to locate with any accuracy. Colvill was supposed to have been located on the border between Carmarthenshire and Pembrokeshire, but in one letter Daniel Rowland mentions travelling to Pembroke and south Carmarthenshire and then to Colvill, which is geographically curious. Since it was, unusually, said to be a bilingual group the members may have divided to join alternative Welsh-medium and English-medium societies.[21] The likely location of Waun-y-groes, established in 1745, is also uncertain. R. T. Jenkins speculated about a field of that name in Cil-y-cwm, once the site of a farm or smallholding, which could have been home to a society. However, the society was under the supervision of William John, who did not have care of the Cil-y-cwm area, and it is far more likely that the society would have been located further towards the south-west of Carmarthenshire where the rest of his circuit lay. Other possbilities, therefore, are Waun-y-groes located just west of Carmarthen town and another in Llansteffan parish.²² Despite these uncertainties, it is clear that over fifty settled societies were set up in Carmarthenshire during this period, with a further twenty-six in Cardiganshire, along with fourteen in north Pembrokeshire.²³

It was the rural regions of the south-west which played host to the more successful early societies. There were of course few large towns to be found in south-west Wales, apart from the county towns of Cardigan, Carmarthen and Pembroke, along with Haverfordwest which had county status and its own MP since 1543. Carmarthen and Haverfordwest are likely to have been the only towns with populations of over 2,000, and Cardigan and Pembroke probably the only towns reaching a 1,000 or more.²⁴ David Howell suggests a hierarchy of towns in the mid-eighteenth century, with Wrexham in the lead, followed by Brecon, Carmarthen, Haverfordwest, Cardiff and Caernarfon.²⁵ This places Carmarthen close to the top as one of the most important and vibrant towns in Wales. There were several dimensions to its influence. The town certainly had a long-standing role as an important adminstrative and legal centre, dating back to its days as effective capital of the Principality of South Wales, after the Statute of Rhuddlan 1284 set up the post-conquest system of government. It was also a vital market town and port, serving the agriculturally productive Tywi Valley, as well as developing additional cultural importance in the fields of education and printing. Members of the gentry had town houses on the more genteel streets, with dinners and dances held for their entertainment, including when the court of Great Sessions assembled in the town. Carmarthen was often referred to as 'the London of Wales', although visitors who had actually been to London admitted to being perplexed by the name as they could detect little similarity, except perhaps the relaxed state of morals in both.²⁶

Haverfordwest was also an important centre, described by Bishop Adam Ottley, in a letter to his wife written during a journey through the diocese, as 'a plentiful place, rich for this country'.²⁷ Even smaller towns like Lampeter and Newcastle Emlyn had an important function in their hinterland. Although invariably described as dirty and unprepossessing, all towns offered more in the way of social and leisure opportunities than the countryside. That usually meant the sort of activities that the Methodists preached against, including travelling theatres, cockfighting, wrestling and dancing. Those whose livelihoods depended on people not always observing the moderate, modest lifestyle advocated by the Methodists were often hostile to visiting exhorters as a result. Towns were generally the centres of the fiercest opposition to the movement, partly because of the greater concentration of population which made it easier to gather an angry mob. The more violent confrontations were usually faced by visiting Methodist preachers in public, but attempts to disrupt the regular activities of societies also seemed more common in the towns, such as efforts by local gentry to silence exhorters in Carmarthen.[28] Similarly, in Lampeter on 9 March 1743, a JP and his servants interrupted a society meeting and arrested the individual who was praying at the time, although he was released shortly afterwards.[29] This was relatively small-scale persecution, but possibly enough to stunt the growth of some societies. It was also probably the case that the movement thrived more in rural areas where there were fewer social activities to compete for time and attention.

Howel Harris admitted to being afraid to even contemplate the towns at times, because of the antagonism he had encountered in some of them.[30] Although it was some of the towns of north Wales which terrified him the most, he had little affection for any in the south either. He referred to Newcastle Emlyn as 'a rebellious Town' and confessed in Haverfordwest in 1743 that he felt greater freedom to speak of Christ in the countryside than the towns, which were reluctant to hear the gospel.[31] He would only enter Carmarthen after fervent prayer and with much trepidation since '... most terrible things do I hear of this Town here they are so full of malice & do so Perjure themselves that they strive to kill each other & offer money for killing so many.'[32] A boisterous town, Carmarthen represented the worst aspects of urban life to Harris, who found a visit to an alehouse there akin to a glimpse into hell itself, full of swearing, roaring, hooting and howling.[33] The society in Carmarthen town was never a particularly flourishing one and was often categorised as lacking both in numbers and in enthusiasm. There were only twelve members at best, and the same number could be found in Ystrad-ffin, one of the most remote societies in Carmarthenshire, in 1744.[34] The local superintendent tended to complain about the disagreements among the members and the general lack of warmth.[35] Whilst a student in Carmarthen Academy, Thomas Morgan of Henllan Amgoed, evidently preferred to travel to the societies which met at Gelli Glyd, Milbourne Bloom's home in Abergwili, or at Bolahaul in Llangynnwr rather than attend the society in town.[36] The earliest mention of the society came in 1741 when William John informed Harris that the Carmarthen society met twice a week and was full of zeal.[37] By 1743, the zeal of the twelve members seemed to have abated, although it was reported that there were some potential new recruits to the society.[38] Opposition hampered the growth of the society, since William John explained in July 1745 that one of the local exhorters had been unable to speak in the town over the previous month, because of the enmity of some of the gentry who tried to prevent them from meeting.[39] Some of the members moved out of the town at the start of 1747, leaving three or four members who were on such bad terms with the superintendent that he did not feel able to continue to visit them.[40] The Association seems to have responded by sending the brothers William and Christopher Mends, since it was they who reported on the society in 1748. Although they had expelled three members for misbehaviour, the two believed that there were signs of growth in the others, which suggests that the numbers had increased by then.[41]

One of the very few towns to have found favour with Howel Harris was Cardigan, one of the largest in the south-west and an increasingly busy port as well as the market town for the Teifi Valley. Harris was asked to visit the town for the first time when he was exhorting nearby in Llechryd on 25 February 1741. He hesitated before agreeing, probably because of his unpleasant experiences in other towns. In order to help him come to a decision, he resorted to his occasional practice of opening the Bible and selecting a random verse in the belief that this would reveal God's will on the subject. His finger fell on Acts 10:20: 'Arise therefore, and get thee down, and go with them, doubting nothing: for I have sent them.' Confident that this was a sure sign of God's blessing, Harris agreed with the urgent request to visit. He was reassured when informed that Daniel Rowland had preached compellingly there and that the inhabitants had accepted his words with great humility, which further inspired him to believe that perhaps not all towns were given over to the Devil after all.[42] He returned to preach in Cardigan on 29 April 1741 and was given a warm welcome, despite his general misgivings about towns: 'I told them I had more Civility here than hardly in any

Town in Wales – that Towns are as it were set against the Word of God'.[43] Curiously, despite the civility Harris claimed to have received, there is no record of any society meeting regularly in the town during the 1740s. On another occasion, Harris mentioned holding a society there until the early hours of the morning on 8 March 1743,[44] so there were seemingly some converts in the town, although they could conceivably have joined with the societies in Llechryd or Ffrwdwenith if they were few in number. After 1744 Harris himself ceased to include Cardigan on any of his visits to the area, but there must have been some further progress as a chapel was built in the town as early as 1760.[45]

The early Methodist movement was undoubtedly strongest outside the towns. Most of the societies were hosted by members in rural farmhouses, sometimes at some distance from any great concentration of population. Societies seem to have only rarely met within villages, but might well be found on the borders of parishes. The society which met at Dygoed was sometimes described as 'Dygoed, Llanarthney' and other times as 'Dygoed, Llanddarog', demonstrating the fact that the house was on the border between the two parishes and very likely drew members from both. Ystrad-ffin society was situated in the furthest reaches of Llanfair-ar-y-bryn parish, on the border with Cardiganshire. These remote and border locations may well have helped the societies to avoid unwelcome attention as they developed, being usually far from the watchful eye of constables and justices of peace. Similar locations had been adopted by early Dissenting groups who sought to escape persecution by providing themselves with escape routes into neighbouring parishes and counties. The society as an institution could be quickly established and just as easily moved to suit the convenience of the members. That flexibility and ability to continue without ordained clergy meant that it worked well as a quick, inexpensive way of organising groups of believers in the thinly populated countryside. It was similarly ideal for the American frontier in the nineteenth century, where it was used by Welsh settlers as a means of establishing a Methodist presence before more formal arrangements were put in place.[46] In that case, the society was used as the first step towards establishing a denominational presence with ordained ministers. That was by no means the intention in eighteenth-century Wales, although it proved to be the eventual outcome.

There were times when some of the larger groups may have found themselves in uncomfortably cramped quarters, as eighteenth-century farmhouses in the south-west were not necessarily generous in size.[47] There are also references to meetings in barns and lofts where there was more space for larger groups to gather. For instance, Richard Tibbott mentioned the Cilcarw society in Llangyndeyrn parish meeting in a barn.[48] Even then, the crowds could be too great to be easily accommodated. Harris literally brought the house down in Talley when one of the rafters in the loft in which he was exhorting collapsed under the considerable assembled weight of the congregation. Harris estimated that those who plummeted to the floor below numbered in the hundreds, but he was prone to exaggerate and cannot be relied upon as an accurate judge of numbers.[49] Some of the more spacious farmhouses provided hospitality as well to the Association meetings and Glanyrafondduganol, Dugoedydd, and Llwynyberllan played significant roles in the history of the early movement in this respect. Their use also demonstrates the way the movement recruited from the substantial middling sorts of rural society, who provided the crucial resources to hold meetings at a time when Methodism had no buildings of its own.

The earliest chapels began to appear quite quickly, however, in Llansawel and Cil-y-cwm, towards the north-eastern part of Carmarthenshire where a number of societies were located. The Association at Abergorlech, Carmarthenshire, decided on 4 September 1744 to set about building a house at Llansawel, for religious and educational purposes.[50] The term 'society houses' was used at this point, rather than churches, chapels or meetings houses, to avoid giving the impression that this was a step towards forming a separate denomination. The houses were to belong to the movement, rather than to individual societies, so all members were asked to contribute. Collecting enough money to put this decision into action took some time, and William Williams was still talking of the intention to build at Llansawel and Cil-y-cwm in a letter to Howel Harris in June 1746.[51] It is not clear precisely when the work was finally completed, but Harris visited the two new houses in July 1747, to exhort at Llansawel and to attend an association meeting at Cil-y-cwm.[52] Harris gave no detail about the size, appearance or usage of the new buildings, but was concerned about the expense, since the two houses, along with another built at Builth in

1748, had cost a total of £240.[53] This showed the willingness of the members to contribute to the movement beyond the confines of their own society, which, along with the existence of these houses can be seen as the earliest foundations of an emerging denomination, despite all efforts to avoid that assumption. They were not registered as meeting houses and were frequently called 'school houses' to emphasise that they were not intended for communion services or any other form of worship. In 1748 James Williams referred to the new 'school house' at Cil-y-cwm as the meeting place for the society.[54] However, such careful use of terminology may have been a futile effort, since by 1755 the curate of Llansawel, Henry Thomas, was referring to 'a large meeting house' in the parish built by the Methodists.[55]

Chapels of Ease

An aspect of the Church's difficulties which may have benefited the Methodists was the way that a number of chapels of ease had been abandoned and could thus be adopted for use by societies. These were chapelries attached to parish churches where additional services had once been provided for communities at a distance from the central parish church. It was often in the largest rural parishes that such chapels had been located and had been especially useful to scattered communities. In some areas this practice had been discontinued, with pluralist clergy unable to spare the time to conduct services in addition to the parish churches. A few chapels had fallen into disrepair, such as Llangynheiddon in Llandyfaelog parish, which may have dated back to the twelfth century.[56] It was said that Peter Williams preached in the graveyard because only the arch above a doorway remained of the building itself.[57] Howel Harris certainly discoursed there although he recorded no details about the surroundings.[58] Erasmus Saunders bemoaned the sad fact that many churches and chapels were fit only to serve as habitations for owls and jackdaws, including Llechryd and Mounton chapels.[59] A few were restored for the use of the Methodists, including Capel Ifan in Llanelli parish.[60] Llanlluan chapel in Llanarthney parish was said to have been rebuilt in 1736 by Philip Lloyd of Heol Ddu, Llanarthney, possibly for the use of the circulating schools in the first instance.[61] The chapel seems to have been further refurbished by Lloyd so that Daniel Rowland could use it for communion services.

Lloyd also donated land for the Independents to build a chapel in Llanddarog, so seems to have been generous to a range of religious causes. Rowland also obtained the permission of John Campbell of Stackpole to preach at Ystrad-ffin, a disused chapelry of Llanfair-ar-y-bryn.[62] This was one of the first places that Rowland had visited to preach outside the near vicinity of his parishes in Cardiganshire, so his influence was important in the area.[63] Despite attempts to forbid the Methodists from using the chapel in 1742, it was there that Howel Harris married Anne Williams in 1744.

Where the buildings were sufficiently intact, the chapels could be used as convenient locations for society meetings. The restored chapel at Llanlluan was being used for twice-weekly society meetings by January 1741.[64] Milbourne Bloom resolved to rent Capel Ifan, in Llanelli parish, to serve as a home to the society on a twenty-one year lease for 30s. in 1742.[65] Abergorlech, attached to Llanybydder parish, was used by a society who seemed to be under the care of William Williams. As consecrated buildings, the chapels could also be used by the ordained clergy in the movement to administer communion. There was unease amongst some of the members about receiving communion from certain clergymen, who they felt were not deserving of their holy orders; and, conversely, some of the parish clergy were reluctant to allow Methodists to receive communion in their churches. In order to stave off any possible defections to the Dissenters as a result of these difficulties, the Methodist leaders ensured that communion would be made available by Daniel Rowland or Howel Davies in some chapels in the south-west. By 1743 Davies and Rowland were arranging monthly communion at Capel Ifan and Abergorlech.[66] Howel Davies also made use of Llechryd by the river Teifi in south Cardiganshire and of Mounton in Pembrokeshire for this purpose. Llechryd had been established as a chapel of ease to Llangoedmor, possibly in the fourteenth century, and Mounton was attached to Narberth and was also of medieval origin.[67] Davies had some misgivings about holding communion services at Llechryd, outside his parish, but Harris reassured him that the only aim of the policy was to keep people inside the Church. He also suggested that Davies should insist that any who received communion should also meet together in private 'to open their Hearts to each other, to watch over each other in the Lord', which sounds like a blueprint for a society meeting.[68]

The adoption of the chapels was controversial. Griffith Jones actually tried to prevent Daniel Rowland from making use of Llanlluan, because he feared it would cause ill feeling and unrest among the local congregations and would distract people from their daily work.[69] By 1744 there were moves afoot by some clergymen to petition Bishop Richard Trevor to forbid the Methodists from using the chapels. The opposition was voiced in a letter from the Revd John Lloyd of Narberth to Bishop Trevor in October 1744, complaining that Howel Davies, despite promises to desist, was administering communion at Mounton Chapel, assisted by Richard Thomas Bateman of Haverfordwest. Bateman was rector of St Bartholomew the Great in London, but was a native of Haverfordwest and sympathetic to the Methodist cause.[70] To strengthen his position, Davies had reportedly bought the lease of the field on which the chapel stood from the current tenant, the land belonging to Sir Thomas Stepney, of Prendergast. This chapel was attached to Narberth, so technically part of Lloyd's benefice. He complained that multitudes were gathering there from all parts of the county to receive communion, a practice which he feared threatened the unity of the Church.[71]

It was decided at Abergorlech Association, 4 September 1744, that the congregation at Abergorlech would send a petition to Bishop Trevor expressing their wish to continue to meet with William Williams of Pantycelyn as their pastor, whatever the consequences.[72] The bishop himself did not seem inclined to create difficulties and appeared very moderate when he discussed the question of the chapels with Davies and Williams.[73] Matters seemed to calm down, and by October 1744 Daniel Rowland was once again administering communion at Abergorlech as before.[74] Some reservations continued, with Howel Davies suggesting in 1748 that the chapels created a bad spirit among the membership, although it is not clear what precisely was meant by this.[75] It may be that Davies remained concerned that the adoption of designated buildings smacked of separation. Their use in some areas was probably reduced, not just because of the threats from the parish clergy, but because of the new society houses which were being constructed in the late 1740s. By 1752, the diocese of St Davids decided to make use of Abergorlech once more, and Henry Thomas was licensed to officiate there.[76] The chapels of ease had proved immensely useful, however, in catering for members who were not happy to take communion in their parish churches, and as meeting places for societies and associations.

The Growth of Literacy

Historians of seventeenth- and eighteenth-century Wales have long since established that William Williams's portrayal of the pre-revival period in deep, dark slumber does not represent historical fact. It does an injustice to the efforts of concerned Anglicans and Dissenters to improve religious knowledge. Attempts to redress the balance began in the eighteenth century with the Baptist Joshua Thomas, who reproved those who believed that there was little or no religion to be had before the revival, citing not only Griffith Jones, but Dissenting ministers and their efforts during the preceding century to publish improving works.[77] Even then, therefore, it was acknowledged by some commentators that the roots of the movement lay further back than the 1730s. More recently, Glanmor Williams has demonstrated that early modern Wales experienced a long, slow process of Reformation, reaching its culmination with the growth of literacy in the eighteenth century. Only with 'the large-scale conquest of illiteracy', he argued, 'could the Reformation really come of age in Wales'.[78] Densil Morgan concurs that by the mid-eighteenth century: 'At long last the Reformation as a popular movement was taking root.'[79] One of the crucial developments which facilitated the emergence of the evangelical movement was this growth in the ability to read, accelerated from the 1740s to 1770s by the influence of the circulating schools. The south-west of Wales, and Carmarthenshire especially, was particularly well-served during this campaign to improve standards of religious knowledge by ensuring that more of the population were able to read the Bible.

Since Wales lacked a university until Aberystwyth was established in 1872, higher education was not readily available in the eighteenth century and was forbidden to those who were not communicating members of the Established Church. Yet, there were opportunities closer to home through grammar schools and dissenting academies, which often offered a good classical education. Carmarthen was something of a centre for such educational opportunities. Carmarthen Grammar School for boys had been founded in 1576, with Griffith Jones and Peter Williams amongst its pupils in the eighteenth century.[80] The town was also the location of the famous Presbyterian College founded there *c.* 1703 by William Evans, the Independent minister of Pencader. When Vavasor Griffiths of Maesgwyn, Radnorshire, took over the academy in 1734, he chose to move it to the quieter rural surroundings of Llwyn-llwyd, Breconshire, but, following his death, the academy was eventually returned to Carmarthen town in 1743.[81] The academy permitted a broad range of religious persuasions amongst its students, so did not just function as a training college for the Dissenting ministry. It was with an eye on a medical career that William Williams attended the academy during its period at Llwyn-llwyd, which is where Howel Harris also studied.[82] The presence of these institutions in the area meant that there was a trickle-down effect with former pupils of the grammar school and academy setting up their own schools locally to provide some instruction for those who could afford it. It is striking how often Edward Tenison noted in his report on the archdeaconry of Carmarthen in 1710 that a proportion of the poor in some parishes were able to read in Welsh. This included some areas where Methodist societies would develop in the 1740s, including around 30 poor people in Merthyr, 20 in Meidrim and 20 in Caeo.[83] It is difficult to know how accurate such assessments were or who exactly was categorised as 'poor', or indeed how these parishioners acquired their literacy in Welsh, since most charity schools tended to be English-medium up until that point. However, more informal instruction in Welsh may have been provided by educated individuals in these areas.

By the eighteenth century, efforts were being made to try to expand this fairly narrow circle of educational opportunities to include more of the middle and lower orders of society, with the desire to raise standards of religious knowledge as the major motivation. The improving agenda was driven by pietistic influences, channelled through societies such as the SPCK (the Society for Promoting Christian Knowledge). The south-west counties benefited greatly from the presence of philanthropically inclined gentry, who became actively involved in such educational charities. Although the SPCK was in many ways a very Anglican venture, it operated through the voluntary efforts of individuals rather than with the backing of the Church as an institution. It sought the approval of the bishop for various initiatives but drew up its own plans and priorities. From the start, the SPCK had strong connections with Wales, with Sir

Humphrey Mackworth of Neath one of the five founders in 1699. During the society's heyday up until around 1740, there was an active group of benefactors of the SPCK amongst the gentry of the south-west area, including John Vaughan of Derllys (1663–1722) and Sir John Philipps of Picton Castle (*c.* 1666–1737). Philipps was one of the most prominent patrons, founding seventeen of the thirty-one SPCK schools in Pembrokeshire, as well as three in Carmarthenshire.[84] It was his efforts that ensured that Pembrokeshire would be one of the leading counties in terms of the SPCK's activities throughout England and Wales. John Vaughan was the father of Bridget Bevan (1698–1779), who continued the family tradition of sponsoring the growth of charity schools. They were joined by John Philipps, the mayor of Carmarthen, and his son, Thomas Philipps, vicar of Laugharne, as well as by Edward Dalton of Llanelli, who became a corresponding member in 1727. Most of the active corresponding members of the SPCK in Carmarthenshire were in holy orders: Edmund Meyrick, Thomas Thomas, Thomas Philipps, David Havard and Griffith Jones.[85] The work of the SPCK locally largely relied upon an alliance between dedicated gentry and clergy, with Thomas Thomas in Carmarthen cooperating closely with John Vaughan, in the same way as Sir John Philipps worked with John Pember, rector of Prendergast, in Pembrokeshire.[86] Edifying English works were suggested for translation and distributed by the members, but probably the greatest contribution was the provision of new editions of the Welsh Bible in 1718, 1727, 1746, 1752, 1769 and 1799, amounting to 80,000 new copies of the Bible in total.[87]

There was an awareness that the SPCK needed to tread carefully so as not to invade the territory of those with more immediate care of souls, that is the clergy.[88] Yet there was also an awareness that they could intervene to help the clergy raise their own standards and improve their ability to guide those under their care. The SPCK thus tried to promote reading habits by setting up lending libraries for clergy and school-teachers to be stocked with Welsh books on suitable religious topics. This was an important development, as previously there were few collections of books in the country, save for the private libraries in gentry households such as Hengwrt and Wynnstay, which were not readily accessible.[89] The SPCK libraries would help improve the standard of the clergy who were not likely to be able to buy many books and would seldom have free access to private libraries. As the secretary, Henry Newman, stated, if the libraries 'don't consist of all these books requisite to make a man a Compleat Scholar yet they may be sufficient to furnish a Divine with Knowledge necessary to his undertaking a Parochial Charge'.[90] After Sir Humphrey Mackworth first mooted the idea, a committee investigated the possibility and proposed that a library should be established in each of the four dioceses. The Society channelled most of its energies and resources into this scheme between 1703 and 1711. Receivers were appointed in different localities to accept gifts of books which could be included in the library. St Davids's library was founded at Carmarthen in 1711 in a house provided by Edmund Meyrick, vicar of St Peter's Church in the town and treasurer of St Davids diocese, with Evan Griffiths as the first librarian.[91] Whereas Bishop Bull approved the setting up of the library, the hard work was undertaken by the corresponding members of the Society. The library was expected to serve the clergy in a ten-mile radius of Carmarthen,[92] but the intention was to try to extend the system to a parochial level once the diocesan libraries were firmly established. Parochial libraries were set up in Llanbadarn Fawr in north Cardiganshire and in Prendergast, near Haverfordwest, in Pembrokeshire.[93]

Gathering, printing and distributing suitable religious literature was one aspect of the Society's work. Another was the drive to found charity schools, in the tradition of the Welsh Trust in the late seventeenth century, which was responsible for 87 schools in Wales in total compared with 96 by the SPCK.[94] The Welsh Trust was the creation in 1674 of Thomas Gouge, minister of St Sepulchre in London until ejected for his Puritan tendencies. Despite some initial success in establishing schools in Wales, suspicions that the schools were promoting Dissent probably led to a fairly rapid decline, and the Trust was wound up following Gouge's death in 1681.[95] Carmarthenshire and Pembrokeshire were amongst the counties with the highest number of schools, perhaps because of the influence of Stephen Hughes, who was Gouge's great ally in the work. Like the SPCK, the Trust's greatest contribution lay in the funding of important publications, including an edition of the Welsh Bible, edited by Stephen Hughes in 1678. Neither organisation was opposed to the Welsh language and both sponsored several publications in Welsh, but the schools they set up favoured the use of English. In north Wales, thanks to the influence of Dean John Jones of Bangor, twelve of the SPCK schools operated in Welsh,[96] but elsewhere they employed English as the medium of instruction. This was the case, for instance, in the charity school set up in Laugharne by the vicar, Thomas Philipps, in 1708, where Griffith Jones was appointed as master. Thomas Thomas of Carmarthen believed that charity schools should be set up in every parish, although that proved far too ambitious an aim.[97] Whilst Pembrokeshire and Carmarthenshire were the two counties with the highest totals of SPCK schools, with 31 in Pembrokeshire and 14 in Carmarthenshire, Cardiganshire did not fare so well, with only two schools in the county, in Llandysul and Eglwys-fach.[98] Despite the good intentions of the patrons, it often proved a struggle to persuade parents to allow their children to attend once the schools were established. John Pember owned that it was difficult to convince illiterate parents that their children might benefit from some measure of education.[99] It was a further struggle to try to teach children who spoke Welsh in their daily lives to learn to read in English. Griffith Jones claimed it could take two years to achieve this, based on his own experiences in Laugharne. The language issue slowed down the impact of the schools, and suspicions that they were fostering Jacobite sentiments may well have led to an overall decline after 1715.[100] They were well intentioned and succeeded in tapping into the real concerns felt by some leading landowners and clerics about the spiritual welfare of the rest of society in south-west Wales.

The SPCK schools also gave Griffith Jones an early, direct experience of elementary schooling. This, combined with his preaching campaign, led him to conclude that the major priority was to teach the skill of reading, so that a greater proportion of the population could come to understand the Bible for themselves. Since parents lacked the knowledge to teach their children to read, Jones foresaw that ignorance would be perpetuated from generation to generation.[101] He feared that his preaching had done little to enlighten his hearers because many of them lacked the basic knowledge required for such preaching to be effective. It was increasingly felt that the written word had a greater permanence than the spoken, which is why some ministers like David Maurice felt prompted to publish sermons.[102] The preaching of a sermon could only do so much, but the ability to read would equip individuals to go on to expand their knowledge thereafter. Griffith Jones embarked on a campaign to address this problem, starting with a school in his own parish in Llanddowror around the year 1731. By 1737, the system of circulating schools had begun to be developed, with peripatetic teachers travelling to parishes to set up classes for a period of three months at a time, during the slackest agricultural period between September and May. It was hoped that parents would be more prepared to send their children to school at a time of year when their labour was not as critically essential as it might be at harvest time. To maximise attendance, evening classes were also provided for adults who were unlikely to be free during the day. Despite being described as 'schools', these were in reality classes conducted in available spaces in churches and farmhouses, a method which cut down costs. Another deliberate policy was the streamlined syllabus which concentrated on reading above all, using the Bible as the text. Children were taught to read in their first language, which in most parts of the country was Welsh, although English-medium schools were also established in areas where that language was commonly spoken. There was a considerable emphasis as well on learning the catechism, in either language. Tuition was free, with costs kept as low as possible in order to make good Jones's boast that he could educate as many as ten poor children for every twenty shillings he received in donations.[103] The single aim behind all the decisions was the need to act swiftly in order to provide knowledge which was considered essential for salvation. It may well have been the outbreak of typhus in the south-west between 1727 and 1731 which proved the deciding factor for Griffith Jones.[104] The high mortality rates as a result of the disease brought it home to him that there was no time to waste, so the result was a deliberately pared-down curriculum, with an emphasis on speed and efficiency. The religious imperative also ensured that both genders would receive equal educational opportunities, since they all had souls which were considered in need of salvation.

By Jones's death in 1761, it is probable that at least 200,000 children and adults had attended 3,325 schools, at a time when the population of the entire country was estimated to be in the region of 480,000.[105] Jones used his annual publication *Welch Piety* to appeal for contributions and to assure his sponsors that their donations had been well spent in a laudable cause. After the death of his brother-in-law, Sir John Philipps, in 1737, his main benefactor was Bridget Bevan, daughter of John Vaughan and wife of Arthur Bevan, the MP for Carmarthen Borough until his death in 1743. She worked alongside Jones and promoted his cause in the genteel circles to which she had entry. She was by all accounts as charming as she was capable, and Howel Harris was evidently enthralled when he met her for the first time: 'I think she is the finest Lady I ever saw in all Respects, twas a taste of Heaven to be with her, she made me a present of a very fine pack of Testaments & encouraged me whatever happens to go on with what I am doing & that I should not want a friend.'[106] After Jones's death in 1761, she continued to manage the schools efficiently from her home in Laugharne until her own demise in 1779.

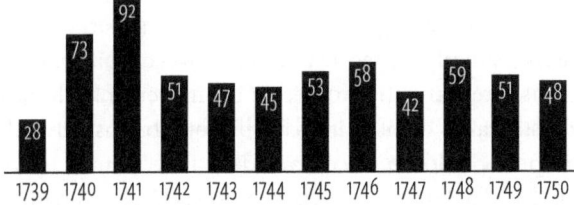

Number of circulating schools in Cardiganshire, Carmarthenshire and Pembrokeshire, 1739–50

The fact that Griffith Jones was based in Carmarthenshire ensured that the south-west would reap the benefits of the circulating schools earlier and more abundantly than other areas. There was a high concentration of schools in Carmarthenshire, but the system also spread quickly to Cardiganshire and to Pembrokeshire, making use of Welsh in the north of the county and English in the south. There were 73 schools in the three counties in 1740 and 92 in 1741, so larger numbers were affected more quickly than elsewhere in Wales. There continued to be in the region of fifty schools each year in the south-west throughout the 1740s, so the teachers undoubtedly reached a substantial proportion of the population, at precisely the same time as Methodism was attracting its converts. As soon as Methodist societies began to sprout in the same part of the country as Griffith Jones's schools had also first emerged, there were suspicions that there was a close connection. Robert Jones, Rhoslan, one of the first historians of the movement, described the schools as the cockcrow signalling the dawn of revival.[107] Jones was dubbed the 'Methodist Pope' in a list of suspected Methodists in the diocesan archive[108] and suspected of being the father figure of the new movement by critics such as John Evans.[109] Evans was the absentee rector of Eglwys Gymyn, Carmarthenshire, who dismissed his curate, Peter Williams, for his Methodist leanings, so was an inveterate enemy of the movement.[110] There was an element of truth in his assumption, since Jones was regarded as a mentor by most of the leading Methodists, who emulated many of his preaching methods. Jones had sympathy with their drive to bring sinners to Christ and wished them well, including sending his greetings to the Tŵr-gwyn Association in 1743.[111] Daniel Rowland considered him as a spiritual father and to a large degree inherited his mantle as the most powerful popular preacher of the mid-eighteenth century. Howel Davies was Jones's curate in Llandeilo Abercywyn, before taking on the parish of Llys-y-frân in Pembrokeshire. Harris regularly visited Llanddowror to consult Jones on various aspects of his career and the progress of the movement. The advice given to Methodists was as blunt as it was to bishops, but usually valuable and highly respected. Jones recommended that Harris refrain from publishing his diaries and concentrate on seeking ordination. He also gave useful advice about which terms might best be used when preaching, suggesting that Harris speak of 'repentance' rather than being 'born again' if he felt audiences might respond better. Jones maintained that the main aim was to bring souls to salvation and if necessary 'to catch them with Guile'.[112] On one visit in March 1741, Harris was derided for his presumption in preaching without ordination not just by Jones, but with his wife and maidservant joining the chorus of criticism of Harris and his brother Methodists. Jones warned that division in the Church would be the only certain outcome and complained that he was being blamed for the Methodist irregularities.[113] Harris was always humbled by Jones and tolerated his criticism in a way that he rarely did with anyone else. He felt a similar respect towards Bridget Bevan, but their relationship was also strained, as Bevan evidently shared Griffith Jones's misgivings about the Methodist influence on the schools. Harris later complained to her that she had prejudiced some of her more genteel contacts in Bath against the Methodists.[114] Despite having much in common, Harris had to conclude that he and Jones, and by association Bevan, were called to serve God in different vineyards.[115]

In addition to this direct influence on the leaders, there was also something of an overlap in terms of personnel, locations and objectives between schools and societies. The advantages of literacy were obviously appreciated, with efforts made to collect money from the societies to fund the printing of Welsh books.[116] Harris generally encouraged his hearers to read Welsh and rejoiced in the growing range of Welsh books available, including, above all, the 1746 SPCK edition of the Bible.[117] It was decided in Watford Association in June 1744 to appoint suitable persons to catechise the society members, in order to reinforce the work of the schools.[118] The movement generally supported the circulating schools and encouraged the less educated among the members to attend. The same farmhouses at times played host to both circulating school and society, including Cwrtycadno, Cynwyl Gaeo; Porthyrhyd, Llanddarog; Cilcarw, Llangyndeyrn; Bolahaul, Llangynnwr and Fron-las, Tre-lech in Carmarthenshire and Dyffryn-saith, Penbryn, and Cwmhowni, Blaen-porth, in Cardiganshire. Some chapels of ease also welcomed both schools and societies, such as Abergorlech, Llanlluan and Ystrad-ffin in Carmarthenshire and Llechryd in Cardiganshire. By 1761, a school was established for the first time in the society house at Cil-y-cwm, which suggests a degree of cooperation between the two movements. One of the schoolmasters in the house at Cil-y-cwm in 1774 was Morgan Rhys, who was also responsible for a school in Llandysiliogogo in Cardiganshire during the winter of 1757–8. Morgan Rhys was one of the foremost hymn writers of the eighteenth century, publishing a series of volumes from the 1750s until his death in 1779. There is an unsubstantiated tradition that he acted as steward of his local society in Llanfynydd,[119] but his Methodism is confirmed in the amounts of money left in his will to the societies of Llanfynydd, Llanegwad, Llansawel, Cil-y-cwm, Caeo, Llandsadwrn and Brechfa, as well as bequests to several of the Methodist leaders.[120] Several of Griffith Jones's other teachers were associated with the Methodist cause, including Richard Tibbott of Llanbrynmair. Tibbott was a protégé of Griffith Jones, who had come under his tuition around the year 1741 and spent two to three years teaching in the Llanddowror area and exhorting local societies.[121] It is not clear whether Anthony Rees of Llandybïe, Carmarthenshire, actually exhorted whilst serving as a schoolmaster in the parish in 1739, but he held meetings on Friday nights for the scholars and others to learn the Psalms and 'to read some godly books'.[122] Howel Harris's own early ventures into exhorting followed along similar lines, but there is no further record of Rees as a Methodist exhorter. Amongst others who definitely combined the roles of exhorters and schoolteachers were David Williams of Llanfynydd and David Evans of Llangwm, Pembrokeshire.[123] During the 1750s John Thomas of Tre-main was responsible for several circulating schools in south Cardiganshire and was also a close adherent of the Methodist cause in the area. At one point, Harris proposed a more formal union between the two movements, suggesting that 'his schools & our Societies should be incorporated wholly & his Chatechumens come among us', an idea which Jones rejected.[124] Most of the early societies in south-west Wales were located in areas where circulating schools were also held, sometimes under the same roof. However, a visit from a circulating school did not necessarily mean that a society would be set up, nor was a well-attended school an indicator of a successful society.

Whilst this connection was encouraged by the Methodist Association in many cases, concerns about losing support for his schools meant that Jones consistently refuted suggestions of links to Methodism. He was utterly reliant on the good will of his patrons, so sought to reassure them in the pages of *Welch Piety* that his schools were untainted by Methodism, Catholicism or any heresy or immorality. This was no easy task for, as he complained to Bridget Bevan, he had only to show common courtesy to one of the Methodists to be accused of offering succour to the movement.[125] In order to impress upon the readers the orthodox Anglican nature of the schools, he requested that parish clergy report to him on the conduct of the teachers and the effect of the schools on their congregations.[126] Many wrote to affirm that the impact of the schools had been highly beneficial, with children mastering their catechism and standards of morality improving. David Havard wrote that the school in his parish at Llandysul, Cardiganshire, had done more good than years of preaching.[127] The curate of Maenclochog in Pembrokeshire, John Howell, approved of the policy of using Welsh:

> This Place being very populous, there are a vast many poor People, having Children, who have not wherewith to bring them up in the English schools, to answer any End; which

would require more Years to learn to read English than months to read Welch, nor could they understand English then where the Conversation is all Welch. Therefore to teach them in their Mother-Tongue, to be sure, is the only and soonest Way to bring them to understand the Principles of Religion, and their Duty to God and Man, and thereby to be useful in their Generation.[128]

Edward Jones, rector of Henllan, Cardiganshire, specifically commended the schoolteacher in the parish because he 'did not use to go out by Night to any private Houses to expound the Scripture, to preach and pray, as some of the modern Methodists use to do'.[129] Jonathan Griffiths, vicar of Bettws, Carmarthenshire, thought it a great shame that some people had turned against the schools just because 'a few of the Masters, by the corrupt Influence or disorderly Example of others, were seduced (in your absence) into some degrees of Irregularity', a reference, presumably, to Methodist activities.[130] George Brook, rector of Eglwyswrw, Pembrokeshire, praised the schools not just for teaching the illiterate to read in their own language, but also for instructing them in the principles of religion, which must make them 'wiser and better' and give them the advantage of being able to read good books.[131] A further term was requested in Ferwig, Cardiganshire, by the curate John Thomas, who added his assessment of the significance of the work: 'And who can tell but that the Salvation of many may, under God, depend upon the Education of one single Child, by the Power of Him who worketh great Things by simple Means, and perfects Strength in Weakness.'[132] The cooperation of such parish priests was often extremely valuable in clearing the reputation of the schools from any insinuation of unorthodoxy or immorality, as well as giving practical assistance with matters such as locating suitable venues for the classes. Many of the schools were held in parish churches or associated buildings and might have struggled without the support of local clergymen. In 1745–6, for instance, schools were housed in the parish churches of Bangor Teifi, Llanddewibrefi, Llechryd and Tregaron in Cardiganshire; Cenarth, Llanddowror, Llanfihangel Rhos-y-corn, Llangynin, Llangynog, Llanwinio, as well as the chapels of Llanlluan and Eglwys Fair Glan Taf, in Carmarthenshire; and Clydau, Llandeilo, Llanglydwen, Llanwrda,

Monington, Moylgrove, Puncheston and Roche in Pembrokeshire.[133] A total of twenty of the fifty-eight schools conducted in the south-west during the course of that year were therefore situated in buildings associated with the Established Church.

More broadly, there is little doubt that the circulating schools did much to improve standards of literacy, which was an important factor in recruiting to Methodism in general. The fact that they were initially developed in the south-west, and so had a particularly strong early influence in the region, was significant for the growth of the Methodist movement. Despite all Griffith Jones's effort to disassociate himself, the suspicions at the time of the influence of his schools on the growth of the revival were not unfounded and have been frequently repeated by historians. The creation of a more literate audience, versed in the Bible, was a key element in the success of revival and was part of a long-term campaign from the sixteenth century onwards to instil greater religious knowledge through education and print in order to ensure that the Protestant faith would be firmly rooted in Wales.

Notes

1. Trevecka MS 1392, Howel Harris to Thomas Adams, 10 January 1746.
2. E. Saunders, *A View of the State of Religion in the Diocese of St David's about the beginning of the 18th* Century (reprint, Cardiff: University of Wales Press, 1949), p. 32.
3. DHH 66, 17 December 1740; 81, 6 November 1741.
4. A. H. T. Lewis, 'The development and administration of roads in Carmarthenshire, 1763–1860' (unpublished MA thesis, University of Wales, 1968), pp. 1–25; H. James, 'The Roman Roads of Carmarthenshire', in H. James (ed.), *Sir Gâr: Studies in Carmarthenshire History* (Carmarthen: Carmarthenshire Antiquarian Society, 1991), pp. 53–77; R. Moore-Colyer, *Roads and Trackways of Wales* (Ashbourne: Landmark Publishing, 2001), passim.
5. A. H. Williams (ed.), *John Wesley in Wales 1739-90* (Cardiff: University of Wales Press, 1971), p. 65.
6. DHH 86, 13 March 1742.
7. NLW 18435B, p. 23, 10 September 1741.
8. Trevecka MS 1071, Daniel Rowland to Thomas Price and the Association, 3 January 1744.
9. DHH 34, 13 November 1738.
10. DHH 35, 29 November 1738.
11. DHH 61, 22 August 1740.
12. DHH 66, 19 December 1740.

13 Trevecca College/1 2957, 25 May 1743.
14 Trevecca College/1 2945, p. 14.
15 Trevecca College/1 2956, 19 May 1743.
16 Trevecca College/1 2945, pp. 13, 51.
17 Trevecca College/1 2945, p. 91.
18 Trevecca College/1 3005, 30 September 1743, James Williams to the Association; 3039, James Williams to the Association, 3 February 1747.
19 Trevecka MS 1240, James Williams to the Association, 3 October 1744.
20 DHH 98, 9 March 1743.
21 Trevecca College/1 3037, William John to the Association, 7 January 1747; Trevecka MS 705, Daniel Rowland to Howel Harris, 20 October 1742. Printed in *Account of Progress of the Gospel*, 2/i (1743), 3–7.
22 R. T. Jenkins, 'Three Early Methodist Societies in Carmarthenshire', *BBCS*, 10 (1941), 332; RCHAMW List of Historic Placenames, https://historicplacenames.rcahmw.gov.uk/placenames.
23 See Appendix for full list.
24 D. W. Howell, *Patriarchs and Parasites: The Gentry of South-west Wales in the Eighteenth Century* (Cardiff: University of Wales Press, 1986), p. 2.
25 D. W. Howell, *The Rural Poor in Eighteenth-Century Wales* (Cardiff: University of Wales Press, 2000), p. 27.
26 Benjamin Malkin, *The Scenery, Antiquities, and Biography of South Wales … 1803* (London: Longman, Hurst, Rees and Orme, second edn 1807), pp. 419, 432.
27 Ottley (Pitchford Hall MSS and Documents)/2671, Bishop Ottley to his wife, 8 September 1717.
28 Trevecca College/1 2945, p. 151.
29 Trevecca College/1 3005, 20 September 1743.
30 DHH 61, 17 August 1740.
31 DHH 98, 8 March 1743; 105, 16 December 1743.
32 DHH 82, 28 November 1741.
33 DHH 36, 15 December 1738.
34 Trevecca College/1 3021, James Williams to the Association, 29 December 1744.
35 Trevecca College/1 3024, William John to the Association, 3 January 1745.
36 NLW MS 5455A, Notebook of Thomas Morgan, 1740–94.
37 Trevecka MS 308, William John to Howel Harris, 14 January 1741.
38 Trevecca College/1 2945, p. 47.
39 Trevecca College/1 2945, p. 151.
40 Trevecca College/1 3037, William John to the Association, 7 January 1747.
41 Trevecca College/1 3067, William and Christopher Mends to the Association, 25 October 1748.
42 DHH 70, 25 February 1741.
43 DHH 72, 30 April 1741.
44 DHH 98, 8 March 1743.
45 C. C. Hughes, *Trem ar Ddwy Ganrif o Hanes y Tabernacl, Aberteifi* (Aberteifi: E. L. Jones, 1960), p. 9.
46 A. K. Knowles, *Calvinists Incorporated: Welsh Immigrants in Ohio's Industrial Frontier* (London, University of Chicago Press, 1997), pp. 138–41.

47 Thomas Lloyd, Julian Orbach and Robert Scourfield, *The Buildings of Wales: Carmarthenshire and Ceredigion* (London: Yale University Press, 2006), pp. 70–7; Thomas Lloyd, Julian Orbach and Robert Scourfield, *The Buildings of Wales: Pembrokeshire* (London: Yale University Press, 2004), pp. 84–8.
48 NLW MS 18435B, p. 22, 9 September 1741.
49 DHH 84, 13 January 1742.
50 Trevecca College/1 2945, p. 111.
51 Trevecka MS 1471, William Williams to Howel Harris (London), 5 June 1746.
52 DHH 127, 21–2, 28 July 1747.
53 Trevecka MS 1763, Howel Harris to John Edwards, 4 February 1748; 1764, Howel Harris to George Whitefield, 4 February 1748.
54 Trevecca College/1 3054, James Williams to the Association, 30 April 1748. Strangely, the society at Llansawel kept to their usual meeting place at Bryniau Bychain farmhouse in 1748 rather than make use of the new house. Trevecca College/1 3068, James Williams to the Association, 26 October 1748.
55 SD/QA/61, 1755.
56 N. Vousden, 'Capel Llangynheiddon, Chapel Site, Bancycapel', RCAMHW, 17 September 2012, *http://www.coflein.gov.uk/en/site/12664/details/capel-llangynheiddon-chapel-site-bancycapel*.
57 NLW, Cwrt Mawr MS 150B, p. 35.
58 DHH 98, 21 March 1743.
59 Saunders, *A View of the State of Religion*, pp. 23–4.
60 NLW, Church in Wales Records, Diocese of St Davids, SD/QA/61.
61 SD/MISC.B/39, *c.* 1735–1780s; Gomer M. Roberts, *Methodistiaeth fy Mro: sef ymchwil i ddechreuad Methodistiaeth yn Nwyrain Myrddin* (Treforus: yr awdur, 1938), p. 24; R. T. Jenkins, 'Nonconformity after 1715: Methodism', in J. E. Lloyd (ed.), *A History of Carmarthenshire, II: From the Act of Union (1536) to 1900* (Cardiff: William Lewis, 1939), pp. 195–6; F. Jones, *Historic Carmarthenshire Homes and their Families* (Newport, Pembrokeshire: Brawdy Books, 2006), p. 94.
62 SD/QA/61.
63 DHH 90 31 May 1742.
64 Trevecka MS 308, William John to Howel Harris,14 January 1741.
65 Trevecka MS 766, John William to Howel Harris, 28 December 1742.
66 Trevecka MS 919, Howel Harris to George Whitefield, 13 July 1743; DHH 104, 1, 27 November 1743.
67 RCAHMW, 'Holy Cross Church, Llechryd', 12 September 2013, *http://www.coflein.gov.uk/en/site/3028/details/holy-cross-church-llechryd*; RCAMHW 'Mounton Chapel; St Michaels Chapel, Mounton, Narberth', *http://coflein.gov.uk/en/site/12170/details/mounton-chapelst-michaels-chapel-mounton-narbeth*.
68 Trevecka MS 561, Howel Harris to Howel Davies, 21 May 1742.
69 DHH 82, 27 November 1741.
70 G. M. Roberts, 'Y Llafurwyr Cynnar', in G. M. Roberts (ed.), *Hanes Methodistiaeth Galfinaidd Cymru, Cyfrol I: Y Deffroad Mawr* (Caernarfon: Llyfrfa'r Methodistiaid Calfinaidd, 1973), p. 205.
71 SD/Let/1183, John Lloyd to Bishop Richard Trevor, 19 October 1744.
72 Trevecca College/1 2945, p. 111, 19 October 1744.
73 Trevecka MS 1224, Howel Harris to Thomas Price, 8 September 1744.

74 DHH 113, 2 October 1744.
75 DHH 132, 21 September 1748.
76 G. M. Roberts, 'Y Methodistiaid a Chapeli Anwes yn Sir Gaerfyrddin', *Carmarthenshire Antiquary*, 2 nos 1, 2 (1945, 1946), 27.
77 Joshua Thomas, *Hanes y Bedyddwyr, ymhlith y Cymry* (Caerfyrddin: John Ross, 1778), pp. 51-2.
78 Glanmor Williams, 'Unity of Religion or Unity of Language? Protestants and Catholics and the Welsh Language 1536-1660', in Geraint H. Jenkins (ed.), *The Welsh Language Before the Industrial Revolution* (Cardiff: University of Wales Press, 1997), p. 229.
79 D. Densil Morgan, *Theologica Cambrensis: Protestant Religion and Theology in Wales, 1: From Reformation to Revival 1588-1760* (Cardiff: University of Wales Press, 2018), p. 377.
80 Malcolm and Edith Lodwick, *The Story of Carmarthen* (Carmarthen: Malcolm and Edith Lodwick, 1954), pp. 51-2.
81 See H. P. Roberts, 'Nonconformist Academies in Wales, 1662-1862', *Transactions of the Honourable Society of Cymmrodorion*, 111 (1928-9), 13-35; Dewi Eirug Davies, *Hoff Ddysgedig Nyth: Cyfraniad Coleg Presbyteraidd Cymru i fywyd Cymru* (Abertawe: Tŷ John Penry, 1976); Noel Gibbard, 'Carmarthen Academy (c.1703-1795)', *Dissenting Academies Online: Database and Encyclopedia*, https://dissacad.english.qmul.ac.uk.
82 Gomer M. Roberts, *Y Pêr Ganiedydd [Pantycelyn], Cyfrol I: Trem ar ei Fywyd* (Aberystwyth: Gwasg Aberystwyth, 1949), pp. 33-4; Davies, *Hoff Ddysgedig Nyth*, pp. 123-4; Derec Llwyd Morgan, 'Harris, Howel (1714-1773), evangelist.' *Oxford Dictionary of National Biography* (Oxford University Press, 2004). Accessed 30 September 2019, https://www.oxforddnb.com/view/10.1093/ref:odnb/9780198614128.001.0001/odnb-9780198614128-e-12392.
83 G. M. Griffiths (ed.), 'A Visitation of the Archdeaconry of Carmarthen, 1710', *National Library of Wales Journal*, 18 (1973), 297-8.
84 M. Clement (ed.), *Correspondence and Minutes of the S.P.C.K. relating to Wales, 1699-1740* (Cardiff, 1952), pp. 1, 329.
85 Meyrick and Thomas were successive vicars of Carmarthen. Meyrick was originally from Merionethshire and connected to the Meyricks of Bodorgan and the Vaughans of Golden Grove, through whose influence he gained several benefices in Carmarthenshire, including Llangathen, Llanegwad and Penboyr.
86 Clement, *Correspondence and Minutes of the S.P.C.K. Relating to Wales*, pp. 8, 15.
87 E. M. White, *The Welsh Bible* (Stroud: Tempus Publishing, 2007), pp. 155-6.
88 Clement, *Correspondence and Minutes of the S.P.C.K. Relating to Wales*, p. 323.
89 Eiluned Rees, 'An Introductory Survey of 18th Century Welsh Libraries', *Journal of Welsh Bibiographical Studies*, X/4 (1971), 197-208.
90 Clement, *Correspondence and Minutes of the S.P.C.K. Relating to Wales*, p. 324.
91 Lodwick, *The Story of Carmarthen*, pp. 53-4; Mary Clement, *The S.P.C.K. and Wales 1699-1740* (London: SPCK, 1954), p. 10.
92 Clement, *Correspondence and Minutes of the S.P.C.K. Relating to Wales*, p. 197.
93 Clement, *The S.P.C.K. and Wales 1699-1740*, pp. 43-7; W. Jacob, 'The State of the Parishes', in G. Williams, W. Jacob, N. Yates and F. Knight, *The Welsh*

Church from Reformation to Disestablishment, 1603–1920 (Cardiff: University of Wales Press, 2007), pp. 150–2.
94 Clement, *The S.P.C.K. and Wales 1699–1740*, p. 160.
95 M. G. Jones, *Charity School Movements: A Study of Eighteenth-century Puritanism in Action* (Cambridge: Cambridge University Press, 1938), p. 284.
96 Clement, *The S.P.C.K. and Wales 1699–1740*, p. 10.
97 Clement, *Correspondence and Minutes of the S.P.C.K. Relating to Wales*, p. 8.
98 Clement, *Correspondence and Minutes of the S.P.C.K. Relating to Wales*, p. 298; Clement, *The S.P.C.K. and Wales 1699–1740*, p. 160.
99 Clement, *Correspondence and Minutes of the S.P.C.K. Relating to Wales*, p. 23.
100 E. M. White, 'Popular Schooling and the Welsh Language', in Jenkins (ed.), *The Welsh Language Before the Industrial Revolution*, p. 321.
101 *Welch Piety* (London, 1740), pp. 15–16.
102 David Maurice, *Cwmffwrd ir Gwan Gristion, neu'r Gorsen Ysyg Mewn Pregeth* (Llundain, 1700), p. vi.
103 *Welch Piety* (London, 1743), p. 2.
104 Geraint H. Jenkins, '"An Old and Much Honoured Soldier": Griffith Jones, Llanddowror', *Welsh History Review*, 11/4 (1983), 459.
105 Jenkins, '"An Old and Much Honoured Soldier": Griffith Jones, Llanddowror', 465; White, 'Popular Schooling and the Welsh Language', p. 331.
106 Trevecka MS 76, Howel Harris to Joseph Harris, [4 June?] 1736.
107 Robert Jones, *Drych yr Amseroedd*, ed. G. M. Ashton (Cardiff: University of Wales Press, 1958), p. 29.
108 SD/MISC/1279, 1744.
109 J. Evans, *Some Account of the Welch Charity-Schools: and of the Rise and Progress of Methodism in Wales, through the Means of them* (London, 1752).
110 Gomer M. Roberts, *Bywyd a Gwaith Peter Williams* (Caerdydd: Gwasg Prifysgol Cymru, 1943), pp. 16–18.
111 DHH 101, 22 July 1743.
112 DHH 54, 9 March 1740.
113 DHH 70, 8 March 1741.
114 DHH 118, 13 October 1745.
115 DHH 84, 12 January 1742.
116 Trevecca College/1 2945, p. 15, 6 April 1743.
117 DHH 49, 13 September 1739; 138, 19 October 1749.
118 Trevecca College/1 2945, p. 84.
119 Tom Beynon, 'Morgan Rhys a Chylch Cilycwm hyd at Ystrad Ffin', *Cylchgrawn Cymdeithas Hanesy Methodistiaid Calfinaidd/Journal of the Historical Society of the Presbyterian Church of Wales*, 20 (1935), pp. 145–7; Gomer M. Roberts, *Morgan Rhys, Llanfynydd* (Caernarfon: Llyfrfa'r Methodistiaid Calfinaidd, 1951), pp. 3–4.
120 NLW, St Davids Probate, SD/1779/116: Morgan Rees, Llanfynydd, yeoman, 1779.
121 E. W., 'Memoir of the Rev. Richard Tibbott, Late Pastor of the Independent Church at Llanbrynmair, Montgomeryshire', *The Evangelical Magazine* (London, 1802), 161–2.
122 Trevecka MS 137, Anthony Rees to Howel Harris, 13 January 1739.
123 Trevecca College/1 2945, pp. 7, 9, 143–4.

124 DHH 124, 31 December 1746.
125 NLW MS 6137, p. 412, Griffith Jones to Bridget Bevan, 19 April 1743.
126 NLW MS 6137, p. 416; Griffith Jones to Bridget Bevan, 19 May 1741.
127 *Welch Piety* (London, 1747), p. 27.
128 *Welch Piety* (London, 1750), p. 63.
129 *Welch Piety* (London, 1741), p. 92.
130 *Welch Piety* (London, 1741), pp. 66–7.
131 *Welch Piety* (London, 1741), pp. 51–2.
132 *Welch Piety* (London, 1752), p. 48.
133 *Welch Piety* (London, 1745), pp. 28–9.

CHAPTER 4

'The Great Shepherd's Little Flock'[1]: The Membership of the Societies

As Derec Llwyd Morgan has stated, 'Very little is known in detail of the vast majority of members in the private societies. They are as it were enveloped in the kind of mist which casts a spell of strangeness over the earth on many a lovely morning.'[2] That strange, lingering mist is very difficult to dispel. Some of the reports to the Association in the 1740s by local superintendents of societies include lists of members, but the names are often far too common for individuals to be easily distinguished. Such membership lists are less frequent than might be expected, and disappear to all extents and purposes for the period after 1745, as the demands on the local superintendents increased. The main purpose of the reports in any case was to provide an account of spiritual progress rather than to count converts. There was a reluctance to take too much interest in statistics as that smacked of 'numbering of the people' which when attempted by David in the Bible was regarded as a sign of sinful pride, and which Harris feared was 'to take God's work out of His Hands'.[3] The surviving information reveals that the average membership of the societies in south-west Wales was around twenty-five. By 1750, over fifty societies had been established in Carmarthenshire alone so there were an estimated 1,250 members in that county on the eve of separation in 1750. The twenty-seven societies in Cardiganshire represented a possible further 675 members by 1750. The Methodists therefore remained a minority group in Wales during the middle part of the eighteenth century. However, since the intention was to form small cells of devoted believers, the emphasis was not so much on numbers as on spiritual growth.

Age and Gender

Although the information about the age of the members is sparse, all the evidence suggests that a large number of the members were contemporaries of the leaders and exhorters, most of whom whose ages are known were in their twenties in the early 1740s. This seems to be the demographic pool from which members were chiefly recruited. When listing those under their care, James Williams and John Richard both on occasion used 'young' and 'unmarried' interchangeably to contrast with 'married' in their reports to the Association.[4] That suggests that the unmarried men and women, who formed the largest groups in most of the societies, were likely to have been young men and women mainly in their twenties. There is the occasional specific reference to an individual as 'old', as if that made them somewhat exceptional, as in the case of John Williams of the Fishguard society in 1743.[5] It is perhaps worth bearing in mind that Wales in the early eighteenth century could generally be deemed a 'young' society, in that only a relatively small proportion of the population lived to a very old age.[6]

The youngest member mentioned in the society reports was Richard Evans of Llanegwad society, who was eight years old in 1744 but was already described as holding deep convictions, according to his superintendent, William John.[7] There was no special provision in the societies for children, so they would have to be mature enough to be able to answer the questions posed to candidates for membership, without any concessions to their youth. There were some precocious young Methodists to be found in the south-west, often the children of devout parents. One young child in the Llangeitho area had come to an awareness of her sinfulness after hearing Harris speak at Ystrad-ffin and was able to discuss her spiritual condition with him in detail.[8] Since she had been taken to hear Harris, she was likely to have been part of a Methodist family who would be familiar with hearing the language of the society, so as to be able to talk of feeling 'ye flesh quite dead'. The same sort of background probably influenced the fifteen-year-old girl from Llanddewibrefi whose father related to Harris her vision of Christ wearing a crown of thorns and telling her that he wore it so that she might wear a crown of glory.[9] Harris also met a youth of fourteen in Llandybïe who had 'the Marks of the New Creature'.[10] Another such young recruit was John Thomas of Myddfai, later of Rhaeadr, who became well-known as a hymn writer. At the age of fifteen, he heard Harris exhort at Rhiwiau, Llanddeusant, the home of

Jeffrey Dafydd Ifan, on 10 October 1745. Harris went on from there to Glanyrafonddu, hoping that his words would prove a blessing to his hearers, unaware that his sermon was to begin the process of conversion for Thomas. Shortly after, Thomas joined the Cefntelych society in the parish of Myddfai.[11] Similar information about the history and timing of joining the society is unknown in the majority of cases, but his story is likely to be representative of others, although it is impossible to gauge how many other teenagers were drawn to the movement. The fact that it was often the younger generation who were recruited was a source of great satisfaction to William Williams, who argued that their conversion could not be attributed to years of study: '…had this Work been begun and carried on only by old learned prudent people; grace should not be so visible to all as tis now had the late reformation been among ye old proffesors and touchd but some of the young men'.[12] The challenging novelty of the movement may well have appealed more to younger people, who were perhaps more prepared to venture and less bound by convention. It was also the case that they were more likely to be drawn to exhorters who belonged to the same generation as themselves.

Although the actual age of members was rarely recorded, there is more information about the gender balance as the early society reports tended to list the members in categories of married and unmarried men and women, revealing a striking preponderance of unmarried women in many societies. William Richard's report on 10 July 1743 listed 200 members in the twelve societies between Llwyndafydd in Cardiganshire and St David's in Pembrokeshire, including 111 unmarried women.[13]

Society	Married men	Unmarried men	Married women	Unmarried women	Total
Total Cardiganshire:					
Dyffryn-saith	4	5	1	14	24
Blaenhownant	1	5	1	5	12
Tŵr-gwyn	2	1	2	5	10
Llwyndafydd	4	0	3	3	10
Aberporth	5	6	0	11	22
Pembrokeshire:					
Longhouse	0	7	0	8	15
St David's	1	3	3	4	11
Fishguard	2	11	0	22	35
Dinas	2	2	0	3	7

Newport	0	4	0	9	13
Pen-caer	0	2	0	4	6
Llwynygorras and Eglwyswrw	2	3	7	23	35
Total	**23**	**49**	**17**	**111**	**200**
Percentage of the membership	11.5%	24.5%	8.5%	55.5%	

The same tendency is to be seen in other areas in the south-west, including in five of the largest societies in Carmarthenshire under James Williams's supervision in 1743, although here the gap between unmarried men and women was not so great:

Society	Married men	Unmarried men	Married women	Unmarried women	Total
Total					
Caeo	1	13	14	21	49
Talley	7	13	15	20	55
Llansawel	4	20	5	17	46
Llangathen	6	13	6	12	37
Cwm-ann	6	8	5	13	32
Total	**24**	**67**	**45**	**83**	**219**
Percentage of the membership	10.9%	30.6%	20.6%	37.9%	

Unfortunately, there are not a large number of such detailed membership lists, and sometimes the converts were listed according to spiritual status rather than gender: those under the law, for instance, and those with a fuller experience of salvation, divisions which would have been more significant in Methodist terms.[14] However, the general consensus was that women formed the majority in many societies and were often an enthusiastic and active majority at that. The obvious presence of women was an acknowledged fact throughout the eighteenth century, as William Williams noted in his *Cyfarwyddwr Priodas* (Guide to Marriage) in 1777 when he declared '*mae mwy o fenywaid yn proffesu nag sydd o wrywiaid*' ('there are more women professing than there are men').[15] As the above tables reveal, it was usually unmarried women who formed the largest group in most societies, despite some exceptions, such as the Pembrey society in south Carmarthenshire, where, at least in 1744, there were no women at all.[16] Married women were less obvious, with none to be found amongst the members at Aberporth,

Longhouse, Fishguard, Dinas, Pen-caer or Newport in 1743. It would have been difficult for wives to attend regularly if their husbands were not also members and there were not a large number of married men either. The predominant groups were obviously the young and unmarried.

Social Status

The traditional view is that the early Welsh Methodists were 'middling sorts',[17] which is also the impression given by the available details for members from the south-west. Since most were to be found outside the towns, they were generally the rural middle rank of society, consisting mainly of farmers and craftsmen and their families. However, attempting to define and identify the 'middling' in society is a perennial problem. There are potential distinctions within the broader category, as yeomen were generally considered the more successful of the rural middling sorts, whereas the term 'husbandmen' was often used to describe farmers of lesser wealth and status.[18] To determine the difference between the social orders is by no means an exact science, for, as Keith Wrightson has pointed out, 'middling' was an elastic category, and the lines between the lesser gentry and wealthy yeomen were often blurred, as were the boundaries between yeomen and husbandmen.[19] In the Welsh context, the terms *iwmon* and *hwsmon* were used at the time and represent the same distinction in standing, however, the income levels reached might be on the low side, especially in south-west Wales. David Howell suggests that the annual income of the lesser gentry in most of eighteenth-century Wales ranged between £100 or under and £400, with many of the middling sorts inevitably falling below that.[20] It is, however, impossible to categorise solely on the basis of wealth. In general, certain elements tend to be regarded as possible signs of more successful middling status, such as higher levels of property and wealth, leading to greater independence, as well as literacy and office-holding, adding up to an overall sense of 'respectability' which is difficult to measure accurately.

A number of early Methodists certainly seem to fit into this middle category, although it is often hard to find information about their social standing. The surviving membership lists are not concerned with such worldly matters as occupation and social rank, so only give names. As so many of these names were very common in the area at the time, it is often only possible to identify individuals who had a firm association with a specific dwelling place, which in order to be named in the records would often be a farmhouse of some size. Methodists who left their mark on the documentary evidence therefore tend to be those of middling rank or above and there may well be other members of lower social status who simply cannot be traced. The respectable rural middling sorts proved essential for maintaining the grass-roots movement as they were able to offer shelter to societies, association meetings and itinerant preachers. The early Dissenters tended to appeal to similar elements in society, often regarded as groups who had greater aspirations to acquire literacy and to improve their levels of religious knowledge. The middling sorts also had potentially greater opportunities for a degree of free time which could be used to read and to attend religious meetings.

Attempts to trace the social and economic status of specific members are hampered by the fact that most of the names were extremely common. For example, there were two women named Mary Evan in the Dyffyn-saith society in 1743, as well as a Thomas John in both the societies of Blaenhownant and Llwyndafydd and a further two in the Aberporth society, all under the supervision of William Richard in south Cardiganshire.[21] The Llanarthney society in 1744 had two men called William Griffith as well as both a David Evan and a David Evans. The women of this society were comprised of two Elizabeth Evans, along with Elizabeth Lloyd, Elizabeth Walter, Catherine Williams, Catherine Powell and Catherine Thomas, names that were likely to be duplicated within the same parish.[22] That was why the names of farms and smallholdings became an essential addition to many personal names in order to provide a distinguishing element, as in the case of William Williams, Pantycelyn. In addition, there can be several variations on the same person's name within the Methodist archive, let alone in other records from the period. Thomas Dafydd, for instance, might also appear in more anglicised form as Thomas David or Thomas Davies. The trend to adopt anglicised first names, at least in their written form, is evident by the mid-eighteenth century, although there still remained an occasional Griffith, Llywelyn, Morgan, Rhys and Gwenllian harking back to Welsh tradition. However, there is evidence that many

Johns would be commonly known as Siôn and several Marys as Mali.[23] Moreover, below the upper levels of society, established surnames on the English model were by no means common. Naming patterns for the lower and middle orders often still favoured the use of the patronymic, making it difficult to determine relationships between husbands and wives, for example, as both spouses might well continue to use the first name of their respective father as their second name. It is possible to see the shift to fixed surnames happening in some of the families involved in Methodism. The name of the father of John Williams of Llwynyberllan, Llandingad, was William John, demonstrating the continued use of the traditional patronymic naming pattern between these two generations. However, John Williams's children used 'Williams' as a surname rather than 'John'. This was, therefore, the precise time that many such respectable middle-ranking families were adopting fixed surnames, so that a whole generation of sons of Johns and Williams were becoming Joneses and Williamses, to the confusion of future historians.

Despite these obstacles, one possible source of information is the probate index for the St Davids diocese, although further problems arise with any such search. Since those with little or nothing to leave were hardly likely to bother with wills, this material inevitably favours wealthier members. It was also the case that far fewer women made wills, widows being the main exception. Although the deaths of thirteen members from the south-west are noted in the society reports during the 1740s, only two can be traced in the probate records: Jenkin David of Crug Ifan and John Parry of Cwmcynon, who apparently died intestate but for whom a letter of administration and inventory of goods survive.[24] It is also possible to locate some known members without a specific date of death simply by searching the relevant parishes. In all too many cases there is no way to determine which particular David Evan or John Jones, if any, is the right one, but it is much easier when the individual's home is known and named in the will. There are very few clues to Methodist leanings in the content of the wills, other than specific bequests to certain individuals and to societies. Margaret Spufford was able to make use of the traditional first bequest which returned the soul to God in order to distinguish religious allegiances in seventeenth-century wills, with references to the Virgin Mary and the saints indicating Catholic tendencies, for instance.²⁵ This bequest is less obviously useful in detecting Methodist influences by the eighteenth century as it appears less frequently. In many cases, the wills would be written, invariably in English, on someone's behalf by a literate person in the parish, often the local clergyman, so there is frequently a common pattern to wills produced in the same parish in the same period. In many cases the bequest of the soul is included as a routine statement along the lines of 'I give my soul to God who gave it', so cannot be considered a unique, individual expression of faith. A few Methodists did take advantage of this opportunity to make a declaration of their beliefs, such as James Williams who left his soul 'into the hands of the Almighty God my Creator hoping through the Mediation of Jesus Christ my Redeemer to be Eternally Saved', and Griffith Evan, Tŵr-gwyn, who left his soul 'into the Hands of Almighty God my maker, hoping through the meritorious Death and Passion of my Saviour Jesus Christ to have free Pardon of all my Sins'. Similar statements about the prospect of pardon through the merits of Christ appear in the wills of John Williams, Llwynyberllan, and Jenkin David, Crug Ifan.²⁶ However, the majority of known Methodists give no indication of their beliefs when disposing of their worldly goods.

Therefore, in the probate index for St Davids diocese only the following thirty-five individuals could be identified with certainty as being involved in the movement in the south-west between 1737 and 1750:

Milbourne Bloom (or Blome), Gelli Glyd, Abergwili, Carmarthenshire, 1766 (exhorter)
Jenkin David, Crug Ifan, Cilrhedyn, Pembrokeshire, husbandman, 1749
Evan Davies, Llwyndafydd, Llandysiliogogo, Cardiganshire, 1787
Isaac Dafydd (or Davies), Dolgynon, Cil-y-cwm, Carmarthenshire, 1793
Griffith Evan(s), Tŵr-gwyn, Troed-yr-aur, Cardiganshire, gentleman, 1775
John Evans, Pen-y-wenallt, Llandygwydd, Cardiganshire, gentleman, 1750
Eaton Griffith, Fishguard, Pembrokeshire, yeoman, 1777

Mary Griffiths, Glanyrafonddu-ganol, Talley, Carmarthenshire, widow, 1785
Thomas Griffiths, Glanyrafonddu-ganol, Talley, Carmarthenshire, gentleman, 1767
Morgan Hughes, Blaen-porth, Cardiganshire, 1792 (exhorter) (letter of administration only)
David James, Llwynyceiliog, Caeo, Carmarthenshire, gentleman, 1754
Mary James, Penrhyn, Cil-y-cwm, Carmarthenshire, widow, 1799
Wiliam John, Llewele Mawr, Llansawel, Carmarthenshire, 1790
David Jones, Maesnonni, Llanllwni, Carmarthenshire, 1743
Griffith Jones, Pantyrhaidd, Cynwyl Elfed, Carmarthenshire, 1763
Theophilus Jones, Blaenplwyf, Llanfihangel Ystrad, Cardiganshire, 1758 (letter of administration only)
John Lewis, Cefncrwth, Meidrim, Carmarthenshire, gentleman, 1751
David Morgan, Llanborth, Penbryn, Cardiganshire, 1770
Enos Owen, Esgaireithin, Penbryn, Cardiganshire, 1789
John Parry, Cwmcynon, Llandysiliogogo, Cardiganshire, 1746 (letter of administration only)
John Pugh, Morfa Bach, Kidwelly, Carmarthenshire, gentleman, 1766
Anthony Rees, Llandybïe, Carmarthenshire, farmer, 1792
David Rees, Clyncoch, Llangrannog, Cardiganshire, 1790
Morgan Rhys (or Rees), Llanfynydd, Carmarthenshire, yeoman, 1779
Evan Richard, Abergwili, Carmarthenshire, 1777 (exhorter)
John Richard, Llansamlet, clockmaker, Glamorgan, 1776 (exhorter)
Thomas Richard, Galltybere, Cil-y-cwm, Carmarthenshire, carpenter, 1788
Daniel Rowland, Llangeitho, Cardiganshire, clerk, 1790
Godfrey Thomas, Tre-lech, Carmarthenshire, 1779
John Thomas, Longhouse, Mathry, Pembrokeshire, gentleman, 1770 (letter of administration only)
Watkin Watkins, Gwndwn, Llangrannog, Cardiganshire, 1777
James Williams, Llanddewibrefi, gentleman, 1764 (exhorter)
John Williams, Llwynyberllan, Llandingad, husbandman, 1744

John Williams, Henllys (and Llwynyberllan), Cil-y-cwm, gentleman, 1791
William Williams, Llanfair-ar-y-bryn, Carmarthenshire, clerk, 1791

This list includes two of the evangelical clergy and five exhorters, as well as three society stewards: Isaac Dafydd of Cil-y-cwm, Thomas Griffiths of Talley and Watkin Watkins of Llwyndafydd and Blaenhownant societies. These were men who needed to be literate as well as capable of showing leadership and gaining respect, so were likely to be of good social standing. Also amongst the names is Morgan Rhys, the hymn writer from Llanfynydd who was a schoolmaster in Griffith Jones's circulating schools between 1757 and 1775, including a school at Cil-y-cwm society house between 1772 and 1774.[27] He also held a school at Llwyndafydd, the home of the local society in Llandysiliogogo parish in south Cardiganshire, and it was Watkin Watkins, the steward of the society, who wrote to Griffith Jones in praise of Rhys's ability to diligently 'draw People of all ages to be taught with Delight and Pleasure'.[28] Born in 1716, Rhys was a native of Cil-y-cwm where he would have been exposed to Methodist preaching from his twenties onwards before moving to Llanfynydd.[29] Tradition has it that his conversion to the cause came as a result of hearing either Harris or Rowland preach at Ystrad-ffin.[30] His devotion to Methodism is apparent in his will, in which he left bequests to several leaders and exhorters, as well as to societies in the region of Llanfynydd. It has been suggested that he acted as steward of Llanfynydd society at some point and may also have exhorted a little, although there is no firm evidence to support this.[31]

Another of the members listed is William John of Llewele Mawr, Llansawel. William John was left a guinea in the will of Morgan Rhys, whilst his daughter Rachel received £5 from Mary Griffiths, Glanyrafonddu-ganol, a member of another staunch Methodist family.[32] William Williams himself wrote an elegy on the death of William John in 1785, emphasising the loss to the movement in Llansawel:

> *Colli un oedd pawb yn garu,*
> *Un oedd tan wir ddwyfol nod,*
> *Neb ni ffeindiodd, neb ni welodd,*
> *Fai'n Llywele Mawr erioed.*[33]

> Losing one whom everyone loved,
> One who was under a true divine mark,
> Nobody ever found or saw
> Any fault in Llywele Mawr.

According to tradition, Williams came to know the family of Llewele Mawr through his wife, Mary or Mali, who was a native of Penlan, Llansawel. It was said that he preached at William John's funeral in addition to composing the elegy in memory of him.[34] These links are illustrative of the network of contacts that were often built up through the Methodist movement and reinforced the sense of fellowship and belonging.

Several of the Methodists who can be identified were prominent members of their communities, especially in the rural areas. Griffith Jones of Pantyrhaidd, Cynwyl Elfed, would be High Sheriff of Carmarthenshire in 1757.[35] Although Jeffrey Dafydd Ifan could not be traced in the probate records, he was included in the grand jury list for 1739 before opening his home at Rhiwiau, Llanddeusant, for the use of the society.[36] Not all noted their occupation or social standing on their wills, but a significant proportion of those who did claimed gentry status, including Griffith Evan of Tŵr-gwyn, Troed-yr-aur, and John Evans of Pen-y-wenallt, Llandygwydd, in Cardiganshire, and in Carmarthenshire, Thomas Griffiths, Glanyrafonddu-ganol, Talley, David James, Llwynyceiliog, Caeo, and John Pugh, Morfa Bach, Cydweli. However, a degree of exaggeration is possible when describing one's own status in a will, which may not always be reproduced elsewhere. Griffith Evan, for example, was downgraded to 'yeoman' on the lease of Tŵr-gwyn Chapel in 1752.[37] Yet, these were obviously men of sufficient status to feel that it was not entirely inappropriate for them to style themselves 'gentleman'. The situation seems to have operated in reverse in the case of John Williams of Llwynyberllan who called himself 'husbandman' in his will.[38] This may have been technically accurate in the sense that his income was derived from husbandry, but it was a term more often used for small-scale tenant farmers, whereas Williams's wealth, property and family connections demonstrated higher social and economic standing. Although Williams was termed a 'plebeian' when his younger son, Rice Williams, entered Jesus College, Oxford, both his father and eldest son were described as 'gentleman' on legal documents.[39] It is difficult to distinguish on purely financial grounds who might be counted a member of the minor gentry and who was a successful farmer, since lineage and lifestyle often played a key role in elevating some less affluent landowners into the upper orders. Williams could probably have claimed gentry status and certainly most of his relatives seem to have done so, without fear of contradiction.

The attention paid by Howel Harris to members of the gentry who showed an interest in the movement suggests that they were not the usual run of converts, as he acknowledged: 'though not many rich are called yet I hope some are.'[40] Harris's attitude veered between a sense of humility, which occasionally verged on the obsequious, and a steadfast refusal to tailor his message to please his hearers. At times he was intimidated, as when David Lloyd of Berllandywyll took him to a coffee house in Cardigan, where he found himself struck dumb amongst the rich array of gentry, out in force for the occasion of the Great Sessions.[41] However, much of the time he fortified himself with the conviction that he was on God's work and therefore had a right to proclaim the gospel to all without being considered inferior to any. Sometimes members of the gentry appeared to come to hear him purely out of a desire to mock, others out of curiosity to seek some diversion. As Harris explained to his brother Joseph in 1743: 'Many of the better sort I believe begin to alter their sentiments of us, and others show themselves to be led by an illnatur'd as well as unwise and rash spirit'.[42] In Lampeter, for instance, Sir Lucius Lloyd of Maesyfelin and 'many ladies' came to hear, so Harris spoke in English for their sake.[43] His efforts seemed to have been wasted on Sir Lucius, who showed no further interest before his early death in 1750, when his estate was passed on to his wife's brother, John Lloyd of Peterwell.[44]

Others were more open to learn something of the movement, such as the unnamed JP's wife in Llannarth, Cardiganshire, who spent some time discussing religious matters with Harris in 1739.[45] Harris was offered hospitality in the homes of several of the minor gentry, including John Williams of Bwlchgwynt, Meidrim, Carmarthenshire, who was mayor of Carmarthen. Harris spent the night at Bwlchgwynt in January 1742, taking advantage of the opportunity to exhort for two hours in the evening.[46] In 1741, he was granted permission to exhort in a field on the estate of Gilfach-yr-heddwch, in Llandingad, by the owner, Leoline Jones, who was respectable enough to be on the grand jury for Carmarthenshire and served as bailiff of Llandovery town in 1743.[47] During one of his tours in Pembrokeshire, Harris spent the nights of 7–8 December 1740 in the company of the Mathias family of Llangwarren, Jordanston, Pembrokeshire, at the invitation of John Mathias, after which he punctiliously wrote to give thanks for the hospitality he received: 'The kind Reception I met with at your House calls for the Return of Gratitude from me; How does it Rejoice my soul that tho not many Mighty are called and chosen, yet there are some that dare own a Persecuted Jesus …'.[48] They had a history of supporting somewhat unorthodox causes, including flirting with Jacobitism in the previous generation. John Mathias had at least thirteen children, one of whom, David Mathias, would go on to become a prominent Moravian.[49] However, the family were apparently merely dabbling briefly with Methodism and there seemed to be no further contact after this visit.

Harris was at times emboldened to believe that some of the gentry could be reeled in, as in the case of Herbert Lloyd who, like his brother-in-law, Sir Lucius Lloyd, came to listen to Harris exhort when he was in the Lampeter area.[50] By 1745, Harris felt assured that Lloyd had indeed been genuinely influenced through Daniel Rowland's preaching.[51] Lloyd resided at Foelallt in Llanddewibrefi, an area where early Methodism flourished, a trend which may have piqued his curiosity. There were also family connections which may have encouraged him to take an interest, as his aunt, Sarah Evans of Peterwell, was married to Marmaduke Gwynne of Garth, who was something of a patron of the movement. Their daughter Sarah, Herbert Lloyd's first cousin, married Charles Wesley in 1749. Although it might be supposed that he was further influenced by the known piety of his second wife, Anne Stedman, a daughter of the Nanteos family whom he married in 1745, his unkind treatment of her makes that unlikely. He went on to inherit the estates of Peterwell and Maesyfelin after the death of his brother John in 1755, and was created a baronet in 1763. He also served as MP for Cardiganshire boroughs in the 1760s, so appeared to be a well-established landowner. However, he became notorious as a ruthless local tyrant who was dismissed as a Justice of Peace in 1755 because of his abuse of power. His ill fame lived on in local legend for centuries after his death in 1769.[52]

Although Methodism seemed to have had only a fleeting influence, when Harris visited Lampeter again in May 1763, Lloyd once again came to hear him.[53]

Other members of the gentry were rather more consistent in their support and can be classed as full members. The Parry family of Cwmcynon, Llandysiliogogo, counted amongst the minor gentry and were active in the Llwyndafydd society. Thomas Parry of Cwmcynon had married the heiress to the nearby Gernos estate in 1711, ensuring that their son John inherited a substantial landholding in south Cardiganshire.[54] That he was regarded as a person of substance by his fellow Methodists is evident from the way he was invariably referred to as 'Mr Parry' rather than the 'Brother Parry' which would be more usual.[55] John and Hester Parry frequently played host to Howel Harris on his visits to the locality. Watkin Watkins, the society steward, was a friend of the family and it was he who wrote to Harris in June 1745 to break the news of John Parry's death:

> Mr Parry of Cwmcynon died, and we are not without some hopes that he is in Glory and he left a good sermon behind, charging his family a little before he departed, to make good of their time, not neglecting the means of Grace, but to go on against all oppositions of their friends and Relation, as they did begun.[56]

The encouragement to stand firm against family opposition shows the general disapproval of the movement among the landowning elite. The family were criticised by friends for attending Llechryd Chapel to receive the sacrament from Howel Davies, rather than remaining loyal to their parish church, especially when they were deemed to have gone there rather too soon after John Parry's death to suit local society. The family suffered a further trial when another member of the family, Elizabeth, died on 28 June 1748, aged 28, after a long illness and in great pain.[57] She was described as 'Miss Parry', and, given her age, it seems most likely that this was John Parry's sister rather than his daughter. Around this time, Hester Parry had been considering the possibility of a second marriage to 'Brother Mends', one of the two brothers, Christopher and William, who were exhorters from Pembrokeshire. Nothing is known of any marriage by William, but Christopher married Ann Twyning of Pembrokeshire, although it is not clear precisely when.[58] For either to have wed Hester Parry would probably have been regarded as a mismatch in wordly terms, although Methodist exhorters did often improve their social and economic lot through marriage. Hester was the daughter of John Howells of Penybeili, Llangynllo, and had apparently brought a £200 dowry to the marriage with John Parry in 1739.[59] The Howells were another lesser gentry family, members of which had served as High Sheriff and Justice of Peace. Harris and Howel Davies were both exercised over the matter, with Davies unable to support the marriage.[60] With Hester herself plagued by doubts, it is not surprising that the marriage did not go ahead. Instead, in 1758 Hester married the old friend of the family, Watkin Watkins, after he lost his first wife Elizabeth.[61] The strong links with Methodism persisted, with Peter Williams acting as a witness to a deed transferring some of Hester Watkins's property to her son, Llywelyn Parry of Gernos, who was High Sheriff of Cardiganshire in 1772.[62] This was therefore one of the most elevated of the Cardiganshire families to show commitment to the movement. However, by the early nineteenth century, Cwmcynon was described as having lost much of its former grandeur.[63]

Amongst those Methodists who identified themselves as of gentry status in their wills was Captain John Evans of Pen-y-wenallt, Llandygwydd, Cardiganshire. He was a slightly unexpected recruit, since his half-brother was Theophilus Evans, an acerbic critic of the movement in his work, *A History of Modern Enthusiasm* (1752). Theophilus Evans had William Williams, Pantycelyn, as his curate in Breconshire for a time before Williams's departure to concentrate on his work with the movement. Given Theophilus's attitude to Methodists, this can hardly have been a congenial relationship for either of the two. As the elder brother, it was John who inherited after the death of their father, returning home from a career at sea to take over the family home of Pen-y-wenallt.[64] Harris was a frequent guest there, a fact which may well have stoked Theophilus Evans's ire against the Methodists even further.

In some areas, there were clusters of families of minor gentry or wealthy farmer rank who offered support and succour for the societies and the exhorters. There was a group in north Carmarthenshire around Llandingad, Cil-y-cwm and Caeo who were crucially important for the development of the societies locally. Prominent amongst them was the family of Llwynyberllan in Llandingad, with father and son both called John Williams. The elder of the two married Barbara, daughter of William Williams of Caron, Cardiganshire, which, although in a different county, was not far from Llandingad as the crow flies.[65] Barbara's brother, Nathaniel Williams, was a friend of John Wesley and Daniel Rowland's son Nathaniel is said to have been named in his honour. Nathaniel Williams lived at Hen Fynachlog, Strata Florida, which was one of the few places in Cardiganshire Harris continued to visit in the immediate aftermath of the split in 1750. Llwynyberllan played host to the second General Association meeting in February 1742, at which time John Williams senior was still alive.[66] According to Harris's diary, a John Williams was appointed to take charge of the societies in the Llandovery area in 1741, and it has been suggested that this was the elder John Williams of Llwynyberllan.[67] A John Williams was to care for the society at Cefntelych, Myddfai, from February 1743, but it is not clear whether this was John Williams of Llwynyberllan. It is certainly geographically feasible. However, the will of the elder of the two John Williams, dated 29 April 1743, states that he was 'sick in Body', which makes it unlikely that he would be taking on the responsibility for a society at around the same time.[68] His son, born around 1720, would have been of an age to become active in the movement by 1741, and he certainly became one of Harris's most loyal supporters by the time of the separation. Williams was also one of the first to welcome Harris back after his return to the movement in 1763, with Harris spending the night of 29 March at Llwynyberllan during his first 'New Round' of the south-west following the reconciliation.[69] It was at Llwynyberllan that Harris had slept on the eve of his wedding to Anne Williams, so his connection with the family was long-standing and close.

The list of names identified in probate records actually includes three members of the Llwynyberllan family: John Williams the elder, along with his son and daughter, namely John Williams, later of Henllys, Cil-y-cwm, and Mary James of Penrhyn, Cil-y-cwm. Mary was a daughter of the Llwynyberllan family who had married William James of Pwllpriddog in Cil-y-cwm, moving to Penrhyn after her husband's death.[70] She bequeathed £100 for the general benefit of the Cil-y-cwm society, so hers was a lifelong commitment to Methodism. One of the witnesses to the will of John Williams of Henllys was Nathaniel Rowland, son of Daniel, demonstrating that he also retained the family links to the Methodist cause. It is not clear how far the rest of the family remained involved. Daniel Williams, brother to Mary, left most of his wordly goods to his nephew John Williams, but there is nothing in his will to indicate Methodist leanings.[71] Mary left £20 to Elizabeth, Daniel's natural daughter, which suggests he had not always kept strictly to Methodist morals. Llwynyberllan evidently represented a considerable accumulation of land, even before the younger John Williams also acquired Henllys in Cil-y-cwm.[72]

A similar web of connections spun around the Thomas family of Longhouse, in Mathry parish in Pembrokeshire. A society of some eighteen souls met in the house, and Harris was a frequent guest and constant correspondent, especially of the two daughters Elizabeth and Anne. They were evidently at the heart of a network of well-connected Methodists in north Pembrokeshire, sending Harris news of Howel Davies and greetings from Catherine Poyer. After Harris visited the Mathias family of Llangwarren in December 1740, he sent a letter directly to John Mathias to express his gratitude, but dispatched a letter to his daughter Mary care of Anne and Elizabeth Thomas, whom he also advised to show 'Molly and Betty Mathias' his letter to them if they thought it would be of benefit.[73] In his letter to Mary, Harris expressed a wish to nurture the positive tendencies he perceived in her when they met, and told her she might write to him via the Longhouse family.[74] There was obviously a friendship between the girls, and it may have been this connection between the families which led to the invitation to Llangwarren, although the Mathiases did not seem to wish to pursue the acquaintance with Harris to the same degree as the Longhouse family did. It has also been suggested that some sort of family connection existed between the Thomas family and the Pugh family of Morfa Bach, Kidwelly, who were also staunch supporters.[75] Elizabeth Thomas was staying there in December 1743, and Catherine Pugh the younger was to return with her to Pembrokeshire.[76] This Catherine, or Kitty, seems to have been her mother's namesake, and Harris was in contact with both, along with the other daughter Mary. He and Howel Davies were frequent visitors at Morfa Bach, which seems to have offered hospitality to Methodists preaching or attending the nearby Capel Ifan, the chapel of ease associated with Llanelli. The Thomas family connections were extended further by the marriages of the daughters: Anne to John Edwardes, Abermeurig in Cardiganshire, and Elizabeth to John Sims of Clyro, Radnorshire.

Other members of the gentry were hearers or sympathisers rather than full members, including David Llwyd or Lloyd of Berllandywyll and Robert Archer Dyer of Aberglasney, both in Llangathen parish. Harris was first invited to Berllandywyll in March 1743 and later in the same month was introduced to Robert Archer Dyer. Both Lloyd and Dyer were extremely useful contacts to make, as both came from well-connected families and were JPs in Carmarthenshire. Lloyd's father had been High Sheriff of the county and the family had links to the families of Peterwell and Maesyfelin.[77] Harris marvelled at how courteously he was received by them: 'I rec'd Civilities amazing here – was respected with uncomon Love – freedom & Respect'.[78] Robert Archer Dyer's grandfather, Robert Dyer, was a lawyer who acted as collector of rents and steward of the courts in the diocese of St Davids.[79] He had made enough money to buy Aberglasney and be termed a 'gentleman' in his will in 1720, before passing on the estate to his son, also Robert.[80] Another son, Benet Dyer, was High Sheriff of Cardiganshire in 1736, and yet another was John Dyer, the poet who famously wrote of the beauties of that part of Carmarthenshire in his poem, *Grongar Hill*.[81] Harris obviously cherished hopes of converting both Robert Archer Dyer and David Lloyd, and spent hours conversing with Lloyd in particular. Although he failed in his efforts, yet he retained the connection, taking his newly wed wife to stay at Aberglasney in July 1744.[82] He visited both men again in January 1745, the last time for some years, although he continued to include Llangathen on his preaching tours.[83] He called at Berllandywyll once more in January 1749, to a warm welcome from Lloyd, although by that time Harris despaired of having any real influence on him.[84]

Mixing in such circles, Harris found he had a choice of highly eligible prospective brides from households in which he was a regular guest on his preaching tours in the south-west, homes which tended to belong to the minor gentry or successful farmers. Daughters of such families had an obvious advantage when it came to contact with the more celebrated Methodist preachers, as in the case of Sarah Gwynne of Garth in Breconshire and Charles Wesley. The eldest daughter of the Mathias family, Mary, or Molly, attracted Harris's interest briefly in 1740, when he spent two nights as a guest at their home, Llangwarren in Pembrokeshire. His initial reaction was disappointment at the rather lukewarm reception he received from the family, but before his departure he came to hope that of the two girls, Mary and Elizabeth, Mary might be won over. After only one day in her company, Harris considered that she might be a more suitable bride than Anne Williams.[85] Although he wrote to her soon after his visit, offering spiritual encouragement and inviting her to respond to his letter, there the correspondence seemed to end.[86] Not much is known of Mary in the future, but Elizabeth and another sister, Anne, later joined the Moravian Brethren in Bristol.[87]

In November 1741, Catherine James, the daughter and heiress of David James, Llwynyceiliog, Caeo, was eager to marry Harris, motivated, she claimed, by a desire to reap the spiritual benefits of being constantly in his company. Harris had to refuse, as he felt himself already committed to marrying Anne Williams, but was tempted by the offer nonetheless:

> I found now I could as freely marry her & she having all spiritual qualifications & less hindrances as to Relations &c but my soul cryd Lord I take now on this Tryal Miss Williams purely because I think Thou has given her to me & on no other reason for here is one quite as agreeable altogether.[88]

In 1744, Catherine James married John Williams, the younger of that name, of Llwynyberllan, Llandingad, later of Henllys, Cil-y-cwm, adding to the links between the landowning Methodist families in the area.[89]

In the meantime, in 1743, Harris was faced with another heiress who seemed amenable to the prospect of marriage, Catherine Poyer of Parciau, Henllan Amgoed, Carmarthenshire. Parciau was another household where Harris was a frequent honoured guest, and he spent many evenings discoursing to the family. A marriage to Catherine presented far fewer problems and had many advantages over a possible match with Anne Williams, whose family disapproved. Harris contemplated the two women's respective virtues and weaknesses in an attempt to decide which would be the better suited to him and the greater ornament to the movement.[90] He concluded that Anne was the more genteel, with the deepest knowledge of her Saviour and resolved to cling to her, asking Catherine to be as a sister to him. Catherine did not lack for eligible Methodist suitors, however, as she went on to marry Howel Davies on 30 April 1744. Catherine, the eldest daughter, inherited Parciau from her maternal grandfather, Griffith Twyning, who left it to her rather than to her widowed mother, Anne Poyer.[91] After Catherine died within a year of the wedding, giving birth to a daughter who died within the space of two years, it was Howel Davies who inherited the property. Such examples of fortuitous marriages led to sarcastic remarks about the tendency of Methodist preachers to marry the pick of the wealthiest young women available to them through the movement.

There is, therefore, a pattern of interlinking families of lower gentry or richer yeoman status, especially in the Cil-y-cwm and Caeo region of north Carmarthenshire. That was an area where there were rather fewer large-scale gentry estates, which tended to be bunched along the banks of the Tywi river, where the fertile land brought higher rents.[92] This seems to fit with Alan Everitt's theory that Dissent did well in 'open' parishes where there was no dominant gentry presence as there was in 'closed' parishes.[93] The regions where the ecclesiastical parishes tended to be large, rural and thinly populated were often also the areas where there were a collection of minor gentry rather than the great houses, such as Dinefwr and Golden Grove. It was in such areas that Methodism seemed to thrive and to receive valuable patronage from families of significant local status. The appeal to those elements in society proved very important in practical terms for the survival of the movement in the long term.

Middling sorts

Another complication with attempting to identify the more successful 'yeoman' middling sorts is that not all were necessarily owner-occupiers, so freehold status is not always an essential qualification. However, lengthy leaseholders of substantial properties would have held similar status to freeholders, often qualifying to vote along with the 40s. freeholder at county constituency elections. Some of the wealthiest members identified were tenants rather than freeholders of all their property, including John Thomas, who held the lease of Longhouse in Mathry from the bishop of St Davids. It was a sizeable property, with a suggestion that it may once have been a grange farm of the episcopal palace.[94] It was estimated to be a 'very considerable thing', worth over £100 a year by 1757.[95] Thomas and Mary Griffiths rented Glanyrafonddu-ganol in Talley from the Edwinsford estate on a three-lives lease, but also owned their own lands, including Llwynyfedwen, Drefach and Tir-y-pab in Llanfynydd parish.[96] Rather lower down the scale came two families who were also tenants of the Edwinsford estate and can be identified among the members in Llansawel. Llewele Mawr was a farm leased by William John, yeoman, for twenty-one years at a rent of £9 a year, having previously been leased to his mother, Catherine Williams, widow, in 1736.[97] Another property leased from Edwinsford was Bryniau Bychain which was home to the Llansawel society for many years and occupied by John David, also described as a yeoman on the lease of the property. Probate material for his son, David John of Bryniau, shows that he left goods worth £19 9s. in 1788, giving an indication of the family's wealth and standing.[98] Amongst the members in the Llansawel area, therefore, there were a number of tenants of Edwinsford, which was striving for position against some of the greater Carmarthenshire estates during the early eighteenth century. The existence of thriving societies in this area seems to argue against the theory that Methodism did not do well in 'closed' parishes where there was a dominant gentry presence. However, the ambitious owner, Sir Nicholas Williams, the first baronet, may have been more concerned with graver matters than a few enthusiastically religious tenants. Winning and holding the Carmarthenshire parliamentary seat between 1724 and 1745 against other Whig as well as Tory families was a considerable achievement in a county of powerful, conflicting gentry interests. His death without issue in 1745 may also have led to a certain discontinuity, which could have allowed Methodism to proceed unhindered in his area of influence.[99]

Both freehold and tenant farmers made a considerable contribution to the movement by playing host to societies and Association meetings, as well as providing hospitality for peripatetic exhorters. In terms of Association meetings in particular, this was not just a question of opening their doors to considerable numbers of people, but often attempting to feed them as well, which would have been a significant undertaking. The growth of the movement owed a great deal to those who were willing to allow the societies to make use of their homes, including Thomas David, Dyffryn-saith, Penbryn; John Lewis, Cefncrwth, Meidrim; and John Williams, Cilcarw, Llangyndeyrn.[100] In a number of areas, the societies were named after the farmhouses in which they met, including Dygoed in Llanarthney, Ffrwdwenith in Aberporth and Ffos-y-ficer in Abercych. Although several were large properties for the period, there must have been occasions when they were uncomfortably full, since some societies had fifty or more members. Between 46 and 51 members regularly met at John David's home at Bryniau Bychain in Llansawel and continued to do so for a time even after the society house was completed in 1748. When the early society houses were built, the land was often acquired through the good auspices of the substantial farmers among the membership. Cil-y-cwm house was built on land bought in 1746 from Dafydd Rhydderch, Dolgynon, father of Isaac Dafydd, the steward of the society. There was a tradition that he had sold the land to the society for a price of 'three peppercorns', but it seems to have actually been a more prosaic ten shillings.[101] The tithe records for Cil-y-cwm list Isaac Dafydd (or Davies) as a farmer, paying £5 5s. in tithe on his corn, wool, lambs, cows and geese in 1775.[102] Isaac left property worth £30 at the time of his death, so he was not necessarily among the very wealthiest of adherents, but squarely in the middling rank of society.[103] The house or chapel at Twr-gwyn was built on land supplied by Griffith Evan, listed as a freeholder of the parish of Troed-yr-aur in 1760 and described as a yeoman on the chapel deeds but as a gentleman in his will. He was the son of Ifan Gruffydd of Twr-gwyn, who was a noted poet in the halsingod tradition in south Cardiganshire. The chapel was to be called 'Capel Evan' and the building with the surrounding parcel of land was conveyed in 1752 for a period of ninety-nine years in an agreement with Daniel Rowland, Howel Davies, William Williams, Peter Williams and other prominent Methodists, on behalf of the movement.[104] There was a tradition that there had been a chapel of ease in the location at one time, which was said to explain Daniel Rowland's willingness to make use of the new building in the 1750s.[105] Twr-gwyn established itself quite early as a centre for the movement's activities in Cardiganshire, with the county's first monthly association held there in July 1743.[106]

It is inevitably easier to find information about the society members who were of the middling sorts or above. There is evidence that some of a lower social standing were also attracted to the movement, but they are rarely named in any of the sources. Howel Harris informed George Whitefield that many of the members were 'poor', but it is difficult to know how he defined poverty.[107] It was also said that many of the members of St David's, Longhouse and Fishguard societies were 'very poor in this world'.[108] Although Thomas Morgan mentioned in his diary that the two maidservants belonging to the household of Owen Evans in Merthyr, Carmarthenshire, were Methodists, he did not give their names and may well not have learnt them.[109] Richard Tibbott spent the night in Llan-y-crwys as a guest of 'a poor man' whose wife explained that they had no nourishment in the house, but could at least offer him shelter if he chose to stay, which he did.[110] Again, these Methodist supporters go unidentified and there are likely to have been more in the same category about whom little information has survived.

Economic Status

Being in possession of wordly wealth was not in itself considered problematic, as money could be extremely useful, if spent wisely and charitably. It has been suggested that John Wesley was influenced by the idea of a 'community of goods' amongst the members, and he certainly urged his followers to 'gain as much as you can, save as much as you can, give as much as you can'.[111] The Welsh Methodists were not so emphatic, but William Williams enouraged members to work diligently in their daily lives in order to have the means to be able to assist those in need.[112] The leaders themselves were generally comfortably situated, despite Howel Harris's occasional protestations of poverty.

Somewhere in the region of £40 annual income has been suggested as a threshold of sorts for the middle rank in society in the early eighteenth century.[113] Since that sort of information is not available for most individuals involved in the movement, it is often only the probate material that offers any indication of wealth. Inventories of goods at the time of death were becoming less common by the mid-eighteenth century, but were generally drawn up by respected members of the community within a short space after death. There was no obligation to do this if the deceased's goods were worth less than £5, so the evidence of inventories reveals more about the better-off in society. Valuations might vary considerably according to those carrying out the assessment, so there is no consistent measure. The 700 sheep owned by John Williams were valued at £70, whereas the 345 sheep owned by David James were valued at £73 7s., although there might possibly be differences in age and quality.[114] There would also be a marked difference in the amount of grain listed in inventories drawn up in early autumn, after harvest, and those towards the end of spring when food stocks would be much depleted. The value of the goods of John Thomas of Longhouse was boosted by corn worth over £200 in October 1770, whereas Eaton Griffith had only £2 10s. 6d worth of corn and hay left in April 1776.[115] Inventories only included movable goods, as well as land rented on lease, so often excluded the most valuable property in people's possession. Since they survive for only a small portion of those who can be identified as members during the period 1737–50, few firm conclusions can be reached about the economic situation of the members in general on this basis, but the evidence offers some interesting insights. There are in addition a number of other individuals, whose wills were proved in the latter years of the eighteenth century, who can be identified as Methodists on the basis of bequests to societies and Methodist preachers. Amongst them was Anne Williams of Glangwenlais, Cil-y-cwm, who left £189 to her son, Samuel, on condition that he pay £10 to the Cil-y-cwm society.[116] Her entire property was worth £200 and her husband, Rhys or Rees, was evidently also a Methodist as his name appears in the subscribers to an edition of Daniel Rowland's sermons and he is named in *Methodistiaeth Cymru* as a known member of Cil-y-cwm society before his death in 1785.[117] However, the movement had expanded considerably by that time and it is impossible to know how early these Methodists were recruited, as they may well be part of the second wave of revival starting in 1762, or even later. It is safest, therefore, only to include those who are known to be connected with the movement prior to 1750.

Value of goods at time of death	£	s.	d
Thomas Richard, Cil-y-cwm, carpenter	6	9	0
James Williams, Llanddewibrefi (exhorter)	9	8	0
Morgan Hughes, Cwmhowni, Blaen-porth (exhorter)	15	0	0
Watkin Watkins, Llangrannog	15	2	4
Eaton Griffith, Fishguard, yeoman	16	19	6

Jenkin David, Crug Ifan, Cilrhedyn, husbandman	19	9	0
John Lewis, Cefncrwth, Meidrim, gentleman	19	10	0
Evan Richard, Abergwili (exhorter)	19	15	0
Isaac Dafydd/Davies, Cil-y-cwm	30	0	0
Anthony Rees, Llandybïe, farmer	30	9	2
William Williams, Pantycelyn, Llanfair-ar-y-bryn	68	0	0
David Jones, Maesnonni, Llanllwni	75	0	6
John Williams, Henllys, Cil-y-cwm, gentleman	105	0	0
John Parry, Cwmcynon, Llandysiliogogo	126	17	0
John Williams, Llwynyberllan, Llandingad, husbandman	132	11	0
David James, Llwynyceiliog, Caeo, gentleman	364	19	0
John Thomas, Longhouse, Mathry, gentleman	686	16	0
Mary James, Penrhyn, Cil-y-cwm, widow	1030	0	0

The average value of goods here is drastically inflated by the the sums for John Thomas and Mary James, but the median value is £30, which would seem to be a likely reflection of the movable wealth of the rural middling sorts.[118] The range of wealth based on farming is apparent, with John Williams of Llwynyberllan owning 700 sheep worth £70, 23 cows worth £25 10s. and 18 calves worth £16, and James Williams owning sheep worth just 8s. and cattle valued at £4 15s. Yet of the two, it was James who called himself 'gentleman' in his will and John who chose 'husbandman'. Eaton Griffith, a yeoman, left behind a cow and a heifer together worth £2 11s. 6d. The terminology therefore does not necessarily reflect the actual wealth involved. David James's inventory lists £220 worth of bonds and notes, the only such mention in any of these inventories, which mainly deal in livestock and implements of husbandry, although John Thomas of Longhouse on the Pembrokeshire coast owned a sloop and shares in a boat worth £55 in total. The only surviving inventory for a craftsman in the movement is that for Thomas Richard, carpenter, who appears to be the poorest of those listed based on the value of his goods.[119] He made very few bequests of money in his will, but left the tools of his trade to be shared between his three sons, although his best two-handed saw was given to his son, William, who was also his executor. He was also able to distribute a quantity of timber oak between his sons and two daughters, some of which timber was said to be still growing. John Richard, the bookbinder-turned-clockmaker, also left his tools to be divided between his two sons, useful bequests which would have helped provide them with the means to make a living.[120]

Despite the difficulties in tracing the financial status of the members, some were obviously affluent and it is apparent that those fortunate enough to have greater worldly wealth felt a responsibility towards more needy members. William Williams regarded wealth as a God-given advantage which should be used to benefit the Church.[121] When Edward Evans, a member of Llangwyryfon society, died on 24 December 1746, the Association was informed of his great generosity towards the poor of the area, both within and outside the society. After his death, his money was left to the society in order to assist the less fortunate, because 'He had a testimony, that His office in the Church was to Distribute towards the necessity of the Brethren – and, so He was Diligently according to His power'.[122] In a similar vein, Mary Griffiths founded a charity to support the poorer members of the societies in the parishes of Talley, Llansawel, Cynwyl Gaeo, Llanfynydd and Llangeitho, and to pay for schoolteachers in those parishes. In 1777, she purchased the farm of Gelliddewi Isaf in Pencarreg, Carmarthenshire from Joanna and David Heron Pugh, the widow and son of the Dissenting minister, Philip Pugh. The rent and profits from the farm were intended to finance the charity for the future. In 1837, the vicar of Llangeitho, then one of the trustees of the charity, attempted to divert the funds to benefit the communicants of the Anglican Church in those areas. The vicar's argument was that the societies had been part of the Established Church when the charity had been set up and that, by leaving the Church, the members had forfeited any claim. However, the legal advice was that he did not have the right to withhold the money.[123]

Several other Methodists left funds to the societies after their death. After a number of individual bequests, Morgan Rhys, the hymn writer from Llanfynydd, left the residue of his property to be sold so that the money could be divided between the deserving poor of the Llanfynydd society. The £30 he set aside for his wife to benefit from its annual interest was, after her death, to be distributed between the societies of Nantgaredig, Llansawel, Cil-y-cwm, Caeo, Llanfynydd, Llansadwrn and Brechfa, suggesting a network of connections established amongst the societies in the region of north Carmarthenshire.[124] Mary James left

£100 for the general benefit of the Cil-y-cwm society.[125] Thomas Griffiths left £20 to the members of Talley society, to be distributed at the discretion of his wife, Mary.[126] Other members preferred to leave money to various individuals belonging to the movement rather than to societies. The evangelical clergy and exhorters were frequent recipients of such bequests, possibly as a sign of appreciation of their contribution. Daniel Rowland was a popular legatee, receiving £3 3s. from Morgan Rhys and £20 from Thomas Griffiths. Griffiths's wife, Mary, also left £100 to Rowland, but topped that by giving his son Nathaniel the sum of £200.[127] Mary Griffiths made her will and set up her charity after the death of her husband, Thomas, who was reputed to have had a more tight-fisted attitude to money.[128] As a widow, she would have had greater freedom to leave her money where she chose. Her only son died at the age of eight, so the closest relatives named in her will are cousins and a nephew, with a good proportion of her wealth left to the Methodist cause.[129] Methodism may well have benefited in particular from members like her and Morgan Rhys who had no children to whom to leave their property.

Charitable giving was not confined simply to fellow Methodists. Despite his reputation as miserly, Thomas Griffiths also left £5 to the poor of the parish of Talley in general and ordered that all his tenants be remitted half a year's rent (with the exception of one William Bailey who may have incurred too many arrears to be granted this favour!).[130] William Williams, Pantycelyn, left £100 in order to set up Welsh-medium charity schools, which he felt were greatly needed.[131] David James of Llwynyceiliog gave the sum of £6 to the poor of the parish of Caeo to be divided up and distributed annually over a period of four years.[132] Griffith Jones of Pantyrhaidd set up an annuity of 20s. a year, half of which was to be transferred to the schoolmaster of the local charity school to be spent on the education of poor children, and the other half for the purchase of four flannel shirts to be bestowed on four boys or girls on Christmas Day.[133] Bequests were not always in the form of money: David Jones of Maesnonni left one bushel of pilcorn each to the parishes of Llanllwni and Pencader, to be distributed amongst the poor.[134] Others showed a rather more cautious attitude, such as Eaton Griffith of Fishguard who appointed his wife Mary to be executor of his will and to manage his property during her lifetime so long as she was not wasteful and did not carry anything away from the premises. If she were to marry again, she would then have 'only sixpence'.[135] This caution may well be an indication of more straitened circumstances calling for greater prudence. Wills drawn up by less affluent individuals often contained more detailed and specific bequests, as there were fewer possessions to divide, making each potentially more valuable to the owner.

Some of those listed here as Methodists in the period 1737 to 1750 later joined the Dissenters, including Morgan Hughes, the former exhorter, and Anthony Rees of Llandybïe. Rees wrote to Harris at a time when he was the schoolmaster of a circulating school in the area in 1738-9. He then appeared to have strong Methodist inclinations, but seems to be one of those for whom Methodism proved a gateway to Dissent. An Anthony Rees acted as a churchwarden and overseer of the poor in the parish of Llandybïe during the 1740s, which seems unlikely to have been the same individual, who would have been under thirty at the time Anthony Rees became churchwarden. Given the uncommon nature of the name in south-west Wales, it may perhaps have been the father of the more Methodistical Anthony Rees. He died in 1792 aged 79, by which time he had evidently become a member of the local Dissenting church of Gellimanwydd established in 1782, since he left money to help the cause there.[136]

Literacy

Of the thirty-two individuals who were Methodist supporters in the 1740s and can be identified as leaving wills, the majority were able to sign. However, the more identifiable the Methodist, the more likely they were to be of a somewhat higher social and economic status than the bulk of the population, which may not lead to a completely accurate cross-section of the membership. A number of them were exhorters and stewards, who would have been required to read and write to carry out their duties. Indeed, the Association in June 1743 passed that one of these stewards, Watkin Watkins, should 'qualify himself to be scribe or Emanuensis' to either Daniel Rowland or Howel Davies, although it is not clear that anything came of this resolution.[137] Those who belonged to the lesser gentry would be expected to have had that level of education as well. The rest seemed to belong to the rural middling sorts, who were increasingly acquiring literacy through the circulating schools. One of these, David Jones, made a stipulation in his will that his younger son and his two daughters should receive schooling until the age of sixteen, indicating a concern for their education.[138] Five of those listed made a mark instead of a signature: Griffith Evan, David James, William John, David Rees and Godfrey Thomas. They were individuals who might be expected to be literate, and it is probably significant that in most cases there was a short space between drawing up the will and probate being granted, suggesting that they were terminally ill and too weak to sign for that reason. David Rees's will actually stipulated that he was sick in body, but of sound memory and understanding. In his case probate was granted on 2 April 1790, a month after the signing of the will on 1 March 1790.[139] There was a gap of under two months between the writing and proving of the wills of Griffith Evan and Godfrey Thomas, and five months in the case of David James. The exception was William John of Llewele Mawr, where five years went by between fashioning the will in 1785 and probate in 1790. However, William Williams's elegy makes it clear that William John died in 1785, so his was also likely to have been a deathbed will, signed with a mark as a result. There is corroborating evidence to suggest that many of these would have been literate in life, with David Rees leaving a Bible in his will and Godfrey Thomas appearing on the list of subscribers to a collection of Daniel Rowland's sermons in 1772. Gomer Roberts suggested that he might be the 'Mr Godfrey, Parcybedw' listed as an exhorter in *Methodistiaeth Cymru*.[140] If so, his preaching career was likely to have started after 1750, as he is not mentioned in that context in the records prior to that.

This was a period which witnessed a general increase in literacy in rural Wales with the new opportunities offered by the circulating schools. There was a corresponding increase in the eighteenth century in the number of subscribers from a range of occupations to Welsh-medium publications.[141] Unfortunately books were rarely assessed as a separate item on inventories, but often included in a broader category such as 'lumber' or 'household goods'. Yet, books might well be considered sufficiently valuable items to be left as individual bequests, especially in the case of Bibles, which were likely to be considered to have worth beyond the purely monetary. Morgan Rhys and David Rees both specifically bequeathed copies of the Welsh Bible to close relations, Rhys to his brother John and Rees to his daughter Elizabeth.[142] Rees also left £5 a year not just to maintain Elizabeth but also to ensure her education. Morgan Rhys gifted his hymn books to the Llanfynydd society, so that they might benefit from the profits from their sale.[143] Watkin Watkins willed his 'phisic books' and a book case to his son David, but shared the remainder of his books between his three sons, John, David and Thomas.[144] Those books would have included a collection of Daniel Rowland's sermons, *Pum Pregeth* (Five Sermons), since Watkins's name appeared on the list of subscribers in 1772.[145] Further down the social scale, Thomas Richard, the carpenter from Galltybere, Cil-y-cwm, left all his English books to one Morgan David, but all his Welsh books to his son Edward. There is no indication how many books there were in total, but as the entire inventory of his possessions came to a total £6 9s. it is unlikely that he had an extensive library, though owning books in two languages suggests a cultured carpenter.

It does seem to have been the literate middling sorts, who overlapped at their upper reaches with the minor local gentry, who were at the forefront of the movement. There may have been an element of attempting to emulate those of higher status who commanded an assured position in connection with the Established Church. In Methodist circles, the middle rank could gain a parallel prominence. This brand of pious patronage may have enhanced their sense of self-worth, in addition to the spiritual comforts provided by membership. Several of those who played host to the movement were householders of an age to have offspring belonging to the same generation as the Methodist leaders. Yet the membership in general seem to have been relatively young, and a number of the gentry who showed an interest tended to be of an age with the leaders and exhorters. In the Lampeter area for instance, Herbert Lloyd was in his early twenties when he went to listen to Howel Harris in the 1740s, and his brother-in-law Lucius Lloyd some ten years his senior. Robert Archer Dyer and John Williams of Llwynyberllan were both in their early twenties when influenced by Methodism, and John Parry of Cwmcynon was also likely to be of a similar age, having married in 1739 and being the issue of a marriage which took place in 1711. These connections ensured that there were members of the ruling elite who must have known from personal experience that the Methodists were not rabble-rousing revolutionaries and possibly saw no harm in allowing a certain leniency. There were a number of members and hearers who were of sufficient wealth and status to play a part in county administration and government at some level, as High Sheriffs and as members of the grand jury. This may have lent the movement a degree of respectability in the area. Especially important perhaps was the number of JPs amongst the more sympathetic gentry, which may well have helped ensure a degree of toleration for the movement in the south-west. Yet those who showed an interest were not usually of a leading rank in the society of south-west Wales, despite the fact that the Mathias family of Llangwarren would later send a son to Harrow.[146] Pre-eminent landowning families such as the Pryses of Gogerddan in Cardiganshire, the Vaughans of Golden Grove in Carmarthenshire and the Philipps of Picton Castle in Pembrokeshire held themselves aloof. Because of the difficulties in tracing members with any degree of accuracy, the social and economic status of the majority remain unknown. It is therefore impossible to judge whether there was in fact a preponderance of respectable middling sorts or whether they were a relatively small, active group providing leadership to larger numbers of lower social status. The middling sorts were certainly vital in establishing the movement, which would go on to recruit more widely throughout the middle and lower ranks of Welsh society as the eighteenth century progressed.

There is no doubt that some sections of society were drawn to Methodism more than others, with the membership lists demonstrating the predominance of the younger generation and of women, both of whom may have had less of a stake in more traditional forms of religion and public worship. The general perception of the respectable 'Methodist fathers' is coloured by later stages of the movement in the eighteenth century and its sober, respectable image in the nineteenth century. However, it was in its earliest phase a movement which was led by young people in their twenties who appealed to their contemporaries. As time went on, those young recruits aged and often brought up their children in the faith, ensuring the continuity and growing respectability of Methodism. There comes a point in the history of every religious movement when it ceases to attract large numbers of fresh recruits and comes to rely chiefly on the next generation produced by its own members to sustain itself. That was not yet the case with the societies prior to 1750, and for many years afterwards fresh waves of revival would draw in new converts.

Notes

1. Trevecka MS 1381, William Williams to Howel Harris, 7 December 1745.
2. Derec Llwyd Morgan, *The Great Awakening in Wales*, trans. Dyfnallt Morgan (London: Epworth Press, 1988), p. 46.
3. DHH 82, 12 December 1741.
4. Trevecca College/1 3005, 30 September 1743; 3009, January 1744.
5. Trevecca College/1 3002, 12 July 1743.
6. G. H. Jenkins, *The Foundations of Modern Wales: Wales 1642–1780* (Cardiff: University of Wales Press, 1987), pp. 91–2.
7. Trevecca College/1 3010, January 1744.
8. DHH 63, 26 September 1740.
9. DHH 63, 22 September 1740.
10. DHH 47a, 6 July 1739.
11. DHH 118, 10 October 1745; J. Thomas, *Rhad Ras neu Lyfr Profiad*, ed. J. Dyfnallt Owen (Cardiff: University of Wales Press, 1949), pp. 28–44; D. Ll. Morgan, 'John Thomas, Awdur *Rhad Ras*', in *Pobl Pantycelyn* (Llandysul: Gomer, 1986), pp. 20–7.
12. Trevecka MS 1381, William Williams to Howel Harris, 7 December 1745.
13. Trevecca College/1 3002, 15 July 1743.
14. For example, Trevecka MSS 2013; Trevecca College/1 2945, pp. 71–4.
15. G. H. Hughes (ed.), *Gweithiau William Williams Pantycelyn, Cyfrol II: Rhyddiaith* (Cardiff: University of Wales Press, 1967), p. 298.
16. Trevecca College/1 3009, January 1744.
17. Jenkins, *The Foundations of Modern Wales*, p. 356.
18. See P. Laslett, *The World We Have Lost – Further Explored* (third edn, London: Methuen, 1983), pp. 43–4; Jenkins, *The Foundations of Modern Wales*, pp. 102–4; H. R. French, *The Middle Sort of People in Provincial England 1600–1750* (Oxford: Oxford University Press, 2007), pp. 1–29.
19. K. Wrightson, *English Society 1580–1680* (London: Hutchinson, 1988 edn), p. 33; K. Wrightson, *Earthly Necessities: Economic Lives in Early Modern Britain, 1470–1750* (London: Penguin, 2002), p. 290.
20. D. W. Howell, *The Rural Poor in Eighteenth-Century Wales* (Cardiff: University of Wales Press, 2000), p. 10.
21. Trevecca College/1 3002, 8–10 July 1743.
22. Trevecca College/1 3009, January 1744.
23. For instance, Morgan Rhys referred to John Parry as 'Siôn' in an elegy, T. Levi (ed.), *Casgliad o hen farwnadau Cymreig, yn dal cysylltiad a chyfundeby Methodistiaid a waned ar ran y Gymanfa Gyffredinol* (Wrexham: Hughes a'i Fab, 1872), p. 55.
24. NLW, Morgan Richardson Collection (Gernos Deeds and Documents) 746, Letters of Administration of the goods of John Parry, 8 July 1747.
25. M. Spufford, *Contrasting Communities: English Villagers in the Sixteenth and*

Seventeenth Centuries (Stroud: Sutton Publishing, 2000), pp. 320–1.
26 NLW, St Davids Probate, SD/1764/132: James Williams, Llanddewibrefi, gentleman, 1764; SD/1775/202: Griffith Evans, Troedyraur, gentleman, 1775; SD/1744/60: John Williams, Llandingad, husbandman, 1744; SD/1749/29: Jenkin David, Cilrhedyn, husbandman.
27 *Welch Piety* (1772), p. 34; (1774), p. 142.
28 *Welch Piety* (1758), pp. 30–1.
29 E. G. Millward, 'Morgan Rhys (1716–1779)', *Oxford Dictionary of National Biography* (Oxford University Press, 23 September 2004). Accessed 30 September 2019, *https://www.oxforddnb.com/view/10.1093/ref:odnb/9780198614128.001.0001/odnb-9780198614128-e-23469*.
30 J. Morris, *Hanes Methodistiaeth Sir Gaerfyrddin* (Dolgellau: E. W. Evans, 1911), p. 16.
31 SD/1779/116: Morgan Rees, Llanfynydd, yeoman, 1779. T. Beynon, 'Morgan Rhys a Chylch Cilycwm hyd at Ystrad Ffin', *Cylchgrawn Cymdeithas Hanes y Methodistiaid Calfinaidd/Journal of the Historical Society of the Presbyterian Church of Wales*, 20 (1935), 145–7; G. M. Roberts, *Morgan Rhys, Llanfynydd*, pp. 8–9; D. H. Jones, 'Emynau Morgan Rhys', *Yr Eurgrawn*, 173 (1981), 83–7.
32 SD/1779/116; SD/1785/245: Mary Griffiths, Talley, widow, 1785. The full name is Glanyrafonddu-ganol, but it is usually referred to in Methodist records simply as Glanyrafonddu. As was often the case, there were a cluster of holdings with the same name, but distinguished by suffixes such as 'c/ganol', 'uchaf' and 'isaf' (middle, upper and lower).
33 Jones (ed.), *Gweithiau Williams Pantycelyn*, p. 552.
34 J. Morris, *Hanes Methodistiaeth Sir Gaerfyrddin* (1911), p. 244; G. M. Roberts, *Y Pêr Ganiedydd*, II, pp. 197–8.
35 J. Buckley, *Genealogies of the Carmarthenshire Sheriffs from 1539 to 1759* (2 vols, Carmarthen: Spurrell, 1910–13), I, p. 219.
36 NLW, Great Sessions, Wales 4, 737/1, 1739.
37 Morgan Richardson Collection (Gernos Deeds and Documents) 749, 1752.
38 SD/1744/60: John Williams, Llandingad, husbandman, 1744.
39 SD/1791/32: John Williams, Henllys, Cil-y-cwm, gentleman, 1791; G. M. Roberts, 'Y Tair Sasiwn Gyntaf, 1742: Dugoedydd, Llwynyberllan a Glanyrafonddu Ganol', *Cylchgrawn Cymdeithas Hanes y Methodistiaid Calfinaidd/Journal of the Historical Society of the Presbyterian Church of Wales*, 26/4 (1941), 97; D. E. Williams, 'Rice Williams: The Contact between Thomas Percy and Evan Evans', *Journal of the National Library of Wales*, 7 (1972), 287.
40 DHH 47a, 8 July 1739.
41 DHH 98, 29 March 1743.
42 Trevecka MS 832, Howel Harris to Joseph Harris, 26 March 1743.
43 DHH 112, 3 August 1744.
44 B. Phillips, *Peterwell: The History of a Mansion and its Infamous Squire* (Llandysul: Gomer, 1981), p. 73; F. Jones, *Historic Cardiganshire Homes and their Families*, ed. Caroline Charles Jones (Newport: Brawdy Books. 2000), pp. 193, 237.
45 DHH 50, 25 October 1739. This may have been Frances, daughter of James Griffiths of Neuadd, Llannarth, and wife of the Revd James Brooke, JP and vicar of Llannarth. Jones, *Historic Cardiganshire Homes*, p. 205.

46 DHH 84, 16 January 1742; F. Jones, *Historic Carmarthenshire Homes and their Families* (Newport, Pembrokeshire: Brawdy Books, 2006), p. 19; The will of John Phillips Williams of Bwlchgwynt, Meidrim, proved in 1778, is that of his son, as the father died in 1747; SD/1778/140: John Phillips Williams, Bwlchgwynt, Meidrim, Carmarthenshire, esquire, 1778.
47 Great Sessions, Wales 4 737/1, 1739; Jones, *Historic Carmarthenshire Homes*, p. 73.
48 Trevecka MS 295, Howel Harris to John Mathias, 10 December 1740.
49 R. T. Jenkins, *The Moravian Brethren in North Wales* (London: Honourable Society of the Cymmrodorion, 1938), 95–9; F. Jones, *Historic Houses of Pembrokeshire and their Families*, ed. Robert Innes Smith, compiled by Caroline Charles-Jones (Newport: Brawdy Books, 1996), pp. 114–15.
50 DHH 84, 12–13 January 1742; D. W. Howell, *Patriarchs and Parasites: The Gentry of South-west Wales in the Eighteenth Century* (Cardiff: University of Wales Press, 1986), p. 210.
51 DHH 115b, 7 February 1745.
52 For a full account, see B. Phillips, *Peterwell: The History of a Mansion and its Infamous Squire* (Llandysul: Gomer, 1981).
53 DHH, 6 May 1763.
54 Morgan Richardson Collection (Gernos Deeds and Documents) 723, 20 December 1714; L. Baker-Jones, *Princelings, Privilege and Power: The Tivyside Gentry in their Community* (Llandysul: Gomer, 1999), p. 47.
55 For instance, DHH 112, 23 July 1744; Trevecka MS 1144, Watkin Watkins to Howel Harris, 9 March 1744; 1337, Watkin Watkins to Howel Harris, 30 June 1745.
56 Trevecka MS 1337, Watkin Watkins to Howel Harris, 30 June 1745.
57 Trevecca College/1 3055, 30 August 1748.
58 *The Evangelical Magazine* (London, 1799), 398.
59 NLW, Haverfordwest (Williams and Williams) MS 25920, John Parry, Cwmcynon, co. Cardigan, Hester Howells, Llanfihangel-ar-arth parish, agreement before marriage, 1739; Jones, *Historic Cardiganshire Homes*, p. 121.
60 Trevecka MS 1760, Howel Davies to Howel Harris, 30 January 1748; DHH 132, 8 September 1748.
61 Morgan Richardson (Gernos), 751, 19 December 1758.
62 Morgan Richardson (Gernos), 765, 29 February 1772; 785, 10 June 1778.
63 S. R. Meyrick, *The History and Antiquities of the County of Cardigan* (London: Longman, 1808), p. 232; Baker-Jones, *Princelings, Privilege and Power*, p. 47.
64 G. M. Roberts, 'Capten John Evans, Pen-y-Wenallt', *Cylchgrawn Cymdeithas Hanes y Methodistiaid Calfinaidd/Journal of the Historical Society of the Presbyterian Church of Wales*, 41 (1956), 76; G. H. Jenkins, *Theophilus Evans (1693–1767): Y Dyn, Ei Deulu a'i Oes* (Aberystwyth: Adran Gwasanaethau Diwylliannol Dyfed, 1993), p. 11.
65 NLW, Neuadd–fawr Estate Records 350, Settlement prior to marriage of John Williams and Barbara Williams, 13 February 1717.
66 Roberts, 'Y Tair Sasiwn Gyntaf', 97–8; Williams, 'Rice Williams: The Contact between Thomas Percy and Evan Evans', p. 288.
67 Roberts, 'Y Llafurwyr Cynnar', p. 249.

68 SD/1744/60.
69 Williams, 'Rice Williams: The Contact between Thomas Percy and Evan Evans', p. 289; DHH 241, 30 March 1763.
70 SD/1799/44: Mary James, Penrhyn, Cil-y-cwm, widow, 1799; SD/1789/34: William James, Pwllpriddog, Cil-y-cwm, 1789; Roberts, 'Tair Sasiwn Gyntaf, 1742', 97; Williams, 'Rice Williams: The Contact between Thomas Percy and Evan Evans', 289; Jones, *Historic Carmarthenshire Homes*, p. 94.
71 SD/1779/79: Daniel Williams, Llwynyberllan, Llandingad, gentleman, 1779. His bequest was to his nephew, the third John Williams of Llwynyberllan.
72 Neuadd-fawr MS 350, 13 February 1717; 351, 11 July 1788.
73 Trevecka MS 293, Howel Harris to Anne and Elizabeth Thomas, 10 December 1740.
74 Trevecka MS 294, Howel Harris to Mary Mathias, 10 December 1740.
75 T. Beynon, 'Morfa Bach, Cydweli', *Cylchgrawn Cymdeithas Hanes y Methodistiaid Calfinaidd/Journal of the Historical Society of the Presbyterian Church of Wales*, 16 (1931), 100–5; T. Beynon, *Allt Cunedda, Llechdwnni a Mwdlwscwm* (Aberystwyth, 1955), pp. 78–83.
76 Trevecka MS 1063, Elizabeth Thomas to Howel Harris, 28 December 1743.
77 J. E. Lloyd (ed.), *A History of Carmarthenshire, II: From the Act of Union (1536) to 1900* (Cardiff: William Lewis, 1939), p. 460; F. Jones, 'Portraits and Pictures in Old Carmarthenshire Houses', *Carmarthenshire Historian*, 5 (1968), 46–7.
78 DHH 99, 23 May 1743; Carmarthenshire Archives, Quarter Sessions Records, QS/1/1, 1748–51; F. Jones, 'The Families of Berllandywyll', *Carmarthenshire Historian* (1978), 43–62.
79 Ottley (Pitchford Hall MSS and Documents) 262, 1 April 1714.
80 His son Robert Dyer, who died in 1752, was referred to 'the old man of the house' by Harris, in contrast to Robert Archer Dyer, the young lawyer whom he had befriended. DHH 98, 24–5 March 1743; Howell, *Patriarchs and Parasites*, p. 42.
81 F. Green, 'The Dyers of Aberglasney', *West Wales Historical Records*, 7 (1917–18), 93–108; F. Jones, 'Aberglasney and its Families', *National Library of Wales Journal*, 21 (1979), 12–14; B. Humfrey, *John Dyer*, Writers of Wales (Cardiff: University of Wales Press, 1980), pp. 5–8.
82 DHH 112, 12 July 1744.
83 DHH 115b, 24 January 1745.
84 DHH133, 4 January 1749.
85 DHH 66, 7–8 December 1740; G. M. Roberts, *Portread o Ddiwygiwr* (Caernarfon: Bwrdd Ymddiriedolwyr y Ddarlith Davies, 1969), p. 93; Howell, *Patriarchs and Parasites*, p. 210.
86 Trevecka MS 294, Howel Harris to Mary Mathias, 10 December 1740.
87 Jenkins, *The Moravian Brethren in North Wales*, p. 97.
88 DHH 82, 33 November 1741.
89 DHH 110, 25 May 1744; Williams, 'Rice Williams: The Contact between Thomas Percy and Evan Evans', 288–9; Jones, *Historic Carmarthenshire Homes*, p. 115.
90 DHH 101, 19–20 July 1743.
91 SD/1742/41: Griffith Twyning, Parke, Henllan Amgoed, gentleman, 1741.
92 See Howell, *Patriarchs and Parasites*.

93 A. Everitt, *The Pattern of Rural Dissent: The Nineteenth Century* (Leicester: Leicester University Press, 1972).
94 S. Lewis, *A Topographical Dictionary of Wales ... Volume Two* (London: S. Lewis & Co., 1833), p. 64; Jones, *Historic Houses of Pembrokeshire*, pp. 108–9.
95 NLW, Lucas Collection 2816, Rental of the estate of the bishop of St Davids in co. Pembroke, post 1759; 3833, Memorandum on leases, post 1757.
96 SD/1767/239: Thomas Griffiths, Talley, gentleman, 1767; SD/1785/245: Mary Griffiths, Talley, widow, 1785; Roberts, 'Y Tair Sasiwn Gyntaf', 99.
97 NLW, Edwinsford Estate Records 2201, 13 October 1736; 2305, 3 August 1758.
98 Edwinsford Estate Records 2292, 21 year lease to John David, Llansawel, yeoman, 10 October 1746; SD/1788/190: David John, Llansawel, 1788.
99 D. L. Baker-Jones, 'Edwinsford', *Carmarthenshire Historian*, 5 (1968), 20–1; Howell, *Patriarchs and Parasites*, pp. 114, 123–5.
100 There were five farmsteads in the hamlet of Cilcarw, so it is difficult to know whether this was Cilcarw Uchaf, Isaf, Fawr, Fach or Ganol (that is Upper, Lower, Greater, Lesser or Middle Cilcarw). D. Williams, 'Cilcarw Uchaf Farm in the Hamlet of Cilcarw in the Ecclesiastical Parish of Llangyndeyrn', *Carmarthenshire Antiquary*, 47 (2011), 145.
101 The house was commonly known as 'Tŷ Newydd' or 'new house' and later became Soar Chapel. Morris, *Hanes Methodistiaeth Sir Gaerfyrddin*, p. 155; E. R. Davies, 'The Deeds of Soar C.M. Chapel, Cil-y-cwm', *Cylchgrawn Cymdeithas Hanes y Methodistiaid Calfinaidd/Journal of the Historical Society of the Presbyterian Church of Wales*, 27 (1942), 1–6; G. M. Roberts, 'Pa bryd y codwyd Capel Soar, Cil-y-cwm?', *Cylchgrawn Cymdeithas Hanes y Methodistiaid Calfinaidd/Journal of the Historical Society of the Presbyterian Church of Wales*, 27 (1942), 106.
102 NLW, D. T. M. Jones Records 2441, c. 1775.
103 SD/1793/38: Isaac Davies, Dolgynon, Cil-y-cwm.
104 Morgan Richardson Collection (Gernos) 749, 1752.
105 G. M. Roberts, 'Methodistiaeth Gynnar Gwaelod Sir Aberteifi', *Ceredigion*, 5 (1964), 7.
106 DHH 101, 22–3 July 1743.
107 Trevecka MS 811, Howel Harris to George Whitefield, 1 March 1743.
108 Trevecca College/1 3057, John Harry to the Association, 2 May 1748.
109 NLW MS 5456A, p. 27b, 25 March 1744.
110 NLW MS 18435B, p. 25, 24 September 1741.
111 J. Walsh, 'John Wesley and the community of goods', in K. Robbins (ed.), *Protestant Evangelicalism: Britain, Ireland, Germany and America, c. 1750–c. 1950: Essay in Honour of W. R. Ward*, Studies in Church History, Subsidia, 7 (Oxford: Blackwell, 1990), p. 35. See also M. A. Noll, *God and Mammon: Protestants, Money and the Market 1790–1860* (Oxford: Oxford University Press, 2001).
112 Hughes (ed.), *Gweithiau William Williams Pantycelyn*, II, p. 240.
113 Wrightson, *Earthly Neccessities*, p. 289.
114 SD/1744/60; SD/1754/6.
115 SD/1770/; SD/1777/53: Eaton Griffith, Fishguard, yeoman, 1777.
116 SD/1788/36: Anne Williams, Glangwenlais (Glanywenlas), Cil-y-cwm, widow, 1788.

117 D. Rowland, *Pum Pregeth* (Caerfyrddin: John Ross, 1772), p. 210; Roberts, 'Tanysgrifwyr Pregethau Cymraeg Daniel Rowland', 44; Hughes, *Methodistiaeth Cymru*, II, p, 451.
118 L. Baker-Jones shows a range of between £19 and £398 as the cash amounts left by the gentry of the Teifi Valley, with little difference between the poorer gentry and richer yeomen. Baker-Jones, *Princelings, Privilege and Power*, pp. 39–41.
119 SD/1778/32: Thomas Richard, Galltybere, Cil-y-cwm, carpenter, 1788.
120 SD/1776/138: John Richard, Llansamlet, clockmaker, 1776.
121 Hughes (ed.), *Gweithiau William Williams Pantycelyn*, II, p. 199.
122 Trevecca College/1 3023, p. 46, 14 January 1747.
123 J. Hughes, *Methodistiaeth Cymru*, II, pp. 425–6; M. H. Jones, 'An Interesting Legal Document, Throwing Light on early Welsh Methodism', *Cylchgrawn Cymdeithas Hanes y Methodistiaid Calfinaidd/Journal of the Historical Society of the Presbyterian Church of Wales*, 15 (1930), 14–23.
124 SD/1779/116: Morgan Rees, Llanfynydd, Carmarthenshire, yeoman, 1779.
125 SD/1799/4: Mary James, Penrhyn, Cil-y-cwm, 1799.
126 SD/1767/239: Thomas Griffiths, Talley, 1767.
127 SD/1785/245: Mary Griffiths, Talley, widow, 1785.
128 Roberts, 'Y Tair Sasiwn Gyntaf, 1742', 98.
129 Hughes, *Methodistiaeth* Cymru, II, p. 425.
130 SD/1767/239.
131 SD/1791/107: William Williams, Llanfair-ar-y-bryn, Carmarthen, clerk, 1791.
132 SD/1754/6: David James, Llwynyceiliog, Caeo, gentleman, 1754,
133 SD/1763/51: Griffith Jones, Cynwyl Elfed, gentleman, 1763.
134 SD/1743/144: David Jones, Maesnonni, Llanllwni, 1743.
135 SD/1777/53.
136 G. M. Roberts, *Hanes Plwyf Llandybïe* (Caerdydd: Gwasg Prifysgol Cymru, 1939), pp. 52, 114, 135, 145.
137 Trevecca College/1 2945, p. 18, 8 June 1743.
138 SD/1743/144.
139 SD/1790/112: David Rees, Clyncoch, Llangrannog, Cardigan, 1790.
140 Rowland, *Pum Pregeth*, p. 210; Hughes, *Methodistiaeth Cymru*, II, p. 319; G. M. Roberts, 'Tanysgrifwyr Pregethau Cymraeg Daniel Rowland', *Cylchgrawn Cymdeithas Hanes y Methodistiaid Calfinaidd/Journal of the Historical Society of the Presbyterian Church of Wales*, 45 (1960), 42. Howel Harris spent the night at Parcybedw, Tre-lech, in 1741, but, as was his common practice, failed to record the name of his host.
141 See E. Rees, 'Pre-1830 Welsh Subscription Lists', *Journal of the Welsh Bibliographical Society*, 11 (1974), 85–119; G. H. Jenkins, *Religion, Literature and Society in Wales 1660–1730* (Cardiff: University of Wales Press, 1978); E. Rees, 'The Welsh book trade from 1718 to 1820', in *A Nation and its Books: A History of the Book in Wales*, ed. P. H. Jones and E. Rees (Aberystwyth: National Library of Wales, 1998), pp. 123–33.
142 SD/1779/116; SD/1790/112.
143 SD/1179/116.
144 SD/1777/138: Watkin Watkins, Gwndwn, Llangrannog, 1777.
145 Rowland, *Pum Pregeth*, p. 210.
146 Howell, *Patriarchs and Parasites*, p. 172.

CHAPTER 5

'Iron Sharpens Iron'[1]:
The Appeal of the Societies

Despite indulging in periodic outpourings of revival up until the last episode in 1904–5, Welsh Calvinistic Methodism managed to establish a solidly sober and respectable image for itself during the nineteenth and twentieth centuries, which has perhaps coloured the perception of the nature of the movement's appeal in the eighteenth century. The established denomination might seem somewhat at odds with the vibrant and novel nature of the early years, during which the movement came up with a portfolio of activities which succeeded in attracting a significant, but far from mass, response. It was select groups that were first recruited, chiefly from certain sections of society. With little headway yet made in north Wales, this was almost exclusively a phenomenon of south Wales before subsequent revivals in the eighteenth century drew in substantial support in the north.

Preaching

Most members were first drawn to the movement by preaching, with the leaders in particular often being cited as the key influence for many converts. There was traditionally a 'taste for sermons' in pre-revival south-west Wales,[2] as evidenced by Erasmus Saunders's description of congregations happy to travel some four miles on foot to hear a sermon, as well as the enthusiastic response to Griffith Jones.[3] A good preacher could draw a sizeable congregation in the area. In the case of Methodist preaching, there were two elements to the attraction: the message and the manner in which it was conveyed. Although it was relatively easy for opponents to depict the Calvinist theology as narrow and forbidding, much of the emphasis at the time was on the more positive theme of grace and atonement. Howel Harris had on several occasions tried his hardest to win over David Lloyd of Berllandywyll, believing that he had never had such power to wrestle for any other soul. He afterwards felt that the experience had taught him that his arguments were worth nothing and that only 'invincible grace' could bring about conversion.[4]

In many descriptions of their preaching, the law and the gospel were commonly contrasted: the one one to do with convincing sinners of their sinfulness and the other to do with mercy and forgiveness.[5] Preaching the law with conviction was part and parcel of Methodist exhorting, including stern warnings that judgement and damnation were the inevitable results of sinfulness. When in this mode, Harris frequently described his own preaching with phrases such as 'most thundering and dreadful', 'terrible and convincing', 'to cut and lash home', 'powerful and cutting', 'horrible and home'.[6] In Caeo in 1740, he apparently spoke specifically to a group of children, showing them 'Happiness in this World & in Death what They shall then see & in Judgmt & to Eternity'.[7] In Brechfa in 1741, he had begun in an effort to speak gently, but soon found himself 'turn'd to ye Law & that in ye most cruel bitter terrible words I could find – I felt in my spirit roughness – denouncing all woes – calling them Dogs – stones &c'.[8] Thomas Morgan heard him speak along similar lines in March 1741, noting that

> His subject was, to show ye corruption of man's nature by ye fall, and ye miserable condition, wherein ye sinner stands in his natural condition, as being whoremongers by ye Lust of ye eye, and being Murderers by hating one another, and loving and fearing ye creature more than God. Here I was tossed, and tumbled, in ye case of my soul, that I knew not whether was I converted or not ...[9]

John Thomas of Rhaeadr heard Harris 'preaching the law' in severe fashion at Rhiwiau in Llanddeusant in 1745, warning his audience that they might have read the Bible for forty years but still know no more of God than would a dog or a pig, and that if they did not let God into their hearts, then devils would rend them asunder on the day of judgement.[10] Those words changed Thomas's life and he would always consider

Harris his spiritual father thereafter. Elaborate metaphors would be used to reinforce the warnings, such as at Cwm-ann on the Carmarthenshire banks of the river Teifi, where Harris warned his audience that they were heading towards hell as if carried by the currents of the river, urging them to leave the water for the safety of the ark.[11] Some of these exhortations obviously succeeded in the aim of making people aware of their sinfulness. That could lead to a state of near despair which might last for some weeks. One young girl who had been influenced by hearing Harris preach at Ystrad-ffin tried to describe her feelings, explaining that she then looked on her own heart as if a cover had been lifted off a tub to reveal the dreadful monsters lurking within.[12] John Thomas evoked a similar response when exhorting on the destruction of Sodom and Gomorrah at Tregaron one evening, when one of the women cried out that she was the greatest of sinners. For the next fortnight, she wandered around in a state of bewilderment until being comforted by a sermon of Daniel Rowland's at Llangeitho.[13]

Daniel Rowland had apparently placed a greater emphasis on the law and the perils of flouting it in the aftermath of his own conversion experience, gaining a reputation as 'the angry cleric'. Richard Tibbott recorded hearing both Rowland and David Jenkins preach on one occasion in Llansawel, summing up the gist of their sermons as mainly 'thundering threats'.[14] William Williams described hearers quaking under the blast of such preaching.[15] Rowland later softened his message to concentrate more on the gospel, on the advice of the Dissenting minister Philip Pugh, who warned that he was likely to kill half the country if he carried on in the same reproving vein.[16] Along with exhortations to repent, there was therefore also a joyous aspect to the Methodist message. Harris referred to this form of preaching as 'evangelising'. Although he was said to describe hell in such detail that he might have been there himself,[17] one of his favourite texts on which to preach was actually 1 John 4:10: 'Herein is love, not that we loved God, but that he loved us, and sent his Son to be the propitiation for our sins.' Rowland would also often dwell on the comfort offered to believers, assuring them that God was fire when cold and Christ food when starving.[18] During the early 1740s, he was gaining fame as one of the greatest preachers of the age and the benchmark by which other performances were judged. As Densil Morgan states, in the case of Rowland, there is 'no doubt that verve, order and extraordinary spiritual power went hand in hand'.[19] When Harris sought to praise a sermon by William Williams he did so by suggesting that some of Rowland's spirit had descended upon his younger colleague.[20] At the age of seventeen, John Elias, who would become one of most prominent Welsh Methodists of the nineteenth century, on hearing of Rowland's death was grief-stricken by the realisation that he would never now have the experience of hearing a sermon from this remarkable preacher.[21]

Since many Methodists were converted as the result of hearing a sermon, there seems to have been a particular attachment to the preacher concerned. As William William's character, Martha Philopur declared, '*mi gofiaf y lle, yr awr, y bregeth a'r pregethwr tra fwyf yn anadlu ar dir y rhai byw*' ('I will remember the place, the hour, the sermon and the preacher while I breathe in the land of the living'),[22] a statement which accords with the testimony of several members who recalled the circumstances vividly. Williams was likely to have heard several such accounts during his time visiting societies and listening to the experiences of the members. A number of them hailed either Rowland or Harris as their spiritual father, as Williams himself did with Harris. Thomas Morgan, Henllan Amgoed, a student at Carmarthen Academy, experienced conversion after listening to Harris exhort and maintained a respect for Harris as a result despite being fairly critical of the Methodists in general.[23]

Preaching by the main leaders of the movement evidently held a particular appeal and there were constant requests for visits, as well as frequent trips to hear them preach in their own vicinity in the case of the beneficed clergy. John Thomas of Tre-main believed that Daniel Rowland's priceless preaching made the journey to Llangeitho always worth the trouble.[24] The Methodists are not to be trusted regarding estimates of their congregations, given a marked tendency to exaggerate beyond the bounds of probability. That is doubtless partly the result of the difficulty at the time in gauging the size of a crowd, a calculation which remains problematic, even with the benefit of film and photographic evidence. There may also have been a desire to make as positive a statement as possible about the impact of the movement. In one week in February 1741, Harris claimed to have addressed 2,000 people in Tre-lech in Carmarthenshire on Monday and 5,000–8,000 in Clydau in

Pembrokeshire on Tuesday. Reaching Cardiganshire on Wednesday, he recorded crowds of 8,000–10,000 in Blaen-porth and 5,000–6,000 in Llechryd, but merely 'some hundreds' in Cardigan town on Thursday and 2,000–3,000 in Newport, Pembrokeshire, on Friday.[25] Since the estimated population of Cardiganshire was around 27,000, Carmarthenshire 42,000 and Pembrokeshire 29,000, these would be extraordinarily large gatherings for such sparsely populated rural areas.[26] Some of the largest crowds attending any Methodist gathering were for communion services held by Rowland at Llangeitho, and Rowland's servant suggested that the numbers were usually in the region of 1,000–1,500.[27] That was probably easier to calculate with rather greater accuracy as the number of places in rotation at the communion table could be counted. It seems unlikely that any of the leaders or exhorters addressed larger crowds than those at Llangeitho, which would have been very substantial for the period.

Preaching was a time-consuming and demanding business, in terms of travel and preparation. Daniel Rowland's daughter noted that it was no easy task to drag her father out of his study, where he devoted a great deal of time to reading and to planning his sermons.[28] Densil Morgan confirms that the printed versions of his sermons were 'reasoned' and 'polished', carefully crafted and subdivided in Puritan mode, clear and direct throughout.[29] Harris seems to have favoured a more impromptu approach, at least at times, as he occasionally decided on the subject of his sermon by opening the Bible and choosing a verse at random.[30] There was a sense of needing to tailor the message to suit the level of experience of the audience, to use the language of 'milk not strong meat' in the first instance.[31] Harris would also sometimes adapt his message to suit his location. In Cardigan, for instance, he explained that it was no more possible to change the course of nature than it was to turn the river Teifi which ran through the town, at least, he concluded, 'till Christ comes in like ye Tyde'.[32] Speaking by the castle walls which held the gaol, and near which condemned felons were hanged in Carmarthen, he was inspired to a lengthy comparison between the offer of God's grace and the prospect of a man awaiting execution receiving not just a King's pardon but the offer of being adopted as a member of the King's own family.[33] A more homely touch was not uncommon, with Daniel Rowland using an extended metaphor relating to the very familiar routine of harvest, with God as the husbandman.³⁴ Although Methodists urged discarding the old man in favour of the new, the term 'new birth' does not figure largely in the accounts of Methodist preaching, whereas 'repentance' does. They may have taken to heart Griffith Jones's advice to use 'repentance' if it seemed a more palatable term than 'new birth'.³⁵

The message of the preaching was part of the attraction, but added to that was the dynamism with which that message was delivered. The written versions or summaries of some of the Methodist sermons cannot convey the power of the delivery, nor reveal the style, mannerisms or vocal tricks employed. There is, however, plenty of evidence of the power of the spoken word when conveyed with the profound enthusiasm which characterised the movement. John Thomas of Rhaeadr found particular pleasure in listening to Methodist exhorters, as they gave the impression that they were speaking directly to him.³⁶ The Parry family of Cwmcynon, Llandysiliogogo, having grown accustomed to the livelier preaching of Daniel Rowland, Howel Harris and Howel Davies, confessed that other preachers struck them as lacklustre in comparison.³⁷ Doubtless some hearers were drawn by curiosity and the prospect of novelty. Archdeacon Edward Tenison noted the attractions of a new preacher in his report on the Carmarthen Archdeaconry in 1710, indicating that parishioners were more tempted to attend Dissenting meetings when an unfamiliar preacher was announced.³⁸ Methodism would have had a similar appeal, especially as in some ways it was more unconventional and less easy to label than Dissent. Since it was not always possible to keep to an exact schedule, congregations often had to be patient and many seemed content to wait as long as necessary for some of the most esteemed of the Methodist preachers. A group at Loughor had to wait for four hours for Harris to arrive to keep his engagement in 1745.³⁹ A large crowd at Caeo in 1740 whiled away the time singing psalms and hymns, the sound of which greeted Harris as he arrived. Their patience was rewarded with a two-hour sermon during which, Harris noted, there was an almost continual groaning and crying.⁴⁰ At least one of the elements of the success of this preaching was the use of the natural language of communication, be it Welsh in most areas of the south-west or English in the more anglicised regions of south Pembrokeshire. Harris occasionally specified in his diary that he spoke in both English and Welsh, for instance in Carmarthen, a town where English was likely to be more familiar than in much of the surrounding countryside. It is very likely that these occasions were notable because they were exceptions to the general trend of using Welsh throughout most of the south-west. The Wesley brothers and George Whitefield were challenged by the lack of knowledge of English in many parts of Wales. When Charles Wesley was announced to preach in Builth in 1748, Harris warned that hundreds of Welsh people would not understand him.[41] Whitefield would usually have a Welsh-speaker accompany him on visits to Wales, often preaching after the great man, as Harris did when he accompanied him on a tour through Swansea, Carmarthen, Cydweli, Laugharne and Narberth in April 1743.[42] It is difficult to know how much of an impact a preacher like Whitefield could have where many would have been unable to understand him, but some aspects such as gestures and modulation of the voice probably transcended the language used.

The joyous responses engendered among some of the hearers gained the Methodists their reputation for heady enthusiasm, along with the nickname 'Jumpers' for their exuberant behaviour. Meetings were often interrupted by cries of *'bendigedig'* ('blessed'), *'gogoniant'* ('glory') and 'hallelujah'. On one occasion in Llanfair-ar-y-bryn, Harris could hardly hear himself preach as those present began weeping and crying fervently for the space of nearly two hours.[43] At times, Harris joined in the exaltations, as in Cil-y-cwm in 1748 when 'I was made to dance to beat and cry allelujah Gogoniant'.[44] At Glanyrafonddu, the shouts were so loud that Harris had to cease speaking, claiming that 'ye Power in me was so great that I did allmost leap over ye Heads of ye People & they continued singing afterward to 1'.[45] There would often be this sort of aftermath to such highly charged occasions, as those affected took time to come to terms and to regain some sort of equilibrium. One man was so strongly affected by hearing Harris at Longhouse, Mathry, in March 1743 that he could not stop weeping copiously after the meeting finished at 3 a.m.[46] On one occasion, Harris was writing letters at 3 a.m. from Rinaston in Pembrokshire, to the sound of three women singing hymns in the distance, the sweetest music he said he had ever heard.[47] Again, at Glanyrafonddu, those assembled continued singing for three hours after Harris had discoursed.[48] Impromptu late night hymn singing seems to have been a fairly common informal postscript to Methodist meetings, with Richard Tibbott recording that he continued to sing hymns with some of the women of the societies until 2 a.m.[49]

Much of the joyful reaction was caused by the preaching about grace and forgiveness. This came as an intense relief for those who had previously come to a conviction of their sinfulness, a state in which they might languish for some time. Conversion could be an extended process, often beginning with a sermon, but sometimes stemming from another influence. David Jones, of Dygoed, Llanarthney, for instance, traced the beginning of his conversion to reading John Bunyan's *Come and Welcome to Jesus Christ*.[50] Howel Davies had felt the love of God so strongly that he was unable to sleep or taste food for a week.[51] William Richard described members in the societies of Dinas and Newport in Pembrokeshire who felt 'they were convinc'd of their Lost & Damned Estate in the first Adam and in themselves & also how all their Hapiness Intirely lie in Him'.[52] A woman from Llanddewibrefi told Harris that she felt the love of God burning constantly in her soul.[53] It was these sorts of experiences that William Williams mined in order to produce the account of conversion offered by his character Martha, who was overcome by fearfulness and despair at her sinfulness in the first instance:

> *Uwchben ffwrn o dân berwedig, tân a brwmstan, mwg pa un sydd yn esgyn i fyny yn oes oesoedd, yr oeddwn yn hongian; nid oedd ond y mymryn lleiaf rhyngwyf a myned at ddiafliaid tros byth. Tebyg'swn fod sawyr Uffern yn codi i fyny yn fy ffroenau; mi anghofiais fwyta fy mara. Nid oedd ond tragwyddol boenau o flaen fy llygaid nos a dydd, ofnau oedd yn fy amgylchu fel byddin.*[54]

> I was hanging over a furnace of boiling fire, fire and brimstone, with the smoke rising up for ever and ever; only the slightest scrap of distance separated me from spending eternity with devils. I imagined that the stench of Hell rose in my nostrils; I forgot to eat my bread. There was nothing but eternal pains before my eyes day and night, fears surrounded me like an army.

After a long period of feeling despair raging within her, and at her very lowest point, she came to see in the space of a minute that her sins were forgiven. Williams has Martha use the same metaphor as Harris also employed of the prisoner under the gallows tree receiving a last-minute reprieve. Since that moment, Martha could not forbear from rejoicing and praising God publicly, something which she would previously have regarded as utter folly.

The *Seiat* and its Activities

Although the initial appeal often came through fervent preaching, it was the *seiat* or society which was the key to keeping hold of the members. The enthusiasm of revival could be a temporary condition, and the function of the society was to maintain the converts in their faith having reached the point of conversion. The origins of the private society as an institution are by no means completely clear, but it was to some extent a practical solution to the necessity of arranging some provision for the converts of Methodist preaching. It emerged in the context of pietistic influences and of the surge in moral reform and religious societies in general by the start of the eighteenth century.[55] These were fuelled by general concerns about lawbreaking, drunkenness and immorality, especially in London, leading to an upsurge in non-state, voluntary initiatives to help address the situation. Although much of the original impetus was associated with efforts to revive the Anglican Church, Dissenters became increasingly involved in such activity after 1689. The work of the Anglican clergyman, Josiah Woodward, *An Account of the Religious Societies in the City of London*, is often cited as a possible influence on the Methodist movement, since it provided guidance on setting up societies.[56] For years, Howel Harris claimed to have started to establish societies before having read the book for the first time in 1739. By 1750, however, he had revised this account and stated on more than one occasion that he arranged the members into private societies as a consequence of reading Woodward's book: 'I shewd how ye first societies were settled by my reading Woodward's Account of Religious Societies.'[57] Geraint Tudur suggests that there may be no inconsistency here, as Harris may have started to set up societies on his own initiative but then organised them more formally after consulting Woodward.[58] There certainly seems to be considerable common ground between Woodward's account and the societies which emerged in Wales. The Welsh Methodist movement published its own guidelines regarding the purpose and conduct of the societies quite early on, in manuscript form in 1740 and in print in 1742. George Whitefield's *A letter from the Rev. Mr. George Whitefield to the religious societies lately set on foot in several parts of England and Wales* (1740) was quickly translated into Welsh in 1740.[59] William Williams would later also address the issue of the aims and procedure of the societies in his *Drws y Society Profiad* (The Door of the Experience Meeting, 1777), one of the most valuable descriptions of the eighteenth-century Methodist society.[60] Unsurprisingly, all these sources argue along very similar lines when it comes to outlining the purpose of and justification for the societies, in tune with Woodward's description of the main aim of religious societies: 'Mutual Assistance and Consolation one of another in their Christian warfare'.[61] In most cases, there was an attempt to cite biblical precedents for such activity in order to provide the societies with a sound foundation. Doubtless bearing in mind the vital importance of Scripture to the Protestant faith, Williams pointed out that many practices which are not specifically ordained as duties in the Bible may yet reasonably be adopted because of their obvious usefulness. He argued that the private society should be regarded in that list of necessary and advantageous undertakings.[62]

One of the main activities designated for the society members was to open their hearts to each other to share their experiences. Fellowship was regarded as essential in order for the members to maintain each other in the faith, without backsliding. Williams suggested that

> *fel y mae haearn yn hogi haearn, felly gŵr sydd yn hogi wyneb ei gyfaill. Y mae gan gyfeillach effaith fawr iawn i'n bywiocáu at dda neu at ddrwg, a pha foddion well i fywiogrwydd nag ymgasglu at ein gilydd i gyd-weddio, cyd-ganu, ac adrodd mor dda bu Duw i un a'r llall wedi'r tro diwethaf?*[63]

> as iron sharpens iron, so a man sharpens the countenance of his friend. Fellowship has a very great effect to invigorate us for good or ill, and what better means to liveliness than to gather together to pray together, to sing together, and to

relate how good God has been to one and another since the last time.

Enthusiasm was infectious, as William Richard testified: 'I find when the Power of God cometh unto a society that it will work upon all one way or other.'[64] Society members were offered ample opportunity to come together to share their experiences. The forty members of Lledrod society in north Cardiganshire, for instance, met twice a week with their private exhorter, David Williams, who exhorted and questioned them on their progress. These regular meetings may have helped ensure that they, as William Williams reported, not only kept up their first love, fire and zeal, but also increased in faith.[65] Richard Tibbott's diaries also provide an insight into the active life of a Methodist convert in Carmarthenshire in the early 1740s, with a network of homes and individuals already established and plenty of meetings to hear preachers and exchange experiences in the society.[66] This evidently continued to be the case in parts of the south-west even after the division in the leadership in 1750, with the diary of John Thomas, Tre-main, demonstrating continued activity and a persistent Methodist network in operation.[67]

Society meetings, like preaching meetings, could be remarkably lively events. William John reported that Llanpumsaint society could not refrain from constantly praising God.[68] William Richard marvelled at the faith of the members of Blaenhownant society, who would spend evenings shouting, crying and praising God. They never met without being overcome with joy, as if 'wattered with the Dew of heaven'.[69] When Harris visited Llechryd society in 1748, he claimed that for two hours they experienced 'nothing but praising, singing *Bendigedig, gogoniant*, allelujah, praises etc'.[70] Watkin Watkins, the steward of Llwyndafydd and Blaenhownant societies, wrote to Harris in 1745 to describe the enthusiasm which characterised those under his care: 'Now a late our societies is in a heavenly flame. He did revive us with His Love a fresh, and more than ever; our work is to prays God, many times, singing Halelujah's from night to morning in an Extasy of Joy in the Holy Ghost.'[71] During a visit to Blaen-porth in 1745, Harris acknowledged that such joy could not easily be contained, a fact which he claimed justified the hubbub of enthusiasm.[72] William Williams summed up the response in his *Drws y*

Society Profiad, when he claimed that the people of the society were so comforted by society meetings that they came from them as happy as *'meddwon o'r gwindy'* ('drunkards from the wine-house').[73]

A good deal of this rejoicing manifested itself through unprompted bursts of hymn singing, which certainly became an element in the appeal of the movement. The hymn became the 'most distinctive, characteristic and ubiquituous feature of the Methodist message'.[74] This period witnessed the development of congregational hymn singing which had not been a major feature of public worship prior to this, apart from the use of metrical psalms. The evangelical revival was chiefly responsible for the real start of the tradition of communal hymn singing in Wales to express a range of emotions from jubilation to anguish. The first rule book, in 1742, suggested that societies should begin their meetings by singing praise, and contains the first attempts at fashioning hymns for the use of the societies.[75] Most of the hymns from the early 1740s were written by Daniel Rowland, Howel Harris and Howel Davies, including those contained in the Llangeitho Manuscript from around 1742.[76] However, it must be said that none of their hymns are still sung and none were included in the official Welsh Calvinistic Methodist hymn book when it appeared in the nineteenth century. That is not to say that they are of notably poor quality, but they were soon eclipsed by William Williams, Pantycelyn, as well as other talented hymn writers produced by the movement during the eighteenth century, such as Morgan Rhys, Llanfynydd, and Ann Griffiths of Dolanog in Montgomeryshire.[77] Several Dissenting hymn writers had also spent time in Methodist circles and were influenced by the revival, including John Thomas of Rhaeadr and the Baptist Dafydd William. It was Williams Pantycelyn, however, who was acclaimed, then and since, as 'the sweet singer' of the revival. His hymns had the power to move congregations and to help inspire fresh spiritual awakenings, as in the 1762 Llangeitho revival.

The significance of communal hymn singing to the movement is apparent in the inclusion of hymns in the first rule book. This was reinforced with the publication of the first book of hymns for the Methodists in 1744, *Hymnau Duwiol Yw canu mewn cymdeithasau Crefyddol* (Godly Hymns to be Sung in Religious Societies). This collection was largely the work of Rowland, but contained two hymns by Williams, whose own first volume of hymns appeared in the same year. Williams would later explain that such hymns were part of a biblical tradition, since songs of praise were to be heard in the temple of Solomon:

Nid yn unig yn gysgod o hyfryd lais yr efengyl, ond hefyd fel moddion yn absenoldeb tywalltiad yr Ysbryd, sef addewid y Tad i ddyrchafu ysbryd addolwyr Dduw i'w ganmol a'i ryfeddu ef. Yr oedd cymaint o leisiau [soniarus] harmony a chydsain yn yr hen deml rhwng tafod a thant, nas gellir yn hawdd gan lawer yn awr gredu na dychymyg.[78]

Not only as a shadow of the lovely voice of the gospel, but also as a means in the absence of an outpouring of the Spirit, the promise of the Father to exalt the spirit of the worshippers of God to praise and marvel at him. There were so many [melodious] voices of harmony and concord in the old temple between tongue and string, that it would be difficult to believe or imagine.

The Methodists preferred to have such biblical precedents for their activities, but their choices were also guided by practicality. The other argument in favour of hymns was that they had a function. They were a memorable expression of faith, which could also convey a degree of religious knowledge, in the tradition of the popular verses of Vicar Rees Prichard. There was evidence of the fondness of the people of south-west Wales for these and for the halsing and carol, poems with religious content and message.[79] Most of the hymnody associated with the evangelical revival relied extensively on biblical content, but went beyond attempts to paraphrase passages of Scripture and related more directly to individual spiritual experience. As Mark Noll concludes, it sought 'to make the drama of personal salvation palpable in every imaginable way'.[80]

Hymn singing provided members with the means to express experiences which could be extremely difficult at times to put into words. Singing and resinging hymns became a characteristic element of Welsh revivals, as a way to channel the heightened emotions produced by sermons and in society meetings.[81] The beneficial effects of communal singing were part and parcel of the attraction for many of the members. The leaders might have found this activity preferable to the more hysterical behaviour which was gaining them notoriety. Although they defended emotional responses such as crying out when they stemmed from uncontrollable joy, they were wary of emotionalism which they feared was not founded on genuine conviction. Richard Tibbott believed that some members could not refrain from such fervour at certain times, but doubted that all the disorder and noise stemmed from a genuine spirit.[82] Methodists in the Llanfihangel Ystrad parish in mid-Cardiganshire were reproved for an excessive zeal which included beating themselves.[83] Harris spoke out in the Association against what he termed 'extravagant' laughing and jumping.[84] He admitted to Griffith Jones that there was 'much of ye Devil and Hypocricy in it', but that others he knew were 'cut so by the power of God's word that they could not help Crying out some by seeing themselves lost and others by seeing they had Pierc'd the Son of God by their Sins'.[85] Daniel Rowland explained to George Whitefield that he had openly disapproved of 'crying out' during Methodist meetings, but at the same time was aware that many of those concerned were deeply affected and could not restrain themselves.[86] Heartfelt singing of approved hymns was a far safer means of releasing that pent-up passion: 'it became the powerful and vigorous possession of more amorphous multitudes, and before long a means by which religious people felt confident to express the abundance of their joy.'[87]

Another important aspect of worship for the Methodists was communion, the approach to which posed something of a challenge throughout the eighteenth century. Although it has been suggested that much of the historical literature on the evangelical revival tends to marginalise the importance of the sacrament, it did have significance for Methodists at the time.[88] Harris was famously moved by Pryce Davies's words at a communion service suggesting to the congregation that if they were not fit to take communion they were not fit to come to church or to live or die.[89] Members were urged to continue to take communion in their parish churches, even though some had misgivings about receiving the sacrament from the hands of ministers they felt were not fulfilling their duties properly. Communion services were conducted in some of the chapels of ease to provide for those with scruples about attending their parish church, so there was a recognition that this was a real stumbling block for some people and an attempt was made to resolve the problem. However, the basic policy was to insist on continuing to take communion in the parish. Harris pointed out to a congregation gathered at Mounton chapel of ease in Pembrokeshire that 'ye Efficacy of ye ordinances dont depend on ye goodness of ye man that administers & the prayer of good people tho' they be not present will be heard'.[90] Even those who did not feel able to take communion, or were barred from doing so, should not leave the Church on that account.[91] Harris received a visit in person at Trefeca from a woman who was troubled about taking communion from a persecuting minister and was considering joining the Dissenters for the sacrament. Her home parish was not named but Harris noted that she could not go to Ystrad-ffin for communion, so she may well have been from that area of north Carmarthenshire. His advice was that she should continue in the Church, citing the example of Christ continuing to attend places of worship despite persecution from the pharisees.[92] Ultimately, it was the importance of the sacrament which led to the final separation from the Church to form the Welsh Calvinistic Methodist Church in 1811.[93] By that time, there were too few evangelical clergy in the movement able to provide communion, so the decision was made to ordain ministers in order to be able to administer the sacrament. The issue had been raised constantly by the exhorters from the 1740s onwards, but had consistently been resisted by the leaders, until it became untenable to continue without being able to offer communion services to the membership.

The Nature of the Appeal

Close fellowship between the members was regarded as an essential element in the growth of a society. The words 'union' and 'brotherly love' were frequently used by superintendents in connection with successful societies, such as Llangeitho and Talley. Conversely, disunity was a sure sign of decline in an individual society, as William Williams noted:

> nid rhaid i eglwys Dduw ond cadw pellter y naill oddi wrth y llall, fe dyf i fyny anghariad fel gwreiddyn, ac oddi wrtho daw pob canghennau truenus, ac nad oes neb a'u distrywia ond Duw yn unig.[94]

God's church need only keep a distance one from another and there grows up uncharitableness like a root, and from thence comes all wretched branches, which none can destroy but God alone.

Harris claimed when speaking at Ystrad-ffin in 1740 that the three factors which hindered the healthy progress of a society were disagreement amongst the members, failure to open their hearts to each other and too much emphasis on the self.[95] All of these related to the importance of fellowship and unity amongst the members. However, disagreements unfortunately occurred with a degree of regularity. Richard Tibbott attended a meeting of the men of the Cilcarw society, Llangyndeyrn, where they had spent their time revealing the prejudices they held against each other, negative feelings which they felt prevented their progress as a society.[96] In 1744, James Williams compared the members of Cwm-ann society to Joseph's brothers because of the prejudice they felt towards each other.[97] William Richard worried in 1746 that Llwyndafydd society lacked the unity evident in the other societies under his supervision, to the point that he feared that some members would choose to leave, since all his efforts to mediate proved useless. There is no further mention of the society in William Richard's later reports to the Association, but it is not clear if this is because of a complete collapse.[98]

The relationship between the leaders and the membership at large illustrated this sense of fellowship. References to the society members as 'the lambs', 'the chicks' and 'the Great Shepherd's little flock' demonstrate the care and fondness felt by the leaders and exhorters.[99] On one occasion, William Richard referred to his circuit as '*y ffordd yr ydwyf yn arferol o ymgyfeillachy a Hwynthwy*' or 'the way I usually keep company with them', which suggests a friendly relationship, in the original Welsh in particular.[100] William Williams faced a practical problem with Llanddewibrefi society, which never exceeded a dozen members and was so close to Llangeitho that Williams could see the sense in uniting the two societies. Yet some fondness or sense of duty seemed to prevent him from making the final decision to dissolve the smaller society. In addition to discussing problems with the local exhorters and superintendents, many of the members felt empowered to write to the leaders directly, a process made easier by the fact that they were relatively close at hand for those in the south-west. Amongst these correspondents, very probably, were some who were the first generation to acquire literacy in the circulating schools. Thus equipped, they were able to ask advice and share experiences, not just with the immediate circle of the society or even the visiting superintendent, but with the leaders of the movement themselves, which reinforced the sense of the importance of each individual. John Williams of Cilcarw in Llangyndeyrn, for instance, wrote to Howel Harris explaining that he was newly married, a relationship which he hoped was of God, and requesting Harris's prayers for him, his family and his society.[101] There was a sense of attachment towards the leaders, stemming from their joint enterprise as part of this novel movement. This is evident in the letter of Llanwinio society to Daniel Rowland, which starts with elaborately formal greetings, but soon resorts to '*Rowlands bach*' or 'dear Rowlands'.[102] This society was located in south Carmarthenshire, not far from the border with Pembrokeshire, which was hardly close to Rowland's main base of operations in Cardiganshire, so this was not the outcome of familiarity caused by frequent contact.

One of the major elements in the appeal was surely the emphasis on the individual and the importance placed on their experience. The retelling of the conversion experience, the new birth, was obviously part of the Methodist culture.[103] Those who could record it in writing often did so, and some of these narratives might be included in publications like the *Weekly History* for the edification of others. At the same time, individuals were encouraged to feel part of a community in the society. This prevented any sense of isolation whilst still placing a premium on the experience of each member who should be assured of being heard and supported by the rest of the group, as well as by the steward, exhorter and superintendent. An importance was placed on the individual's contribution which was rarely found in other Protestant denominations in Wales at the time. Yet this happened in the context of a community of believers who had shared similar experiences and could sympathise with each other and reinforce each other's spiritual progress.[104] The societies worked as groups, not just as collections of individuals. When they united they were often greater than their parts. The superintendents in their reports would invariably refer to the condition of the societies as a whole in addition to assessing the individual members.

There were signs of frustrations with some societies, such as William Williams with Tan-yr-allt, near Tregaron, whose apathy threatened to extinguish the spirit of even this most zealous of Methodists.[105] Although, even then, Williams remained confident of this recalcitrant society's eventual, gradual progess. In other cases there was obvious affection, with James Williams referring fondly to the small group which met at Galltybere, near Ystrad-ffin, as 'our little sister'.[106] The society at Lledrod were so easy to deal with that they must have come as a relief to William Williams, who consistently praised their excellence and honesty.[107] The members were encouraged to regard themselves as part of a select group, a close community of believers who were distinct from the ungodly wider world. There were comparisons to the early Church described in the New Testament, who formed small cells meeting privately in the face of indifference or hostility from the rest of society. The social aspect was an important factor in the appeal of the movement, especially in the sparsely populated rural areas of the south-west, where opportunities for sociability were limited. Although the late seventeenth and early eighteenth centuries witnessed a growing number of voluntary associations in England and Wales, they were chiefly located in urban settings, with few such groups to be found in the rural south-west, especially beneath the level of gentry society.[108] The members were kept occupied with meetings and would often arrange additional activities such as travelling together to hear some of the leaders preach or to receive sacrament from Daniel Rowland or Howel Davies. The society thus provided them with a network of contacts and activities to fill any spare time they might have. This combination of emphasis on both the individual and the close-knit religious community was also characteristic of the Moravians, who were part of the revival milieu and had a significant influence on many of the Methodist leaders, although the links between them grew rather looser during the 1740s.[109]

The sense of community was not confined to the individual society or even to the local group of societies or to Wales, since the membership were reminded that they were part of a broader revival, bearing witness to God's work in the world. In his *Aurora Borealis* in 1774, William Williams referred to the fire of revival lighting up the northern parts of the globe, like the northern lights. The Welsh societies were taught that they were part of that remarkable, unearthly fire.[110] Scheduled days of prayer and fasting for Methodists elsewhere in the world reinforced that sense of broader fellowship. Welsh Methodists were persuaded out of fellow feeling to donate to the orphanage established by George Whitefield at Bethesda in Georgia, with over £41 collected in the south-west during February 1748.[111] News of the progress of the gospel elsewhere was welcomed; as Howel Harris stated, 'tis natural for one part of God's Family to rejoice in hearing of ye other Part, and if one Member suffers, all ye members suffer with it.'[112] The English-speaking Methodists made use of published magazines to spread joyful news about the progress of revival across the world. Welsh Methodists had access to this network through the leadership and exhorters. The *Weekly History* was certainly received and distributed in the south-west, although it is difficult to know just how widely the contents were disseminated; but a single copy might serve several Methodists. Harris sent copies from London to Rowland with instructions that they should be passed on to the Longhouse family, who should pass them on to Howel Davies, who if he saw fit, might give them to Griffith Jones.[113] It is entirely feasible that the accounts it contained were relayed in Welsh to some of the societies by superintendents who were obviously fluently bilingual in most cases.

The membership were also encouraged to feel a direct sense of responsibility towards each other, not just for their spiritual wellbeing, but also for more worldly considerations. This was a general preoccupation of Methodism in both Wales and England.[114] The rules stated that society members were expected to carry each other's burdens, which frequently meant offering assistance to those in difficulties.[115] However, subjects of charity had to be felt to be genuinely in need of assistance, and there was little sympathy for those who were considered poor because of their own lazy or prodigal nature.[116] Hard work was important to avoid the perils attendant on idleness, including gossip and bringing the movement into disrepute.[117] In that respect, the Methodists were not out of step with much of the established view of poverty at the time. Bequests in wills demonstrate the willingness of the wealthier members to provide for those in need. Much of the charity was directed towards the immediate needs of fellow members of the society or local community, but members would also provide help where needed to sustain the movement beyond their individual society. They were called on, for instance, to contribute to the building of society houses, even if they were not situated close enough to be able to make use of the buildings themselves. The houses built at Llansawel and Cil-y-cwm were regarded as belonging to all the members, not just those who met there, so contributions were sought from societies more widely for the good of the movement as a whole. Harris angrily barred anyone from leaving a society held at Glanyrafonddu in April 1748 until they had contributed to the building costs, which were hampering the completion of the work.[118] There would also be occasional requests for contributions towards legal cases when they arose. For example, in 1748, the Association asked the societies in the south-west to help with the costs incurred by Methodists in Denbighshire and Merionethshire who were seeking to prosecute some of their fiercest opposers.[119] It was expected that societies would wish to help each other in such eventualities and would then be able to expect support in return if it were required. The members were called upon to contribute more and more as the movement expanded. By 1748, Harris recommended establishing weekly collections in the societies in order to maintain a central fund which the Association could draw on in order to respond to requests from those in need. Harris insisted that there was a Scriptural precedent for this and that it had been the practice of the early Church.[120] Every member was asked to set aside a penny or two a week for this fund, an amount which it was felt was not so demanding that they were not also able to contribute to other specific causes when the need arose. Money may not have always been so readily to hand at the time, and it may well have been the case that it was easier for members to provide help in kind than in cash. Wealthier members, such as Edward Evans of Llangwyryfon society, seem to consider it part of their responsibility to help other members who were less fortunate.[121] The society therefore was a source of practical support in addition to spiritual sustenance, which would have added to its attractions.

At its best, the society offered support and fellowship, but there are signs that it did not succeed in all cases. Richard Tibbott was greatly grieved to hear one woman in Llangyndeyrn declare that she regretted ever having joined the society.[122] Those attracted to the movement tended to be quite serious-minded and some of the emphasis on introspection and self-examination seems to have proved problematic for a few of these individuals. An elderly blind woman from Twˆr-gwyn used to weep all night out of distress for her sinful state.¹²³ It was weeping for the sins of others, however, which kept a girl from Myddfai awake at night; should she neglect this duty she felt as if she was burning in the fires of hell.¹²⁴ There were some who had been made aware of their sinfulness by the Methodist message but seemed then to lose hope of being worthy of forgiveness. One man from Caeo had lapsed into such a state of melancholy that he could not speak a word when Harris visited him.¹²⁵ William Harry of Llanfynydd fell to such despair that he could neither read nor pray. William Harry of Caeo became convinced that God required him to maintain a state of perpetual motion. His attempts to obey this perceived instruction led him to utter exhaustion and bewilderment, culminating in him beating his horse, quarrelling with his wife and concluding that only hell awaited him.¹²⁶ Such stories are far outnumbered in the surviving sources by more uplifting accounts of the joy which accompanied being a member of the society, although it must be said that the experiences of those who turned their backs on the movement for various reasons are unlikely to appear in the records.

In addition to fellowship and support, it seems that one of the chief attractions of the movement was that it offered some comfort in the face of fear of death and judgement. It was not just death which was to be feared, but what followed, with tales evidently circulating of the Devil coming to claim his own. Howel Harris was told the story of John Morgan, from Cwm near Myddfai, Carmarthenshire, who saw the Devil standing at his side as he was dying.¹²⁷ Another man in Pembrokeshire was said to have died knowing 'he had no part in Christ' and screaming 'murder' as he saw the Devil approaching to seize him.¹²⁸ Life was precarious for many in rural south-west Wales, with the constant threat of epidemic disease, malnutrition and fatal accident. The growing population from the 1740s onwards also inevitably brought greater pressures to bear. Part of Griffith Jones's motivation for establishing the circulating schools was the concern caused by the number who died from typhus in the epidemic which struck the south-west between 1727 and 1731. Such outbreaks brought the reality of sudden death very close, along with fear about what might follow. It has been suggested that some nineteenth-century revivals may have been prompted in part at least by epidemics of cholera.¹²⁹ It is difficult to trace a direct correlation between mortality crises and the growth of the evangelical revival, but the hard winter of 1739–40 led to food shortages and riots, which might have had some effect on those drawn to the movement. Harris found himself having to counter accusations in the south-west that the dearth experienced in 1741 was some sort of outcome of the Methodist activity, possibly a punishment on them.[130] Even the Methodist John Sparks of Haverfordwest worried that the bad weather might be a 'Rod of God'.[131] However, the situation seems to have been far more serious in north Wales than in the south-west.[132]

The support network provided for members by the society lasted until their final moments on earth. Caring for the seriously ill in the early modern period inevitably fell to the family, so the extension of the kinship group in this respect to include the members of the society might have been a significant relief.[133] The local superintendent and exhorters, as well as the society steward and fellow members, would visit to pray with the terminally ill and to offer comfort and encouragement. Even the support of the leaders could be requested. When Thomas David, the steward of Dyffryn-saith society in south Cardiganshire, was too ill to attend meetings in his last months, he was able to send a message via William Richard that he would welcome a visit from Howel Harris.[134] The attitude was that death was not something to fear but to be welcomed, since it meant leaving behind the troubles of this world for a better existence. There was an acceptance that grief was the natural reaction of bereaved friends and relatives, but also a constant reiteration that the departed were in a better place. This was a consistent theme, not just in letters and society reports but in the elegies composed by Methodist poets in the eighteenth century. Morgan Rhys, for instance, in his elegy to John Parry of Talley, an exhorter, who died at a young age in 1770, imagined him saying:

> Fe ddarfu holl gystuddiau f'oes,
>   A chario'r groes a phechu,
> Ffarwel priodi a marw mwy,
>   Heb boen na chlwy' 'rwy'n canu,
> I'r Oen a laddwyd ar Galfaria,
> Efe yw'n holl hyfrydwch yma,
> Ni all angelion nefoedd draethu
> Maint fy mraint anfeidrol heddy'.[135]

All the sufferings of my life are ended,
   And carrying the cross and sinning,
Farewell now to marrying and dying,
   Without pain or wound I sing,
To the Lamb who was killed on Calvary,
He here is all our joy,
Heaven's angels cannot tell
How great my infinite privilege is today.

William Williams spoke in a similar vein in his elegy to William Richard, the superintendent from Llanddewibrefi who died in 1771:

Nid oedd arno hiraeth ronyn,
Am na gwraig, na char, na phlentyn,
   Ond 'r oedd wedi llwyr anghofio
'R ddaear fawr a'i llwyth yn gryno,
Fel pe buasai erioed heb berchen
Ar un dim o tan y wybren,
Gwel'd y bedd mewn rhyw hedd, hyfryd ei rinwedd,
Ac ymestyn mewn gorfoledd
A llawenydd at y diwedd.[136]

He felt no grain of longing,
For wife, or loved one, or child,
   But had completely forgotten
All the world and its tribe,
As if he had never owned
Anything under the sun,
Seeing the grave in peace and lovely virtue,
Reaching out in jubilation
And joy towards the end.

Another element of consolation was the idea that those who had passed could rejoice in the company of the saints in heaven. Williams described John Parry of Talley feasting with the saints and the Cardiganshire Methodists whom he mourned in an elegy in the late 1750s being warmly greeted by fellow believers who had gone before.[137] Howel

Davies on his death joined a host of ten thousand souls who were 'void of pain' in the comfort of heaven.[138]

Williams began writing elegies by the end of the 1750s, the very earliest of which were largely in memory of society members he had come to know in his capacity as superintendent for Cardiganshire, including Theophilus Jones of Blaenplwyf, Llanfihangel Ystrad, in whose home Howel Harris stayed on several occasions. He would write a considerable number as more and more of the young people who were drawn to the movement in the 1740s aged and passed away: a total of thirty-one in Welsh, four in English and three dedicated to groups of believers from particular areas, including Cardiganshire.[139] The most poignant of all his elegies was the one he wrote to his baby daughter, Maria Sophia, who died when she was just a fortnight old. Even in this case, he took comfort from the belief that by dying so young the little girl had been spared all the trouble that life could bring. From time to time, he would tell himself that he should forgo the practice of writing elegies, as these were individuals who he was confident were now in a blessed state, but at the same time he could not stop himself from wanting to express his sense of loss. Although he suggested that colleagues like William Richard would not miss their lives on earth, he acknowledged that they were often sorely missed by those left behind.

Such elegies generally came rather later in the history of the movement as there were only a few deaths recorded during the early phase of revival. There is some information about these individuals, however, thanks to reports provided by local superintendents, who mostly gave the reassuring news of what would be considered a good death in Methodist terms. This usually involved maintaining a firm grasp on faith, despite pain, often with an expression of confidence that heaven was at hand. There was an interest in the topics of conversation which engaged those near death, since this revealed much about their preoccupations at the end. A woman from Llechryd, for instance, who was dying of consumption, was said to have talked constantly of 'the Saviour's love to sinners'.[140] The last words spoken held a particular significance and would be recounted to the Association. It is interesting that, on a visit to Cardiganshire, Howel Harris was told of the last words of Daniel Rowland's grandparents, which shows how such statements were cherished and circulated as signs of piety.[141] There seems to have

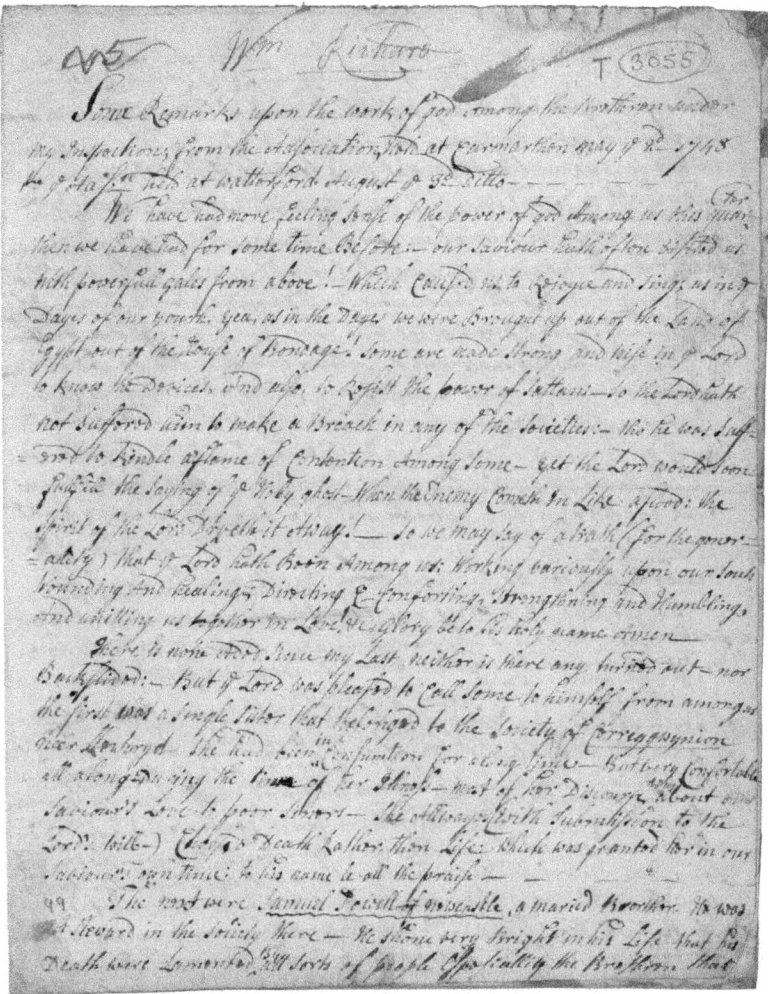

William Richard's report to the Association, May-August 1748 (Trevecca College/1 3055).

been some prompting of the terminally ill, who might have been considered to have valuable insights to offer when poised between this world and the next, to give an account of how they felt, almost as a continuation of the practice of sharing experiences in a society meeting. William John was at the bedside of one member of the Blaenhyfer society three to four minutes before he died, at which point when questioned he said he felt assured in his faith and had no fear.[142] William John also described Margaret John, an elderly woman from Llanwinio society being questioned by her son about her spiritual state:

> *ei mab a ofynnodd iddi os gallai ddyweid pa fodd roedd gyda hi y pryd hyn'y hi attebodd y gallai ai bod yn hyfryd iawn arni, fel y dywedodd or blaen ar ffordd yn rhydd ac yn oleu, yna, ebe hi dyma fi yn landio fry nawr yn y nefoedd ac ar y gair hi a ymadawodd, felly marwolaeth ei saints sydd werthfawr yn golwg yr arglwydd a choffadwriaeth y cyfiawn sydd fendigedig.*[143]

her son asked her if she could say how it was with her at that time. She answered that she could and that it was very lovely, as she had said before, and that the way ahead was clear and light. Then she said 'Here I am landing now above in heaven', and on that word she departed, so the death of his saints is valuable in the eyes of the Lord and the memory of the just is blessed.

Some Methodists were in too much pain to say very much at the end, including Elizabeth Parry of Cwmcynon, Llandysiliogogo, whose final illness lasted just nine days.[144] Samuel Powell, the blacksmith from Newcastle Emlyn who was married to Daniel Rowland's sister, regretted that he was too short of breath to sing praises on his deathbed.[145] Jenkin David of Crug Ifan was able to speak during an illness which lasted four weeks, but seemed unable to find a form of words to express himself.[146] In such cases, verses from the Scripture might well prove useful. Thomas David of Dyffryn-saith died with verses from the Bible on his lips, including the uplifting 'Blessed are they that dwell in thy house: they will be still praising thee.'[147] Several of those whose deaths are recorded seemed to have faced their end with unflinching bravery, as did William James of Tre-lech, who insisted that death could not hurt him. Mary Nicholas, a widow from Llwynygorras society in Pembrokeshire, was another whose experience offered consolation to others. Having suffered from a cancer in her breast for four years, she was frequently in great pain, but, nonetheless, died in great peace of mind in 1748.[148] Such accounts would be an inspiration and comfort to others, which was doubtless part of the reason for preserving and passing on these details.[149]

Such examples offered a positive message but there were others that served as a warning of what to seek to avoid, such as the death of Dafydd Jenkin of Meidrim society. According to his former superintendent, William John, he had neglected the society in order to keep 'corrupt company', which meant that he died in fearful misery, without the support of his fellow members.[150] Howel Harris was also struck by a tale told by Edmund Jones, of a man who drew up a written agreement between him and God only to abandon religion shortly after. He died in a state of overwhelming sadness, having realised on his deathbed that he had broken every single word of his agreement.[151] Such was the outcome of neglecting the society, it was suggested.

The Women of the Societies

Many of the elements in the appeal of the movement seem to have resonated particularly with women in the rural south-west. The reports reveal the high proportion of women in many societies and it was acknowledged that female piety was often a significant driving force in the movement. William Williams noted, for instance, that the women of Tan-yr-allt society in Cardiganshire showed greater signs of zeal and progress than the men.[152] Yet the history of these Elizabeths, Marys, Annes, Sarahs and Catherines remains even more shrouded in mist than that of their male contemporaries. Historians have struggled to uncover and analyse their experiences.[153] The same has been true to a large extent of the Methodist movement in England, save for some obvious exceptions such as the Countess of Huntingdon and Mary Bosanquet. The significance of the relationship between women and religion has been noted more generally, especially their loyalty to what might be termed minority causes. The perceived religiosity of women as a recurring theme throughout the early modern period has been identified, although, as Gail Malmgreen has suggested, it has until recently not been studied widely either by religious historians or those interested in the history of women.[154] Women preachers have been the focus of some attention from historians, including Wesley Swift's work on early women preachers in Wesleyan Methodism, Deborah M.

Valenze's study of working-class women preachers in the cottage tradition of nineteenth-century evangelicalism, and Jennifer Lloyd on their opportunities in the nineteenth century.[155] More recent works have looked more broadly at women's religious experiences, such as Linda Wilson's study of female spirituality amongst nineteenth-century Nonconformists.[156] Historians of Methodism are now much more inclined to consider the active participation of women as part of their studies of the movement in general, with David Hempton having regularly drawn attention to the fact that 'the history of Methodism is really a history of female preponderance'.[157]

Although the surviving sources give clear indications that women were numerous in the societies, their authentic voice remains elusive. Their experiences are usually relayed indirectly through the reports of the superintendents or in the writings of Harris and Williams. One can speculate about the possible factors which were likely to have drawn them to the movement, including the greater opportunity for lay participation and the chance to have their voices heard, at least within the close community of the private society. It was also the case that it was women who had the responsiblity of caring for the sick and dying, so any consolation offered in that regard might have had a particular relevance to those who had witnessed at first hand the often painful process of dying. Women were also especially vulnerable to the perils of childbirth and attendant infections, so faced additional risks to the ordinary dangers of disease and disaster which stalked much of the population at the time.[158]

There are a number of elegies written to Methodist women in the eighteenth century, but they generally dwell on the hospitality provided in their homes to exhorters, societies and Association meetings.[159] William Williams did acknowledge that 'a myriad of women' had reached heaven to sit alongside Protestant heroes such as Luther and Cranmer.[160] This is part of his elegy to Grace Price of Watford, a place where Williams had stayed many times and which played host to some historic Association meetings. He confessed to a deep affection for Grace and penned his poem in a single rush of grief lasting into the early hours of the morning. There is a vivid description of Grace looking through Williams's books and reading sermons, but in another verse it is her skill as a needlewoman which is lauded, with specific reference to her home-made curtains.[161] Grace herself, of course, might have been pleased by this tribute, and Williams as her friend was likely to have been aware of that, but it strikes the modern ear rather strangely and in stark contrast to the elegies dedicated to the men of the movement. Yet, it was their capacity to care for others in very practical ways which usually earned women praise. This is apparent in Morgan Rhys's elegy to Esther, the wife of William John of Llewele Mawr in Llansawel, who died in 1770.[162] It is stated that she had maintained her faith and regularly attended sermons over a period of twenty-nine years having been converted around 1741 at the age of twenty-six, but it is her role as helpmeet to her husband and comfort to those in need which is emphasised. Esther is depicted spotting visitors at a distance and busily preparing to cater for their needs. The widow and orphan would always find a friend and confidante in her. These were the qualities which led even her enemies to acknowledge that she lived and died as a Christian. It is hardly surprising that it is the stereotypical female virtues which were highlighted here. Yet women such as Esther who lived in houses which played host to the societies and visiting preachers had a particular advantage when it came to gaining a personal influence. They tended to have direct access to the leaders and exhorters and could potentially sway some of their decisions, even if on relatively minor matters such as where else to stay or preach in the area. They could also become involved in local organisation, passing on information about meetings and helping with the general arrangements. Catherine Pugh of Morfa Bach, Cydweli, certainly seems to have played an active role in this way, with Thomas Morgan noting in his diary in 1744 that she had come to call on him in his lodgings to arrange a preaching engagement.[163] Richard Tibbott also visited and stayed at Morfa Bach on several occasions. Armed with a strong personality, a woman could exert a significant degree of influence in organisational matters, especially perhaps if her social status was of the lesser gentry or substantial middling sorts.

But were any of the Welsh Methodist women really able to exercise agency beyond the domestic arrangements? One of the movement's main attractions was the opportunity it offered its members to make an active contribution to the societies, a development which opened doors for women, at least to some degree. It also brought them into contact with like-minded women. As Phyllis Mack has argued, the associational religious life offered by Methodism provided women with friendship networks and increased self-confidence.[164] This was one of the few opportunities available to women to participate in any sort of society, since most of the clubs and associations which were so fashionable by the early eighteenth century were exclusively male.[165] Methodist women were expected to describe and analyse their experiences in the societies, so this was a rare chance to speak in a semi-public setting. There is little evidence to show to what extent Welsh societies adopted the same practice as existed in England of dividing societies into separate bands for men and women so that they could discuss more freely the issues more relevant to them. Many of the Welsh societies may have been too small for that to be practical. Even so, the fact that women often formed the majority may have made speaking out a more reassuring and less intimidating experience than if they had been in the minority. Their contribution was not restricted to relating their experiences alone, although the level of engagement open to them remained a matter for debate. Only Sidney Griffith was permitted to attend the Association, and that was highly controversial. Daniel Rowland had provoked some fierce opposition in the Llandyfaelog area of Carmarthenshire in 1741 when he had asked a woman to pray in public.[166] During a conversation over breakfast on a visit to London in 1743, Harris found himiself at odds with the Whitefield household, who were more inclined to favour the prospect of women preaching.[167] Harris also had fixed ideas about the role of wives in the family: '... shewd of Husbands being Kings Priests & Prophets & ye wives being not Heads else that is putting ye man to walk on his head'.[168] Although Harris was not a strong advocate of women taking on prominent roles, he seemed to accept in principle that they should be free to pray in the societies. At Llwynyberllan in May 1744, he noted in his diary that women had been selected to pray, but there are no further details about who and in what circumstances.[169] Harris became much more of a supporter of women's involvement by the end of the decade, by which time he insisted that both men and women should have the opportunity to pray in societies.[170] He turned to the Bible to reveal how women had been active in the Church.[171] When Richard Tibbott had scruples over two biblical texts regarding women speaking in the churches, Harris was able to explain them in a way which reassured Tibbott that it was acceptable.[172] However, that is likely to have been the result of a desire to shore up Sidney Griffith's position rather than to enforce women's status more generally. Harris compared her to Deborah in the Old Testament and Phoebe in the New, which may well have been the biblical examples he used to explain to his hearers that women could legitimately be given roles within the church.

In general, Methodists were not keen supporters of women preaching, partly because it was a step which would potentially have distanced them from the Established Church who did not countenance such a role for women. The Welsh movement seemed less open to the idea of women preaching than the Wesleyans, who would allow the occasional woman who claimed 'an extraordinary call' to exhort.[173] Only one woman in Wales was recorded being given even limited scope to exhort during the first wave of revival. This permission was granted in the years prior to the finalising of the rules for the exhorters in the Association, and approval was given on a temporary basis. When Harris visited Blaen-porth in south Cardiganshire in April 1741 he stayed the night at Cwmhowni where he heard of the local society:

> I find some do meet but ye men being not gifted a poor humble experienced Loving broken soul a Woman is stird up to speak a little & finds great Effect & had Scruples on her mind about it – I said she may I thought when ye Lord gave her Power, Love and success discourse a little in a Society private till ye Lord should send some body fitter – I could not discourage her when I saw her spirit.[174]

It might have been difficult for Harris to resist in this case since, as a layman, his authority to preach in effect rested on the same principle of 'an extraordinary call' as did the justification for women preaching. In June 1742 Harris received a letter written in English from Elizabeth Thomas on behalf of the Blaen-porth society, which demonstrates that she was educated and articulate, with considerable authority in the society.[175] Although Harris had not previously named her in his diary it would seem that this was the woman he had authorised to exhort. W. G. Hughes-Edwards suggested that she was a widow who allowed the society to meet in her house, possibly on the evidence of a letter from William Richard to Harris in September 1742 explaining that 'Betty Thomas' was experiencing difficulties from the Dissenters who threatened to expel her for receiving the Methodists into her home.[176] This may or may not be the same Elizabeth Thomas, as no specific society or location is mentioned in relation to her. It is worth noting that the only surviving membership list for Blaen-porth is from 1743, in which Elizabeth Thomas appears as a single woman, a category which might conceivably include widows, if they were not listed separately.[177] There are indications that Elizabeth Thomas of Blaen-porth had Dissenting tendencies, as she recommended administering the sacrament in the societies. The Blaen-porth society usually met at Cwmhowni, a farmhouse where Harris stayed quite frequently on his visits to the locality, which was not at that point owned by a widowed Elizabeth Thomas, although an Elizabeth Thomas inherited Cwmhowni from her uncle, Jenkin Lewis. When Lewis wrote his will in 1741, his niece was named as Elizabeth Thomas, daughter of Thomas Griffiths, so presumably was unmarried at that point. However, when the will was proved in 1770, administration was granted to Elizabeth Thomas, wife of Morgan Hughes of Blaen-porth.[178] This Morgan Hughes was the former Methodist exhorter who settled in Cwmhowni, and whose wife is also named as Elizabeth in the letters of administration following his death in 1792.[179] If this is, as seems almost certain, the same woman as the exhorter, her level of literacy becomes rather more understandable. Her uncle, Jenkin Lewis, was resident in Fareham in Hampshire and left lands in London and Westminster to his wife. Her aunt, Catherine Lewis, presumably Jenkin's sister, also held properties in Blaen-porth and Aberporth, including Neuadd Fawr, which she left to Morgan Hughes, her nephew-in-law.[180] These would seem to be Elizabeth's relations on her mother's side and the family was obviously relatively wealthy, which might account for her own education and self-confidence. She does not appear again in the Methodist records after 1742, and it is possible that her permission to discourse would have been rescinded as the Association imposed greater order on the exhorters. In addition, if she were Morgan Hughes's wife, she might have left the society to worship exclusively with the Dissenters. Although it is difficult to be completely sure of her identity, she was evidently an exceptional character, but even she failed to continue to exhort in the movement once the rules of the Association were imposed. As Jennifer Lloyd points out, the history of the involvement of women in Methodism was not necessarily a history of progress, since doors which opened could also close when more strict organisation was adopted.[181]

One area where women were able to make a consistent and seemingly uncontroversial contribution was in the development of the tradition of hymn singing, which became a vital element in the movement's attractions and activities. Richard Tibbott, during his time in Carmarthenshire, had great pleasure when attending the Cilcarw society in Llangyndeyrn in hearing Dorothy (Doriti or Doli) Jones and some of the other women singing hymns.[182] It was this musical talent which ensured that she was selected to visit societies in order to teach the members suitable tunes to which they might sing William Williams's hymns.[183] Such opportunities allowed at least some of the women in the societies to put their talents to use in a way which was likely to have boosted their self-esteem. Dorothy took a step further and began to compose verses to describe her sense of closeness to Christ, although she had not shown any poetic talents prior to joining the society. Her extraordinary zeal impressed Howel Harris.[184] A handful of her verses have survived, recorded by Richard Tibbott, and may well have been among the hymns sung by Dorothy and her friends as they travelled to Methodist meetings. Although they are not of the same quality as those of Ann Griffiths later in the century, they are written from a woman's perspective and may therefore have had a special appeal to the women in the societies:

> *O disgwil ferch o disgwil di*
> *O disgwil fy Anwilid i*
> *Myfi a ddaw ith dynu mas*
> *O dan lywodreth pechod cas.*

> *Myfi yw y mab ath rhytha di*
> *O disgwil disgwil wrtho fi*
> *Mi ath gar di a chariad rhad*
> *Gwna it Angofio tu dy dad.*[185]

Wait, girl, oh wait
Wait my beloved
I will come to pull you out
From the rule of hateful sin.

I am the son who frees you
Oh wait, wait for me
I will love you with free love
To make you forget your father's house.

However, the dominant figure in early Methodist literature was William Williams of Pantycelyn, firstly becoming recognised for his talents as a hymn writer but also developing to be one of the most important prose writers of the revival, whose works provide a vital insight into Methodist thought. Having long since identified the enthusiastic participation of women in the societies, Williams chose to use a fictional woman, Martha Philopur, as the voice of all Methodist converts in his first prose work, *Llythyr Martha Philopur* (The Letter of Martha Philopur), in 1762. He was moved to write in an attempt to explain the nature of the recent Llangeitho revival and to justify some of the emotional outbursts associated with it. The work takes the form of a letter from Martha to her mentor and adviser, Philo-Evangelius. Thus Martha speaks for all the converts as she outlines the nature of her conversion and her response to it. This is something of a second-hand conversion narrative, as it is probably an amalgam of many first-hand accounts from a number of enthusiastic women Williams would have encountered during his visits to the societies. Williams also uses her to provide scriptural precedents for the exuberant behaviour of those influenced by the revival, an impassioned response which was invoking considerable suspicion and criticism. By choosing a female character as his representative Methodist convert, Williams was reflecting the actual situation in most societies, yet it was still something of a departure from convention, especially in his first published prose work. However, there was a more traditional overarching format, as Martha was writing to the older and wiser Philo-Evangelius, whose reply to her letter in Williams's next publication made this into a dialogue between the young pupil and the wiser mentor, a literary device with a long pedigree which established that the leadership roles still belonged to the men in the movement.

The charismatic appeal of the leaders and exhorters to young women in particular has been pointed to as a possible factor in their recruitment to the movement. There certainly seem to have been times when some of the more well-known figures were subject to adulation verging on stalking. During February and March 1741 Harris was pursued around Carmarthenshire by Betty Rees (or Rice) Jones, who claimed to be taking her inspiration from Mary Magdalene following Christ. Harris tried to reason with her and implored her to stay at home, to no avail, so resorted to warning her of the prospect of hellfire if she did not desist. Embarrassed by her public devotion, he feared he was being blamed for misleading her: '... she drawing all to blaspheme allmost – weakening my Hands offending ye Weak – many saying how could I say such Words & so delude her others scoffing'.[186] Betty insisted that she acted in obedience to God's will, but Harris suspected that she was possessed by a legion of devils. By 12 March, all patience exhausted, he called on a constable in Llanddarog to restrain her so that he might have time to escape. He was not the only exhorter to be troubled by her presence, as Richard Tibbott described her in his diary as 'a clear picture of an image of a Hypocrite' ('*darluniad eglyr o ddelw Rhagreithwr*') who professed profound faith, without any true experience of it.[187] He stated, with an uncharacteristic note of sarcasm, that she claimed to have great anxiety about sin, such deep convictions, such concern for the truth, but had no more sense of these in reality than would an animal.

It is conceivable that women might be attracted by the charisma of a Methodist preacher or the prospect of widening their social circle. However, the expectations of society members meant that any long-term affiliation demanded a commitment which was not entered into idly or easily maintained for shallow reasons. To a large extent the attractions for the men of the society were similar to women's: a chance to belong, to contribute, to be supported and not to have to cope alone with their experiences. Yet a wider range of opportunities to participate in the movement would have been more readily available to the men, who, even as unordained laymen, could claim a spiritual calling without having to plead extraordinary circumstances. Leadership roles in the societies were almost without exception open to the men only, so they had far greater scope to take advantage of opportunities to gain self-confidence, experience and standing in the local community. As Mark Noll summarises: 'important as women always were for evangelicalism on the ground, the public movement was driven by men.'[188] Methodism did open up possibilities for lay participation but still in gendered ways, so it was far from a social revolution, nor did it ever show any aspirations in that direction.

Despite numerous attempts to define the nature and appeal of Methodism, both in Wales and beyond, it remains a challenge. It is really only possible to conclude that there were a number of factors involved which seemed to attract certain sections of society in particular. Many were initially attracted by the active preaching mission, but the close network of support provided by the system of societies helped to retain the converts in the longer term. There were also particular circumstances at the outset of the revival which aided its ultimate success, including the emergence of voluntary religious and moral reform societies, as well as the growth of literacy and print culture. The movement was quick to take advantage of the burgeoning print industry through the medium of Welsh, publishing guidebooks and hymn books in the 1740s. Yet, although the printed word was important, the spoken word remained completely crucial to the movement's appeal, through sermons, society discussions and hymns.

Notes

1 G. H. Hughes (ed.), *Gweithiau William Williams Pantycelyn, Cyfrol II: Rhyddiaith* (Caerdydd: Gwasg Prifysgol Cymru, 1967), p. 188.
2 G. H. Jenkins, *Literature, Religion and Society in Wales 1660–1730* (Cardiff: University of Wales Press, 1978), p. 13.
3 E. Saunders *A View of the State of Religion in the Diocese of St David's About the beginning of the 18th Century* (reprint, Cardiff: University of Wales Press, 1949), p. 32; J. Morgan-Guy, 'Sermons in Wales in the Established Church', in K. A. Francis and W. Gibson (eds), *The Oxford Handbook of the British Sermon 1689–1901* (Oxford: Oxford University Press, 2012), p. 185.
4 DHH 98, 25 March 1743.
5 For further discussion of the law and gospel, see R. L. Maddox, *Responsible Grace: John Wesley and Practical Theology* (Nashville: Kingswood Books, 1994); K. Ganske, 'Preaching Christ: John Wesley's Definition of the Gospel, 1746–51', *Wesley and Methodist Studies*, 11/2 (2019), 113–42.

6   For instance, DHH 70, 26 February 1741; 66, 10 December 1740; 48, 23 August 1739; 82, 12 December 1741.
7   DHH 54, 4 March 1743.
8   DHH 72, 13 May 1741.
9   NLW MS 5456A, p. 3b, 11 March 1741.
10 J. Thomas, *Rhad Ras neu Lyfr Profiad*, ed. J. Dyfnallt Owen (Cardiff: University of Wales Press, 1949), pp. 28–9.
11 DHH 98, 27 February 1743.
12 DHH 63, 24 September 1740.
13 Thomas, *Rhad Ras*, p. 78.
14 '*tarany bwgwthion*', NLW 18435B, p. 25, 27 September 1741.
15 N. Cynhafal Jones (ed.), *Gweithiau Williams Pant-y-celyn, Cyfrol I* (Treffynnon: P. M. Evans & son, 1887), p. 582.
16 J. Owen, *Coffhad am y Parch. Daniel Rowlands, gynt o Langeitho, Ceredigion* (Caerlleon: Edward Parry, 1839), pp. 17–18; D. J. Odwyn Jones, *Daniel Rowland, Llangeitho (1713–1790)* (Llandysul: Gwasg Gomer, 1938), p. 19.
17 Owen Thomas, *Cofiant y Parchedig John Jones Talsarn* (Wrexham: Hughes and Son, 1874), p. 799.
18 DHH 90, 23 May 1742.
19 D. D. Morgan, 'The Welsh Sermon, 1689–1901', in Francis and Gibson (eds), *The Oxford Handbook of the British Sermon 1689–1901*, p. 205.
20 Trevecka MS, 803, Howel Harris to George Whitefield, 14 February 1743.
21 Goronwy P. Owen (ed.), *Hunangofiant John Elias* (Penybont ar Ogwr: Mudiad Efengylaidd Cymru, 1974), pp. 55–6.
22 Hughes (ed.), *Gweithiau William Williams Pantycelyn*, II, p. 1.
23 NLW MS 5456A, p. 59a.
24 NLW MS 20515C, 15 April 1759.
25 DHH 70, 23–7 February 1741.
26 D. W. Howell, *Patriarchs and Parasites: The Gentry of South-west Wales in the Eighteenth Century* (Cardiff: University of Wales Press, 1986), p. 2.
27 Jones, *Daniel Rowland, Llangeitho*, p. 69.
28 Jones, *Daniel Rowland Llangeitho*, pp. 114–15.
29 Morgan, 'The Welsh Sermon, 1689–1901', p. 205.
30 For example, a verse from Ephesians 6 on one occasion at Haverfordwest. DHH 122, 14 April 1746.
31 DHH 95, 25 March 1743.
32 DHH 96, 10 December 1742.
33 DHH 131a, 5 May 1748.
34 DHH 121, 22 January 1746.
35 DHH 54, 9 March 1740.
36 Thomas, *Rhad Ras*, p. 37.
37 Trevecka MS 1144, Watkin Watkins to Howel Harris, 9 March 1744.
38 G. M. Griffiths (ed.), 'A Visitation of the Archdeaconry of Carmarthen, 1710', *National Library of Wales Journal*, 18 (1973), 321.
39 DHH 121, 18 January 1745.
40 DHH 54, 4 March 1740.
41 DHH 131b, 3 August 1748.
42 Trevecka MS 856, Howel Harris to John Lewis, 18 April 1743.

43 DHH 62, 31 August 1740.
44 DHH 129, 27 April 1748.
45 DHH 122, 21 April 1746.
46 DHH 98, 11 March 1743.
47 Trevecka MS 756, Howel Harris to George Whitefield, 14 December 1742; DHH 96, 14 December 1742.
48 DHH 118, 11 October 1745.
49 NLW MS 18435B, p. 17, 19 August 1741.
50 Trevecka MS 299, David Jones to Howel Harris, 20 December 1740.
51 DHH 68, 21 January 1741.
52 Trevecca College/1 3016, William Richard to the Association, 20 June 1744.
53 DHH 68. 18 January 1741.
54 Hughes (ed.), *Gweithiau William Williams Pantycelyn*, II, p. 1.
55 P. Clark, *British Clubs and Societies 1580–1800: The Origins of an Associational World* (Oxford: Oxford University Press, 2000), pp. 64–6, 74–5; B. S. Sirota, *Christian Monitors: The Church of England and the Age of Benevolence, 1680–1730* (New Haven: Yale University Press, 2014), pp. 1–5.
56 First published in 1697, a second enlarged edition appeared in 1698. J. Woodward, *An Account of the Rise and Progress of the Religious Societies in the City of London, &c, And of the Endeavours for Reformation of Manners Which have been made therein* (London: JD for the author, 1698).
57 DHH 145, 28 June 1750; see also, DHH 144, 19 April 1750.
58 G. Tudur, *Howell Harris: From Conversion to Separation* (Cardiff: University of Wales Press, 2000), pp. 667.
59 George Whitefield, *Llythyr oddiwrth y Parchedig Mr. George Whitefield at societies neu gymdeithasau crefyddol, a osodwyd yn diweddar ar droed mewn amriw leoedd yng Nghymru a Lloeger* (Pont-y-pool: Argraph-Wasg Newydd, 1740).
60 There is a translation into English: William Williams, *The Experience Meeting*, trans. Mrs Lloyd-Jones (Bryntirion: The Evangelical Movement of Wales, 1973).
61 Woodward, *An Account of the Rise and Progress of the Religious Societies*, p. 50.
62 Hughes (ed.), *Gweithiau William Williams Pantycelyn*, II, p. 188.
63 Hughes (ed.), *Gweithiau William Williams Pantycelyn*, II, p. 188.
64 Trevecca College/1 3023, p. 18, William Richard to the Association, January 1746.
65 Trevecca College/1 3025, William Williams to the Association, January 1745.
66 NLW MS 18435B, 1741–2; Trevecka College MS 1/3187, February–May 1744.
67 NLW MS 22070B, Diary of John Thomas, Tre-main, 1756–60.
68 Trevecca College/1 3023, p. 9, William John to the Association (copy), October 1745.
69 Trevecca College/1 3027, William Richard to the Association, 2 July 1746.
70 DHH 129, 7 February 1748.
71 Trevecka MS 1337, Watkin Watkins to Howel Harris, 30 June 1745.
72 DHH 156, 4 February 1745.
73 Hughes (ed.), *Gweithiau William Williams Pantycelyn II*, p. 188.
74 D. Hempton, *The Church in the Long Eighteenth Century* (London: I. B. Tauris, 2011), p. 158. See also D. Ll. Morgan, *The Great Awakening in Wales* (London:

Epworth Press, 1988), pp. 267–97; Mark A. Noll, 'The Significance of Hymnody in the First Evangelical Revivals, 1730–1760', in D. W. Roberts (ed.), *Revival, Renewal and the Holy Spirit* (Milton Keynes: Paternoster, 2009), pp. 45–64.

75 *Sail, Dibenion a Rheolau,'r Societies neu'r cyfarfodydd neullduol a ddechreuassant ymgynnull yn ddiweddar yn Nghymru* (Bristol: Felix Farley, 1742), p. 84.

76 NLW MS 19044A; see also Goronwy P. Owen (ed.), *Canu Cynnar y Diwygiad Methodistaidd: Agweddau ar emynau Llawysgrif Llangeitho* (Caernarfon: Ymddiriedolwyr y Ddarlith Davies, 2016).

77 See H. A. Hodges, *Flame in the Mountains: Williams Pantycelyn, Ann Griffiths and the Welsh Hymn*, ed. E. Wyn James (Talybont: Y Lolfa, 2017).

78 Hughes (ed.), *Gweithiau William Williams Pantycelyn II*, p. 21.

79 Saunders, *A View of the State of Religion in the Diocese of St David's*, p. 33; E. Wyn James, 'The Evolution of the Welsh Hymn', in I. Rivers and D. L. Wykes (eds), *Dissenting Praise: Religious Dissent and the Hymn in England and Wales* (Oxford: Oxford University Press, 2011), pp. 235–6.

80 Noll, 'The Significance of Hymnody in the First Evangelical Revivals, 1730–1760', p. 58.

81 James, 'The Evolution of the Welsh Hymn', pp. 239–47.

82 Trevecka College 1/3187, fol. 11.

83 DHH 105, 3 December 1743.

84 DHH 112, 25 July 1744.

85 Trevecka MS 338, Howel Harris to Griffith Jones, 15 May 1741.

86 Trevecka MS 792, Daniel Rowland to George Whitefield, 2 February 1743.

87 Morgan, *The Great Awakening*, p. 268.

88 J. Coffey, 'Between Puritanism and Evangelicalism: "Heart-work" in Dissenting Communion Hymns, 1633–1709', in J. Coffey (ed.), *Heart Religion: Evangelical Piety in England and Ireland, 1690–1850* (Oxford: Oxford University Press, 2016), pp. 29–30.

89 Howell Harris, *A Brief Account of the Life of Howell Harris, Esq.* (Trevecka: Trevecka Press, 1791), p. 10; G. Tudur, *Howell Harris: From Conversion to Separation 1735–1750* (Cardiff: University of Wales Press, 2000), pp. 15–16.

90 DHH 134, 19 March 1748.

91 DHH 84, 7 January 1742.

92 DHH 53a, 18 October 1740.

93 See D. C. Jones, B. S. Schlenther and E. M. White, *The Elect Methodists: Calvinistic Methodism in England and Wales 1735–1811* (Cardiff: University of Wales Press, 2012), pp. 223–32.

94 Hughes (ed.), *Gweithiau William Williams Pantycelyn, II*, p. 189.

95 DHH 62, 31 August 1740.

96 NLW MS 18435B, p. 22, 9 September 1741.

97 Trevecca College/1 3013, James Williams to the Association, March 1744; 3014, James Williams to the Association, January 1744.

98 Trevecca College/1 3032, William Richard to the Association, 9 April 1744; 3036, William Richard to the Association, 2 October 1746.

99 For instance, Trevecka MS 745, Howel Harris to George Whitefield, 5 December 1742; 962, William Richard to Howel Harris, 2 September 1743; 1381, William Williams to Howel Harris, 7 December 1745.

100 Trevecca College/1 3048, William Richard to the Association, 26 January 1748.
101 Trevecka MS 403, John Williams to Howel Harris, 27 October 1741.
102 Trevecca College/1 3110, Llanwinio society to Daniel Rowland, 1748.
103 See B. Hindmarsh, *The Evangelical Conversion Narrative: Spiritual Autobiography in Early Modern England* (Oxford: Oxford University Press, 2005).
104 See also D. W. Bebbington, *Evangelicalism in Modern Britain: A History from the 1730s to the 1980s* (London: Routledge, 1989), p. 24.
105 Trevecca College/1 3049, William Williams to the Association, 28 January 1748.
106 Trevecka MS 1240, James Williams to the Association, 3 October 1744.
107 Trevecca College/1 3078, William Williams to the Association, 1750.
108 P. Clark, *British Clubs and Societies 1580–1800*, p. 3.
109 D. Hempton, *Methodism: Empire of the Spirit* (London: Yale University Press, 2005), pp. 13–16; J. Morgan-Guy, 'The Moravian Church', in R. C. Allen and D. C. Jones (eds), *The Religious History of Wales* (Cardiff: Welsh Academic Press, 2014). See also C. Podmore, *The Moravian Church in England 1728–1760* (Oxford: Clarendon Press, 1998).
110 Hughes (ed.), *Gweithiau William Williams Pantycelyn*, II, pp. 178–9.
111 DHH 129, notes inside front cover.
112 Trevecka MS 695, Howel Harris to Daniel Rowland, 15 October 1742.
113 Trevecka MS 633, Howel Harris to Daniel Rowland, 14 September 1742.
114 See, for instance, Henry Rack, *Reasonable Enthusiast: John Wesley and the Rise of Methodism* (London: Epworth Press, 1980), pp. 442–3; Rebekah L. Miles, 'Happiness, holiness, and the moral life in John Wesley', in R. L. Maddox and J. E. Vickers (eds), *The Cambridge Companion to John Wesley* (Cambridge: Cambridge University Press, 2010), p. 210.
115 *Sail, Dibenion a Rheolau*, p. 3; Hughes (ed.), *Gweithiau William Williams Pantycelyn*, II, p. 190.
116 Hughes (ed.), *Gweithiau William Williams Pantycelyn*, II, p. 200.
117 Hughes (ed.), *Gweithiau William Williams Pantycelyn*, II, p. 200.
118 DHH 130, 27 April 1744.
119 Trevecca College/1 2986, 3 February 1748.
120 DHH 134, 12 March 1749. Harris gave Acts 11:27–30 as an example, which contained the history of the church in Antioch sending contributions via Paul and Barnabas to help their co-believers in Judaea during a time of food shortages. The instructions regarding collection for the saints in 1 Corinithians 16:1–4 was also cited.
121 Trevecca College/1 3023, pp. 45–6, 14 January 1747.
122 NLW 18435B, p. 14, 9 August 1741.
123 DHH 101, 23 July 1743.
124 DHH 46, 20 July 1739.
125 DHH 54, 6 March 1740.
126 DHH 46, 18 July 1739.
127 DHH 50, 18 December 1739.
128 DHH 54, 14 March 1740.
129 W. R. Lambert, *Drink and Sobriety in Victorian Wales c.1820–c.1895* (Cardiff: University of Wales Press, 1983), pp. 128–9; R. Davies, *Hope and Heartbreak: A*

Social History of Wales and the Welsh, 1776–1871 (Cardiff: University of Wales Press, 2005), p. 333.
130 DHH 72, 28 April 1741.
131 DHH 49, 10 September 1739.
132 D. W. Howell, *The Rural Poor in Eighteenth-century Wales* (Cardiff: University of Wales Press, 2000), pp. 178–80.
133 S. Cooper, 'Kinship and Welfare in early modern England: Sometimes charity begins at home', in A. Borsay and P. Shapeley (eds), *Medicine, Charity and Mutual Aid: The Consumption of Health and Welfare in Britain, c. 1550–1950* (Aldershot: Ashgate, 2007), pp. 55–69.
134 Trevecka MS 1388, William Richard to Howel Harris, 2 January 1745.
135 T. Levi (ed.), *Casgliad o hen farwnadau Cymreig, yn dal cysylltiad a chyfundeby Methodistiaid a wnaed ar ran y Gymanfa Gyffredinol* (Wrexham: Hughes a'i Fab, 1872), p. 55.
136 Jones (ed.), *Gweithiau Williams Pant-y-celyn, Cyfrol I*, p. 479.
137 Jones (ed.), *Gweithiau Williams Pant-y-celyn, Cyfrol I*, pp. 434, 483.
138 Jones (ed.), *Gweithiau Williams Pant-y-celyn, Cyfrol I*, p. 650.
139 See R. Geraint Gruffydd, 'Marwnadau William Williams Pantycelyn', *Llên Cymru*, 17 (1993), pp. 254–71; Cathryn A. Charnell-White, 'Galaru a Gwaddoli ym Marwnadau Williams Pantycelyn', *Llên Cymru*, 26 (2003), pp. 40–62.
140 Trevecca College/1 3055, William Richard to the Association, 3 August 1748.
141 DHH 41, 2 March 1739.
142 Trevecca College/1 3066, William John to the Association, 20 October 1748.
143 Trevecca College/1 3027, William John to the Association, 2 July 1745.
144 Trevecca College/1 3055, William Richard to the Association, 3 August 1748.
145 Trevecca College/1 3055, William Richard to the Association, 3 August 1748.
146 Trevecca College/1 3065, William Richard to the Association, 19 October 1748.
147 Trevecca College/1 3027, William Richard to the Association, 2 July 1745; Psalms 84:4.
148 Trevecca College/1 3055, William Richard to the Association, 3 August 1748.
149 For similar themes in nineteenth-century obituaries, see David Bebbington, 'The Deathbed Piety of the Victorian Evangelical Nonconformists', in Coffey (ed.), *Heart Religion*, pp. 215–22.
150 Trevecca College/1 3040, William John to the Association, 20 July 1747.
151 DHH 36, 20 December 1738.
152 Trevecca College/1 3025, William Williams to the Association, January 1745.
153 See E. M. White, '"Myrdd o Wragedd": Merched a'r Diwygiad Methodistaidd', *Llên Cymru*, 20 (1997), 'Women in the Early Methodist Societies in Wales', *Journal of Welsh Religious History*, 7 (1999), and 'Women, Work and Worship in the Trefeca Family, 1752–1773', in P. Forsaith and G. Hammond (eds), *Religion, Gender and Industry* (Eugene, Oregon: Wipf and Stock, 2012).
154 K. Thomas, 'Women and the Civil War Sects', *Past and Present*, 13 (1958); P. Mack, *Visionary Women: Estatic Prophecy in Seventeenth-century England* (London: University of California Press, 1992); P. Crawford, *Women and Religion in England, 1500–1720* (London, Routledge, 1996), pp. 73–86; G. Malmgreen, *Religion in the Lives of English Women, 1760–1930* (London: Croom Helm, 1986), p. 1; W. J. Sheils and D. Wood (eds), *Women in the Churches*, Studies in Church History, 27 (Oxford: Blackwell, 1990).

155 W. Swift, 'The Women Itinerant Preachers of Early Methodism', *Proceedings of the Wesley Historical Society*, 28/5 (1952), 29/4 (1953); D. M. Valenze, *Prophetic Sons and Daughters: Female Preaching and Popular Religion in Industrial England* (Princeton: Princeton University Press, 1985); J. M. Lloyd, *Women and the Shaping of British Methodism: Persistent Preachers 1807–1907* (Manchester: Manchester University Press, 2009).
156 L. Wilson, *Constrained by Zeal: Female Spirituality among Nonconformists 1823–1875* (Carlisle: Paternoster Press, 2000). See also S. Morgan, *Women, Religion and Feminism in Britain 1750–1900* (Basingstoke: Palgrave Macmillan, 2002); S. L. Apetrei, *Women, Feminism and Religion in Early Enlightenment England* (Cambridge: Cambridge University Press, 2010); A. M. Lawrence, *One Family under God: Love, Belonging and Authority in Early Translatlantic Methodism* (Philadelphia: University of Pennsylvania Press, 2011).
157 Hempton, *Methodism: Empire of the Spirit*, p. 137.
158 D. Cressy, *Birth, Marriage and Death* (Oxford: Oxford University Press: 1997), pp. 15–54.
159 Kathryn Jenkins, 'Pantycelyn's Women Fact and Fiction: An Assessment', *Journal of Welsh Religious History*, 7 (1999), 77–94.
160 Jones (ed.), *Gweithiau Williams Pant-y-celyn, Cyfrol I*, p. 526.
161 Jones (ed.), *Gweithiau Williams Pant-y-celyn, Cyfrol I*, p. 525.
162 Levi (ed.), *Casgliad o hen farwnadau Cymreig*, pp. 57–8.
163 NLW MS 5456A, 11 August 1755.
164 P. Mack, *Heart Religion in the British Enlightenment* (Cambridge: Cambridge University Press, 2008), pp. 167–9.
165 Clark, *British Clubs and Societies 1580–1800*, p. 3.
166 DHH 70, 8 March 1741.
167 DHH 21 August 1743.
168 DHH 134, 5 March 1749.
169 DHH 110, 21 May 1744.
170 DHH 144, 19 April 1750.
171 DHH 145, 14 July 1750; 146, 3 December 1750.
172 DHH 146, 27 September 1750.
173 G. Malmgreen, 'Domestic discords: women and family in East Cheshire Methodism, 1750–1830', in J. Obelkevich, L. Roper and R. Samuel (eds), *Disciplines of Faith: Studies in Religion, Politics and Patriarchy* (London: Routledge and Kegan Paul, 1987), p. 58; Lloyd, *Women and the Shaping of British Methodism*, p. 5.
174 DHH 72, 29 April 1741.
175 Trevecka MS 569, Elizabeth Thomas to Howel Harris, June 1742.
176 Trevecka MS 642, William Richard to Howel Harris, 16 September 1742; W. G. Hughes-Edwards, 'The developments and organization of the Methodist Society in Wales 1735–50' (unpublished MA, University of Wales, 1966), 172.
177 Trevecca College/1 3004, 19 September 1743.
178 NLW St Davids Probate, SD/1770/220: Jenkin Lewis, Fareham, Hampshire (Blaen-porth), 1770.
179 SD/1792/9: Morgan Hughes, Blaen-porth, 1792.
180 SD/1770/6: Catherine Lewis, Blaen-porth, 1770. 'Mrs Lewis Blaneporth' was one of the places William Richard arranged for Howel Harris to visit in May

1742, although it is not clear if there is a connection here. Trevecka MS 550, William Richard to Howel Harris, 7 May 1742.
181 Lloyd, *Women and the Shaping of British Methodism*, p. 2.
182 NLW MS 18435B, p. 12, 31 July 1741.
183 T. Beynon, 'Morfa Bach, Cydweli', *Cylchgrawn Cymdeithas Hanesy Methodistiaid Calfinaidd/Journal of the Historical Society of the Presbyterian Church of Wales*, 16 (1931), 102; T. Beynon, *Allt Cunedda, Llechdwnni a Mwdlwscwm* (Aberystwyth, 1955), p. 82; G. M. Roberts, *Y Pêr Ganiedydd: (Pantycelyn), Cyfrol II: Arweiniad i'w Waith* (Llandysul: Gwasg Gomer, 1958), p. 27.
184 DHH 83, 17 December 1741.
185 NLW MS 18435B, p. 57.
186 DHH 70, 12 March 1741.
187 NLW 18435B, p. 41, 4 June 1742.
188 M. A. Noll, *The Rise of Evangelicalism: The Age of Edwards, Whitefield and the Wesleys* (Downers Grove, Illinois: InterVarsity Press, 2003), p. 141.

CHAPTER 6

'The World, the Flesh and the Devil'[1]: Order and Discipline

The major appeal of Methodism lay in the intense preaching and the close fellowship of the society, with its host of activities and fervent communal singing. It is these aspects which have tended to draw the interest of historians most of all. However, it should not be forgotten that careful planning was also required in order to make sure that this outburst of revival was channelled into an organised administrative structure. It has been suggested that early Calvinistic Methodism in Wales and Wesleyan Methodism in England were better organised and thus fared better in the long term than English Calvinistic Methodism.[2] Certainly, a degree of 'organisational coherence' and 'religious discipline' was evident amongst the Wesleyan movement,[3] and Welsh Calvinistic Methodism also managed to combine the heady enthusiasm of revival with more practical considerations of how best to organise the converts and to continue to oversee them in the societies. Since those issues had largely been resolved in the 1740s, there was a process in place by which to receive new members during subsequent periods of revival. It was this framework of rules and procedures which helped ensure Methodism's survival as a religious movement and ultimately a nonconformist denomination.

Long before it became a denomination, therefore, Welsh Methodism had recognised the need to devise its own rules and regulations in order to provide a structure for the converts, with clear guidelines to follow. The movement was carefully monitored and regulated by the system of stewards, exhorters and superintendents, all of whom ultimately reported to the Association and carried out its decisions. All these positions commanded authority, which was considered to be ultimately derived from God, so those who held them should be able to expect obedience and respect.[4] The basic framework was the result of discussions in the early 1740s, but rules and policies were also formulated subsequently in response to particular problems which arose among the members. Underlying all of the structures, rules and regulations was the need to keep alive the faith and enthusiasm of the members, as well as guard them from the temptations of the world, the flesh and the Devil.

The Order of the Societies

The earliest sets of rules were chiefly concerned with explaining the aims of the societies and justifying their existence through demonstrating their usefulness and tracing possible biblical precedents for such activities. The Welsh translation of George Whitefield's letter to the societies was published in 1740. A list of 'Rules of the Private Society' (*Rheola'r Socyaty Neilltuol*) was drawn up in 1740 but not published. There is also a collection of rules used in the Cardiganshire societies in the Llangeitho Manuscript, dating from 1741–4. There are very few actual rules in any of these collections, and they largely focus on exhorting members to meet together to help one another maintain the faith and to reinforce each other to resist temptation. Potential rules were discussed during 1741, and by 1742 the results of these discussions appeared in the first official rule book, *Sail, Dibenion a Rheolau,'r Societies* (The Foundation, Aims and Rules of the Societies).

This book concentrated on the aims of the society as an insitution and it echoes many statements found in the Llangeitho Manuscript. However, there were also instructions regarding accepting new members. Candidates for membership should appear before a society meeting having submitted his or her name to the previous meeting, along with testimony of good behaviour from some of the existing members. There is evidence of this procedure in action, for instance in July 1743, when three men and five women had put forward their names to the Fishguard society to be examined at the next meeting.[5] They were asked ten questions in order to gather detailed information relating to their spiritual condition. Most of these questions were concerned with personal experience, in an attempt to ensure that the individual was committed to being a member of the society. In terms of ideology, the new member was advised to avoid controversial subjects such as infant baptism and ecclesiastical organisation during meetings. New members were asked to agree to the teachings of the Church of England on the 'fundamental truths', namely the Trinity, election, original sin, justification by faith and continuing in a state of grace.

If the answers to these questions proved satisfactory, the candidate could then be admitted on trial to the general or public society. For example, St David's society had twelve members in July 1743 and an additional three men on trial, and Longhouse society had fifteen members with another three women on trial.[6] Acceptance to the private society followed if the new member passed muster during the trial period in the general society and after a further eight questions listed in the rule book were answered in an appropriate fashion. The second set of questions called for evidence of spiritual growth as a result of attending meetings. Having spent time in the environment of the society, the candidate was expected to demonstrate an increased sense of God's love, more sympathy with the sins of others, and a deeper conviction of their salvation through God's grace. After this the candidate might be accepted as a full member of the private society. Any applicant who was, in the opinion of the local superintendent, truly in search of faith should be received on trial. However, those who were not prepared to relinquish their old way of life or whose request to join the society was not deemed to be genuine might be rejected. The trial period could at times be extended over weeks or months, if the superintendent was not satisfied with the spiritual development of the candidate. In July 1743, for instance, William Richard decided to extend the trial period for Jane Edward, of Llwyndafydd society, because of her lack of knowledge.[7] Some who sought membership were not even considered suitable to be allowed a trial period, so fell at the first hurdle. William Richard absolutely refused to accept one man to the Llangeler society, although the reasons for the rejection are not recorded.[8] Howel Harris rejected an applicant to Carmarthen society because, although he seemed humble, 'I could not feel his spirit broken nor feel spirit in his Words'.[9] The need for witnesses to their good behaviour may have caused problems in some cases. Although many accounts of Methodist conversions dwell on prior sinfulness, there is often a tendency to emphasise what might be regarded as relatively minor transgressions. It is not clear how much of a barrier previous failings might be. In Cynwyl Elfed, Harris met 'a miserable object, a poor woman left entirely to herself', her isolation the result of disobeying her father and taking a lover. Presumably abandoned by the lover and having lost her former beauty, she was now the object of derision, with children throwing dung at her as she passed. Harris spoke with her more than once, read the Bible with her and prayed for her, yet seemed to feel that she was not serious enough about her own spiritual condition.[10] It was noted that Philip Pugh, the Dissenting minister, was taking her case 'seriously to consideration', so she may have been regarded as a suitable object of charity. Admission was not readily available to all, therefore, and it was generally accepted that it was not to the benefit of the movement to welcome someone as a member unless there was strong reason to feel confident that they would not lapse into apathy and backslide. However, in theory anyone who showed genuine signs of repentance and conviction was given an opportunity, and many societies were largely made up of those who were still striving to achieve a settled state of faith.

William Williams also drew up a set of questions for new members in his *Drws y Society Profiad* in 1777, based on his years of experience in societies. Many of these are very similar to those in *Sail, Dibenion a Rheolau,'r Societies*, including questions on justification by faith, awareness of the need for salvation and a willingness to abandon what was previously important. One difference is the lack of reference to the articles of the Church of England and the lack of a second set of questions for those already received on trial. Williams adds a number of additional questions relating to behaviour having joined the society, an issue which may not have received as much attention in 1742 as some of these problems had probably not come to fore by that point. These extra questions concern being prepared to contribute generously to the needy in the society and to suffer every persecution for the faith. Williams emphasises that all these questions are suggestions for use and not firm requirements, but he was obviously producing a guidebook for leaders of societies to follow so his questions may well have been put into practice. Their similarity to the list from 1742 suggests that the same basic themes were still regarded as highly important, even if there might be some developments in additional aspects.

Once accepted into the private society, all members were expected to be faithful to all its activities, an obligation which Howel Harris would remind members to observe on some of his visits.[11] He scolded members at Trefin in Pembrokeshire, for instance, for their lack of commitment in allowing a little rain to prevent them from meeting.[12] Methodists were expected to show a little more hardiness and determination than that or they would never contrive to meet in west Wales. The timing and frequency of meetings varied according to what was convenient to members in different areas and would have been influenced by factors such as distance to travel. The only firm rule was that meetings should not take place at the same time as church service. Society meetings would generally be lengthy affairs, perhaps especially so for a visit by one of the leaders such as Howel Harris. Harris spent two hours in a private society in Llechryd in 1748, and four hours, until 3 a.m., in Longhouse society in 1743.[13] On such occasions, the societies might delay the start of their meeting until after Harris had exhorted, so inevitably carrying on into the early hours. Most societies met in the evening at the end of the working day, which may well have involved late nights in any case. There were some exceptions, such as Haverfordwest society which met at 9 a.m. on two occasions when Harris joined them, although that again may have been a special arrangement to coincide with his visit.[14] Most societies met once or twice a week; Llanddeusant society, for example, held two meetings of the public society and one of the private society each week.[15] Intense local persecution could interrupt the usual routine of some societies. Carmarthen society was unable to meet regularly in 1745 because of the hostility of some local gentry.[16] Yet the major hurdle was usually the distance to travel, especially in winter, when some members were faced with difficult journeys and would have to spend considerable time trying to reach the meeting and return home afterwards. The societies of Merthyr and Tre-lech rarely met during 1745 because the members lived at a considerable distance from each other and found it difficult to gather together.[17] James Williams condemned the members of Caeo, Talley and Llansawel in 1746 for their laziness in suggesting that it might be better to split each of their societies in half in order to reduce the distance they had to travel to meetings.[18] On the other hand, William Richard arranged for the eighteen members of Llechryd society who lived in Pembrokeshire to meet separately in order to make it easier for them to attend more regularly.[19]

All these groupings were termed societies in exactly the same way, although in England the geographical divisions of the Llechryd society might have been considered 'class meetings'. Those subdivisions do not seem to have been adopted as commonly in Wales, and Harris explained to Whitefield, at the time when much of the organisation was being decided, that the societies in Wales were too scattered to make it possible to follow the same order as prevailed in London.[20] Howel Harris reported that he had divided those gathered to hear him at Ystrad-ffin in 1740 into bands and ordered the leaders to report to Daniel Rowland, but it is not clear if at that relatively early date these groups were bands within societies or newly formed societies.[21] The Association later decided that men and women should meet in separate bands 'as Spirit of the Lord should lead them'.[22] Despite that ruling, the practice does not seem to have been widespread, although there are stray references to bands in some societies, including Llwynygorras and Llanpennal.[23] There are indications of more systematic use elsewhere, including Richard Tibbott's societies in Montgomeryshire. He had evidently arranged the forty members of Llandinam society into separate bands for married and unmarried women and established separate bands for the twenty men and women in Llanllugan society.[24] The latter case was hardly a resounding success since the women apparently harboured considerable 'prejudice' towards each other. The distribution of societies to some extent, therefore, depended on the policy of the local superintendent who might prefer to group the members into smaller units, even if that increased the number of societies which had to be visited regularly. The contrast is obvious between the circuits under the supervision of William Richard and James Williams, with William Richard overseeing a cluster of relatively small cells quite close together in south Cardiganshire and north Pembrokeshire and Williams organising his flock into larger groups of over fifty members located at greater distance from each other.

When members did congregate, there were no strict regulations about what order to follow, since it was believed that the spirit should determine such matters and that the members should pray for guidance on what activities might be most appropriate.[25] If any activity was not proving beneficial, then another should be tried instead, which meant that the pattern the society followed could vary considerably. *Sail, Dibenion a Rheolau,'r Societies* did advise opening with a hymn and prayer before following the guidance of the spirit thereafter.[26] That was certainly the order followed in the societies attended by John Thomas of Tre-main in south Cardiganshire, in the 1750s, which was likely to be a continuation of the common practice in the 1740s. For instance, he described a society meeting at Tre-main in 1757 which began with the singing of a hymn, followed by prayers from four of the brethren and the subsequent exchange of experiences.[27] Harris would at times find hymn singing particularly beneficial in societies, but admitted that on occasion he felt dull and uninspired when questioning the members.[28]

As might be expected, prayer was one of the most fundamental elements of the society and would often begin a meeting. There were a number of standard subjects, including the continued success of the societies and the progress of Protestantism in general, especially when confronted with any challenge from Catholicism. Prayers were routinely offered on behalf of the King and the government of the day, in the face of any enemies, such as the Jacobite Pretender and his supporters. God's blessing was sought on some quite specific matters, such as the two-day fast Harris urged on the members of Eglwyswrw society in Pembrokeshire in 1748 in order to offer prayers against both the King of France and Sir Watkin William Wynn of Wynnstay, one of the fiercest persecutors of Methodism in north Wales.[29] The Welsh Methodists were generally very supportive of the government and firmly opposed to all attempts to depose the Hanoverian monarchy in 1745, despite being suspected of all sorts of nefarious associations and disloyalty to the Crown. Some of the Methodists in the south-west expressed their willingness to take up arms in defence of the King and showed their ardent support for him in prayer, as William Williams explained in a letter to Harris who was in London at the end of 1745: 'here are some fears by reason of the rebellion in the north but it would fill your soul with Love to God to see how fervent the poor Despised Methodist Pray for King George the Second and the Present Government.'[30] Although some such prayers might be fairly routine, there were occasions when prayer sparked off waves of enthusiasm. Members of societies in the Fishguard area apparently became so moved when saying grace before eating that their prayers lasted for three hours.³¹ The Association would from time to time instruct the societies to pool their resources by joining in a day of humiliation, which was set aside to fast and pray for a particular cause. This was a practice mentioned by Josiah Woodward as necessary in order to confess the public sins of the nation and to pray for improvement.³² It was resolved in June 1744 to keep the first such day for 'a variety of things'.³³ A Monthly Association meeting later the same year ruled that one day in each month should be set aside for fasting and prayer for the sins of the world.³⁴ Some days were dedicated to specific topics, such as 1 November 1744 to the commemoration of the persecution suffered by Methodists in Leominster.³⁵ On 19 March 1745, prayers were to be focused on healing the divisions in the movement in England and on countering any sense of apathy throughout Wales and England.³⁶

Prayer was naturally an essential element not just in society meetings but in the daily lives of the members. Harris was inclined to pray for God's guidance on all manner of decisions, including in May 1745 on whether or not he should buy a horse; even knowing that it would be of immense practical use, he did not feel able to go ahead without having sought divine approval.³⁷ The general attitude adopted by the Methodists was that God was involved in every aspect of their lives and no subject was too trifling to be the subject of prayer. Harris in particular felt that human reason was too flawed to be reliable, so that he could not decide on the basis of his own judgement alone. That was the motivation for drawing lots or allowing a verse selected at random from the Bible to determine how to proceed. Harris followed this course at Llwynyberllan in June 1750 soon after the separation, when he found that Rowland had arrived there also. Caught unawares and unsure how to deal with this unexpected situation, he sought guidance by opening the Book, as he termed it, and felt emboldened to stand his ground as a result.³⁸ Howel Davies apparently followed a similar trend of not trusting to human reason, according to the tradition that his New Chapel in Pembrokeshire was built on a site which he selected by throwing his whip in the air and laying the foundations where it chanced to fall.³⁹

Around the year 1742, there was an attempt to introduce the love-feast, a Moravian practice which seemed more popular in England than Wales.⁴⁰ This entailed a simple meal of bread and water which was shared between the members of the private society only.⁴¹ It was not intended to emulate a communion service but instead to reinforce the sense of fellowship between the membership. The first love-feast in Wales was held on 18 May 1742 at Longhouse, Mathry, home of the local society and a place Harris visited frequently.[42] Harris presided over this love-feast and was eager to establish the practice throughout the Welsh societies, who did not seem to share his enthusiasm. In September 1742, William Richard, despite being superintendent over Longhouse society which had played host to a love-feast, was asking quite fundamental questions about the significance of the love-feast and how it should be conducted.[43] It is significant that the only reference to a love-feast being held at an Association is at the Monthly Association at Trefeca in January 1745, since Harris could ensure that this went ahead when the meeting took place under his own roof.[44]

The activity which occupied most of the society's time was the relating of experiences often in response to questioning by a steward or exhorter. Any exhorter who visited a society where he was not already the designated private exhorter or superintendent tended merely to exhort and not to question the members.[45] Richard Tibbott, for instance, generally stated that he discoursed on verses from the Scripture when he visited societies in south Carmarthenshire, over which he had no regular authority.[46] Harris would often take advantage of such visits to explain the purpose of the society in general or to outline the organisation of the movement, although as general superintendent he was also in a position to conduct an ordinary society meeting and question members about their experiences. In Fishguard society in 1743, he explained the need for discipline within the movement and the vital importance of watching over each other.[47] In Cefntelych in Carmarthenshire in October 1748 Harris urged the members to interrogate him, and he responded to their questions about his place and authority in the movement, as well as the reasons for remaining loyal to the Church.[48] At this juncture, with tensions within the movement increasing, Harris may have been trying to allay fears by allowing members to ask him questions in a seemingly open fashion.

It was more customary for a steward to lead the society on most occasions, and this role was of fundamental importance to the entire system,[49] ever since it was formally resolved in Glanyrafonddu Association on 1 March 1743 to appoint a steward to each society.[50] The word *stiward* in Welsh was borrowed from the English movement, although there was also the occasional use of the Welsh word *blaenor* or leader. Wiliam Williams used *blaenor* to describe the steward of Llangwyryfon society and William John used the same term for the stewards of Llanegwad in 1747.[51] Howel Harris used 'leaders' on several occasions in 1740, which was another term borrowed from the movement in England, but not one which was much used subsequently, with steward becoming adopted as the usual term. This was not an elected role and a steward would usually be selected by the superintendent on the basis of merit. The direct responsibility for the society fell on the shoulders of the steward, but he was answerable to the private exhorter and the superintendent. He was required to provide a report to the monthly society, either in Pembrokeshire or in Carmarthenshire and Cardiganshire, where the local superintendents, exhorters and stewards met to consult each other about the work.[52] It was the steward who passed on the instructions of the Association and sought to carry them out in his society. He had to keep a register of those present, take responsibility for the weekly collections, ensure assistance to those in need and act as a mediator if any conflict arose between members.[53]

Most societies in the south-west were led by one steward, although the rules stated that it was possible to appoint more than one if the society was a large one, or the members were geographically scattered.[54] There was evidently a strong pastoral element to the role, which required visits to the homes of members as well as taking the lead in the meetings. Only three societies appear to have had two stewards in 1743, although they were by no means the largest in number: Fishguard with 35 members, Aberporth with 22 members and Llanddeusant with 28 members.[55] In the same year, Watkin Watkins was operating as steward over three societies in south Cardiganshire under William Richard: Llwyndafydd with 16 members, Blaenhownant with 12 members and Tŵr-gwyn with 11 members.[56] Although all three were fairly small societies, visiting each twice a week would mean a major commitment, and Watkins not unreasonably complained that this was causing him substantial difficulties. There seemed to be a degree of inconsistency of practice here, but much depended on the talents of the members of individual societies, and some smaller societies may have struggled to find anyone suitable to take on the position on a long-term basis. As with the role of exhorter, it was demanding in terms of time and travel, and could draw individuals away from their daily labours. Watkin Watkins was a well-to-do farmer verging on the lesser gentry, so might have been better placed to manage this than most, but even then was evidently struggling.

A capable steward was a great asset to a superintendent. It was the steward, along with the private exhorter, who spent most time with the society and would have a better knowledge of the members than anyone else. There is very little evidence of any problems arising in relation to the stewards, whose work was another vital element in the success of the movement. Morgan John Lewis, the superintendent who had care of Llanddeusant society in east Carmarthenshire, feared in 1744 that neither stewards nor private exhorters were fulfilling their duties conscientiously so that the movement was not recruiting new members as it should have done.[57] Yet, this seems to have been a lone expression of discontent and William Williams freely acknowledged the importance of a good steward to a society:

> Nid oes un teulu heb ben arno, nac un eglwys heb weinidog, nac un plwyf heb warden, ac mor anaddas bod society heb ben neu stiward arni.[58]

> There is no family without a head, nor a church without a minister, nor a parish without a warden, and how inappropriate that a society should be without a head or steward.

Williams portrayed the steward in his prose and poetry through stalwart, astute characters such as Theophilus in *Drws y Society Profiad* and Dr Alethius in his epic poem *Theomemphus*.[59] Williams outlined the multiple talents required by a steward, which included true godliness in order to be in a position to rebuke and advise members, a fearless spirit, genuine affection for all the society members and a large measure of religious zeal.[60]

In addition to all the practical aspects to a steward's duties, his primary responsibility was to take the lead in the society meetings and to question the members on their experience, helping them to analyse their spiritual condition. This activity was at the heart of the society's very existence and reflected the importance attributed to personal experience. A large number of the questions listed in the first rule book to be used to test candidates for the society begin with the words '*A ydych chi yn profi*? (Do you experience?).[61] It was considered vitally important for the members to relate their experiences so that they might then receive assistance to reflect on them and analyse their significance. The need to open their hearts to their fellow members was a constant refrain in most of the literature produced for the societies. George Whitefield advised setting aside time to confess faults and share experiences, in addition to other activities such as hymn singing and prayer.[62] The rules contained in the Llangeitho Manuscript and in *Sail, Dibenion a Rheolau,'r Societies* agreed with this suggestion:

> ... *bod ini agoryd ein Calonnau, yw gilydd ag adrodd yn Symlrwydd ein Calonnau yr hyn oll o'r drwg a'r Da yr ydym yn ei weled oddifewn ini, yn ôl y cymmorth a gaffom.*[63]

> ... that we open our hearts to each other and recite in the simplicity of our hearts, according to the help we receive, all of good and ill that we see within us.

This honest sharing was intended to provide the members with a forum in which they could express their innermost thoughts with an assurance of a sympathetic hearing from those who had often been through similar experiences. When all was well within a society, this could be joyous recounting of spiritual triumphs, as in Aberporth society where God, according to William Richard, 'is often pleas'd to take them into the Banqueting House and his Baner over them is Love, he dandles them upon his Knee and shows them many tokens of his Especiall Love!'[64]

Unlike the English Wesleyan societies, the Welsh societies had no set list of queries to ask regular members routinely once they were accepted. It may be that some of the questions for those on trial were repeated, especially perhaps the question regarding what lessons they had been taught since the previous meeting and how much of the deceit of Satan and the grace of God had they detected in their hearts.[65] The questions listed were far from as brief and direct as those drawn up for the Wesleyan bands.[66] William Williams hoped that experienced members would not need specific questions and could be moved to share their experiences without prompting. However, he did include examples of what might be asked, which are likely to be based on his own practice when conducting societies. These nine questions include several which are very similar to the eight questions listed for candidates for membership at the end of their trial period, reflecting the same urge to reflect on their progress. Williams emphasised the need for members to examine themselves carefully to ensure that they were growing in grace, acting out of the correct motives and making use of the talents they had received to the glory of God and the benefit of his Church.[67]

The rules stated that members were expected when opening their hearts to speak of the ill they saw as well as the good. Part of the rationale behind this was to prevent resentment from festering between members.[68] If such ill feeling remained unspoken it could increase and cause tension, so it was believed that raising such issues in the society could nip quarrels in the bud. Richard Tibbott described a meeting of Cilcarw society in Llangyndeyrn where the members openly discussed the prejudices they had harboured against one another.[69] Similar grievances emerged between some of the members of Fishguard society in 1744, but William Richard resolved the tensions by insisting that the members admit their faults and apologise for any cross words.[70] Airing a complaint against another member of the society was considered healthy, because if it was justified then some reprimand was required. However, if the accusation was unfounded, then it was a sure sign that the complainant harboured ill feelings and was guilty of a lack of brotherly or sisterly love, which needed to be addressed.

When confessing any temptations, a society member ought to feel sure of receiving support from the rest of the group. Part of the purpose of the society was to organise the members so that they were able to strengthen each other to resist temptation. The Methodists were in a constant state of war against their major enemies: the world, the flesh and the Devil, with the society designed as a means to arm them for battle. Howel Harris urged anyone who felt the temptations of nature threatening to defeat them to turn to the society and to pray for the strength to overcome.[71] By declaring their faults, they should come to know themselves better and to mature as Christians. James Williams praised Llanfynydd society in 1744 for growing in the ability to identify evil in their own hearts.[72] William Williams recommended asking the members if they felt themselves growing in grace as they examined their own hearts more carefully. More experienced Methodists should be able to detect in themselves the first signs of sin, before it had the chance to poison them completely.[73] Williams believed that such perception of their own weakness should make them more inclined to take a sympathetic view of any failings in their fellow members and to realise the need for God's forgiveness for their sins. The society did not offer any absolution, but could help any of its members to pray for God's forgiveness. After careful self-reflection, members were asked if they felt:

> mwy o oleuni ysbrydol o'u mewn yn datguddio iddynt fwy o burdeb y gyfraith, sancteiddrwydd Duw, pla eu calonnau, drwg pechod, gwerthfawrogrwydd cyfiawnder Crist, a holl addewidion y cyfamod newydd, ynghyd â'r aneirif ddichellion sydd gan y byd, y cnawd a'r diafol i'w denu oddi wrth Dduw?[74]

> more spiritual light within them revealing to them more of the purity of the law, the sanctity of God, the plague of their hearts, the evil of sin, the value of Christ's justice, and all the promises of the new covenant, along with the innumerable deceits which the world, the flesh and the devil have to draw them away from God?

It was the role of the questioner, who was usually but not always the society steward, to ensure that there was a balance between good and ill, celebration and complaint, for the benefit of the entire society.[75] There was an art to leading society discussions, which called for wisdom and discretion. One golden rule was that nothing that was discussed in the society should ever be repeated. It was also judged that there were some confidential matters that it was best not to air before everyone and would be better discussed in private with the steward. Other issues to be avoided were fleeting temptations which had little impact, or sins which had already been confessed and overcome. It was also considered inappropriate for a husband and wife to complain of each other before the society. For the rest, it was for the steward to ensure that everyone was treated equally and that no favouritism was shown to those of higher social status. Everyone should be included and have their opportunity to speak. To that end, it was important to ask a range of questions which were appropriate to everyone, as there would be different problems and preoccupations according to age, gender and spiritual experience. There were a number of considerations involved in leading a successful experience meeting, including how to analyse the experiences and offer appropriate guidance. Thus, as William Williams suggested:

> *trwy brofiadau y dyn a holir mae'r holiedydd yn ennyn canwyll o ddisgleirdeb nefol i'r holl gymdeithion ac yn gwneud iddynt ddysglaid o fwyd melys, o bosibl o brofiad tlawd ac anniben.*[76]

> through the experiences of the man questioned the questioner lights a candle of heavenly brilliance for all the fellows and prepares for them a bowl of sweet food, possibly from a poor and untidy experience.

Moreover, the same group could require a very different approach at different times so it was important to judge the mood of the society at each meeting. On one occasion in a society in Llan-non in Carmarthenshire, Howel Harris sensed that there was 'a Judas' in their midst and those present were speaking from head knowledge rather than from their hearts, which was an important distinction in the eyes of the Methodists.[77] Moses John of Llwyndafydd society, for instance, was said to have 'much knowledge but very little experience'.[78] It was necessary to judge the capacity of those present at the society and tailor the discussion to suit them all in some way.

The society developed its own terminology to categorise the experiences of its members, inevitably borrowing from the Bible. The same sorts of phrases were used by different superintendents to describe the different stages of experience and in some reports the members would be divided not by gender and marital status but by spiritual condition. The two major distinctions were between those under the law and those freed by their faith in Christ, although there were variations on the wording to describe each state.[79] In 1743, for example, James Williams declared that twenty-seven of the sixty members of Caeo society were free and the rest still under the law.[80] There were a number of members in each society who were categorised as 'under the law', 'under the power of unbelief', 'under the spirit of captivity' or 'in bondage', yet were eligible for membership on the basis that they were genuinely seeking new birth, such as James Evan of Newport, Pembrokeshire, who was 'under ye Law, has tasted some love and begins to see his own vileness'.[81] Others were designated as 'searching for the pearl', such as Evan Hugh, Thomas John and Thomas Francis from Aberporth society in 1743.[82] Similar categories were those who were 'looking for a saviour' or 'thirsting for God's word', who were considered to be on the right path. The other major category were the 'experienced Christians', who were 'justified' or 'in freedom', such as Thomas John from Llanarthney society, who was said to be justified and 'walking very worthfull'.[83] The entire society at Lledrod in north Cardiganshire had achieved a similar state by 1745 and, according to William Williams, shone forth like a city on a hill.[84] Similarly, Llan-non in 1746 had triumphed over the world, the flesh and the Devil.[85] On occasion, rather than writing a full description of the spiritual state of some of the members, references to verses from the Bible were noted in order to indicate their condition. So in Dyffryn-saith in 1743, Anne David, Anne Jenkins and Elizabeth Thomas were grouped together under Luke 15, a chapter which contains the parables of the lost sheep, the lost coin and the prodigal son.[86] Nothing further needed to be said to an audience familiar with their Bible. Some reports expanded further than just the reference to specific verses, with John Richard noting in 1744 that several in the societies of Llan-non, Llanarthney, Cilcarw and Pembrey who had previously been justified were now in doubt because, as in Galatians 15, they had come to misunderstand and pervert the gospel.[87]

In many ways, the relationship between members in the societies was similar to that of a family, with the steward as paterfamilias. The Methodists generally called each other 'brother' and 'sister', as a sign of the close unity within the movement. Yet, the Methodists were often believed to create conflict with the biological family, who might disapprove of their relatives' religious choices. The ideal was to recruit the entire family, who might then engage in family devotions and maintain the standards of holy living within the household. Although that might be the case in some families, like the Thomas family of Longhouse, there were obviously other instances where it was the younger family members who were attracted to the societies, leaving them at odds with their closest relatives.

Discipline and Authority

Discipline in itself is not a topic which has received a great deal of attention from Methodist historians,[88] but it was an essential element in the organisation of the movement from the start. Every society needs its rules, along with a system to enforce them and to punish those who transgress. Discipline within the societies was intended to guard the members against falling into temptation and to help them ward off the wiles of the Devil, who it was believed was intent on drawing them to destruction.[89] It was therefore a serious matter, or, as Harris insisted, 'an awfull thing'.[90] The society members were warned constantly about the very real threat represented by the Devil – Satan, the enemy or the serpent as he was also called. Fear of the Devil's actual presence seemed to persist into the eighteenth century in rural Wales, along with a tendency to attribute evil deeds to his instigation.[91] He was a nagging, dangerous tempter who had to be resolutely resisted. John Thomas's spiritual autobiography is littered with references to 'the enemy', with every fleeting temptation or error attributed to his guile.[92] It was believed that he was thwarted by the societies,[93] but, without their backing, the members were felt to be terrifyingly vulnerable to his attacks. As Eusebius in *Drws y Society Profiad* urged his friend and mentor, Theophilus,

> *Cofiwch amdanof fi a'm society fechan. Nid ynt hwy na minnau ond eiddilod gweinion, a Satan yn hen ac yn gyfrwys.*[94]

> Remember me and my little society. Neither they nor I are more than frail weaklings, and Satan is old and cunning.

The superintendents would often attribute any prejudice or dispute within the bounds of a society to the machinations of the Devil and would consider any positive outcome to such troubles to be a direct victory over him, as in Llangathen in 1741 where it was said that 'the enemy and his instruments raged' but to no avail.⁹⁵ Part of the guidance offered in the society was to help the members become familiar with those tendencies within them which the Methodists considered to stem from the Devil and his temptations. James Williams hoped in October 1744 that his societies were succeeding in doing so:

> ... *fy mod yn cael lle i gredu fod yr Arglwydd Iesu yn dwyn ei waith yn y blaen a hwynthe yn cael ei dysgu yn fwy manol a phrofiadol ag yn cael ei goleyo i weled mwy o ddrwg ei calone, a nabod mwy o ddichellion y gelyn diafol, ag yn teimlo mwy o nerth ysbryd Duw yn ei cynnal ag yn ei gwaredy tan ei holl brofedigaythe.*⁹⁶

> ... that I have reason to believe that the Lord Jesus carries his work forward and that they are taught in a more detailed and experience way and are enlightened to see more of the evil of their hearts, and know more of the deceits of the enemy the devil, and feel more of the strength of God's spirit supporting them and sparing them through all their tribulations.

In order to protect the society members from temptation, they were encouraged to keep the ungodly world at arm's length, with strict discipline established to try to enforce this. Membership involved more than simply attending meetings, but being prepared to change one's way of life to maintain a standard of holy living in keeping with the Methodist way. The rules and regulations were also intended to safeguard the reputation of Methodism as a whole, to avoid any individual bringing shame on the entire movement. Critics of Methodism would snatch at any signs of misdoing or immorality as evidence of underlying hypocrisy. The leaders hoped that such scandals could be avoided and that the societies would instead shine forth like candles, lighting up their vicinity.⁹⁷

If any member were to offend against the Methodist rules, then they could be punished by receiving either a reprimand from the steward in private or in front of the society, or, in more serious cases, being excluded for a period from the private society and relegated to the public society.

For example, a complaint about the behaviour of Thomas Hugh, Lettice Hugh and Martha Owen from Fishguard society led to them being relegated for a month on trial, primarily because they sought to hide their faults when questioned rather than confessing openly. All three were unmarried but there is no further information about their offence, other than a statement that they had 'walked uncivil'.[98] The responsibility for any such discipline rested in the first place with the steward, who decided if the society needed to be told of any transgression. When more serious offences occurred, the steward would consult the superintendent and it was the latter who would make decisions about excluding members completely from the society. Howel Harris, as general superintendent, and the evangelical clergy in the movement also had the authority to expel members and did so on occasion when consulted by the superintendent. The first time Harris expelled someone was in Llan-non in south Carmarthenshire in 1744, when he turned out one of the men for breaking the rules by marrying without the permission of the society.[99] There was some difference of opinion among the leaders on the question of expulsion, with Harris clashing with both Daniel Rowland and William Williams in the Association on this point.[100] Harris would complain that at times Daniel Rowland was willing to offer communion to individuals that Harris had already excluded, which he felt showed a lack of consistency and undermined his position.[101] It was decided by the Association in 1747 that if Harris, or one of the clergy, or the local superintendent had taken the decision to expel a member then none of the others should reverse that decision, although they might raise the issue with the person responsible if they had reservations.[102] In that way, they would not be seen to disagree and question each other's authority. Harris was chiefly responsible for fashioning the regulations and tended to be rather more assiduous in adminstering the rules than some of his colleagues. He was convinced that in such matters he was carrying out God's will, so to question him was tantamount to challenging God.[103] Rowland and William Williams seemed rather more lenient on such matters. In a sermon on '*Cerydd a Chariad Brawdol*' ('Punishment and Brotherly Love'), Rowland advised those responsible for discipline to be absolutely certain of guilt before doling out any punishment. Even then, he advocated mercy:

Da yw fod cymmaint o boethder mewn cerydd, ag y codo efe ymaith y blew, ond nid mor boeth ag yr ysgaldano ef y croen. Fe wnaeth Eliseus fwy â chusan, nag a wnaeth ei was ef â ffon: anwylyd, os gwna cusan y tro, gochelwch gario dannedd yn eich tafodau.[104]

It is good that a rebuke is hot enough to lift the hairs, but not so hot as to scald the skin. Elisha did more with a kiss than his servant with a stick: dearest, if a kiss will do, refrain from carrying teeth in your tongues.

Williams, through the character of Theophilus in *Drws y Society Profiad*, judged that it was not appropriate to dismiss anyone save for

achosion mawrion a diarbed, sef gweled dyn yn myned ymlaen yn ei bechod, ei garu, ymbleseru ynddo, a mynych gwympo iddo, heb edifarhau, ond yn hytrach ymgaledu, gan ddiystyru arghoeddiadau Duw a dynion.[105]

great causes, namely seeing a man going ahead in his sin, loving it, taking pleasure in it, falling frequently into it, without repenting, but rather hardening, ignoring the convictions of God and men.

Harris agreed that the 'incorrigible' should be disowned.[106] According to Williams, it was best to offer a tender word of reproof and show mercy to those who fell into sin for the first time, or who surrendered to a fleeting temptation without fully realising the import of their actions. He employed a number of examples from the New Testament to justify such a lenient approach, including Christ forgiving Peter's denial and his merciful attitude to the woman caught in adultery, as well as Paul's advice to attempt to restore a fellow believer who was at fault. However, if someone persisted in their transgression, without repenting and learning to hate their sin, then they should be reprimanded before the whole society as a warning to others. If the fault was known to the outside world, then a more public penance was appropriate in order to demonstrate that the movement did not countenance such behaviour. If any member of the society acted in a way which was contrary to the standards of the society and in tune with the world of unbelievers, then a stern rebuke was required, with the threat of expulsion if there was no improvement. Williams's system of discipline therefore showed a twofold concern with the spiritual condition of the members and the perception of the movement given to the outside world, two considerations which seemed to govern much of the thinking regarding discipline in general.[107]

Expulsion was the most extreme form of punishment, but it did not have to be final, since anyone who showed genuine signs of remorse, in the opinion of the steward and superintendent, could be allowed to return, with the consent of the other members. This happened in the case of one woman who was expelled by William John from Carmarthen society for unbecoming conduct but who was allowed to return after she showed repentance.[108] In other cases, the society could lose members on a permanent basis, either because they resented the measures taken and resolved not to return, or because the superintendent was not convinced that they were truly sorry. For instance, William Richard refused to accept the return of two members of Llwyndafydd society in south Cardiganshire who had been guity of an unspecified sin which 'brought shame to religion', because he did not feel the two were genuinely penitent.[109] However, a group of members excluded from Meidrim society for selling goods on a Sunday felt so aggrieved at their treatment that they made no request to return.[110] There was always the possibility that some would rebel against the authority of the societies in this way, and it may have been one of the potential dangers of the emphasis on individualism. Discipline was always a balancing act between maintaining standards and risking the loss of some followers. However, the priority of the movement overall seemed to be the need to keep to the established moral code even if that meant a reduction in numbers.

This was particularly apparent when it came to matters of love and romance. The most common cause for expulsion throughout the south-west – and beyond – was for marrying or planning to marry against the wishes of the society or without its consent. That this was an issue should come as no surprise, bearing in mind William Williams's description of the people of the society as:

cwmpeini o lanciau hoenus a gwrol, tyrfa o ferched yn eu grym a'u nwyfiant, dynion y rhan fwyaf ohonynt ag sy gan Satan le cry i weithio ar eu serchiadau cnawdol, ac i'w denu at bleserau cig a gwaed.[111]

a company of lively and manly youths, a crowd of girls in their heyday, people, most of them, upon whose carnal desires Satan can work, and to draw them to the pleasures of the flesh.

The superintendents were very aware of the problem, as James Williams noted: '*... ar ffordd fwa dichellgar yr wyf yn ei weled gan Satan i lygry ac i weithio rhagfarn ydyw cary cnawdol*' ('... and the most deceitful means I see Satan has to corrupt and to work prejudice is carnal love').[112] Richard Tibbott confessed in his diary that 'impure thoughts' had often prevented him from feeling free to exhort and share experiences with women in the societies in the same way as the men.[113]

By maintaining the focus of the members on the society and its activities and, to a degree, isolating them from the outside world, the movement tended to restrict their scope when it came to choosing partners. Other religious groups who were concerned about marriage to outsiders encountered similar difficulties. The Society of Friends also disowned more members because they were unable to abide by the rules on marriage than for any other reason during the eighteenth century.[114] The prospect of marrying a non-member caused alarm as it might be difficult to continue to attend in such circumstances, unless the spouse could also be drawn into the movement. Richard Tibbott noted that several members were lost to the societies in Carmarthenshire because they were drawn away by romantic attachments, or 'carnal love' to use the Methodist terminology.[115] William Williams was deeply concerned that the same situation prevailed in north Cardiganshire as well.[116] The problem had become sufficiently troubling by 1747 for the Association to judge that rules and regulations were needed to provide the superintendents with guidelines to follow when faced with these issues.[117] The ruling was that no society member was to make an offer of marriage without first consulting his superintendent, and anyone who broke this rule could be expelled automatically. If the superintendent was unsure whether or not to approve the match, he should seek the advice of Howel Harris as general superintendent or of one of the evangelical clergy. The decision to marry was a serious undertaking which should not be entered into lightly and there was little leeway allowed for a change of heart. If one of the couple were to change their mind in advance of the wedding, they would not then be considered free to marry anyone else while the other still lived. The decision of the superintendent was paramount, and the parents of the young people concerned had no voice and there was no expectation that they should be consulted until after the matter was aired with the society. Howel Harris believed that parents had no right to prevent their children from marrying or to force them to marry against their will, although his opinion might conceivably have been skewed by the opposition of his wife's family to their proposed marriage.[118]

The superintendents had to adminster these rules fairly regularly and tended to take a stern approach. William Williams, generally regarded as one of the most human and sympathetic of the Methodist leaders, ruthlessly warned a man from Lledrod to give up his relationship with a woman who was not a fellow believer, or bid farewell to the society.[119] He was deeply disappointed as well at what he considered the folly of an elderly woman from Llangwyryfon who parted company with the society in order to marry a non-believer.[120] William John felt forced to expel a young woman from Llanegwad society because he claimed she was keeping 'carnal company' with a number of young men.[121] The Methodist language tends to make these affairs sound more scandalous than they may have been, as 'carnal', or '*cnawdol*' in Welsh, tended to be used for any relationship that was not regarded as stemming from God or sanctioned by him and the society.

As these examples indicate, forming suitable relationships was more of a problem for the women in the societies, who usually outnumbered the men. The result was that several were placed in the invidious position of being forced to choose between love and faith. It was the dilemma which faced several of the sisters in the society which prompted William Williams to write his guidebook on marriage in 1777, *Ductor Nuptiarum neu Gyfarwyddwr Priodas* (*Ductor Nuptiarum* or a Guide to Marriage). Despite the growth in moral and didactic literature through the medium of Welsh in the eighteenth century, there were none of the guidebooks on marriage and women's role in society which appeared elsewhere in Europe, so Williams was something of a pioneer in this respect. Derec Llwyd Morgan considers this to be the first substantial discussion in Welsh on the role of women in society or on the female psyche.[122] It is known that Williams had a copy in his library of the English translation of the work of the French feminist author, Poulain de la Barre, *The Woman as Good as the Man, or the Equality of Both Sexes* (1677).[123] However, Williams cannot really be considered a feminist ahead of his time. As with all his publications, his guiding motivation was the needs of the people of the societies, and he had been well aware of the complications surrounding the question of marriage since he was first appointed superintendent over north Cardiganshire in the 1740s. He was a man who seemed to have a genuine respect for women, undoubtedly fed by a successful marriage and a happy home life where capable women were consistently in the majority, surrounded as he was by his wife Mary and their four daughters, as well as his mother Dorothy, who remained with the family until her death in 1784 at the age of 95.

The focus of this work was the problem of 'unequal' marriages with those outside the faith. It took the form of four dialogues, the first three between two old friends, Mary Eugamus and Martha Pseudogam, who encounter each other for the first time after a gap of some years, and the last between Pamffila and Evangelius, her mentor. The dialogue was a traditional device to convey essential information in a more lively format to make it more accessible to the reader. The fourth dialogue between Pamffila and Evangelius was more conventional in that it concerned a less experienced character seeking advice from an authority figure who was male. In the other three dialogues, the wiser voice was Mary, who was a contemporary of Martha's, but a more experienced and committed member of the society who had followed the approved path on the question of marriage and could thus offer advice to her less fortunate sister. It was unusual for such a dialogue to be exclusively female, but the advice was primarily aimed at women, and the two female characters were able to compare their experiences of marriage in order to provide an example to aspire to and a pitfall to avoid. The discussion is also as a result more frank than it might have been possible for the author to write between male and female characters. Both women had been members of the same society so knew each other of old, but Martha had flitted away from religion in order to marry the young man who had beguiled her. Their affection was based on physical desire and disappeared 'like mist before the wind' as Martha's figure coarsened as a result of childbearing. Mary, by way of contrast, had married Philo Alethius with the consent of the society having sought God's blessing above all. Their love had deepened since as a result of the joy they found in each other's devotion to the faith:

> *Dyma'r cariad sydd gennym ni yn awr; cariad gwastad, dwfn yw, fel y môr, ag a ddwg feichiau mawrion y naill dros y llall, fel yr ym heddiw ond un cnawd, un enw, un interest, un diben, un farn, un goleuni; yr un peth ydym yn gasáu, yr un peth ydym yn chwennych.*[124]

> This is the love we have now; it is a deep, constant love, like the sea, which carries great burdens, one for the other, so that we are today but one flesh, one name, one interest, one aim, one opinion, one light; we hate the same thing, we want the same thing.

Having established the misery of Martha's marriage and the contentment experienced by Mary, the third dialogue consists of Mary's advice to Martha on how to salvage her marriage by showing her husband renewed respect and affection in order to regain influence over him. Williams advised the use of feminine wiles since even the wisest of men would be susceptible to this approach:

> *Mae gallu gan ein sex ni, O Martha, yn enwedig os byddant ond glân a hawddgar, a chyfrwystra nid bychan i demtio y doethaf, y callaf, a'r cryfaf o wyr, fel mae yn anodd iawn dianc o'n rhwydau, oni atal gras y nef ... Ein traed, ein dwylo, ein gruddiau, a phob rhannau eraill o'n cyrff ... a wnawn ni yn faglau a rhwydau llwyddiannus i ennill pob gwrywaid ond efnuchiaid ...*[125]

> Our sex has power, O Martha, especially if they are but pure and amiable, and no little cunning to tempt the wisest, the

most sensible and the strongest of men, so that it is very difficult to escape our snares, unless heavenly grace intervenes ... Our feet, our hands, our cheeks, and all other parts of our bodies ... we make into successful traps and snares to win all males save eunuchs ...

By winning over her husband in this way, Martha may then be able to persuade him to follow the faith. The advice in the fourth dialogue is equally forthright, with Pamffila expressing her desire to marry, stating that flesh and spirit were at war within her night and day. However, she is advised to remain single rather than risk her faith through marriage to an unbeliever. This frank discussion of female sexuality proved too much for the more prudish nineteenth century and, despite Williams's fame, this volume was considered too indecent to be reprinted.

Whilst marriage between fellow members could be beneficial so that they might support each other's faith, there was always the possibility of an unsuitable attachment. A brother from Llanwinio society married a sister from Cilrhedyn society and both proved a blessing to each other, which was the ideal situation.[126] A young woman from Llanpumsaint society married a Methodist from the Llanddowror area, but instead of sustaining each other in the faith their relationship was said to have brought shame on religion.[127] There was considerable pressure to try to establish whether the relationship would be beneficial, and sometimes the superintendent concerned struggled with the decision. John Richard agonised for some time over the proposed marriage of two members in his area.[128] The problem was that the two were lodging in the same house and were already in the throes of a physical relationship so that the woman in particular felt bound to marry in order to try to salvage her reputation. Although they had informed the society of their plan to marry, John Richard was reluctant to give his approval without further evidence of a real commitment which was not based solely on physical desire. After seeking guidance through prayer, he concluded that they could be forgiven their behaviour, but he did not feel free to sanction the marriage without consulting Harris, whose ultimate opinion is not recorded. This is a case which may also draw on customary attitudes to practices such as bundling, which allowed courting couples a degree of familiarity, with the possible acceptance that there could be consequences which would have to lead to immediate marriage.¹²⁹ Yet, here John Richard's response was not to act hastily in order to maintain a degree of respectability, but to concentrate on the nature of the relationship itself. Methodist courtship could be a very complicated and protracted process as a result, with many young couples struggling to conclude decisively that their feelings of affection were not temptations sent by the Devil. This was also apparent in the story of John Thomas, Tre-main, in the 1750s.¹³⁰ He spent an entire year praying for guidance whether he should marry the girl he loved. He delayed discussing the matter with the society or his superintendent, William Richard, because he was not convinced that he could answer their questions with a clear conscience. After much soul-searching, he concluded that the relationship was the work of God and gained the approval of the society and the consent of his beloved. There was to be no turning back after this momentous decision was finally reached, not even when the unfortunate John fell ill with smallpox three days before the wedding. The intense introspection that was required in matters of the heart could lead to this sort of indecision and may explain E. P. Thompson's dismissal of the very notion of a passionate Methodist lover![131]

Although marriage and relationships were the cause of most expulsions from the society, there were a range of other problems which led to members being excluded or reprimanded. John Harry in south Pembrokeshire expelled several from the societies for drunkenness although they were subsequently allowed to return.[132] Evan Rees Reynold was cast out of Llangwyryfon society by William Williams in 1750 for deceit.[133] Several members of Meidrim society were expelled for breaking the Sabbath by selling goods on Sunday.[134] Harris seemed also to disapprove of fiddlers, and on occasion reproved those who allowed dancing in their houses or sent their children to dancing schools.[135] He had harsh words for the inhabitants of Carmarthen for indulging in riotous behaviour at election time, which was something of a tradition of the tumultuous politics of the town.[136] Complaining about bad weather affecting the harvest was a fault he detected in the people of Tre-lech, although one suspects it was far more widespread, considering the vital importance of a successful harvest.[137]

Converts were questioned before being accepted into the society whether they were ready to reject all those things which had been precious to them beforehand.[138] In reality, there were many converts who confessed they found it difficult to give up all their bad habits on joining the society and that there lurked a danger of falling prey to their besetting sin, whether it be dancing, cockfighting, smoking or worse. It was especially difficult to observe the rules when it came to practices which were generally considered socially acceptable and even at times expected of a member of a community. A particular problem troubling the societies in south Cardiganshire and north Pembrokeshire by 1748 was the dictate forbidding attending a *neithior* or wedding feast. The Methodist line on this was that such occasions involved drinking and dancing in the company of unbelievers, and there was therefore a very real risk of yielding to temptation. Howel Davies was faced with this problem time and time again in Pembrokeshire and believed that 'many of ye Brethren that frequent them are generally drawn aside by Satan some way or other before they depart & which greatly hinders ye Success of ye Gospel among us.'[139] Several members rebelled against this ruling, arguing that there was no scriptural basis for avoiding weddings, and that this was just a whim on the part of the leaders.[140] They also felt a social imperative, as such bidding feasts were the custom in the south-west which helped enable young couples to gain the wherewithal to set up house. Family, friends and neighbours brought gifts to help furnish the marital home and would find the favour returned when the time came. To opt out of participating was to ostracise oneself from the local community in a way which could have made life very awkward. The Methodist leaders were unyielding in the matter, however, and John Harry expelled some members in his societies in the south of the county who refused to pay heed to his and Howel Davies's warnings.[141]

Another conflict of opinion arose along the west coast over the attitude to smuggling and looting shipwrecks. These were practices which were popularly regarded in a very different light from the official view, which designated them as capital offences in the mid-eighteenth century. Looting shipwrecks was held to be a traditional right of those who lived near the sea, although it was at odds with the letter of the law.[142] Most of the activity in the south-west was not the outcome of deliberate wrecking, a fact which supported the argument that this was just a matter of taking advantage of unfortunate accidents rather than actively breaking the moral code. However, John Harry expelled six south Pembrokeshire members for intentionally luring a ship to be wrecked in order to steal the cargo.[143] That was a rare occurrence, and most other instances seemed to be a matter of opportunistic stealing. Even that was enough for Howel Harris to threaten to expel any society member who went anywhere near a shipwreck with any thought except to help those on board to safety.[144] He vented his wrath in particular to the inhabitants of Penbryn in south Cardiganshire and Hayscastle in Pembrokeshire, with warnings often coupled with diatribes against smuggling. It is not clear just how much free trading was carried on in the area, although there are traditions of smugglers along the coast in the vicinity of Penbryn.[145] The autobiography of William Owen of Narberth (1717–47) shows that there were some daring smugglers flouting the authorities in the Cardigan and north Pembrokeshire area at the time.[146] The Cardiganshire coast in particular was associated with such illegal activities and gained an unsavoury reputation, as seen in the description of the people of Aberporth by their vicar, David Jones: 'The inhabitants of this Neighbourhood are mostly Seafaring Men, which, of all People here, as in other Maritime Places, are the most rude Folks as concerning good Parts and manners ...'[147]

It was difficult for the Methodists to persuade their followers that smuggling was a great evil, as the common perception was that tolls and taxes were unreasonably high on imported goods, so that there was justification for avoiding them. It was probably viewed as a victimless crime, but Harris tried to explain that it was serious theft, as it was essentially robbing the government of its rightful dues, with the ultimate effect of leaving Britain unable to finance the defence of its coastline.[148] The fact that this was a fairly consistent theme throughout the 1740s suggests that the inhabitants of the seaside proved difficult to persuade or command on this point. It seems that people in Cornwall and other coastal areas of England demonstrated a similarly intransigent attitude to Methodist preaching against smuggling and looting, to the point that John Wesley published his *Word to a Smuggler* in 1767.[149] The level of resistance to Methodist preaching against these practices suggests a deeply held popular belief that these habits were legitimate and should not be condemned as sinful.

Other worldly preoccupations also caused concern, and the movement frowned on a lack of concentration on spiritual matters.

Harris declared himself willing at all times to expel any member who gave too much thought to the world.[150] Isolation from the bustling world of daily commerce was difficult to achieve, especially for members who earned their living as craftsmen and farmers, and could not necessarily pick and choose from whom they bought and to whom they sold. Harris was also cutting to those who did business with 'the carnal' rather than with their fellow Methodists, and suggested they were often cheated as a result.[151] There were attempts via the English evangelical magazines to promote business within Methodist circles so as not to have to deal with the outside world, but this was far less feasible in a Welsh context where the societies were more widely dispersed. It was nigh on impossible to use only Methodist craftsmen and tradesmen exclusively as a result, even had one wished to do so.[152]

Methodists should also guard against profligate spending on what were considered 'superfluities' or luxuries. They were asked to question themselves rigorously before spending out of pride and consequence on items that were not strictly necessary. Essentials were permitted, and even to a degree what might be considered 'decencies' or 'conveniences', which did not reach the level of luxury items but suggested a degree of comfort above the basic requirements.[153] Overindulgence was to be strictly avoided, with moderation, rather than total abstinence, advocated in food, drink and general habits. Harris roundly condemned celebrating Christmas by indulging in finer food and drink rather than concentrating on the spiritual side of the festival.[154] Even the normally abstemious leaders sometimes fell foul of their own strictures, being accused of too much feasting during the Association meeting at Porth-y-rhyd, Carmarthenshire, in October 1744, when fasting would have been more becoming.[155] Worse than overindulgence in food and drink, however, was a fondness for 'superfluities' such as tobacco and snuff. Inhaling snuff was regarded as rather more genteel than smoking tobacco as it avoided generating smoke and ash, though encouraging further expenditure on ornate snuff boxes. The Methodists regarded them in the same light as wasteful indulgence. William Williams was scathing about those who were addicted to the 'leaf from the Virginian fields' or preferred 'draughting frothy beer, sweet wine, punch, toddy or rum' rather than devoting their thoughts to higher matters.[156] Tea, however, was a fashion more readily adopted by most Methodists, even if Williams also criticised those who professed religion but wasted their time chattering over teacups. Such social occasions were always an opportunity for light conversation and gossip, which should probably not be a favoured occupation in a serious convert.

Harris insisted that rules were broken not just by outward immorality but by inward spiritual faults,[157] which were often more difficult to police and correct. Spiritual pride was a weakness which many other religious groups detected in the Methodists. Griffith Jones wished that they had a more 'modest and humble opinion of themselves' and 'did not think themselves wiser than all the rest'.[158] It was a tendency of which they needed to beware,[159] which may account for the deliberate humility of some of their language and self-descriptions, including calling themselves 'the worst of sinners'[160] or the convention of signing letters in self-effacing terms such as *'y dwsdyn gwael anghymwys i fynt i blith neb o saints Duw'* (the wretched speck of dust unfit to go amongst any of God's saints).[161] Unregulated spiritual pride was often associated with antinomianism, the belief that Christians were released by grace from the obligation to observe moral law. There were certainly signs of this in the movement, with Harris having to expel one member in Carmarthenshire for holding antinomian principles. He also expelled an unnamed exhorter in the area who claimed he had been made perfect and could not sin.[162] The case of the exhorter caused real concern as he was said to have 'infected some' through his teaching. In such cases of misguided beliefs, there was little hesitation over expelling those concerned in order to protect the other members from the spread of misguided ideas. It was also important to ensure that such teaching did not gain the Methodists as a whole a reputation for antinomianism, a fault which many opponents believed plagued them.

Methodists were also expected to engage in constant self-searching to identify any signs of lukewarmness or backsliding. Harris would often note in his diary that he had 'fallen', which would usually mean that he had not been wholeheartedly concerned with godly matters, but had strayed to thoughts of this world.[163] Even though there was no outward sin, therefore, such a lack of concentration could lead the mind into temptation so there was a need for vigilance to root out such weakness. To a large degree, this was a matter of self-regulation and the subject of prayer, but also something which the superintendents would try to monitor. William Richard, for instance, feared in 1747 that wordly matters, such as pride, lack of moderation, discord, gluttony, drunkenness and thoughts of marriage, had overcome many of the members under his care, at the expense of love and unity in the societies.[164]

Slipping into a state of apathy seemed to be a danger which overcame both individuals and entire societies and was very difficult to remedy. In one sermon, Daniel Rowland explained that lukewarmness prevented spiritual growth as rocks blocked the current of a river, but preaching against it did not automatically bring about a solution.[165] If society members abandoned the meetings, there was little to be done but to pray for their restoration.[166] There was the possibility of expelling members who were not attending faithfully,[167] but that was to admit failure to some extent, and it was even more difficult to know how to act towards those who continued to attend but without engaging fully or taking any benefit from the meetings. Whilst society reports showed many members gaining in faith, others were struggling. Mary John, a single woman from Dyffryn-saith society in south Cardiganshire, was reported to be full of certainty of faith in July 1743, but only two months later was under dark clouds and beset by storms.[168] She was by no means the only one floundering. Judith Jenkin, a married woman from Eglwyswrw, was 'under conviction, with many ups and downs not knowing where she is'.[169] William James of Tre-lech was described as justified early in 1744, but by June had lapsed into a state of captivity under the law. He fell ill at the end of the year and struggled to keep his faith during his illness. He asked for the prayers of his fellow members, which were forthcoming, and, according to William John's report in January 1745, he died in a state of unshakeable faith, no longer doubting God's love and able to state that death had no power to harm him.[170]

Several society members went through such ebbs and flows. There was an awareness that enthusiasm could wane and that there might also be some losses amongst those whose conversion was not wholly genuine. In his *Atteb Philo-Evangelius*, which was written as a result of the revival of 1762, Pantycelyn warned that it should be expected that some who joined during a revival might later withdraw, for, as he said,

> pan y fo awelon o argyhoeddiad neu ddiddanwch yn disgyn fel glaw ar y gwir dduwiol, mae sŵn y gwynt yn cwrdd â'r

rhagrithwyr hefyd, ac yn gweithio rhyw chydig ar eu nwydau naturiol; ac yna y maent fel llong o flaen y gwynt, heb un balast ond tan gyflawn hwyliau, ac mewn perygl o gael ei briwio gan y creigydd, neu ei gyrru i mewn i aberodd amherthnasol.[171]

when breezes of conviction or consolation fall like rain on the truly godly, the sound of the wind meets the hypocrites also, and works a little on their natural passions; and then they are like a ship before the wind, without any ballast but in full sail, and in danger of being damaged on the rocks, or of being driven into irrelevant estuaries.

The primary purpose of the society was to keep the fires of faith burning, but this was difficult to achieve if the entire society at times lapsed into an apathetic routine of observing meetings with little zeal. Williams had witnessed such struggles in some of the societies under his care in the 1740s, including Tan-yr-allt near Tregaron, which consisted of some twenty members, with the women more committed and enthusiastic than the men. In 1748 he complained that their lack of enthusiasm was having a disheartening effect on him:

Mae society Tan yr allt yn farw ag yn glaiar iawn ac fel hyn mae er pan wi yn eu nabod. Maent megis wedi rhyw ymwirioni mewn digalondid a marweidd-dra ag mae eu claiarineb yn diffodd fy zel inne pan fwi yn eu mysc.[172]

Tan-yr-allt society is very dead and lukewarm and has been so since I have known them. They seem to have become as it were infatuated with dejection and apathy and their lukewarmness quenches my zeal when I am with them.

By 1750, he felt some slight hope for the revitalisation of Tan-yr-allt, which was making slow progress although labouring hard for every inch of ground gained, '*yn wthio gan ei pwyll bach tua'r nefoedd fel assen tan ei baich*' (pressing bit by bit towards heaven like an ass under its burden).[173]

Membership of the society was a demanding and serious business, therefore. To opponents of Methodism, the movement might seem narrow and judgemental, but the leaders would argue that they were protecting those under their care from harm. Howel Harris assured the members of Cilcarw society that it was deep love and concern for their welfare which led the movement to forbid them from engaging in sports and popular pastimes like their neighbours.[174] The members of the societies were presented with clear boundaries and guidelines to follow. There was no expectation of gaining salvation as a result of observing discipline and maintaining holy living, but it was a sign of a commitment to the faith and an example to the ungodly of how true Christians should conduct themselves. It can seem like enforcing strict rules to repress enthusiastic and emotional young people, but there was a degree of autonomy in making the choice to observe the restrictions. Moreover, members played a part in decisions about whom to receive back into the society after exclusion. The movement bowed to group dynamics by stating that the members needed to consent to welcome back any errant colleagues. One woman from Blaenhownant society in south Cardiganshire had been expelled for spreading 'lies and gossip', and her eagerness to return had not been met with a corresponding enthusiasm from her fellow members.[175] In such cases, it would be disruptive to impose on a society a fellow member with whom they could not feel any unity or trust, so consent was required. At its worst, this could mean ruthlessly alienating an unpopular member, and it is impossible to know how satisfactorily the system operated in the eyes of the members, but ultimately membership was voluntary and people could choose to conform to the rules or decide to leave.

Notes

1. *Sail, Dibenion a Rheolau,'r Societies neu'r cyfarfodydd neullduol a ddechreuassant ymgynnull yn ddiweddar yn Nghymru* (Bristol: Felix Farley, 1742), p. 3; G. H. Hughes (ed.), *Gweithiau William Williams Pantycelyn, Cyfrol II: Rhyddiaith* (Cardiff: University of Wales Press, 1967), p. 191.
2. M. J. McClymond, 'Revival', in A. C. Thompson (ed.), *The Oxford History of Dissenting Traditions, Volume II: The Long Eighteenth Century, c.1689–1828* (Oxford: Oxford University Press, 2018), p. 230.
3. D. Hempton, *The Church in the Long Eighteenth Century* (London: I. B. Tauris, 2011), p. 155.

4 DHH 132, 19 September 1748.
5 Trevecca College/1 3002, William Richard to the Association, 15 July 1743.
6 Trevecca College/1 3002, William Richard to the Association, 15 July 1743.
7 Trevecca College/1 3002, William Richard to the Association, 15 July 1743.
8 Trevecca College/1 3065, William Richard to the Association, 19 October 1748.
9 DHH 141, 24 February 1750.
10 DHH 41, 25–7 February 1739.
11 Hughes (ed.), *Gweithiau William Williams Pantycelyn*, II, p. 215; DHH 129, 27 April 1748.
12 DHH 82, 8 December 1741.
13 DHH 98, 11 March 1743; DHH 129, 7 February 1748.
14 DHH 99, 18 April 1743; DHH 118, 18 October 1745.
15 Trevecca College/1 3001, Morgan John Lewis to the Association, 29 June 1743.
16 Trevecca College/1 2945, p. 151, William John to the Association, 3 July 1745.
17 Trevecca College/1 3023, p. 35, William John to the Association, 4 April 1746.
18 Trevecca College/1 3023, pp. 40–1, James Williams to the Association, 4 April 1746.
19 Trevecca College/1 3004, William Richard to the Association, 2 October 1743.
20 Trevecka MS 811, Howel Harris to George Whitefield, 1 March 1743.
21 DHH 63, 28 September 1740.
22 Trevecca College/1 2945, p. 16, 11 May 1743.
23 Trevecca College/1 3016, William Richard to the Association, 20 June 1744; 3023, pp. 21–2, William Williams to the Association, 7 January 1745.
24 Trevecka MS 2008, Richard Tibbott to the Association, January 1744.
25 Hughes (ed.), *Gweithiau William Williams Pantycelyn*, II, pp. 207–8.
26 *Sail, Dibenion a Rheolau,'r Societies*, p. 4.
27 NLW MS 20516C, 2 March 1757.
28 For instance, DHH 96, 10 December 1742; DHH 127a, 11 August 1747.
29 DHH 129, 7 February 1748.
30 Trevecka MS 1381, William Williams to Howel Harris, 7 December 1745.
31 Trevecka MS 756, Howel Harris to George Whitefield, 14 December 1742.
32 J. Woodward, *An Account of the Rise and Progress of the Religious Societies in the City of London, &c, And of the Endeavours for Reformation of Manners Which have been made therein* (London: JD for the author, 1698), p. 24.
33 Trevecca College/1 2945, p. 92, 27 June 1744.
34 Trevecca College/1 2945, p. 127, 18 October 1744.
35 Trevecca College/1 2945, p. 127, 18 October 1744.
36 Trevecca College/1 2945, p. 144, 23 January 1745.
37 DHH 117, 13 May 1745.
38 DHH 145, 28 June 1750. The verses he found were Ecclesiastes 10:6–8: 'Folly is set in great dignity, and the rich sit in low place. I have seen servants upon horses, and princes walking as servants upon the earth. He that diggeth a pit shall fall into it; and whoso breaketh an hedge, a serpent shall bite him.' He seemed to take these verses as reassurance that those who appeared in the ascendancy were not unassailable.
39 J. M. Jones and W. Morgan, *Y Tadau Methodistaidd, I* (2 vols, Abertawe: yr awdur, 1895 and 1897), p. 134.

40 D. L. Watson, *The Early Methodist Class Meeting* (Nashville, 1985), pp. 119–20; K. M. Watson, *Pursuing Social Holiness: The Band Meeting in Wesley's Thought and Popular Methodist Practice* (Oxford: Oxford University Press, 2014), pp 53, 131.
41 DHH 95, 20 October 1742.
42 DHH 90, 18 May 1742.
43 Trevecka MS 642, William Richard to Howel Harris, 12 September 1742.
44 Trevecca College/1 2945, p. 141, January 1745.
45 Hughes (ed.), *Gweithiau William Williams Pantycelyn*, II, pp. 218–19.
46 See Richard Tibbott's diary, NLW MS 18435B.
47 DHH 98, 10 March 1743.
48 DHH 132a, 28 October 1748.
49 G, M. Roberts, 'Datblygiad Trefn', in G. M. Roberts (ed.), *Hanes Methodistiaeth Galfinaidd Cymru: Cyfrol I: Y Deffroad Mawr* (Caernarfon: Llyfrfa'r Methodistiaid Calfinaidd, 1973), p. 167; Watson, *The Early Methodist Class Meeting*, pp. 98–104.
50 Trevecca College/1 2945, p. 11, 1 March 1743.
51 Trevecca College/1 3078, William Williams to the Association, 1750; Trevecca College/1 3040, William John to the Association, 20 July 1747. The term *blaenor* became common by the nineteenth century for elders or deacons in Nonconformist chapels.
52 Trevecca College/1 2945, pp. 143–4, 23 January 1745.
53 Trevecca College/1 2992, 16 January 1745; DHH 134, 5 March 1749; G. M. Roberts, 'Datblygiad Trefn', p. 185.
54 Trevecca College/1 2945, p. 11, 1 March 1743; Hughes (ed.), *Gweithiau William Williams Pantycelyn*, II, p. 197.
55 Trevecca College/1 3001, Morgan John Lewis to the Association, 29 June 1743; 3002, William Richard to the Association, 15 July 1743.
56 Trevecca College/1 3004, William Richard to the Association, 2 October 1743.
57 Trevecka MS 1207, Morgan John Lewis to the Association, [*c*. 1 October] 1744.
58 Hughes (ed.), *Gweithiau William Williams Pantycelyn*, II, p. 197.
59 D. Ll. Morgan, *Williams Pantycelyn* (Caernarfon: Gwasg Pantycelyn, 1983), pp. 29–30.
60 Hughes (ed.), *Gweithiau William Williams Pantycelyn*, II, pp. 198–9.
61 *Sail, Dibenion a Rheolau,'r Societies*, pp. 6–14.
62 Whitefield, *Llythyr oddiwrth y Parchedig Mr George Whitefield*, p. 23.
63 *Sail, Dibenion a Rheolau,'r Societies*, p. 4.
64 Trevecca College/1 3016, William Richard to the Association, 20 June 1744.
65 *Sail, Dibenion a Rheolau,'r Societies*, p. 13.
66 Quoted in Kevin M. Watson, *Pursuing Social Holiness: The Band Meeting in Wesley's Thought and Popular Methodist Practice* (Oxford: Oxford University Press, 2014), pp. 193–4.
67 Hughes (ed.), *Gweithiau William Williams Pantycelyn*, II, pp. 198–9.
68 *Sail, Dibenion a Rheolau,'r Societies*, p. 3.
69 NLW MS 18435B, p. 22, 9 September 1741.
70 Trevecca College/1 3019, William Richard to the Association, 3 October 1744.
71 DHH 132, 11 September 1748.
72 Trevecca College/1 3014, James Williams to the Association, January 1744.

73 Hughes (ed.), *Gweithiau William Williams Pantycelyn*, II, pp. 216–17.
74 Hughes (ed.), *Gweithiau William Williams Pantycelyn*, II, pp. 216–17.
75 Hughes (ed.), *Gweithiau William Williams Pantycelyn*, II, pp. 229–32.
76 Hughes (ed.), *Gweithiau William Williams Pantycelyn*, II, p. 208.
77 DHH 105, 20 December 1743.
78 Trevecca College/1 3004, William Richard to the Association, 2 October 1743.
79 For instance, Trevecca College/1 3037, William John to the Association, 7 January 1747. See also D. Ll. Morgan, *The Great Awakening*, trans. D. Morgan (London: Epworth Press, 1988), pp. 98–9.
80 Trevecca College/1 3005, James Williams to the Association, 30 September 1743.
81 Trevecca College/1 3002, William Richard to the Association, 15 July 1743.
82 Trevecca College/1 3004, William Richard to the Association, 2 October 1743.
83 Trevecca College/1 3010, William John to the Association, January 1744.
84 Trevecca College/1 3025, William Williams to the Association, January 1745.
85 Trevecca College/1 3023, p. 38, John Richard to the Association, 9 April 1746.
86 Trevecca College/1 3004, William Richard to the Association, 2 October 1743.
87 Trevecca College/1 3017, John Richard to the Association, 20 June 1744.
88 See T. E. Frank, 'Discipline', in W. J. Abraham and J. E. Kirby (eds), *The Oxford Handbook of Methodist Studies* (Oxford: Oxford University Press, 2009), pp. 245–61.
89 Hughes (ed.), *Gweithiau William Williams Pantycelyn*, II, pp. 186, 188–9.
90 DHH 109, 18 April 1744.
91 G. H. Jenkins, 'Popular Beliefs in Wales from the Restoration to Methodism', *Bulletin of the Board of Celtic Studies*, 27 (1977), 443; R. Suggett, *A History of Magic and Witchcraft in Wales* (Stroud: History Press, 2008), pp. 51–5.
92 See J. Thomas, *Rhad Ras neu Lyfr Profiad*, ed. J. Dyfnallt Owen (Cardiff: University of Wales Press, 1949).
93 Trevecca College/1 3003, John Harries to the Association, 22 July 1743.
94 Hughes (ed.), *Gweithiau William Williams Pantycelyn*, II, p. 236.
95 Trevecca College/1 3000, James Williams to Howel Harris, 2 October 1741.
96 Trevecka MS 1240, James Williams to the Association, 3 October 1744.
97 Hughes (ed.), *Gweithiau William Williams Pantycelyn*, II, p. 241.
98 Trevecca College/1 3004, William Richard to the Association, 2 October 1743.
99 DHH 109, 18 April 1744.
100 DHH 129, 4 February 1748.
101 DHH 131a, 17 May 1748; Evans, *Daniel Rowland*, p. 277.
102 Trevecca College/1 2982, 21 July 1747.
103 DHH 139, 22 November 1749.
104 D. Rowland, *Deuddeg o Bregethau* (Aberystwyth: Samuel Williams, 1814), p. 44.
105 Hughes (ed.), *Gweithiau William Williams Pantycelyn*, II, p. 221.
106 DHH 152, 19 September 1748.
107 Hughes (ed.), *Gweithiau William Williams Pantycelyn*, II, pp. 221–6.
108 Trevecca College/1 3067, 25 October 1748.
109 Trevecca College/1 3016, 20 June 1744.
110 Trevecca College/1 3023, p. 35, William John to the Association, 4 April 1746.
111 Hughes (ed.), *Gweithiau William Williams Pantycelyn*, II, p. 186.

112 Trevecca College/1 3018, James Williams to the Association, 20 June 1744.
113 Trevecka College/1 3187, fol. 5.
114 R. C. Allen, 'Quakers' in Thompson (ed.), *The Oxford History of Dissenting Traditions, Volume II: The Long Eighteenth Century*, p. 85.
115 NLW MS 18435B, p. 44, 29 July 1742.
116 Trevecca College/1 3049, William Williams to the Association, 28 January 1749.
117 Trevecca College/1 2982, 21 July 1747; G. M. Roberts, 'Datblygiad Trefn', p. 184.
118 DHH 84, 9 January 1742; 104, 1 November 1743.
119 Trevecca College/1 3078, William Williams to the Association, 1750.
120 Trevecca College/1 3078, William Williams to the Association, 1750.
121 Trevecca College/1 3040, 20 July 1747.
122 D. Ll. Morgan, *Williams Pantycelyn* (Cardiff: University of Wales Press, 1983), p. 44.
123 G. T. Hughes 'Llyfrgell Pantycelyn', in *'Yr Hen Bant': Ysgrifau ar William Pantycelyn* (Talybont: Y Lolfa, 2017), pp. 92–3.
124 Hughes (ed.), *Gweithiau William Williams Pantycelyn*, II, p. 260.
125 Hughes (ed.), *Gweithiau William Williams Pantycelyn*, II, p. 268.
126 Trevecca College/1 3037, William John to the Association, 7 January 1747.
127 Trevecca College/1 3040, 20 July 1747.
128 Trevecka MS 1318, John Richard to Howel Harris, 29 April 1745.
129 See Anna Brueton, 'Illegitimacy in south Wales 1660–1870' (unpublished PhD, University of Leicester, 2015); Angela Muir, 'Illegitimacy in Eighteenth-century Wales', *Welsh History Review*, 26/3 (2013), 351–88.
130 NLW MS 20515C, 9–12 January 1759; R. G. Gruffydd, 'John Thomas, Tremain: Pererin Methodistaidd', *Cylchgrawn Cymdeithas Hanes y Methodistiaid Calfinaidd/Journal of the Historical Society of the Presbyterian Church of Wales*, 9 (1985–6), 65–6.
131 E. P. Thompson, *The Making of the English Working Class* (Harmondsworth: Penguin, 1970), p. 405.
132 Trevecca College/1 3062, John Harry to the Association, 30 July 1748.
133 Trevecca College/1 3078, William Williams to the Association, 1750.
134 Trevecca College/1 3023, p. 35, 4 April 1746.
135 DHH 98, 4 March 1743; 134, 13 March 1749.
136 DHH 98, 4 March 1743.
137 DHH 113, 1 October 1744.
138 *Sail, Dibenion a Rheolau,'r Societies*, p. 4.
139 Trevecka MS 1760, Howel Davies to Howel Harris, 30 January 1748.
140 Trevecca College/1 3069, John Harry to the Association, 26 October 1748.
141 Trevecca College/1 3062, John Harry to the Association, 30 July 1748.
142 C. Emsley, *Crime and Society in England 1750–1900* (second edn London: Longman, 1996), p. 4; R. W. Ireland, *Land of White Gloves? A History of Crime and Punishment in Wales* (Abingdon: Routledge, 2015), p. 45.
143 Trevecka MS 1866, John Harry to the Methodist Societies, 19 May 1749.
144 DHH 105, 6 December 1743; DHH 134, 12 March 1749.
145 J. Geraint Jenkins, *Maritime Heritage: The Sailors and Seamen of South Cardiganshire* (Llandysul: Gomer Press, 1982), p. 7; G. I. Hawkes, 'Illicit

Trading in Wales in the Eighteenth Century', *Cymru a'r Môr/Maritime Heritage*, 10 (1986), 89–107; D. W. Howell, *The Rural Poor in Eighteenth-century Wales* (Cardiff: University of Wales Press, 2000), pp. 189–91.
146 NLW MS 21834B, A smuggler's autobiography (online version: *https://www.library.wales/discover/digital-gallery/manuscripts/modern-period/smugglers-autobiography/*; Glyn Parry, 'Autobiography of a Smuggler', *National Library of Wales Journal*, 24 (1985), 84–92.
147 *Welch Piety* (London: J. Oliver, 1752), p. 60; M. Benbough-Jackson, *Cardiganshire and the Cardi, c.1760–c.2000* (Cardiff: University of Wales Press, 2011), pp. 65–7.
148 DHH 98, 30 March 1743.
149 H. Rack, *Reasonable Enthusiast: John Wesley and the Rise of Methodism* (London: Epworth Press, 1989), p. 445.
150 DHH 132, 18 September 1748.
151 DHH 134, 5 March 1749.
152 E. M. White, 'The Material World, Moderation and Methodism in Eighteenth-century Wales', *Welsh History Review*, 23/3 (2007), 47.
153 See L. Weatherill, 'The meaning of consumer behaviour in late seventeenth- and early eighteenth-century England', in J. Brewer and R. Porter (eds), *Consumption and the World of Goods* (London: Routledge, 1993), pp. 207–8; W. D. Smith, *Consumption and the Making of Respectability, 1600–1800* (London: Routledge, 2002), pp. 63–8; M. Berg, *Luxury and Pleasure in Eighteenth-century Britain* (Oxford: Oxford University Press, 2005), pp. 31–7.
154 DHH 98, 4 March 1743; 133, 3 January 1749; 134, 13 March 1749.
155 Trevecka MS 1311, James Beaumont to Howel Harris, 6 April 1745.
156 Hughes (ed.), *Gweithiau William Williams Pantycelyn*, II, p. 240.
157 DHH 131a, 6 May 1748.
158 NLW MS 6137D, Griffith Jones to Bridget Bevan, 19 April 1743.
159 Morgan, *The Great Awakening*, pp. 165–6.
160 For example, DHH 82, 9 December 1741.
161 Trevecca College/1 3074, James Williams to the Association, 8 May 1750. See also Trevecka MS 642, William Richard to Howel Harris, 12 September 1742; 766, John William to Howel Harris, 28 December 1742; 897, John Jones to Howel Harris, 26 June 1743; 1337, Watkin Watkins to Howel Harris, 30 June 1745; 1388, William Richard to Howel Harris, 2 January 1749.
162 Trevecka MS 1167, Howel Harris to George Whitefield, 28 April 1744.
163 DHH 101, 15 July 1743.
164 Trevecca College/1 3042, William Richard to the Association, 14 July 1747.
165 DHH 90, 23 May 1742.
166 Hughes (ed.), *Gweithiau William Williams Pantycelyn*, II, pp. 226–7.
167 DHH 130, 27 April 1748.
168 Trevecca College/1 3002, William Richard to the Association, 15 July 1743; 3004, William Richard to the Association, 2 October 1743.
169 Trevecca College/1 3002, William Richard to the Association, 15 July 1743.
170 Trevecca College/1 3024, William John to the Association, 2 January 1745.
171 Hughes (ed.), *Gweithiau William Williams Pantycelyn*, II, p. 15.
172 Trevecca College/1 3049, William Williams to the Association, 28 January 1748.

173 Trevecca College/1 3078, William Williams to the Association, 1750.
174 DHH 98, 22 March 1743.
175 Trevecca College/1 3048, William Richard to the Association, 26 January 1749.

CHAPTER 7

'This Furnace of Affliction'[1]: Trials and Tribulations

It could be said that the very name 'Methodist' was an affliction to be borne with as much patience as possible. Howel Harris declared that it was 'a name given in derision' and that the people of the societies belonged to the Established Church no less than anyone else.[2] 'The people called Methodists' devised no name for themselves, and it was no compliment to award them the same nickname as had been attributed to the Wesley brothers. Harris opposed all such individual labels for religious groups that he felt should be known simply as 'Christians', with the only distinction being between 'believers' and 'non-believers'.[3] Even so, despite all resistance, they were stuck with 'Methodist' as a label, following the tradition of a name given in jest ultimately becoming officially adopted by a religious group. Although they came to own the name with pride, it was one sign of the opposition the movement encountered in its early days.

The history of Welsh Methodism prior to 1750 was by no means a smooth progress. In addition to problems with maintaining both enthusiasm and discipline amongst the membership, it also faced a number of obstacles, with problems emerging from within the movement and hostility threatening from without. The movement was never without its enemies and obviously stirred up considerable ill feeling for a number of reasons. There were tensions arising from their relationship with both the Established Church and Dissenters. External hostility was to be expected, judging from the prior experiences of the early Dissenters, and members were often reminded of the need to prepare themselves for opposition and for a lack of understanding of their aims and motives.

Such outside opposition to some extent may have been easier to deal with than the internal disputes, which created considerable challenges for the leadership and the superintendents who had charge of the societies in the south-west. It was possibly easier to arm themselves mentally to meet outside challenges than to face problems caused by friends and colleagues within the movement.

By the end of the 1740s, the superintendents and exhorters in the south-west spoke increasingly of a decline in the fortunes of the societies and their members. The superintendents' reports tended to dwell on the apathy of the members and a nostalgia for the heady days of the early outbreak of revival. Amongst them was William Richard, who feared in July 1747 that the work was not progressing as it once had and that the societies were further away from God than before.[4] Howel Davies suggested in 1748 that the term 'Ichabod' – the glory of God is departing – might be appropriate to sum up that stage in the movement's history.[5] Although the societies under John Richard's care continued to meet, by 1750 he feared it was to little avail as most of them were shrouded in 'a dark night'.[6] John Harry suggested that a similar situation prevailed in both the Welsh- and English-medium societies in Pembrokeshire at the beginning of 1748:

> *Rhay ac ymddangosodd unwaith in wresog ac yn seliws – sydd ai cydwybodau fel pe baint gwedy ei sero a haearn poeth in ymroddy y ddrwgiony ac in aneimladwy ohono ... may genim Rhay Eilwaith sydd in gid fined y dy dduw a chenthint Rhith Duwioldeb Eithir gwedy gwady ei grim hy – a chin belled ac ir wify in Duall nid oes dim delins neilltyol Rhingthint a duw – ac maint yn anwibodus o Ewillis duw tiac atint hwy.*[7]

> Some who once appeared warm and zealous now have their consciences as if seared with a hot iron surrendering themselves to evil and insensible of it ... we have some secondly who go together to God's house with an appearance of godliness but having denied its power – and as far as I understand there are no particular dealings between them and God – and they are ignorant of God's will toward them.

Complaints about members becoming indifferent about their faith were not uncommon in various societies throughout the 1740s, but it seemed to become a more consistent theme by the end of the decade. It is not entirely clear just how far this sense of an ebb in the spiritual progress of the societies was accompanied by a dip in actual numbers. The surviving reports reveal that the movement grew from 1737 onwards, reaching a sort of plateau around 1743–4, after which the reports tend not to record the numbers. Some sort of cooling-off might be inevitable after the first few years of revival had recruited those most likely to be affected, but there were still some indications of growth. In May 1749 William John listed two new members and one more on trial in Llanegwad society, although one existing member had backslid and been lost; one new member and one on trial in Llanarthney; a new member on trial in both Llanpumsaint and Henllan Amgoed; and one new member and one on trial in Blaenhyfer, which had also lost a member who had recently died. All the other societies under his care had witnessed no change in numbers. That was a total of potentially nine members gained and two lost. In addition, he noted that a new society had been set up in Laugharne with fifteen members, although it is not clear if the Laugharne society constituted the reformed remnants of the society previously cared for by the Mends brothers, or a completely new cause.[8] The story from this area of south Carmarthenshire thus seemed to be a positive one even this late in the decade. However, where the reports provide full figures of membership for the societies, they invariably show a decline by 1748–50. One of the most striking occurred in Llansawel where the numbers fell from 51 in 1744 to 25 in 1748. The society in Daniel Rowland's parish of Llangeitho seems to have been an exception, according to surviving records, and there is considerable evidence of continued activity in the area, which would not have been as affected by the withdrawal of Howel Harris. Internal disputes between the leaders may well have been a factor in the decline by the end of the 1740s therefore.

THE WELSH METHODIST SOCIETY

Caeo Society:

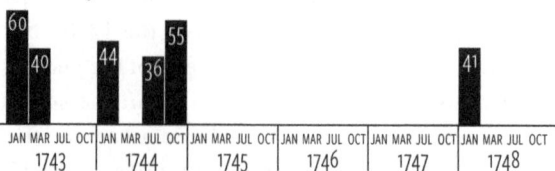

Cil-y-cwm Society:

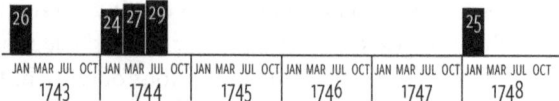

Llansawel Society:

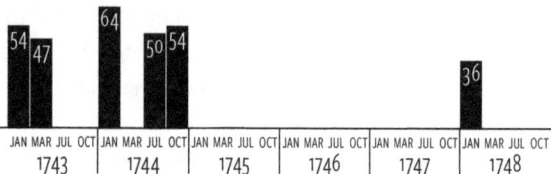

Llanfynydd Society:

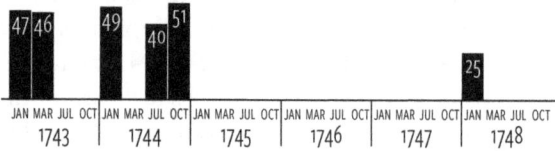

Meidrim Society:

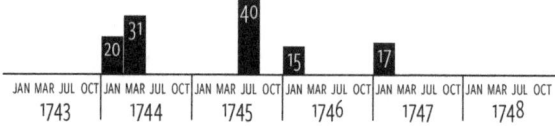

Talley Society:

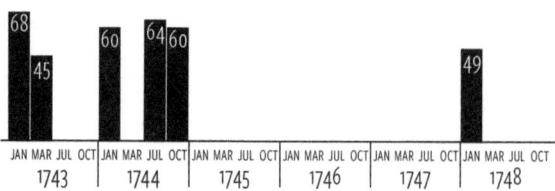

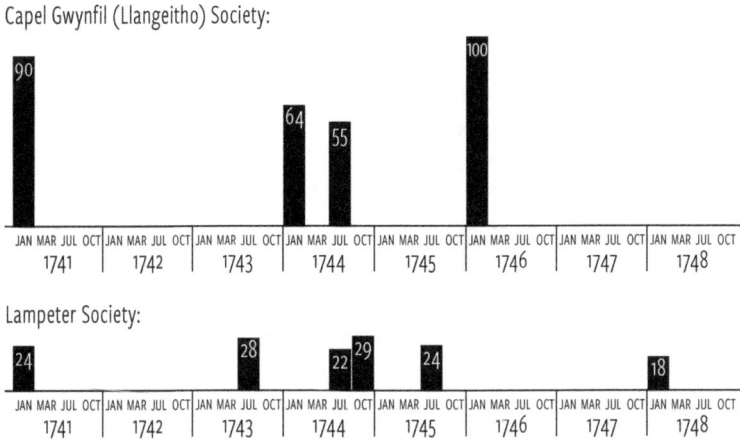

Doctrinal Difficulties

One of the consequences of the dispute leading to the separation in 1750 was the decline in Harris's visits to the south-west, which he seemed to regard as the territory of his opposition within the movement, the evangelical clergy, Daniel Rowland, William Williams and Howel Davies. Harris's personal influence in the area had been considerable, and many members regarded him as their spiritual father. Several of the local exhorters complained about his absence and its effects. John Harry rejoiced that a visit from Harris had shaken the societies in Pembrokeshire out of their apathy and breathed new life into the cause.[9] At the same time, despite his positive impact as a preacher and visitor to societies, there is no denying the fact that Harris had become a divisive figure by the end of the 1740s. Some of the exhorters in the south-west were uneasy about the effects of the conflict between the leaders on the societies in general. John Richard reported in 1750 that the news of the dispute had caused consternation in the societies under his supervision. Unsurprisingly, he turned to the Bible for some precedent, believing that the movement was witnessing the fulfilment of Paul's prophecy to the elders amongst the Ephesians: 'Also of your own selves shall men arise, speaking perverse things, to draw away disciples after them.'[10] This would seem to be a reference to the accusations of heresy against Harris, which may also have been implied in James Williams's report to the last Association prior to the separation in 1750:

ofni yr wyf fod rhyfig yn agos, rhai gwedy myned i ymresymy ynghylch amryw bethe yn Enwedic ynghylch gwaed y bendecedic Iesu, rhai a hayrant mae trwy waed yr oen, heb rinwedd nag Effeth, rhay a fynant mae y rhinwedd o hono ar olwg arno trwy ffydd a dynodd ei heneide ar ol ef.[11]

I fear that presumption is close, some are given over to reasoning about various things especially to do with the blood of the blessed Jesus, some insist that it was through the blood of the lamb, without virtue or effect, others insist that that virtue and the sight of it through faith drew their souls to follow him.

There was obviously some disquiet about the possible spread of confusion and misapprehension amongst the members.

Arguments over doctrine were hardly a new development in the movement in the late 1740s. The split between Arminian and Calvinistic Methodism did not mean a major division in the Welsh movement as it had in England, but there were other issues which caused considerable difficulties. One of these was the question of assurance of faith, which for many evangelicals was an automatic outcome of conversion, but which to others seemed presumptuous.[12] This was a new emphasis, developed by Jonathan Edwards and embraced by John Wesley. Harris insisted that it was essential and so found himself at odds with some of his colleagues, including some of the Dissenters, who argued that it was possible to be in a state of grace without knowing it for certain, and that many had gone to heaven without feeling any such assurance. As Geraint Tudur has pointed out, Harris seemed to be overlooking the fact that he himself lacked that conviction of salvation for a period between 1736 and 1739, but now expected it of others.[13] It was an issue which caused problems within the movement, with Daniel Rowland and William Williams less persuaded by a doctrine that seemed 'foreign to the pastoral theology of moderate Calvinism'.[14] The theological standpoint of Welsh Dissent was largely moderate and centrist Calvinism, which the Methodists had found compatible, but this was an issue that challenged that quiet consensus. Discussions over the matter in the Association in March 1742 were fraught, with Rowland and Harris at odds in a way which was an indication of future divisions. Rowland felt that Harris was creating too stern a test of faith for the newly converted, whereas Harris believed that Rowland's policy would allow those who were not true believers to join the societies. A compromise was achieved with an agreement that when called, a Christian was aware of having something but would not know it to be justification by faith by name until it was explained to him. Harris optimistically reported to Whitefield after the Association that they had achieved union despite the Devil's attempts to create division over the question of assurance.[15] However, Harris continued to brood on the subject and hoped that Whitefield might write some guide, which could be translated into Welsh, since so many still held that assurance was not necessary.[16] The issue had therefore been smoothed over to some extent, but not wholly resolved.

Achieving a real certainty that they were saved was a challenge for many of the society members as well, as becomes obvious in some of William Wiliams's hymns. There were complaints that his first volume of hymns in 1744, *Aleluja*, expressed a confidence and assurance of faith that not all were able to share, leaving them uneasy about joining the singing with sincerity and zeal.[17] A major milestone in Williams's career as a hymn writer was the publication in 1762 of a collection revealing an increased depth and maturity to his work, *Caniadau (y Rhai sydd ar y Môr o Wydr yn gymmysgedig a than, ac wedi cael y maes ar y bwystfil i Frenhin y Saint* ('The Songs of those on the sea of glass mixed with fire and who have defeated the beast, to the King of the saints').[18] In response to earlier criticisms, Williams claimed that these hymns were largely prayers for strength and guidance, which could be sung by all Christians regardless of experience. The fresh outbreak of revival in 1762 is partly credited to the influence of this volume which contained a number of Pantycelyn's most popular hymns.[19] Williams consciously ensured that these were hymns that did not require a complete assurance to be sung with gusto. As a result, they are full of references to overcoming doubts and difficulties and contain a number of images of pilgrims wandering through the desert towards the promised land, including the original Welsh version of what would become Williams's most popular hymn in English, 'Guide me, O Thou great Jehovah'.

The issue of assurance was one of those which caused tension in the relationship between the Methodists and Dissenters. David Hempton's description of Methodism as 'a clever parasite', which often initially established itself through symbiosis, is one that some Welsh Dissenters would recognise.[20] Although the Methodists may have seemed to have been most reliant on the Anglican Church, they also gained a good deal of ground through invitations to preach by Dissenters who were keen to establish mission activity in the hope of spiritual renewal. There had been a warm welcome for the Methodists from leading figures such as Edmund Jones of Pontypool, who was happy to support a Calvinist revival of this kind. The Dissenters, and the Independents in particular, gained a good deal in the long term from the momentum created by the evangelical revival. In the initial phase, they seemed to recognise the potential to add to their own numbers and were prepared to encourage the young Methodist exhorters.[21] Rees Davies of Abergavenny and James Davies of Cwm-y-glo were other Independent ministers in the south-east who invited Methodist visits. In the south-west, the Independent ministers Philip Pugh in Cardiganshire and Henry Palmer of Henllan Amgoed, as well as the Baptist minister Enoch Francis of Newcastle Emlyn, offered a friendly welcome. However, it did not take long for the differences between them to become apparent, as the Methodist leaders insisted on their loyalty to the Church. Harris stated in his diary: 'I see I know nothing about Church Government but it seems that Independency to me is not right.'[22] The Methodists favoured a more centralised system which did not allow for the primacy of the individual congregation in the same way as the Independents did. There were accusations of partisanship on both sides, with some of the Dissenting members in the societies caught in the middle.[23] David Williams of Pwll-y-pant had eagerly invited Harris to his area of Glamorgan in 1738 and arranged various very successful preaching engagements on his behalf. However, the relationship soured when the two disagreed over the question of assurance. Harris wrote a lengthy letter to Williams, in which he stated that many Christians who had been awakened by him were now under Williams's care, so he had an interest in the gospel they were receiving and was concerned to hear that Williams had preached that one could be a good Christian without knowing it.[24] Williams felt that his ministry had a sufficiently firm foundation that he did not need to be put on trial by Harris. As other people would later also suggest, he felt that Harris was too inclined to believe ill and based his criticism on the remarks of a few prejudiced individuals who were reporting back to him.[25] There would be no further correspondence between them for seven years, when Williams's bitterness at Harris's behaviour was revealed in a letter criticising the Methodists for having taken unscrupulous advantage of the generosity shown them by many Dissenters in the early years of revival. He accused Harris of starting out with good intentions but then transforming into a dictator and 'Lord Inquisitor' who would brook no opposition. He was deeply disappointed in the way Harris used the Dissenters in the first instance to gain a foothold in many areas and then abandoned them when their support was no longer required.[26]

That was not the only personal dimension to the disagreement, since Howel Harris caused considerable offence to many of the Dissenters through his behaviour to Christmas Samuel. Samuel had been minister of Pant-teg in Carmarthenshire since 1711 and was one of the most revered figures amongst the Welsh Independents. He was sixty-eight in 1742, when Harris seemed to question the value of his entire ministry, to the consternation of all those who heard of the accusation. Harris had never been afraid to censure his colleagues, as Daniel Rowland and William Williams could testify, but such an attack on a cherished minister in another denomination shocked many. It was inevitably particularly harmful in the Carmarthenshire area where Christmas Samuel was best known. Harris did attempt to undo some of the damage by writing immediately to Samuel to explain himself. His explanation was that when he heard the description of Samuel as sent by God, which formed part of an announcement of a forthcoming preaching engagement, he felt stirred by his conscience to question it. He insisted that he had not actually said that Samuel lacked grace or that his ministry was dead and worthless, but acknowledged his fault if he was wrong.[27] It was not an abject apology by any means, although rather more than some others who had been offended by Harris had ever received. It was quite characteristic for Harris to question the idea of how to judge who was sent by God, but in the context it might have been wiser and more civil to have allowed it to pass as polite words about a respected minister.

Tensions also arose within individual societies where there was a mixture of Anglicans and Dissenters. The overall perception of the leaders that Methodism was a movement within the Church of England may have alienated some of the members who did not belong to that Church, and it may have been difficult to sustain a sense of unity within the societies themselves. A sign of the general attitude may be detected in James Williams's telling description of the members of Llanllwni society: 'they are mixt of our friends and Dissenters'.[28] Over half of Tŵr-gwyn society were Dissenters in September 1743, but some of them left after a quarrel with the Anglican members.[29] There were suspicions that the presence of Dissenters in the societies would infect others by drawing them away from the Church. However, although there were some examples of individual society members joining a Dissenting cause, such as one unnamed member from Llanegwad in 1747,[30] it does not seem to have happened to any great extent. James Williams suggested that there was greater consensus in Caeo after the Dissenters had left the society by October 1745, but problems persisted in Llanllwni, where the society remained mixed.[31] As the relationship grew more strained, fewer Dissenters were to be found in the societies, with William John declaring that most had left the societies in his superintendency by April 1746.[32] Some areas experienced greater problems than others, depending on the relative strength of Dissent. William John's area of south-west Carmarthenshire covered some bastions of the Dissenting faith, including Henllan Amgoed, where an early Independent chapel had been established in 1697. The minister, Henry Palmer, had initially been receptive to Methodism, but had died in 1742, to be succeeded in 1746 by Thomas Morgan, converted after hearing Harris preach, but generally at odds with the Methodist movement. His influence may be detected in William John's report in May 1748 that any remaining Dissenters in Henllan Amgoed had left because threatened with expulsion from their church.[33] Yet, there were still some stray examples of Dissenters joining the movement, including one in Henllan Amgoed in 1749, but certainly fewer than previously.

None of the societies in the south-west chose to leave the movement in order to establish themselves as dissenting causes, as happened with the Groes-wen, Aberthin and New Inn societies during the 1740s.[34] Yet Dissent had its attractions for both exhorters and members, as it offered the prospect of the right to administer communion. The Toleration Act of 1689 permitted Protestant Dissenting groups to register their meeting houses as places of worship separate from the Established Church and thus ordain their own ministers and conduct their own services. Several exhorters argued in favour of taking advantage of the terms of the Act in order to be able to offer communion services to the members. Preaching, prayer and pastoral care could already be supplied in the societies, but the sacrament was missing. Elizabeth Thomas of Blaen-porth, the only woman to be allowed to exhort at the time, argued strongly in favour of dissenting in order to take advantage of the opportunity to administer the sacrament:

> I hope to have the sacraments ministered in our society by one of the Brethren if the Lord permits and I hope without any presumption or party zeel but in love and meekness and in the simplicity of our harts for you will own other assemblies to be part of the church as well as conformists and why should not we have the Liberty of conscience seeing the goverment allows it.[35]

The official stance of the movement was that members should continue to receive communion regularly in their parish churches, however many had reservations about taking communion from certain parish clergy, and some clergy also refused to accept known Methodists. The use of the chapels of ease was an attempt to offer some alternative in such instances, but could not provide for all.

There were sound reasons for Dissent to attract Methodist exhorters, therefore, and a number of the more gifted lay leaders of the movement in the south-west ended their days as Independent ministers, including Milbourne Bloom, Richard Tibbott and Morgan John Lewis. Lewis had always been a strong advocate of registering the societies as meeting houses in order to have the right to administer the sacrament. Although he agreed to accept the decision of the Association to remain in the Church, he maintained his reservations about the wisdom of that choice. He was not alone in that respect. Several of the members under John Harry's care in Pembrokeshire strongly desired to leave the Church and complained of the leaders' reluctance to take this step.[36] According to James Williams, his members in October 1747 were in uproar, some unwilling to go to the Church, some unwilling to turn to the Dissenters and others waiting for 'the Lord to open a door'.³⁷ That degree of uncertainty about their status to some extent was unavoidable whilst they resisted the temptation to dissent from the Church until the final separation came in 1811.

Opposition and Persecution

When joining the society, members were warned to expect to have to endure opposition and hostility, since, as Daniel Rowland stated, the cross was the way to the crown.³⁸ William Williams reminded them that persecution was the inheritance of all true Christians, so that in a sense it was proof that their cause was correct.³⁹ It was also a test of faith to be endured courageously. Howel Harris preached that persecution acted as the lancets and probes of 'the Great Physician'; therefore, however painful, it was ultimately of benefit.⁴⁰ The same principle lay behind the image of the purifying furnace, which was used on more than one occasion as a metaphor for the decline and persecution which seemed to be troubling the movement by the end of the 1740s. John Harry took comfort, believing:: 'is not our Captain ye only wise God that nows how to make all things to work for our advantage – for I am perswaded that we shall loos nothing in this furnace of affliction but our dross.'⁴¹ Daniel Rowland introduced the same idea in one of his printed sermons in which he explained that there is no gold or silver that is not first refined in the cauldron of suffering.⁴² Having suffered the process, the Methodists would be a refined and purified product.

Williams summed up the enemies and methods of attack in his *Atteb Philo-Evangelius* in 1767:

> *Rhyfelir â hwynt weithiau â'r tafod, weithiau â'r pin sgrifennu, yn fynych â'r argraffwasg. Esgobion ac offeiriaid, mawrion a thlodion, gwŷr llên a gwŷr lleyg yn cytuno yn un yn erbyn y bobl a elwir 'Methodistiaid'.*⁴³

> War is waged with them sometimes with the tongue, sometimes with the writing pen, often with the printing press. Bishops and priests, great and poor, men of letters and laymen all agreed against the people called 'Methodists'.

The Methodists' own accounts of their sufferings need to be approached with caution, as they may well have exaggerated on occasion out of a natural desire to provide themselves with a history of heroism. Many stories of the early leaders and exhorters dwell on their bravery in the face of enmity, with the underlying message that they endured it all in Christ's name. William John, for instance, was praised for his persistence in overcoming all manner of trials:

Fe gurwyd gan ei frodyr, fe gurwyd gan y byd,
Fe nerthwyd hyd y diwedd er gwrthwynebau gyd
Yn awr mae gwlad ac eglwys oll yn ei gyfiawnhau,
Gan gofio ei ffyddlondeb hyd angeu yn parhau.[44]

He was beaten by his brothers, beaten by the world,
He was strengthened until the end despite all the opposition
Now Church and country all justify him,
And remember his faithfulness unto death.

Many of the Methodist preachers did encounter considerable opposition and life was far from easy at times, although the levels of persecution in south-west Wales were probably not as serious as in some other regions of Wales and England. The institution most concerned with the growth of Methodism was the Established Church. In the diocese of St Davids, there was little concerted, centralised opposition to the movement. Bishop Nicholas Claggett was followed in 1743 by Bishop Richard Trevor, but both were absent for much of the time, and neither seemed overly inclined to impose draconian measures against the Methodists. Claggett had reacted angrily towards Harris's request for ordination, and had also, rather ominously, sent Daniel Rowland a copy of the *The New Weekly Miscellany* which contained an anonymous attack on Rowland's unorthodox activities.[45] He took little further action, however, and Bishop Trevor was apparently quite well disposed to Daniel Rowland on his arrival in the diocese, as well as adopting a moderate stance towards William Williams and Howel Davies over the matter of the chapels of ease.[46] It was also said that he had no opposition to zeal as long as it operated within the bounds of the law.[47] Thomas Herring, bishop of Bangor (1737–43), was also supposed to be fairly lenient, having written to George Whitefield to explain that he had no wish to follow a policy of persecution in his diocese.[48] Nevertheless, John Owen, the chancellor of the diocese, pursued a much harsher approach in the bishop's absence and was more than willing to excommunicate anyone who could be charged with exhorting in private societies.[49] In St Davids diocese, the one real step taken as a measure to restrict the growth of Methodism was to refuse ordination to those involved in the movement. Fortunately for Daniel Rowland, his full ordination to priest's orders in 1735 had preceded his new birth as a leading Methodist, so his position was safe, at least until he lost his curacies in 1763 for refusing to limit himself to the confines of his parishes.[50] Although already ordained as a deacon, William Williams was refused further ordination in 1743 because of his role in the movement.[51] John Jones of Llowes in Glasbury, Radnorshire, had to apologise humbly for his connection with the movement before his application for orders was approved by Bishop Trevor in 1745.[52] Howel Harris was refused ordination four times, in the first instance possibly because he was still under the usually required age of twenty-three, but subsequently because he was a notorious Methodist.

The ordained evangelical clergy were at risk of being called before the Church courts if their activities seemed too out of line with their clerical duties. William Williams, as curate of Llanwrtyd and Llanddewi Abergwesyn, was reported by the churchwardens of the parishes in 1742 and 1743 for neglecting his duty.[53] The accusations on the second occasion included not visiting the sick, not conducting baptism, catechism or burial, and being absent from his parishes. He was found guilty on 26 January 1744, but by then had already chosen to leave his curacies to take on the full-time role as assistant to Daniel Rowland.[54] Had there been a campaign to persecute him as a Methodist he might well have been found guilty the first time, but he was then refused full ordination, so was obviously not in any great favour. His history perhaps shows the lack of a consistent policy when it came to the attitude to Methodism in the diocese. Eifion Evans suggests that the prime mover against Williams was not the bishop but the chancellor, Edward Jones, who was likely to have been responsible for the list of names of Methodists preserved in the diocesan archive.[55] As in Bangor, resident senior clergy were likely to have been highly influential in determining the reaction in the diocese.

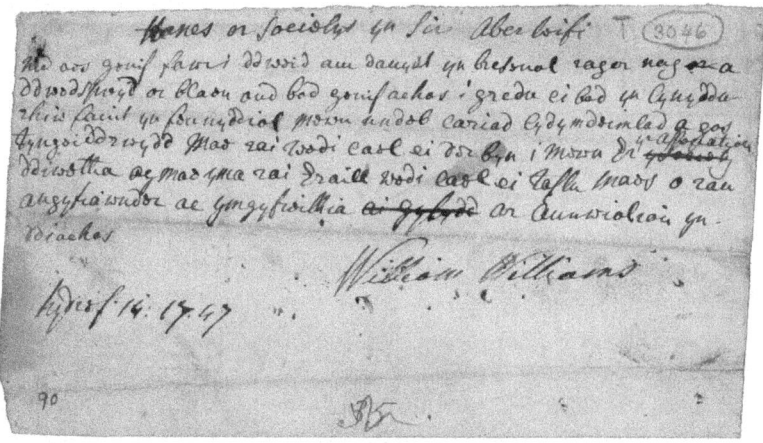

William Williams's report to the Association, 14 October 1747 (Trevecca College/1 3046)

It often fell to individual clergymen to determine how to respond to Methodist societies and preaching in their parishes. It was the exhorters who perhaps particularly aroused their anger since they would cut across the accepted territorial parish boundaries without asking consent in the way which was considered normal practice and common courtesy between clergy. John Tilsley of Llandinam was one of those who objected to Harris preaching in his parish without consulting him and showing disrespect for the Church by exhorting in highways and fields.[56] Harris believed that some of the clergy resented him for his success, like 'common tradesmen who when they see some have more Custom than the rest are not to be wondered at for being angry'.[57] There was also a resentment of ill-educated and unqualified exhorters daring to suppose that they were the equal, if not superior, of the ordained clerics.[58] Harris clashed with Anthony Jones of Llanegwad who hindered him from speaking in his parish in 1741, with Harris concluding that he was 'very busy to pervert ye minds of ye weak'.[59] In answer to Jones's challenge to explain by what right he came there, Harris maintained that the number of converts in the area confirmed that his mission had been God's will. William John was stopped from exhorting in the parish of Laugharne by the vicar, Thomas Phillips, sending a constable to prevent him.[60] Yet a new society was formed in Laugharne by 1749 despite Phillips's opposition. Some societies also encountered antagonism from local clergy, including at St David's, where the clergy were said to rage against the society.[61] Problems persisted, with William Richard complaining of the 'preaching, threatening and persuading' against the cause in St David's.[62] These particular difficulties may have been caused by the presence nearby of the concentration of cathedral clergy, who might well be annoyed at the existence of such a meeting on their doorstep.

There were reasons why the Methodists invoked suspicion and resentment from the clergy, often with the support of the local gentry. One of their problems was that they inevitably evoked memories of the seventeenth-century revolution, with its associations with social upheaval and challenge to authority. Some sort of folk memory of those events lingered, including grief at the loss of the king and bewilderment over the changes to the church. In north Wales, the Methodists were referred to as 'Cariadogs' after Walter Cradock the Puritan leader, which shows how the awareness of the seventeenth-century developments had persisted.[63] It was assumed that the Methodists were Puritans revived, with the same intent to turn the world upside down, as Harris was accused of in Haverfordwest: 'our preaching in ye Highway &c & turning ye World upside down &c this is fulfilling ye Scripture'.[64] The reality was that the movement had no political aspirations other than promoting loyalty to the secular powers that be, as those placed in their position by God. The rule book noted that the duty of the poor in society was to be content with their lot and to be faithful and industrious in their labours.[65] That political disinterest explains why the Methodists have been considered part of the reason for a lack of the sort of revolution that was experienced in France in the eighteenth century.[66]

Ironically, at the same time as being accused of being seventeenth-century Puritans revived, the Methodists were also suspected of being closet Catholics. This accusation appeared in print in the work of George Lavington, bishop of Exeter, *The Enthusiasm of Methodists and Papists Compared* (1749–51), in which John Wesley was compared to the founders of Catholic orders like the Dominicans.[67] The idea of the Catholic connection may also have been at play in the suspicions that the Methodists were staunch Jacobites, yearning for the success of the Pretender, James Stuart, son of the former James II.[68] The Stuart attempt to dethrone the Hanoverian monarchy in 1745 came to nothing, and

Welsh support was conspicuous by its absence, but it was a period when the Society of Sea Sergeants in the south-west could toy with the idea of deposing George II.[69] The SPCK seem to have suffered similar unfounded opposition at the time of the 1715 uprising, so Jacobitism created an air of conspiracy, which meant that any societies meeting in private might be regarded with suspicion. The spectre of Catholicism aroused strong emotions in Wales, based on the preconception that its restoration would mean the triumph of superstition and the loss of the Bible in Welsh. Since Methodism appeared ambiguous to outsiders, it may have been convenient to associate it with a familiar enemy. The Blaen-porth society, for instance, met with hostility locally because they were believed to be covert Catholics.[70] One of the superintendents, John Richard, had reservations about the practice of examining the state of souls in the society because he felt it smacked of Catholicism and the confession: 'examining into the particular state of souls was Popish.'[71] He was not the only one to come to such a conclusion, as Saunders Lewis famously and controversially argued that the society was indeed a revival of the Catholic confessional, although his theory has not generally been accepted.[72]

As there was no consistent policy in the Church when it came to attitudes to Methodism, so too there was inconsistency amongst the county authorities and gentry in general. Much of the government at the time operated at a county level, so the Justices of Peace in each of the three counties had considerable leeway to decide on their approach. It is perhaps remarkable how much tolerance there was in the area for the new movement. Several members of the gentry such as Edward Dalton, whilst never fully committing to the movement, were prepared to take a lenient attitude and not to show any open opposition. It may be that the existence of movements like the Society for Promoting Christian Knowledge led some to believe these new societies were simply part of that wave of well-intentioned pietism. They may have been viewed as harmless in the first instance as a result. For many magistrates, Methodism could have been a temporary fad which would fall from fashion, so hardly worth taking any active effort to remove it. There was also a tradition of ineffective persecution of minorities in Wales, which might stem from an attitude of tolerance or from plain idleness. There had been little appetite either for hunting down Dissenters in the age of persecution in the seventeenth century, or for bringing witches or Catholic recusants to book because the law dictated it.[73]

More importantly, there were also a number of gentry who provided a degree of patronage and protection, including Marmaduke Gwynne of Garth and his connections, which spread into Carmarthenshire. However, his brother, Roderick Gwynne of Glanbrân, Breconshire, was a fierce opponent who challenged Howel Harris and William Williams in the vicinity of Ystrad-ffin in 1743. The confrontation was evidently something of an embarrassment for Marmaduke Gwynne, who apologised to Harris for his brother's unkind behaviour.[74] This must have been on the Breconshire side of the border with Carmarthenshire, as Ystrad-ffin was located close to the borders with Cardiganshire and Breconshire, creating a jurisdictional uncertainty. As a Breconshire JP, Gwynne read the Riot Act, in response to which Harris argued that the law allowed them an hour in which to disperse, but Gwynne insisted that they move on immediately. Harris was eager to recommence exhorting on the highway nearby, but was again prevented. The crowd moved a further distance and Harris began discoursing again on the subject of persecution, only for Gwynne to read the Riot Act once more. In the face of such determined hostility, there was little choice but to disperse, or face being arrested for riot. Harris had obviously gained some familiarity with the law on riot and had put up a spirited defence:

> I said I had business & could not go & did plead the Magna Charta of England that I was a Britton & did plead ye Protection of ye Law – if I had offended or behav'd disrespectfull or Unbecoming that I was willing to sufer but that I would not go away as a Thief or Murtherer or a Villain. He said I was no better than a Vagabond I said he was welcome to call me what he pleased.[75]

The Methodists in the south-west did not suffer as much from legal action against them as those in other areas. Nevertheless, if a magistrate was determined to put obstacles in the way, life could be very difficult. There was always the possibility of having travelling preachers arrested for vagrancy, forcing the accused to prove that they had a fixed abode and livelihood before they could be released. Technically, also,

Methodists could be accused of holding unlawful assemblies under the terms of the Conventicles Act, which forbade groups of more than five persons to gather together to worship outside of the Church. This had been part of the code of persecution directed at the Dissenters, who were no longer affected by it since they could register their causes as meeting houses under the terms of the Toleration Act of 1689. The irony was that the Dissenters were exempt from the harshness of the Act, but the Methodists, who claimed that they were loyal to the Church, were not. The societies were in an ambiguous position and could be regarded as falling foul of the Conventicles Act, although the leaders insisted that it had been intended specifically to target those who refused to conform to the Church.[76]

The only exhorter in the area who was brought before the courts was Morgan Hughes, the first superintendent over north Cardiganshire. He was imprisoned in Cardigan during the first week of March 1743 to appear before the court of Great Sessions on charges of vagrancy and holding an unlawful assembly, brought by Richard Stedman of Strata Florida, a gentleman whose widow was to marry Herbert Lloyd of Peterwell shortly after.[77] This would seem, therefore, to be related to his exhorting in the north of the county, but the Sessions met in the county town of Cardigan. The first charge was essentially vexatious and easy to disprove, but the second represented a challenge, and if Hughes were found guilty, then many more Methodists might be at risk from the law in this way. Aware of the potential danger, the Methodists sought to muster as much support as possible, making use of friends and connections to seek legal advice and promises of assistance. Howel Harris consulted his lawyer acquaintances, including in Carmarthenshire, David Lloyd of Berllandywyll and Robert Archer Dyer of Aberglasney.[78] He was confident that the societies could not be proved to be unlawful assemblies, but was obviously doing all he could to persuade others of this in advance of the case. He wrote to Marmaduke Gwynne, asking for both practical advice and prayers on behalf of Hughes.[79] Thomas Price of Watford sent money to help with any costs and suggested having the case moved to the Westminster courts, promising further financial assistance.[80] The entire movement seemed to be mobilised to pray for the exhorter and to provide whatever other assistance they could. The appeal to Marmaduke Gwynne proved successful, as he contacted his nephew, John Lloyd of Peterwell, whose father Walter was the King's attorney in the circuit, to seek his help with the case.[81]

Harris was grateful that the case came before the Sessions in Cardigan and not Carmarthen, which might have been a more riotous occasion, given the general behaviour of Carmrthen crowds. He saw the hand of providence at work in arranging this: 'how wisely good has Jesus ordered this little nothing Tryal in a moderate Town where there is no Enmity open whereas it might have been in many Towns where Life had been in danger.'[82] The hopes for a 'little nothing Tryal' turned out to be justified, since when Morgan Hughes appeared before the court on 31 March, Richard Stedman was not present to prosecute. He may have thought better of it or was not sufficiently concerned to see it through to the end, but was forced to pay costs.[83] In response, Harris decided to drop the accusation of assault on the highway which he had intended, on Thomas Price's advice, to bring against those who arrested Hughes. Gwynne's contacts proved immensely useful, but the experience may have prompted Hughes towards the Dissenters rather than face similar charges in future.

The Methodists showed themselves in this case to be quite capable of employing the law to their benefit and of making use of whatever worldly influence they had. There was a similar attitude on display in their determination to respond to the far fiercer persecution in the north by bringing a case against Sir Watkin Williams Wynn of Wynnstay for his mistreatment of Peter Williams, contributions to pay for which were requested from the societies in the south-west.[84] There was a sense that they needed to prepare their defences for any possible legal threat gainst them, which could take various forms. When Harris wrote to inform Daniel Rowland of Hughes's predicament, he warned him that there were rumours of a writ against Rowland for riot, but these seem to have come to nothing.[85] There were also threats of taking action to eradicate the Methodists by pressing them into military service. The stalwart William Richard resolved to follow the example of Daniel and continue to venture into the lion's den, come what may.[86] There may have been rather less of a threat to him in Cardiganshire than Carmarthenshire, where the press gang did seem to have been in action against the Methodists. William John reported in 1745 that some of the gentry broke into society meetings with armed assistance in order to press those present, although they had later been released.[87] James Williams claimed to have been much threatened with the press gang, and Richard Tibbott confessed to quaking with dread at the prospect.[88] For some of the exhorters, this seemed like an additional motivation to register as Dissenting causes, but the Association simply advised those under threat, such as John Richard, to try to avoid the areas where the danger was greatest, which may not have been wholly reassuring.[89] There was real cause for concern, since Howel Harris's assistant James Ingram was snatched from Trefeca on 4 May 1744. Harris had also been threatened, but could establish his credentials as a property owner, having bought Trefeca from his brother Joseph. After a spirited defence, Ingram was released, but his imprisonment meant that he is the only Welsh Methodist whose exact height is known, being too short for the army at 5 foot, 2½ inches.[90]

The frequent description of some of the gentry 'raging' or 'roaring' against the Methodists seems appropriate in many cases. There were many threats of legal action but few were carried through, although it is not clear whether that was because those involved did not feel strongly enough to take action, or because more moderate voices intervened to restrain them. A magistrate in Lampeter interrupted the society to arrest the person who happened to be praying at the time, and although the unfortunate individual was later released, the magistrate continued to utter threats.[91] It was often in the towns that such persecution was at its height, since it was there that the gentry could often count on hostile crowds to back up their threats. The Association was prevented from meeting in Llandovery in January 1741 because of local opposition.[92] Harris was forbidden to exhort in Cydweli, in Carmarthenshire, by order of the mayor and had to move out of his jurisdiction before resuming his sermon.[93] Opposition there was led by Sir Edward Mansel of Trimsaran, Pembrey, and the Gwynne family of Gwempa, Llangyn-deyrn, who were highly influential in the area.[94] Mansel interrupted Harris when he attempted to exhort in Llangyndeyrn, urging the hearers to ignore such a mad creature. He warned Harris not to return to any of what he termed 'his parishes' again, unless he wished to be arrested for inciting riot. Harris's uncompromising response to him and to other gentlemen who sought to oppose the Methodists was: 'if they Imprisoned me I should be in Time set free att least by Death but when would they be set free from Hell's Dungeon when they should burn together as they sin together.'[95]

Angry crowds in towns and villages were often the source of the fiercest persecution, sometimes with the encouragement of the local gentry. Folk memories of the prevailing confusion felt under Oliver Cromwell's rule reinforced loyalty to the Church and hostility to its rivals. Anti-Methodist disturbances in eighteenth-century Wales can indeed be classed among 'Church and King riots' where the participants felt themselves to be operating in defence of the status quo in state and religion.[96] There were also other factors behind the antagonism in towns in particular, since the Methodist preaching against indulging in entertaintments may have seemed a direct threat to the livelihood of innkeepers and others who relied on people seeking some sort of recreation in their free time.[97] Resentment was also caused by the perception that the Methodists were causing divisions within families, with young people being encouraged to defy their parents by attending the societies.

Much of the anti-Methodist activity seemed to be aimed at making a mockery of the exhorters and generally making life awkward for any Methodists attempting to gather together. There was often no need to bother with reading the Riot Act, as various tricks could be played to frustrate the exhorters' efforts to preach. In Newport in Pembrokeshire, a large number of dogs had been brought together and set to barking to drown out the Methodists.[98] Harris had to compete with the church bells in Llandeilo, which were rung especially to silence him.[99] Dirt, dung, eggs and stones were regularly thrown to distract and deter the exhorters. The most ferocious attacks occurred elsewhere, however, but even then only on occasion did they become truly serious, as when William Seward died as a result of injuries suffered at Hay-on-Wye. Daniel Rowland and Williams were beaten at Tresaith, on the Cardiganshire coast, by a crowd egged on by a local gentleman.[100] Even before he was arrested, Morgan Hughes was targeted for his Methodist activities. He was set upon by a servant of William Price of Pigeonsford, Llangrannog, whose son would later marry Dorothy, the daughter of James Bowen of Llwyn-gwair, one of the supporters of the Methodist cause in Pembrokeshire, an alliance which would change the family's attitude quite radically.[101] When Eliza, the daughter of George and Dorothy Price, died at the age of seventeen, William Williams himself wrote an elegy in her memory, based on an obvious familiarity with the house and family.[102] Hughes apparently had another potentially violent encounter at Ffair-rhos in north Cardiganshire, when the house in which he was exhorting was surrounded by armed men led by Richard Stedman, who would later prosecute Hughes for vagrancy and unlawful assembly. Hughes informed Harris that he had only escaped intact because the persecutors felt too ashamed to continue when they heard the fervent prayers of the Methodists in the house.[103] All in all, it may be little wonder that Morgan Hughes preferred the relative safety of life as a Dissenter to the heroics expected of a Methodist exhorter!

Although prepared to arm themselves with legal defences and counter-suits when taken to court, in cases of direct, and occasionally brutal, violence, the Methodists chose not to retaliate. They might flee if all else failed, but the aim was to try to persevere with their message as long as possible. Harris sometimes did think twice about daring to visit some places where he had heard that enemies awaited him. He usually prayed for strength and sang his own translation of John Wesley's translation of a hymn by Johann Joseph Winckler:

> A raid i mi rhag ofon dyn
> Wrthnebu Ysbryd Duw ei hun,
> A digaloni ar air na gwaith
> Rhag bod yn dyst i'm Harglwydd maith?[104]
>
> Shall I, for fear of feeble man,
> The Spirit's course in me restrain?
> Or undismayed in deed and word,
> Be a true witness to my Lord?[105]

It was not just the leaders and exhorters who suffered at the hands of the gentry and others for their loyalty to the movement. Hostile landlords had almost unchecked power to evict or threaten to evict tenants who joined the societies. One elderly woman who was in frail health was visited by Howel Davies during her illness and was much distressed at receiving a warning to quit her house as a result.[106] William John, although not in any arrears of rent on his home at Glancothi, in Llanegwad, was required by his landlord to pay £12 on the grounds that he thought he was a 'Presbyterian'. This William John took as a sign that he was accounted worthy to suffer in the name of Christ and resolved to endure with patience:

> I was not mov'd against Them in ye less motion and I desir'd my heavenly father to forgive them for they knew not, prais'd be god who give me patience to forbear with Joy, believing all things doth work for my good, for He doth strengthen me that I can rejoce under tribulations and afflictions for there the love of Christ is more sweet rejoceing that I am accounted worthy to suffer for his name sake.[107]

There are few such examples in the south-west, compared to the north, where William Griffith of Cefnamwlch, for instance, was said to avenge himself on all Methodists for his wife's association with Howel Harris by evicting any tenants of that persuasion on his estate. Masters of servants could also set obstacles in the way of membership by preventing their employees from attending societies if they boarded where they worked, as many farmservants did. Not all employers were as tolerant as Owen Evans of Merthyr, who permitted his two maidservants to attend the local society regularly. He was a Dissenter and may well be the Owen Evan who joined the Merthyr society a few months later and was described by William John as 'an old Proffesor among the Dissenters'.[108]

Possibly the worst opposition to have to bear was that of family, friends and neighbours, who could not understand the religious new birth that seemed to alienate them from each other. Anthony Rees feared to pass through the villages in the region of his home in Llandybïe in east Carmarthenshire because of the constant provocation he claimed to face.[109] Methodism could divide families, as in the case of Theophilus Evans and his half-brother, Captain John Evans of Pen-y-wenallt, as well as Marmaduke and Roderick Gwynne, who held vastly different opinions and behaved in radically different ways. Such rifts in families inevitably fuelled accusations that the Methodists were intent on luring people away from their families in order to take advantage of them, either financially or sexually. The very fact that the majority of the members were young led to almost automatic suspicion in some quarters. Since some of the young men and women who joined the societies did so despite the disapproval of their parents, this led to an obvious resentment of a religious movement which seemed to be steeling the younger generation to defy their elders and disregard their families.[110] This could result in distressing scenes between family members. Nicholas Griffith of Cil-y-llyn, Llansawel, was sternly rebuked and mocked by his father and elder brother for his Methodist beliefs which led to a split in the family. It is not known whether the division was healed before Nicholas's father, John, died in 1740.[111] Some parents took extreme measures to dissuade their children, such as one mother who tied her daughter up and beat her to stop her from attending the society at Glancothi.[112] Few were so brutal, however, and several relied on threats of disinheritance or disowning to try to change their children's views. One girl in the society of Dygoed, Llanarthney, who was convinced after hearing a sermon by Howel Davies, was threatened with being cut out of her father's will, which meant forfeiting a substantial inheritance, for her father was said to have 'much of this world to give'. Her superintendent, John Richard, prayed that she would have the fortitude to keep to her faith and sacrifice her inheritance.[113] More mundane opposition from friends and neighbours who mocked or ostracised society members could also have been painful on a daily basis, so some strength of character was often required not to yield to persuasion and abandon the society.

These were the kinds of themes that anti-Methodist literature revelled in exploring. There was no Welsh equivalent to William Hogarth and his caricatures of Methodist preachers gulling the credulous, and it is not surprising that opposition to Methodism in Wales turned to traditional Welsh forms of expression through verse and popular culture. It used the *anterliwt* or interlude, that cross between morality play and pantomime which was performed at fairs to suit the tastes of popular audiences.[114] Interlude humour was rowdy and ribald, taking pot shots at popular targets that were sure to raise a laugh, such as lawyers, misers and Methodist preachers. The surviving anti-Methodist interlude, *Ffrewyll y Methodistiaid* (The Scourge of the Methodists, 1746) by William Roberts, was written and performed in north Wales where there was far greater antagonism towards the Methodists.[115] But the very fact that they were considered worthy subjects for such an attack might be deemed a mark of success and a sign that their influence was spreading. Even in 1783, Huw Jones, one of the most famous writers of popular ballads and interludes in north Wales, was still making jokes about Harris and Whitefield.[116]

There was nowhere near as much anti-Methodist literature, or defence against it, in Wales as there was in England, and many of the authors and poets concerned were located in north Wales rather than the south. There was some verse in the south-west attacking the Methodists, with Daniel Rowland an obvious target, but that was mainly rather later in the century. Rowland was probably the unnamed minister in Ifan Thomas Rhys's verse, 'Y Maen Tramgwydd' (The Stumbling Block) from c. 1757–61. Rhys (1710–70) was a popular poet and cobbler from Llanarth in mid-Cardiganshire, not too far from Llangeitho, so an area that would have felt the ripples of the revival. As a member of the Arminian congregation of Llwynrhydowen, it is not surprising that Rhys poured scorn on the doctrine of election in his ballad. He also composed a verse in response to a dispute between Rowland and Dafydd Llwyd, his own minister at Llwynrhydowen, in which he mocked Rowland as one who thought that it was he, and not Christ, who judged who was justified and who should be sent to hell.[117] Ioan ap Hywel (or John Howell, 1774–1830) from Abergwili seemed to seek conciliation between Methodists and the Church in his work, but he also reminded his readers that God did not appear to Elijah in the earthquake, or the powerful wind or the fire, but in the still, small voice. As a result he could not help but enquire how God's kingdom could be carried on by commotion and convulsions, which seemed much more like the work of the Devil.[118] These poetic attacks were fairly restrained and centred on matters of differences in belief and practice, rather than focusing on presenting some of the popular accusations against the Methodists.

It was through the medium of prose, therefore, that the more virulent attacks on Methodists in south-west Wales appeared, produced by some of Wales's most prominent authors at the time. Lewis Morris was one of the foremost scholars of Welsh literature and history in the mid-eighteenth century, but also penned the satirical piece, 'Young Mends the Clothier's Sermon' in 1743.[119] Although Morris was originally from Anglesey, he spent many years in Cardiganshire and for a period between 1737 and 1743 was engaged in surveying the Welsh coastline, during which time he may very well have chanced to hear a sermon by one of the two brothers William and Christopher Mends, both exhorters in south Carmarthenshire with their roots in Pembrokeshire. Their father was actually a clothier, so Morris may have heard some gossip about the pair on the occasion he heard one or the other speak.[120] Although unpublished, the mock sermon is one of the most effective works of anti-Methodist literature because of the telling satire which exaggerates the style of the Methodist exhorter. It draws on biblical language in a similar way, but twists it to convey a less sincere message. There are clear echoes of the Song of Songs in a section which insinuates that the Methodist preacher was intent on seducing the women who came to hear:

> The Lambs of the Lord are willing to play, they are Beautiful to the Eye, they have Velvet Thighs, their Skins are soft, their wool is white Like Cotton, yea like the Cotton of America. Their Blushes are like wool dyed with Madder of which we make the Garments of the Righteous in Roose and Castlemartin.
>
> I give you Leave to play, my Lovely Lambs, Receive the Spirit within you with Eagerness and Love. Dance and skip about for I will absolve you from your sins. But whatever you do, do in the dark, that our Enemies may not triumph over us, for the Eyes of the wicked Peep into every corner.[121]

Here are also some of the repeated references in the sermon to materials and garments, referring back to what might be regarded as the exhorters' lowly origins, which made them ill-suited for their present occupation. 'Mends' bemoans the lack of any clothier amongst Christ's disciples and aspires to fill the gap: 'My name is Mends and if I mend the souls of the Roose folks with my Tongue and mend their Evil Habits by making Cloth with my Hands, How am I less than the rest of the Apostles?'[122] One of the abiding themes, however, is the desire to take advantage of the women in the societies, by inducing them to part with their money or their virtue. In the sermon, Mends makes the point that Howel Davies had married well and that he might aspire to do the same by entrancing the young women who came to listen to him, who should find him more attractive than the church clergy who 'are fat in Body, but Lean in spirit,

I am Lean in Body but Fat in spirit'.[123] This was a common accusation amongst the enemies of the movement, with Howel Harris's relationship with Sidney Griffith feeding the suspicions further. Since the societies contained a mixture of young men and women and met at night, there were fears that this could lead to immoral behaviour. William Roberts in his interlude claimed that the timing of the meetings provided an opportunity for 'whoring' on the sly.[124] John Evans of Eglwys Gymyn, whilst mainly concerned with Griffith Jones's perceived failings, also charged the Methodist societies with being 'Nurseries of Fornication, Adultery, and all Kind of Lewdness; of false Doctrine, Heresy and Schism'.[125]

The sermon also shows another characteristic of the criticism of the exhorters: the accusation that they were uneducated and often drawn from other walks of life, but claiming the call of the spirit to justify their preaching, even though their words were ill-informed and unwise. The description of Mends as a clothier emphasised his lack of ordination or qualification to preach to others. For such men to seek to proclaim the word of God seemed to be a sign of disorder and chaos. Most of the exhorters were farmers or craftsmen with no great claims to learning, and may have seemed unsuited to their calling in the eyes of many supporters of the Church. This trend is reminiscent of the anti-Puritan literature of the seventeenth century, which issued similar attacks on itinerant preachers who had previously been ordinary craftsmen before being elevated to the pulpit during the Commonwealth period.[126] The exhorters, like the Puritan itinerants, were portrayed as deceitful and ignorant hypocrites, intent on turning the world upside down, with just enough cunning to dupe the innocent to believe in them. In *Ffrewyll y Methodistiaid*, Harris and Whitefield agree between them to strip the kingdom of its wealth by charming the gullible, although they end up being snatched away by the press gang. The Methodists were naturally aware of these accusations and were concerned to improve the exhorters' levels of education. Even so, Harris believed that the fact that 'very mean & unlearned men not in ye usual way'[127] were chosen for the work was a sign of its divine provenance, and William Williams reminded his readers that the only real qualification to preach was the influence of the spirit:

> *er mai seiri, cryddion a chobleriaid, fel y dywedoch, oeddent yn ddiweddar, nid ŷnt un gronyn gwaeth o hynny ... Ac mi wn fod rhai pregethwyr ag oedd o'r fath grefftau tlodion â hynny o'r blaen, heddiw yn gwir ddosbarthu gair y bywyd.*[128]

> although they were lately, as you say, carpenters, shoemakers and cobblers, they are not one jot the worse for that ... And I know that some preachers who were of such poor trades as that, today truly distribute the word of life.

Lewis Morris's satire was one of the few works produced prior to 1750, and most anti-Methodist literature is of a later date, when the movement was becoming more of a presence throughout Wales.[129] It was in the 1750s that one of the other best-known authors of the period turned his attention to the Methodists, as Theophilus Evans published his *A History of Modern Enthusiasm* in 1752. Evans had demonstrated his precocious talent when he published his hugely popular account of the history of Wales, *Drych y Prif Oesoedd* (The Mirror of the Primitive Ages), in 1716, later modified and expanded in 1740.[130] He had already translated Bishop Gibson of London's letter of advice against enthusiasm into Welsh in 1740 and his prejudices against the Methodists were probably only reinforced by the experience of having William Williams, Pantycelyn, as his curate.[131] Although the two are amongst the most famous literary figures in eighteenth-century Wales, it is unlikely that they had much in common, as they saw the country, its religion and history from very different perspectives. There is no suggestion that Evans had any hand in the charges against Williams before the ecclesiastical courts, but he certainly seems to have done nothing to help. In *A History of Modern Enthusiasm*, he cast an eye over various heretical sects which had emerged since the Protestant Reformation, adding the Methodists to the list, especially in the second edition of the work in 1757. He accused them of pride in considering themselves to have a special relationship with God and believed that their emphasis on justification through faith led inevitably to antinomianism and a disregard for morality. He painted them as a highly dangerous element in a dangerous tradition of groups who claimed enthusiasm as a cover for their heresy. Surprisingly perhaps, he had little to say about the Welsh

Methodists specifically, but they were obviously included in the general criticism.[132]

The accusation of excessive enthusiasm and irrational emotionalism was one frequently levelled by enemies of Methodism. Some modern historians have also detected in the movement generally a rejection of reason and a tendency to espouse belief in the supernatural.[133] There are elements of truth, as the Methodists did firmly believe in the direct intervention of God and the Devil, and saw signs and omens at work in the world, which they attributed either to providence or to diabolical power. In some ways, the willingness to believe in such forces might be a response to scepticism and a commitment to heart religion. Edmund Jones, the Independent minister, collected tales of devils, fairies and spirits for that very reason.[134] Superstitious stories and practices lingered in rural Welsh society, and travelling preachers heard hair-raising tales in many places. Some of these may have appealed because they suggested some form of retribution for the ungodly. For instance, James Williams heard of the death of a man who had collapsed with blackened tongue and face after a bout of profuse swearing in a tavern.[135] Other accounts hinted at almost miraculous divine intervention, such as the sixty-year-old woman, wife of William Samuel of Llanllwni, who found herself able to produce milk to feed an orphan child for which she was caring.[136] Although Harris judged sightings of corpse candles in south-west Wales to be 'truth real', there was generally no comment on the veracity of such hearsay tales.[137] Methodist correspondence and literature seemed to prefer uplifting examples of remarkable conversions, providential influences and good deaths. Yet such superstitious beliefs were obviously still a part of popular culture, and the Methodists were not wholly immune.

A fervent belief in the work of providence was characteristic of the movement, and any escape from persecution was interpreted as the protection of providence. Howel Harris believed that providence had ensured that there were powerful friends in place to defend the movement, especially Marmaduke Gwynne, whose influence spread into the south-west through family connections and who was their main protector when it came to court cases such as that facing Morgan Hughes.[138] Harris detected the same power at work when some persecutors seemed to encounter difficulties themselves, which he regarded as divine retribution. A gentleman from Cwrt Hendre, near Neath, who stole his horse was subsequently said to have lost two of his own horses and suffered ill health.[139] A young gentleman from Cwm-ann who had been a persecutor fell ill and died believing that he was heading straight to hell.[140] In a similar example, Harris felt sympathy for John Jones, a doctor from Llandovery who had been a ferocious enemy to the Methodists, but on his deathbed in desperation begged for Harris's prayers.[141] The Methodists saw providence operating in little ways to ease their path, convincing them that God was on their side. Harris, for instance, rejoiced that some kind soul he encountered at the Bear in Llandovery chose to give him a pair of boots, 'my feet having been wet all this winter for want of dry Boots'.[142] Even the weather at times was believed to have been altered in their interest, with Harris recording a number of instances in the south-west where foul weather improved suddenly for the duration of his preaching.[143]

The members and exhorters found similar inspiration to help them perseverse through various trials. John Richard also wrote a hymn aimed at uplifting the society members to press on regardless of obstacles:

> *O frodyr a chwiorydd glân,*
> *Dewch awn ar ôl ein brawd trwy'r Tân;*
> *Heb ofni dwyn y Groes:*
> *Mil o flynderau ni awn trwy:*
> *Pam ofnnwn lid un Gelyn mwy?*
> *Gorchfygu wnawn trwy rhinwedd Grâs.*[144]

> O good brothers and sisters,
> Come let us follow our brother through the fire;
> Without fearing carrying the Cross:
> A thousand troubles we'll go through:
> Why fear we more the anger of any Enemy?
> Through the virtue of Grace, we will overcome.

Despite many brave statements of determination to carry on despite opposition, there were inevitably moments of doubt. Richard Tibbott, for instance, confessed privately to his diary that the threat of the press gang made him feel dissatisfied with God for 'suffering his children to have such afflictions and persecutions in the world' (*'godde yw blant gail y fath flindere ag erlidie yn y byd'*).[145] Yet, even on the eve of the separation, with the future of the movement uncertain, James Williams felt unshakeably convinced that 'the Lord Jesus is in the little societies' still.[146] John Harry in Pembrokeshire saw signs of decline all around him in 1748, but still insisted that the Lord would know his own, come what may.[147] With that obstinate belief, many of them were convinced that any difficulties could be overcome and were simply sent to purify their faith even further.

Notes

1 Trevecca College/1 3062, John Harry to the Association, 30 July 1748.
2 DHH 132, 16 September 1748.
3 For examples see Trevecka MS 447, Howel Harris to John Powell, 19 December 1741; 658, Howel Harris to George Whitefield, 23 September 1742; 736, Howel Harris to William McCulloch, 23 November 1742; 854, Howel Harris to William McCulloch, 15 April 1743.
4 Trevecca College/1 3042, William Richard to the Association, 14 July 1747.
5 Trevecka MS 1760, Howel Davies to Howel Harris, 10 January 1748; a reference to 1 Samuel 4:21.
6 Trevecca College/1 3082, 3083, John Richard to the Association, 1750.
7 Trevecca College/1 3051, John Harry to the Association, 30 January 1748.
8 Trevecca College/1 3073, William John to the Association, 24 May 1749. For the Mends and Laugharne, see Trevecca College/1 3067, 25 October 1748; Carmarthenshire Archive, Quarter Session Records, QS1/1, p. 57.
9 Trevecca College/1 3057 John Harry to the Association, 2 May 1748.
10 Trevecca College/1 3081, John Richard to the Association, 1750. Acts 20:30.
11 Trevecca College/1 3074, James Williams to the Association, 8 May 1750.
12 D. W. Bebbington, *Evangelicalism in Modern Britain: A History from the 1730s to the 1980s* (London: Routledge, 1989), pp. 6–7, 42–50.
13 G. Tudur, *Howell Harris: From Conversion to Separation* (Cardiff: University of Wales Press, 2000), pp. 155–8.
14 D. D. Morgan, *Theologia Cambrensis: Protestant Religion and Theology in Wales, I: From Reformation to Revival 1588–1760* (Cardiff: University of Wales Press, 2018), p. 371.
15 Trevecka MS 501, Howel Harris to George Whitefield, 23 March 1742.
16 Trevecka MS 532, Howel Harris to George Whitefield, 5 April 1742.
17 N. Cynhafal Jones (ed.), *Gweithiau Williams Pantycelyn, Cyfrol II* (Newport: W. Jones, 1891), pp. 22–3; Gomer M. Roberts, *Y Pêr Ganiedydd [Pantycelyn], Cyfrol II: Arweiniad i'w Waith* (Llandysul: Gwasg Gomer, 1958), p. 67.
18 Derec Llwyd Morgan, *Williams Pantycelyn* (Caernarfon: Gwasg Pantycelyn, 1983), 17–19, 54–65; G. T. Hughes, *Williams Pantycelyn* (Cardiff: University of

Wales Press, 1983), pp, 75–124; Kathryn Jenkins, *Cân y Ffydd: Ysgrifau ar Emynyddiaeth*, ed. Rh. Griffiths (Caernarfon: Gwasg y Bwthyn, 2011), p. 98.
19 R. Geraint Gruffydd, 'Diwygiad 1762 a William Williams o Bantycelyn', *Cylchgrawn Cymdeithas Hanes y Methodistiaid Calfinaidd/Journal of the Historical Society of the Presbyterian Church of Wales*, 54 (1969), 68–75; (1970), 4–13; E. M. White, '"I will once more shake the heavens": The 1762 Revival in Wales', in *Revival and Resurgence in Christian History*, Studies in Church History, 44, ed. Kate Cooper and Jeremy Gregory (Woodbridge: The Boydell Press, 2008), p. 158; E. M. White, '"Yr Ysbryd Canu": Diwygiad Llangeitho, Williams Pantycelyn a'r Emyn', *Y Traethodydd*, CLXVIII (2013), 226–40.
20 D. Hempton, *Methodism: Empire of the Spirit* (London: Yale University Press, 2005), pp. 11–31.
21 Tudur, *Howell Harris: From Conversion to Separation*, pp. 43–4; Morgan, 'The Welsh Sermon, 1689–1901', in Francis and Gibson (eds), *The Oxford Handbook of the British Sermon 1689–1901* (Oxford: Oxford University Press, 2012), pp. 203–4.
22 DHH 82, 2 December 1741.
23 R. Tudur Jones, *Congregationalism in Wales*, ed. Robert Pope (Cardiff: University of Wales, 2004), pp. 110–13.
24 Trevecka MS 288, Howel Harris to David Williams, 26 November 1740.
25 Trevecka MS 303, David William to Howel Harris, *c.* 25 December 1740.
26 Trevecka MS 1268, David Williams to Howel Harris, ?1747.
27 Trevecka MS 564, Howel Harris to Christmas Samuel, 3 June 1742.
28 Trevecca College/1 3023, p. 41, James Williams to the Association, 4 April 1746.
29 Trevecca College/1 3004, William Richard to the Association, 2 October 1743.
30 Trevecca College/1 3040, William John to the Association, 20 July 1747.
31 Trevecca College/1 3023, pp. 8–9, James Williams to the Association, October 1749.
32 Trevecca College/1 3023, p. 35, William John to the Association, 4 April 1746.
33 Trevecca College/1 3059, William John to the Association, 3 May 1748.
34 Jones, *Congregationalism in Wales*, p. 112; Tudur, *Howell Harris*, p. 116.
35 Trevecka MS 569, Elizabeth Thomas to Howel Harris, June 1742.
36 Trevecka MS 1866, John Harry to the Association, 19 May 1749.
37 Trevecca College/1 3045, James Williams to the Association, 10 October 1747.
38 D. Rowland, *Pum Pregeth* (Carmarthen: John Ross, 1772), p. 34.
39 G. H. Hughes (ed.), *Gweithiau William Williams Pantycelyn, Cyfrol II: Rhyddiaith* (Caerdydd: Gwasg Prifysgol Cymru, 1967), p. 29.
40 DHH 109, 18 April 1744.
41 Trevecca College/1 3062, John Harry to the Association, 30 July 1748.
42 D. Rowland, *Pum Pregeth*, p. 36.
43 Hughes (ed.), *Gweithiau William Williams Pantycelyn*, p. 29.
44 T. Dafydd, *Coffadwriaeth am y Cyfiawn* (Caerfyrddin: John Ross, 1776), p. 2.
45 E. Evans, *Daniel Rowland and the Great Evangelical Awakening in Wales* (Edinburgh: Banner of Truth Trust, 1985), pp. 326–7.
46 Trevecka MS 973, William John to Howel Harris, 10 September 1743; 1224, Howel Harris to Thomas Price, 8 September 1744.
47 DHH 122, 14 April 1746.

48 Trevecka MS 776, Howel Harris to Griffith Jones, 10 January 1743.
49 Trevecka MS 990, Griffith Evan Lewis and Griffith Evans to Howel Harris, September 1743.
50 Evans, *Daniel Rowland*, pp. 326–7.
51 SD/MISC/1279, a list of candidates for orders with names of alleged Methodists on dorse, c. 1744; G. M. Roberts, *Y Pêr Ganiedydd [Pantycelyn], Cyfrol I: Trem ar ei Fywyd* (Aberystwyth: Gwasg Aberystwyth, 1949), pp. 56–67.
52 SD/Let/1810, 22 February 1745.
53 W. T. Morgan, 'William Williams, Pantycelyn, Before the Bishop's Court', *Cylchgrawn Cymdeithas Hanes y Methodistiaid Calfinaidd/Journal of the Historical Society of the Presbyterian Church of Wales*, 33 (1948), 2–12; G. M. Roberts, *Y Pêr Ganiedydd*, pp. 56–67; D. Ll. Morgan, *Williams Pantycelyn*, p. 7.
54 Trevecca College/1 2945, p. 13, 6–7 April 1743.
55 Evans, *Daniel Rowland*, p. 221.
56 Trevecka MS 178, John Tilsley to Howel Harris, 2 August 1739.
57 DHH 12, 30 March 1736.
58 See G. Tudur, 'Gwir Ffrewyll y Methodisitiaid', *Y Cofiadur*, 46 (1981), 8; Tudur, *Howell Harris*, pp. 119–30.
59 DHH 72, 12 May 1741, 14 May 1741; 84, 15 January 1742.
60 Trevecca College/1 3104, 23 June 1746.
61 Trevecca College/1 3004, William Richard to the Association, 2 October 1743.
62 Trevecca College/1 3016, William Richard to the Association, 20 June 1744.
63 For instance in W. Roberts, *Ffrewyll y Methodistiaid, neu Buttein-glwm Siencyn ac Ynfydog* (Shrewbury, 1746), p. 29.
64 DHH 105, 15 December 1743.
65 *Sail, Dibenion a Rheolau,'r Societies* (Bristol: Felix Farley, 1742), p. iv.
66 E. P. Thompson, *The Making of the English Working Class* (Harmondsworth: Penguin, 1970), pp. 385–440; D. Hempton, *Religion and Political Culture in Britain and Ireland from the Glorious Revolution to the Decline of Empire* (Cambridge: Cambridge University Press, 1996), pp. 25–48; Royle, *Revolutionary Britannia? Reflections on the Threat of Revolution in Britain, 1789–1848* (Manchester: Manchester University Press, 2000), pp. 164–7.
67 J. D. Walsh, 'Methodism and the Mob in the Eighteenth Century', in G. J. Cuming and D. Baker (eds), *Popular Belief and Practice*, Studies in Church History, 8 (London: Cambridge University Press, 1972), pp. 226–7.
68 G. H. Jenkins, *The Foundations of Modern Wales: Wales 1642–1780* (Cardiff: University of Wales Press, 1987), pp. 358–9.
69 D. W. Howell, *Patriarchs and Parasites: The Gentry of South-west Wales in the Eighteenth Century* (Cardiff: University of Wales Press, 1986), pp. 115–19.
70 Trevecka MS 642, William Richard to Howel Harris, 12 September 1742.
71 Trevecca College/1 2945, p. 19, 30 June 1741.
72 S. Lewis, *Williams Pantycelyn* (Llundain: Foyle's, 1927), pp. 47–9, 60–1. For a full discussion of his theory and responses to it, see S. Lewis, *Williams Pantycelyn*, ed. D. Densil Morgan (Cardiff: University of Wales Press, 2016).
73 E. M. White, 'From Ejectment to Toleration in Wales, 1662–89', in A. P. F. Sell (ed.), *The Great Ejectment of 1662: Its Antecedents, Aftermath and Ecumenical Significance* (Eugene, Oregon: Pickwick Publications, 2012), p. 150.
74 Trevecka MS 823, Marmaduke Gwynne to Howel Harris, 21 March 1743.

75 DHH 98, 25 February 1743.
76 D. Hempton, 'Methodism and the Law, 1740–1820', *Bulletin of the John Rylands Library*, 70 (1988), 94–5.
77 DHH 98, 9 March 1743; Trevecka MS 816, Howel Harris to Daniel Rowland, 9 March 1743; 821, Howel Harris to John Lewis, 17 March 1743; G. M. Roberts, 'Methodistiaeth Gynnar Gwaelod Sir Aberteifi', *Ceredigion*, 5 (1964), 5–6; B. Phillips, *The History of a Mansion and its Infamous Squire* (Llandysul: Gomer, 1981), pp. 52–3.
78 DHH 98, 25 March 1743; Trevecka MS 832, Howel Harris to Joseph Harris, 26 March 1743; 833, Howel Harris to Thomas James, 26 March 1743.
79 Trevecka MS 817, Howel Harris to Marmaduke Gwynne, 12 March 1743.
80 Trevecka MS 824, Thomas Price and William Howel to Howel Harris, 23 March 1743.
81 Trevecka MS 823, Marmaduke Gwynne to Howel Harris, 21 March 1743.
82 DHH 98, 28 March 1743.
83 DHH 98, 31 March 1743; Trevecka MS 849, Howel Harris to Susannah Harris, 5 April 1743.
84 G. M. Roberts, *Bywyd a Gwaith Peter Williams* (Cardiff: University of Wales Press, 1943), pp. 31–5.
85 Trevecka MS 816, 9 March 1743.
86 Trevecca College/1 2986, 3 February 1747.
87 Trevecca College/1 2945, p. 151, William John to the Association, 3 July 1745.
88 Trevecca College/1 2945, p. 150, James Williams to the Association, 3 July 1745; Trevecca College/1 3187, p. 67, 16 April 1744.
89 Trevecca College/1 2945, p. 147, 3 July 1743.
90 Trevecka MS 1171a, Howel Harris to John Williams, 5 May 1744; Trevecka MS 1193, James Ingram to anon., 19 June 1744. Printed in *Christian History*, 5/iv (1744), 68–9.
91 Trevecca College/1 3005, James Williams to the Association, 1743.
92 DHH 68, 18 January 1741.
93 DHH 66, 18 December 1740.
94 F. Jones, *Historic Carmarthenshire Homes and their Families* (Newport, Pembrokeshire: Brawdy Books, 2006), pp. 88–9, 189.
95 DHH 70, 9 March 1741.
96 See J. Walsh, 'Methodism and the Mob in the Eighteenth Century'; J. Stevenson, *Popular Disturbances in England, 1700–1832* (second edn, Harlow: Longman, 1992), pp. 173–9.
97 Hempton, 'Methodism and the Law', p. 98; G. Tudur, 'Gwir Ffrewyll', p. 98; Stevenson, *Popular Disturbances in England*, p. 32.
98 DHH 70, 26 February 1741.
99 DHH 70, 11 March 1741.
100 DHH 97, 11 February 1743; Evans, *Daniel Rowland*, pp. 216–17.
101 DHH 96, 7 December 1742.
102 N. Cynhafal Jones (ed.), *Gweithiau Williams Pant-y-celyn, Cyfrol I* (Treffynnon: P. M. Evans & son, 1887), pp. 578–80.
103 DHH 96, 7 December 1742.
104 G. M. Roberts, *Portread o Ddiwygiwr* (Caernarfon: Bwrdd Ymddiriedolwyr y Ddarlith Davies, 1969), pp. 56–7.

105 *The Works of John Wesley, Volume 7: A Collection of Hymns for the Use of the People called Methodists*, ed. F. Baker (Oxford: Clarendon Press, 1975), p. 416; first published in *A Collection of Psalms and Hymns* (1738).
106 DHH 90, 11 May 1742.
107 Trevecka MS 308, William John to Howel Harris, 14 January 1740.
108 NLW MS 5456A, p. 27b, 25 March 1744; Trevecca College/1 2945, p. 105, William John to the Association, 27 June 1744.
109 Trevecka MS 137, Anthony Rees to Howel Harris, 13 January 1739.
110 See G. Malmgreen, 'Domestic discords: women and family in East Cheshire Methodism, 1750–1830', in J. Obelkevich, L. Roper and R. Samuel (eds), *Disciplines of Faith: Studies in Religion, Politics and Patriarchy* (London: Routledge and Kegan Paul, 1987), pp. 63–4.
111 Trevecka MS 179, 3 August 1738; Jones, *Historic Carmarthenshire Homes and their Families*, p. 34..
112 DHH 54, 8 March 1740.
113 Trevecca College/1 3023, p. 38, John Richard to the Association, 9 April 1746.
114 D. G. Jones, 'The Interludes', in B. Jarvis (ed.), *A Guide to Welsh Literature c. 1700–1800* (Cardiff: University of Wales Press, 2000), pp. 210–55.
115 See W. Roberts, *Ffrewyll y Methodistiaid*, ed. A. C. Lake (Cardiff: Cardiff University Press, 1998).
116 A. C. Lake (ed.), *Anterliwtiau Huw Jones o Langwm* (Caernarfon: Cyhoeddiadau Barddas, 2000), pp. 228–32.
117 E. G. Millward, 'Rhai Agweddau ar Lenyddiaeth Wrth-Fethodistaidd y Ddeunawfed Ganrif', *Cylchgrawn Cymdeithas Hanes y Methodistiaid Calfinaidd/Journal of the Historical Society of the Presbyterian Church of Wales*, 60 (1975).
118 NLW MS 6238A, p. 350.
119 See A. R. Jones, 'Vermin who creep into all corners through the least crevices: Lewis Morris and the Methodists', *Transactions of the Cymmrodorion Society*, new series, 5 (1999), 24–35; G. H. Jenkins, 'Lewis Morris: "the fat man of Cardiganshire"', *Ceredigion*, 14/2 (2002), 1–23.
120 *Evangelical Magazine* (1799), 397.
121 NLW MS 67A, pp. 60–1.
122 NLW MS 67A, p. 54.
123 NLW MS 67A, pp. 59–60.
124 Roberts, *Ffrewyll y Methodistiaid*, p. 20.
125 J. Evans, *Some Account of the Welch Charity-Schools: and of the Rise and Progress of Methodism in Wales, through the Means of them* (London, 1752), p. 79.
126 See G. H. Jenkins, *Protestant Dissenters in Wales 1639–1689* (Cardiff: University of Wales Press, 1992), pp. 39–56; J. Morgan-Guy, '"Tinkers and other vermin": Methodists and the established church in Wales 1730–1800', in D. W. Roberts (ed.), *Revival, Renewal and the Holy Spirit* (Milton Keynes: Paternoster, 2009), pp. 27–35.
127 DHH 122, 21 April 1746.
128 Hughes (ed.), *Gweithiau William Williams Pantycelyn*, II, p. 204.
129 See P. H. Williams, 'Jumpers: Blessed Enthusiasts or Bizarre Episodes?', *Cylchgrawn Cymdeithas Hanes y Methodistiaid Calfinaidd/Journal of the Historical Society of the Presbyterian Church of Wales*, 29–30 (2005–6), 43–72.

130 G. Thomas, 'Two Prose Writers: Ellis Wynne and Theophilus Evans', in B. Jarvis (ed.), *A Guide to Welsh Literature c. 1700–1800* (Cardiff: University of Wales Press, 2000), pp. 54–63.
131 T. Evans, *Llythyr Addysg Esgob Llundain at y Bobl o'i Esgobaeth; yn eu rhybuddio yn erbyn Claiarwch o'r naill du; a zêl danbaid nid ar ôl Gwybodaeth o'r tu arall* (Caerloyw, 1740).
132 G. H. Jenkins, *Theophilus Evans: Y Dyn, Ei Deulu a'i Oes* (Llandysul: Gwasg Gomer, 1993), pp. 18–19.
133 H. D. Rack, 'Doctors, Demons and Early Methodist Healing', in W. Sheils (ed.), *The Church and Healing*, Studies in Church History, 19 (Oxford: Basil Blackwell, 1982), pp. 137–8.
134 E. Jones, *The Appearance of Evil: Apparitions of Spirits in Wales*, ed. J. Harvey (Cardiff: University of Wales Press, 2003), p. 6; A. Coward, 'Magic and the supernatural in eighteenth-century Wales: the world of the Rev. Edmund Jones (1702–1793)' (unpublished PhD thesis, University of Wales, Newport, 2012), pp. 151–3.
135 DHH 97, 2 March 1743.
136 DHH 41, 28 February 1739.
137 DHH 41, 1 March 1739; 70, 26 February 1741.
138 DHH 98, 3 March 1743.
139 DHH 121, 18 January 1746.
140 DHH 98, 27 February 1743.
141 DHH 50, 16 December 1739.
142 DHH 69, 16 February 1741.
143 DHH 46, 10–11 July 1739; 49, 11 September 1739.
144 J. Richard, *Hymnau Buddiol a Chymm[w]ysyw canu ar amryw achosion gan Gristnogion, gwir brofiadol* (Caerfyrddin: Samuel Lewis, 1747), p. 14.
145 Trevecca College/1 3187, p. 84.
146 Trevecca College/1 3074, James Williams to the Association, 8 May 1750.
147 Trevecca College/1 3051, James Harry to the Association, 30 January 1748.

Conclusion

Eighteenth-century Welsh Methodism remains a difficult movement to define, as indeed it was for many commentators at the time. It existed primarily through the *seiat*, the society, along with the Association to provide oversight. It did not work for everyone, as it demanded unwavering devotion and perseverance. It was a movement of combinations and contrasts. The secret of its success lay to a large degree in the combination of emphasis on both the individual and the community. It also combined the effects of the growth of literacy with the importance of the spoken – and sung – word. Enemies could at the same time pour scorn on both its emotionally excessive exuberance and its ridiculously narrow-minded rules. To outsiders it could thus seem like several sorts of madness combined. A certain degree of resilience was required in order to maintain membership of the early Methodist societies, both in respect of the demands placed on the individual and as a result of the enmity faced in families and local communities, although it must be said that opposition was far less fierce in the south-west than it was elsewhere. Success also rested on a combination of inspired leadership from the Methodist 'fathers' and diligent pastoral care from the superintendents. The movement was both hierarchical and representative, with exhorters and society stewards regularly attending meetings of the Association, but being assigned quite tightly defined roles, with careful distinctions maintained between private and public exhorters and superintendents. The lack of ordained clergy forced the societies to be somewhat self-reliant, but they created a leadership of their own, which threw up the occasional woman like Elizabeth Thomas, but, more commonly, young farmers and craftsmen, such as William Richard,

James Williams, William John and John Richard, who combined steadfast practicality and hard work with a strong spiritual streak. Their dedication to the cause is sometimes staggering, bearing in mind the distances they had to travel and the number of societies under their care. The movement gave them the opportunity for a spiritual fulfilment they seemed not to find elsewhere, and also the chance to deploy their undoubted talents.

Although some accounts of the effects of the evangelical revival may have been exaggerated, there is no doubt that it had a profound and lasting impact on a group of people, who increased substantially in number over the duration of the eighteenth century. Writing in 1774, William Williams marvelled at the changes he had witnessed over the previous forty years, since the outbreak of revival. What had begun, he said, as a small seed had flourished into a stately tree with wide branches in which birds could nest. He had seen similar progress, he claimed, not just in Wales, but also in England, Scotland, Ireland and north America.[1] By 1774, he could securely talk of substantial growth and permanency, as the influence of the movement had spread far more widely throughout Wales as a result of recurrent outpourings of revival. In 1750, that outcome was far from certain, although even then Methodism was revealing itself to be remarkably tenacious and capable of surviving bouts of doctrinal disagreements and external opposition. At the time of the division between the supporters of Rowland and Harris in 1750 the future looked extremely uncertain, with Methodism remaining very much a minority movement. Yet a firm structure had been set in place through the careful organisation and oversight of societies and exhorters. In spite of all difficulties, Methodism survived as a result of a number of factors, chief amongst them the nature of the society itself, as a flexible creation which could be set up without any need for building work or consecration, and as a meeting which offered fellowship and support to sustain members and provide them with opportunities to socialise and to contribute. The organisation of the movement remained in place, despite subsequent changes in leadership and character. Harris was reconciled to the movement in 1763, but his dominant role in the Association would never be fully restored. New members and exhorters had been recruited in his absence who knew him only by somewhat doubtful reputation, with the result that the Methodists had become far more 'Rowland's people' than his. When the first generation of leaders had all died by 1791, the leadership fell largely to Thomas Charles, a native of Carmarthenshire but resident in Bala in north Wales, signifying an important shift in the geographical support.

A century after the doubtful days of separation, by the Religious Census of 1851, Calvinistic Methodism commanded more worshippers than any other religious denomination in Wales. The roots of the eighteenth-century Welsh movement lie partly in local circumstances, such as the influence of the circulating schools, but also in the common factors which have been identified behind the evangelical revival as a whole. It drew on the same European pietistic roots and on Anglican spirituality as well as seventeenth-century Puritan influences. It remains difficult to explain why Methodism had a far greater impact in Wales than it did in England, but it may be related to the growth in literacy and the natural use of the Welsh language. It was the first version of Protestantism which was intrinsically Welsh from the outset, not needing to overcome the same obstacles of language and communication as sixteenth-century Anglicanism and seventeenth-century Puritanism. This may have been particularly relevant in the south-west of the country, which benefited greatly from the circulating schools initiative from the 1730s onwards, and also from the emerging role of Carmarthen as a central hub for the growth of print culture from the 1720s. It was possibly the very lack of opportunities in the area previously which had prompted voluntary societies and individuals to concentrate on attempting some improvement in these counties in particular. Some concerned individuals in the region identified the deficiencies and sought to address them. This was also true in the case of the early Methodist movement, which relied very much on the labours of a group of dedicated recruits to ensure that the early societies were established on a firm footing to survive into the second half of the century.

Many of those dedicated recruits belonged to the middle ranks of society, with sufficient financial security to feel able to make their own choices in terms of religion. A degree of patronage or at least tolerance from the local gentry allowed the movement space in which to grow, but it gained most from the support of the rural middling sorts. Their growth in number and influence is an important aspect of eighteenth-century Wales which still requires further examination. The networks of farming families who became actively involved were crucial in providing resources and personnel for the movement. Their prominence suggests the development of a community leadership, which was forming as an alternative to some of the absentee landowners of the period. As increasing numbers of the population were drawn to Methodism during the eighteenth century, its leaders would gain considerable status and influence in Welsh society. That was generally a neutral influence in the political arena, at least until well into the nineteenth century when the Methodists would be spurred into action by the desire to respond to the criticisms contained in the controversial Blue Books.[2]

By the mid-nineteenth century, Sunday school processions would march in a show of confidence along the very streets where eighteenth-century Methodist preachers had been derided and assaulted.[3] Methodism played its part in creating that assertive Nonconformist culture, through use of the print industry and public meetings. Although there are signs of Enlightenment influence in eighteenth-century Wales, a public sphere of coffee houses and political debate is more difficult to discover.[4] Where the Methodists did intrude into public space, preaching in fairs and marketplaces, they often met a hostile reaction. Yet, with perseverance, that public perception changed. The movement led the way amongst Welsh religious groups in terms of the use of the periodical press in order to create a sense of unity and fellowship through a common readership. The publication of *Trysorfa Ysprydol* (Spiritual Treasury) in 1799 is regarded as the start of a new era in the history of the periodical press in Wales, an example which Nonconformist denominations would soon emulate.[5] The impact on the public sphere was considerable, not least through the growth of communal hymn singing, a popular activity which spread beyond societies and chapels to *eisteddfodau* and sporting crowds.

However, it could also be argued that the greatest influence was on a more private sphere. The Methodists had always made a distinction between the public and private, but placed importance on both aspects. There were public and private exhorters, both with essential skills, but appointed after trial to the position deemed best to suit their talents. Membership of the private society was achieved after a period of careful examination and allowed for entry into confidential discussions. The movement encouraged individuals to look inwards to analyse their own responses and emotions. Prys Morgan notes that the University of Wales Dictionary lists some 348 words beginning with the prefix 'hunan-' (self), 'the great majority of which first appeared in the eighteenth and early nineteenth centuries', some of them listed as appearing for the first time in works by Daniel Rowland, Peter Williams and William Williams.[6] Self-expression through the medium of Welsh was becoming more necessary and more detailed, partly in response to the discussions of the *seiat*. Silent, individual reading was also becoming increasingly common with the rise of literacy and for some Methodists was the trigger for a conversion experience, as with David Jones reading John Bunyan's *Come and Welcome to Jesus Christ*.[7] The individual experience was therefore given special importance, but within the context of a religious community.

There is no doubting the remarkable transformative long-term influence of the evangelical revival, even if it should more correctly be attributed to 'revivals' in the plural. It was not an instantaneous success, but established itself through years of determined mission activity and committed pastoral care. Waves of revival consolidated and spread the initial gains throughout the country. The 1762 revival proved that the first outburst was repeatable, and thereafter prayers for a fresh outpouring of the spirit would occur at fairly regular intervals after an intermission of quiet routine. Key to this was the society as an institution, as the means by which enthusiastic conversion was transformed into steady, committed membership. Even after the Calvinistic Methodist denomination was founded and the society became a weekly evening activity, attended in addition to the potential three services on a Sunday, membership of the *seiat* remained a badge of honour and a sign of faith.

Notes

1 G. H. Hughes (ed.), *Gweithiau William Williams Pantycelyn Cyfrol, II: Rhyddiaith* (Cardiff: University of Wales Press, 1967), pp. 177–8.
2 See R. Pope, 'The Methodists and Society, 1814–1914', in J. G. Jones (ed.), *The History of Welsh Calvinistic Methodism, III: Growth and Consolidation (c.1814–1914)* (Historical Society on behalf of the Presbyterian Church of Wales, 2013), pp. 168–92.

3 P. O'Leary, *Claiming the Streets: Procession and Urban Culture in South Wales, c.1830–1880* (Cardiff: University of Wales Press, 2012), pp. 127–30.
4 R. J. W. Evans, 'Was there a Welsh Enlightenment?', in R. R. Davies and Geraint H. Jenkins (eds), *From Medieval to Modern Wales: Historical Essays in Honour of Kenneth O. Morgan and Ralph A. Griffiths* (Cardiff: University of Wales Press, 2004), pp. 142–59.
5 H. Walters, 'The Periodical Press to 1914', in P. H. Jones and E. Rees (eds), *A Nation and its Books: A History of the Book in Wales* (Cardiff: University of Wales Press, 1998), pp. 198–9.
6 P. Morgan, 'A Private Space: Autobiography and Individuality in Eighteenth- and Early Nineteenth-Century Wales', in Davies and Jenkins (eds), *From Medieval to Modern Wales*, pp. 160–1, 173–4.
7 Trevecka MS 299, David Jones to Howel Harris, 20 December 1740.

APPENDIX

Early Methodist Societies in South-west Wales

Superintendents Listed as Responsible for the Societies
MB: Milbourne Bloom
JH: John Harry
MH: Morgan Hughes
WJ: William John
MJL: Morgan John Lewis
Mends: Christopher and William Mends
JR: John Richard
WR: William Richard
JW: James Williams
WW: William Williams

Date First Mentioned in Records
CARDIGANSHIRE

Aberporth	WR	1743
Blaen-porth	WR	1743
Blaenhownant (Penbryn)	WR	1743
Bron-y-mwyn (Tregaron)	MH	1744
Capel Gwynfil (Llangeitho)	JW	1743
Caron (Tregaron)	MH	1743
Coed-y-brain (New Quay)	WR	1744
Cwm Meurig	WW	1745
Dyffryn-saith (Penbryn)	WR	1743
Felinfach	JW	1747
Ffrwdwenith (Felinwynt, Aberporth)	WR	1745
Lampeter	JW	1743

Llanddewibrefi	WW	1748
Llanfairorllwyn	WR	1743
Llangwyryfon	JW>WW	1744
Llanilar	MH?	1743
Llanllwchaearn	WR	1744
Llanpennal (Blaenpennal)	WW	1746
Llechryd	WR	1743
Lledrod	WW	1743
Llwyndafydd (Llandysiliogogo)	WR	1743
Llwynybeudy	WW	1748
Nant-y-llys (Tregaron)	WW	1745
Pen-y-lan (Tregaron)	WW	1745
Rhydfendigaid	WW	1743
Tan-yr-allt (Tregaron)	WW	1745
Twr-gwyn (Rhydlewis)	WR	1743

CARMARTHENSHIRE

Abergorlech	WW (Llanybydder parish)	1743
Abergwili (at Gelli Glyd)	MB/WJ	1743
Aber-nant	WR	1748
Bontgarreg	WJ	1747
Caeo	JW	1743
Capel Ifan	JR	1746
Carmarthen	WJ (1748 Mends)	1743
Cefncrwth (Meidrim)	WJ	1744
Cefntelych (Myddfai)	JW	1743
Cilcarw (Llangyndeyrn)	JR	1743
Cilypostau (Cil-y-cwm)	JW	1743
Cil-y-cwm	JW	1743
Colvill (Pembrokeshire border)	WJ	1745
Crug Ifan/Evan (Cilrhedyn)	WR	1746
Cwmaman (Llandeilo)	MJL/JR	1743
Cwm-ann	JW	1744
Cwrtycadno (Caeo)	JW	1748
Cynwyl Elfed	WJ	1747
Dygoed (Llanarthney/Llanddarog)	JR	1745
Fforest (Cil-y-cwm)	JW	1743

Glynbedw (Caeo)	JW	1748
Henllan Amgoed	WJ	1748
Laugharne	Mends	1748
Llanarthney	WJ	1744
Llandafen (Llanelli)	JR	1743
Llanddarog	JR	1743
Llanddeusant	MJL/JR	1743
Llandeilo	(Mends)	1748
Llandyfaelog	JR	1743
Llanegwad (at Glancothi)	WJ	1741
Llanfihangel Aberbythych	WJ	1743
Llanfynydd	JW	1743
Llangathen (at Cilsan)	JW	1743
Llangeler (at Trefelin)	WR	1744
Llangynnwr (at Bolahaul)	WJ	1744
Llanlluan	WJ	1741
Llanllwni (at Maesnonni)	JW	1743
Llan-non	JR	1744
Llanpumsaint	WJ	1744
Llansadwrn	JW	1743
Llansawel (at Bryniau (bychain))	JW	1743
Llanwinio	WJ	1745
Llanwrda	JW	1743
Llanybydder (at Penrhiw)	JW	1748
Merthyr	WJ	1745
Nant-bai (Rhandirmwyn) (Llanfair-ar-y-bryn)	JW	1743
Newcastle Emlyn	WR	1744
Pembrey	JR	1743
Rhandir Isaf (Llanfair-ar-y-bryn)	JW	1743
Talley	JW	1743
Tre-lech	WJ	1744
Waun-y-groes	WJ	1745
Ystrad-ffin/Galltybere (Llanfair-ar-y-bryn)	JW	1744

APPENDIX: LIST OF SOCIETIES

NORTH PEMBROKESHIRE

Blaenhyfer	WR	1747
* Cerrig Gwynion (Llechryd)	WR	1748
Cilrhedyn	WR	1744
Dinas	WR	1743
Dygoed (Clydau)	WR	1743
Eglwyswrw	WR	1743
Ffos-y-ficer (Abercych)	WR	1744
Fishguard	WR>JH 1748	1743
Llwynygorras	WR	1743
Longhouse (Mathry)	WR>JH 1748	1743
Manordeifi	WR	1744
Newport	WR	1743
Pen-caer	WR	1743
St David's	WR>JH 1748	1743

* Cerrig Gwynion ('white stones') seems likely to be Carregwen ('whitestone') a hamlet over the river Teifi from Llechryd, so in Pembrokeshire. (J. Evans, *Hanes Methodistiaeth Rhan Ddeheol Sir Aberteifi* (Dolgellau: E. W. Evans, 1904), p. 340 suggests that there was a cause established at Carregwen after Howel Harris preached in the area around 1740.)

Bibliography

PRIMARY SOURCES
National Library of Wales, Aberystwyth
CALVINISTIC METHODIST ARCHIVE (CMA), TREVECKA COLLEGE: TREVECKA LETTERS, MANUSCRIPTS AND RECORDS (GROUP 1)
Trevecka Letters 1–2944
Trevecca College 1/2945–99 Association records
Trevecca College 1/3000–85 Society reports
Trevecca College 1/3187 Diary of Richard Tibbott, February–May 1744
Howell Harris Diaries and Manuscripts 1735–78

RECORDS OF THE CHURCH IN WALES
ST DAVIDS DIOCESAN RECORDS
Visitation Returns SD/QA/1–15, 61, 129, 180–200
Correspondence SD/Let/1–1972
Miscellaneous Papers SD/MISC/1–1470
Consistory Court Records, Archdeaconry of Carmarthen SD/CCCm(G)/241, 287, 289–90, 296, 303, 312, 326, 348, 349, 351–2, 354

BANGOR DIOCESAN RECORDS
Visitation Returns B/QA/2–12

LLANDAFF DIOCESAN RECORDS
Visitation Returns LL/QA/10
Consistory Court Records LL/CC/G/918, 952

GREAT SESSIONS RECORDS
Wales 4 737/1, 1739: 4/739/5, 8 January 1770

BIBLIOGRAPHY

NATIONAL LIBRARY MSS
67A 'Young Mends the Clothier's Sermon', Lewis Morris, 1743
6203E Papers relating to Isaac Williams, c.1764–1805
6238A 'Y Gell Gymysg', miscellany of prose and verse, 1785–99
9145F List of the Clergy at Bishop's Visitation, 1745
12388 Pant-teg Church registers
18435B Diary of Richard Tibbott, 1741–2
19044A Llangeitho MS, c.1742
202515–6C Diary of John Thomas, Tre-main, Cardiganshire
21834B A Smuggler's autobiography (William Owen of Narberth, 1717–47), online version, https://www.library.wales/discover/digital-gallery/manuscripts/modern-period/smugglers-autobiography

PANTON MANUSCRIPTS
2009B 'The Grievances of the Church in Wales' (c. 1765)

HENLLAN MANUSCRIPTS
5455A Notebook of Thomas Morgan, 1740–94
5456A Diary of Thomas Morgan, 1–7414

GWYNFRYN MANUSCRIPTS
6137D Transcripts of letters of Griffith Jones, Llanddowror

GILBERTSON PAPERS
6203E Papers relating to Isaac Williams, c. 1764–1805
NLW Deposit MS 127A (Rhydwilym)

SPECIAL COLLECTIONS
Cwrt Mawr Manuscripts
150B Autobiography of Peter Williams, written c. 1794, transcribed by Peter Bailey Williams.
182B Freehold Book, 1760

D. T. M. Jones (Solicitors) Records
2441 Tithe Account, parish of Cil-y-cwm, co. Carmarthen, c. 1775

Edwinsford Estate Records
2201 13 October 1736
2292 21-year lease to John David, Llansawel, yeoman, 10 October 1746
2305 3 August 1758

Haverfordwest (Williams and Williams)
25920 John Parry, Cwmcynon, co. Cardigan, Hester Howells, Llanfihangel-ar-arth parish, agreement before marriage, 1739

Lucas Collection
2816 Rental of the estate of the bishop of St Davids in co. Pembroke, post 1759
3833 Memorandum on leases, post 1757

Morgan Richardson Solicitors Collection
Gernos Deeds and Documents
723 20 December 1714.
746 Letters of Administration of the goods of John Parry, 8 July 1747
749 Demise for 99 years ... Capel Evan, 1752
751 19 December 1758
765 29 February 1772
785 10 June 1778

Neuadd-fawr Estate Records
350 Settlement prior to marriage of John Williams and Barbara Williams, 13 February 1717
351 Surrender of one half of properties specified in no. 350, between John Williams the elder of Henllys Cil-y-cwm, gentleman, and John Williams the younger of Llwynyberllan, Llandingad, 11 July 1788

Ottley (Pitchford Hall MSS and Documents)
24 Articles against Owen Evans, clerk, rector of Llangoedmor, 1707
30 Letters of Privy Seal ... of arrears of the accounts of the temporalities, 21 May 1707
89 Thomas Philipps, Laugharne, to Bishop Ottley, 29 October 1718
100 Griffith Jones, Laugharne, to Bishop Ottley, 11 July 1715
126–8 Articles against Samuel Williams, vicar of Llandyfrïog and rector of Llangunllo, and related correspondence, 18–21 February 1719
262 Appointment of Robert Dyer, Aberglasney, 1 April 1714
Manuscript Volume VI/Valuation of Livings. A copy of a return to an inquiry made within the diocese of St Davids, *c.* 1708
2671, Bishop Ottley to his wife, 8 September 1717
3230 Adam Ottley to Mrs Ottley, 10 January 1723

BIBLIOGRAPHY

CARMARTHENSHIRE ARCHIVES
Quarter Sessions Records QS/1/1, 1748–51

PRINTED PRIMARY SOURCES

A. B., *Annerch Difrifol a Charedig at y Bobl a elwir Methodistiaid* (London: Siôn a William Oliver, 1765).

Account of the Most Remarkable Particulars relating to the Present Progress of the Gospel, 2, i (1743).

Baker, Frank (ed.), *The Works of John Wesley Volume 7: A Collection of Hymns for the Use of the People called Methodists* (Oxford: Clarendon Press, 1975).

Beebe. Keith Edward (ed.), *The McCulloch Examinations of the Cambuslang Revival (1742): A Critical Edition: Conversion Narratives from the Scottish Evangelical Awakening* (Woodbridge: The Boydell Press, 2013).

Bowen, Ivor (ed.), *The Statutes of Wales* (London: T. Fisher Unwin, 1908).

Calamy, Edmund, *A Continuation of the Account of the Ministers ... who were Ejected and Silenced*, (2 vols, London: R. Ford, R. Hett and J. Chandler, 1727).

Camden, William, *Britannia*, ed. R. Gough (3 vols, London: T. Payne and Son, 1789).

Clement, Mary (ed.), *Correspondence and Minutes of the S.P.C.K. relating to Wales, 1699–1740* (Cardiff: University of Wales Press, 1952).

Dafydd, Thomas, *Coffadwriaeth am y Cyfiawn, Mewn Hanes byrr o Fywyd dichlynedd a dedwydd Farwolaeth William Sion, ym Mhlwyf Llanegwad, yn Sir Gaerfyrddin, ynghyd ag amryw eraill a hunasant yn yr Arglwydd, yn y Flwyddyn 1776* (Caerfyrddin: John Ross, 1776).

Davies, J. H. (ed.), *The Letters of Lewis, Richard, William and John Morris, of Anglesey, (Morrisiaid Môn), 1728–1765* (2 vols, Aberystwyth: the author, 1907–9).

Denning, R. T. W. (ed.), *The Diary of William Thomas of Michaelston-super-Ely, near St Fagans Glamorgan 1762–1795* (Cardiff: South Wales Record Society, 1995).

The Evangelical Magazine (London, 1799, 1802).

Evans, John, *Some Account of the Welch Charity-Schools: and of the Rise and Progress of Methodism in Wales, through the Means of them* (London, 1752).

Evans, Theophilus, *A History of Modern Enthusiasm from the Reformation to the present times* (London: W. Owen and W. Clarke, 1752).
Evans, Theophilus, *Llythyr Addysg Esgob Llundain at y Bobl o'i Esgobaeth; yn eu rhybuddio yn erbyn Claiarwch o'r naill du; a zêl danbaid nid ar ôl Gwybodaeth o'r tu arall* (Caerloyw: R. Raikes, 1740).
Griffiths, G. M. (ed.), 'A Visitation of the Archdeaconry of Carmarthen, 1710', *National Library of Wales Journal*, 18 (1973), 19 (1975-6).
Harris, Howell, *A Brief Account of the Life of Howell Harris, Esq* (Trevecka: Trevecka Press, 1791).
Hughes, G. H., (ed.), *Gweithiau William Williams Pantycelyn, Cyfrol II: Rhyddiaith* (Cardiff: University of Wales Press, 1967).
Jones, Edmund, *The Appearance of Evil: Apparitions of Spirits in Wales*, ed. J. Harvey (Cardiff: University of Wales Press, 2003).
Jones, Griffith, *A Further Account of the Progress of the Circulating Welsh Charity-Schools: in a letter to a friend* (London: J. Hutton, 1740).
Jones, Griffith, *An Address to the Charitable and Well-Disposed: in behalf of the poor in the Principality of Wales* (London, James Hutton, 1741).
Jones, N. Cynhafal (ed.), *Gweithiau Williams Pantycelyn, Cyfrol I* (Treffynnon: P. M. Evans & son, 1887); *Cyfrol II* (Newport: W. Jones, 1891).
Jones, Robert, *Drych yr Amseroedd*, ed. G. M. Ashton (Cardiff: University of Wales Press, 1958),
Lake, A. C. (ed.), *Anterliwtiau Huw Jones o Langwm* (Caernarfon: Cyhoeddiadau Barddas, 2000).
Levi, Thomas (ed.), *Casgliad o hen farwnadau Cymreig, yn dal cysylltiad a chyfundeby Methodistiaid a waned ar ran y Gymanfa Gyffredinol* (Wrexham: Hughes a'i Fab, 1872).
Lewis, Morgan John, *Cynhwysiad Byr o Feddyliau'r Eglwys a Ymgorpholodd dan y Drefn hon yn Sir Fonwy: Pa un sy'n ymgyfarfod yn bennaf, yn y Neuad yn y Pant-teg, gerllaw Pont-y-pool: yn agos ir modd y Proffesswyd hwynt ar Ddydd ein Hordeinassiwn, sef Dydd y llun y Sulgwyn, 1756* (Bala: John Rowlands, *c.* 1761).
Malkin, Benjamin, *The Scenery, Antiquities, and Biography of South Wales...1803* (second edn, London: Longman, Hurst, Rees and Orme, 1807).
Maurice, David, *Cwmffwrd ir Gwan Gristion, neu'r Gorsen Ysyg Mewn Pregeth* (Llundain, 1700).

Meyrick, Samuel Rush, *The History and Antiquities of the County of Cardigan* (London: Longman, 1808).
Owen, Goronwy P. (ed.), *Hunangofiant John Elias* (Penybont ar Ogwr: Mudiad Efengylaidd Cymru, 1974).
Richard, John, *Hymnau Buddiol a Chymm[w]ysyw canu ar amryw achosion gan Gristnogion, gwir brofiadol* (Caerfyrddin: Samuel Lewis, 1747).
Roberts, Gomer M. (ed.), *Gweithiau William Williams Pantycelyn, Cyfrol I* (Cardiff: University of Wales Press, 1964).
Roberts, William, *Ffrewyll y Methodistiaid*, ed. C. Lake (Cardiff: Cardiff University Press, 1998).
Rowland, Daniel, *Deuddeg o Bregethau* (Aberystwyth: Samuel Williams, 1814).
Rowland, Daniel, *Pum Pregeth* (Caerfyrddin: John Ross, 1772).
Rowland, Daniel, *Ymddiddan rhwng Methodist uniawn-gred ac un camsyniol* (Bristol: Felix Farley, 1750).
Sail, Dibenion a Rheolau,'r Societies neu'r cyfarfodydd neullduol a ddechreuassant ymgynnull yn ddiweddar yn Nghymru (Bristol: Felix Farley, 1742).
Saunders, Erasmus, *A View of the State of Religion in the Diocese of St David's about the Beginning of the 18th Century* (reprint, Cardiff: University of Wales Press, 1949).
Thomas, John, *Rhad Ras neu Lyfr Profiad*, ed. J. Dyfnallt Owen (Cardiff: University of Wales Press, 1949).
Thomas, Joshua, *Hanes y Bedyddwyr, ymhlith y Cymry* (Caerfyrddin: John Ross, 1778).
Welch Piety (London: J. Oliver, 1737-79).
Whitefield, George, *Llythyr oddiwrth y Parchedig Mr. George Whitefield at societies neu gymdeithasau crefyddol, a osodwyd yn diweddar ar droed mewn amriw leoedd yng Nghymru a Lloeger* (Pont-y-pool: Argraph-Wasg Newydd, 1740).
Whiteman, Anne (ed.), *The Compton Census of 1676: A Critical Edition* (Oxford: Oxford University Press, 1986).
Williams, A. H. (ed.), *John Wesley in Wales 1739–1790* (Cardiff: University of Wales Press, 1971).
Williams, Moses, *Pregeth a Barablwyd yn Eglwys Crist yn Llundain* (Llundain: Printwyr y Brenin, 1718).

Williams, Samuel, *Amser a Diwedd Amser* (Llundain: Ebenezer Tracy, 1707).
Williams, William, *Drws y Society Profiad wedi ei agor o led y pen* (Aberhonddu: E. Evans, 1777).
Williams, William, *Marwnad Er Coffadwriaeth am Mr. Howel Harries, yr hwn oedd un o'r rhai cyntaf a ddechreuodd y Diwygiad mawr yng Nghymru: ac a ymdawodd a'r byd hwn, Gorphenhaf yr 21, yn y Flwyddyn, 1773* (Aberhonddu: E. Evans, 1773),
Williams, William, *Marwnad William Richard o Abercarfan* (Caerfyrddin: John Ross, 1771).
Woodward, Josiah, *An Account of the Rise and Progress of the Religious Societies in the City of London, &c, And of the Endeavours for Reformation of Manners Which have been made therein* (London: JD for the author, 1698).

SECONDARY SOURCES
Abraham, W. J., and J. E. Kirby (eds), *The Oxford Handbook of Methodist Studies* (Oxford: Oxford University Press, 2009).
Allen, Richard C. and David C. Jones (eds), *The Religious History of Wales* (Cardiff: Welsh Academic Press, 2014).
Apetrei, S. L. *Women, Feminism and Religion in Early Enlightenment England* (Cambridge: Cambridge University Press, 2010).
Atwood, Craig D., *Community of the Cross: Moravian Piety in Colonial Bethlehem* (University Park: Pennsylvania University Press, 2004).
Baker-Jones, D. L., 'Edwinsford', *Carmarthenshire Historian*, 5 (1968).
Baker-Jones, L. *Princelings, Privilege and Power: The Tivyside Gentry in their Community* (Llandysul: Gomer, 1999).
Bassett, T. M., *The Welsh Baptists* (Swansea: Ilston House, 1977).
Bebbington, David W., *Evangelicalism in Modern Britain: A History from the 1730s to the 1980s* (London: Routledge, 1989).
Benbough-Jackson, M., *Cardiganshire and the Cardi, c.1760–c.2000* (Cardiff: University of Wales Press, 2011).
Bennett, Richard, *Methodistiaeth Trefaldwyn Uchaf, Cyfrol I: Hanes Cyfnod Howel Harris, 1738–1752* (Y Bala: R. Evans a'i Fab, 1929).
Berg, Maxine, *Luxury and Pleasure in Eighteenth-century Britain* (Oxford: Oxford University Press, 2005).

Berg, Maxine and Helen Clifford (eds), *Consumers and Luxury: Consumer Culture in Europe, 1650–1850* (Manchester: Manchester University Press, 1999).
Beynon, Tom, *Allt Cunedda, Llechdwnni a Mwdlwscwm* (Aberystwyth: Tom Beynon, 1955).
Beynon, Tom, *Cwmsêl a Chefn Sidan* (Caernarfon: Llyfrfa'r Methodistaid Calfinaidd, 1946).
Beynon, Tom, *Golud a Mawl Dyffryn Tywi* (Caerfyrddin: Cyngor Sir Caerfyrddin, 1998).
Beynon, Tom, 'Morfa Bach, Cydweli', *Cylchgrawn Cymdeithas Hanes y Methodistiaid Calfinaidd/Journal of the Historical Society of the Presbyterian Church of Wales*, 16 (1931).
Beynon, Tom, 'Morgan Rhys a Chylch Cilycwm hyd at Ystrad Ffin', *Cylchgrawn Cymdeithas Hanesy Methodistiaid Calfinaidd/Journal of the Historical Society of the Presbyterian Church of Wales*, 20 (1935).
Bidgood, R., 'The Lewis and Bowen Families of Cefntrenfa, Cilycwm', *Carmarthenshire Antiquary*, 48 (2012).
Borsay, Anne and Peter Shapeley (eds), *Medicine, Charity and Mutual Aid: The Consumption of Health and Welfare in Britain, c. 1550–1950* (Aldershot: Ashgate, 2007).
Brewer, John and Roy Porter (eds), *Consumption and the World of Goods* (London: Routledge, 1993).
Brown, Roger L., 'Bishop William Basil Tickell Jones (1822–1897)', *Ceredigion*, XVI/4 (2012).
Brown, Roger L., *Evangelicals in the Church in Wales* (Welshpool: Tair Eglwys Press, 2007).
Brown, Roger L., *In Pursuit of a Welsh Episcopate: Appointments to Welsh Sees 1840–1905* (Cardiff: University of Wales Press, 2005).
Buckley, James, *Genealogies of the Carmarthenshire Sheriffs from 1539 to 1759* (2 vols, Carmarthen: Spurrell, 1910–13).
Charnell-White, Cathryn A., 'Galaru a Gwaddoli ym Marwnadau Williams Pantycelyn', *Llên Cymru*, 26 (2003).
Clark, Peter, *British Clubs and Societies 1580–1800: The Origins of an Associational World* (Oxford: Oxford University Press, 2000).
Clement, Mary, *The S.P.C.K. and Wales, 1699–1740* (London: SPCK, 1954).

Coffey, John (ed.), *Heart Religion: Evangelical Piety in England and Ireland, 1690–1850* (Oxford: Oxford University Press, 2016).

Cooper, Kate and Jeremu Gregory (eds), *Revival and Resurgence in Christian History:* Studies in Church History, 44 (Woodbridge: The Boydell Press, 2008).

Crawford, Patricia, *Women and Religion in England, 1500–1720* (London, Routledge, 1996).

Cressy, David, *Birth, Marriage and Death* (Oxford: Oxford University Press: 1997).

Cuming, G. J., and D. Baker (eds), *Popular Belief and Practice* Studies in Church History, 8 (London: Cambridge University Press, 1972).

Currie, R., 'A Micro-theory of Methodist Growth', *Proceedings of the Wesley Historical Society*, 36 (1967).

Davies, Dewi Eirug, *Hoff Ddysgedig Nyth: Cyfraniad Coleg Presbyteraidd Cymru i fywyd Cymru* (Abertawe: Tŷ John Penry, 1976).

Davies, E. R., 'The Deeds of Soar C.M. Chapel, Cil-y-cwm', *Cylchgrawn Cymdeithas Hanes y Methodistiaid Calfinaidd/Journal of the Historical Society of the Presbyterian Church of Wales*, 27 (1942).

Davies, R. R. and Geraint H. Jenkins (eds), *From Medieval to Modern Wales: Historical Essays in Honour of Kenneth O. Morgan and Ralph A. Griffiths* (Cardiff: University of Wales Press, 2004),

Edwards, Owen M., *Cartrefi Cymru* (Wrecsam: Hughes a'i Fab, 1896).

Emsley, Clive, *Crime and Society in England 1750–1900* (second edn, London: Longman, 1996).

Evans, Eifion, *Bread of Heaven: The Life and Work of William Williams, Pantycelyn* (Bridgend: Bryntirion Press, 2010).

Evans, Eifion, *Daniel Rowland and the Great Evangelical Awakening in Wales* (Edinburgh: Banner of Truth Trust, 1985).

Evans, John, *Hanes Methodistiaeth rhan ddeheuol sir Aberteifi o ddechreuad y 'Diwygiad Methodistaidd' yn 1735 hyd 1900* (Dolgellau: E. W. Evans, 1904).

Evans, Neil and Huw Pryce (eds), *Writing a Small Nation's Past: Wales in Comparative Perspective, 1850–1950* (London: Routledge, 2013).

Evans, Non, 'Stephen Hughes: The Family Man', *Carmarthenshire Antiquary*, 37 (2001).

Everitt, Alan, *The Pattern of Rural Dissent: The Nineteenth Century* (Leicester: Leicester University Press, 1972).

Fawcett, A., *The Cambuslang Revival: The Scottish Evangelical Revival of the Eighteenth Century* (Edinburgh: Banner of Truth Trust, 1971).
Forsaith, P. and G. Hammond (eds), *Religion, Gender and Industry* (Eugene, Oregon: Wipf and Stock, 2012).
Francis, Keith A. and Gibson, William (eds), *The Oxford Handbook of the British Sermon 1689–1901* (Oxford: Oxford University Press, 2012).
French, H. R., *The Middle Sort of People in Provincial England 1600–1750* (Oxford: Oxford University Press, 2007).
Ganske, Karl, 'Preaching Christ: John Wesley's Definition of the Gospel, 1746–51', *Wesley and Methodist Studies*, 11/2 (2019).
Gibson, William, *Church, State and Society, 1760–1850* (London: Macmillan, 1994).
Gibson, William and John Morgan-Guy (eds), *Religion and Society in the Diocese of St Davids 1485–2011* (Farnham: Ashgate, 2015).
Gillespie, Michele and Robert Beachy (eds), *Pious Pursuits: German Moravians in the Atlantic World* (Oxford: Berghahn Books, 2007).
Goodhead, Andrew, *A Crown and a Cross: The Rise, Development, and Decline of the Methodist Class Meeting in Eighteenth-century England* (Eugene, Oregon: Wipf and Stock, 2010).
Green, Francis, 'The Dyers of Aberglasney', *West Wales Historical Records*, 7 (1917–18).
Gruffydd, R. Geraint, 'Diwygiad 1762 a William Williams o Bantycelyn', *Cylchgrawn Hanes y Methodistiaid Calfinaidd/Journal of the Historical Society of the Presbyterian Church of Wales*, 54/3 (1969), 55/3 (1970).
Gruffydd, R. Geraint, *Y Gair a'r Ysbryd: Ysgrifau ar Biwritaniaeth a Methodistiaeth*, ed. E. Wyn James (Bangor: Gwasg Bryntirion, 2019).
Gruffydd, R. Geraint, 'John Thomas, Tre-main: Pererin Methodistaidd', *Cylchgrawn Cymdeithas Hanes y Methodistiaid Calfinaidd/Journal of the Historical Society of the Presbyterian Church of Wales*, 9 (1985–6).
Gruffydd, R. Geraint, 'Marwnadau William Williams Pantycelyn', *Llên Cymru*, 17 (1993).
Hawkes, G. I., 'Illicit Trading in Wales in the Eighteenth Century', *Cymru a'r Môr/Maritime Heritage*, 10 (1986).

Haykin, Michael A. G. and Kenneth J. Steward (eds), *The Emergence of Evangelicalism: Exploring Historical Continuities* (Nottingham: Inter-Varsity Press, 2008).

Hempton, David, *The Church in the Long Eighteenth Century* (London: I. B. Tauris, 2011).

Hempton, David, 'Methodism and the Law, 1740–1820', *Bulletin of the John Rylands Library*, 70 (1988).

Hempton, David, *Methodism: Empire of the Spirit* (London: Yale University Press, 2005).

Hempton, David, *Religion and Political Culture in Britain and Ireland from the Glorious Revolution to the Decline of Empire* (Cambridge: Cambridge University Press, 1996).

Hindmarsh, Bruce, *The Evangelical Conversion Narrative: Spiritual Autobiography in Early Modern England* (Oxford: Oxford University Press, 2005).

Hodges, H. A., *Flame in the Mountains: Williams Pantycelyn, Ann Griffiths and the Welsh Hymn*, ed. E. Wyn James (Talybont: Y Lolfa, 2017).

Howell, David W., 'The Agricultural Community of Cardiganshire in the Eighteenth Century', *Ceredigion*, VII/1 (1993).

Howell, David W., *Patriarchs and Parasites: The Gentry of South-west Wales in the Eighteenth Century* (Cardiff: University of Wales Press, 1986).

Howell, David W., *The Rural Poor in Eighteenth-century Wales* (Cardiff: University of Wales Press, 2000).

Howells, Brian, 'Social and Agrarian Change in Early Modern Cardiganshire', *Ceredigion*, VII/3-4 (1974/5).

Hughes, C. C., *Trem ar Ddwy Ganrif o Hanes y Tabernacl, Aberteifi* (Aberteifi: E. L. Jones, 1960).

Hughes, G. H., 'Thomas Dafydd, Un o Emynwyr Sir Gaerfyrddin', *Journal of the Welsh Bibliographical Society*, 7 (1950).

Hughes, Glyn Tegai, '*Yr Hen Bant*'; *Ysgrifau ar Williams Pantycelyn* (Talybont: Y Lolfa, 2017).

Hughes, Glyn Tegai, *Williams Pantycelyn* (Cardiff: University of Wales Press, 1983).

Hughes, John, *Methodistiaeth Cymru* (3 vols, Wrecsam: R. Hughes a'i Fab, 1851–6).

Humfrey, B., *John Dyer*, Writers of Wales (Cardiff: University of Wales Press, 1980).
Ireland, Richard W., *Land of White Gloves? A History of Crime and Punishment in Wales* (Abingdon: Routledge, 2015).
James. H. (ed.), *Sir Gâr: Studies in Carmarthenshire History* (Carmarthen: Carmarthenshire Antiquarian Society, 1991).
Jarvis, Branwen (ed.), *A Guide to Welsh Literature c. 1700–1800* (Cardiff: University of Wales Press, 2000).
Jenkins, Geraint H., *Cadw Tŷ mewn Cwmwl Tystion* (Llandysul: Gwasg Gomer, 1990).
Jenkins, Geraint H., *The Foundations of Modern Wales: Wales 1642–1780* (Cardiff: University of Wales Press, 1987).
Jenkins, Geraint H., 'Lewis Morris: "the fat man of Cardiganshire"', *Ceredigion*, 14/2 (2002).
Jenkins, Geraint H., *Literature, Religion and Society in Wales 1660–1730* (Cardiff: University of Wales Press, 1978).
Jenkins, Geraint H., '"An Old and Much Honoured Soldier": Griffith Jones, Llanddowror', *Welsh History Review*, 11/4 (1983).
Jenkins, Geraint H., *Protestant Dissenters in Wales 1639–1689* (Cardiff: University of Wales Press, 1992).
Jenkins, Geraint H., *Theophilus Evans (1693–1767): Y Dyn, Ei Deulu a'i Oes* (Aberystwyth: Adran Gwasanaethau Diwylliannol Dyfed, 1993).
Jenkins, Geraint H., 'Yr Eglwys "Wiwlwys Olau" a'u Beirniaid', *Ceredigion*, 10 (1985).
Jenkins, Geraint H. (ed.), *The Welsh Language Before the Industrial Revolution* (Cardiff: University of Wales Press, 1997).
Jenkins, Geraint H. and Ieuan Gwynedd Jones (eds), *Cardiganshire County History, Volume III: Cardiganshire in Modern Times* (Cardiff: University of Wales Press, 1998).
Jenkins, J. Geraint, *Maritime Heritage: The Sailors and Seamen of South Cardiganshire* (Llandysul: Gomer Press, 1982).
Jenkins, Kathryn, *Cân y Ffydd: Ysgrifau ar Emynyddiaeth*, ed. Rh. Griffiths (Caernarfon: Gwasg y Bwthyn, 2011).
Jenkins, Kathryn, 'Pantycelyn's Women Fact and Fiction: An Assessment', *Journal of Welsh Religious History*, 7 (1999).
Jenkins, R. T., 'The Moravian Brethren in Carmarthenshire', *Cylchgrawn*

Cymdeithas Hanes y Methodistiaid Calfinaidd/Journal of the Historical Society of the Presbyterian Church of Wales, 21 (1936).

Jenkins, R. T., *The Moravian Brethren in North Wales* (London: Honourable Society of the Cymmrodorion, 1938).

Jenkins, R. T., 'Three Early Methodist Societies in Carmarthenshire', *BBCS*, 10 (1941).

Jones, Alun R., 'Vermin who creep into all corners through the least crevices: Lewis Morris and the Methodists', *Transactions of the Cymmrodorion Society*, new series, 5 (1999).

Jones, D. C., B. S. Schlenther and E. M. White, *The Elect Methodists: Calvinistic Methodism in England and Wales 1735–1811* (Cardiff: University of Wales Press, 2012),

Jones, D. H., 'Emynau Morgan Rhys', *Yr Eurgrawn*, 173 (1981).

Jones, D. J. Odwyn, *Daniel Rowland Llangeitho (1713–1790)* (Llandysul: Gwasg Gomer, 1938).

Jones, David J. V., *Rebecca's Children: A Study of Rural Society, Crime, and Protest* (Oxford: Clarendon Press, 1989).

Jones, E. D., 'Llyfr Eglwys Pant-teg', *Y Cofiadur*, 23 (1953).

Jones, E. D., 'Phylip Pugh', *Diwinyddiaeth*, 15 (1964).

Jones, Francis, 'Aberglasney and its Families', *National Library of Wales Journal*, 21 (1979).

Jones, Francis, 'The Families of Berllandywyll', *Carmarthenshire Historian* (1978).

Jones, Francis, *Historic Cardiganshire Homes and their Families*, ed. Caroline Charles Jones (Newport: Brawdy Books. 2000).

Jones, Francis, *Historic Carmarthenshire Homes and their Families* (Newport, Pembrokeshire: Brawdy Books, 2006).

Jones, Francis, *Historic Houses of Pembrokeshire and their Families*, ed. Robert Innes Smith, compiled by Caroline Charles-Jones (Newport: Brawdy Books, 1996).

Jones, Francis, 'Portraits and Pictures in old Carmarthenshire Houses', *Carmarthenshire Historian*, 5 (1968).

Jones, Ieuan Gwynedd, *Explorations and Explanation: Essays in the Social History of Victorian Wales* (Llandysul, Gwasg Gomer, 1981).

Jones, Ieuan Gwynedd, *Mid-Victorian Wales: The Observers and the Observed* (Cardiff: University of Wales Press, 1992).

Jones, J. Gwynfor (ed.), *Hanes Methodistiaeth Galfinaidd Cymru, Cyfrol*

III: Y Twf a'r Cadarnhau (c.1814–1914), (Caernarfon: Gwasg Pantycelyn, 2011).

Jones, J. Gwynfor (ed.), *The History of Welsh Calvinistic Methodism, III: Growth and Consolidation (c.1814–1914)* (Historical Society on behalf of the Presbyterian Church of Wales, 2013).

Jones, J. M. and Morgan, W., *Y Tadau Methodistaidd* (2 vols, Abertawe: yr awdur, 1895–7).

Jones, M. G., *Charity School Movements: A Study of Eighteenth-century Puritanism in Action* (Cambridge: Cambridge University Press, 1938).

Jones, M. H., 'An Interesting Legal Document, Throwing Light on Early Welsh Methodism', *Cylchgrawn Cymdeithas Hanes y Methodistiaid Calfinaidd/Journal of the Historical Society of the Presbyterian Church of Wales*, 15 (1930).

Jones, M. H., *The Trevecka Letters or the Unpublished MSS Correspondence of Howell Harris and his Contemporaries* (Caernarfon: C.M. Bookroom, 1932).

Jones, O. W. and Walker, D. (eds), *Links with the Past: Swansea and Brecon Historical Essays* (Llandybïe: Christopher Davies, 1974).

Jones, P. H., and E. Rees (eds), *A Nation and its Books: A history of the Book in Wales* (Aberystwyth: National Library of Wales, 1998).

Jones, R. Tudur, *Congregationalism in Wales*, ed. Robert Pope (Cardiff: University of Wales, 2004).

Knowles, Ann Kelly, *Calvinists Incorporated: Welsh Immigrants in Ohio's Industrial Frontier* (London, University of Chicago Press, 1997).

Lambert, W. R., *Drink and Sobriety in Victorian Wales c.1820–c.1895* (Cardiff: University of Wales Press, 1983).

Laslett, Peter, *The World We Have Lost – Further Explored* (third edn, London: Methuen, 1983).

Lawrence, Anna M., *One Family under God: Love, Belonging and Authority in Early Translatlantic Methodism* (Philadelphia: University of Pennsylvania Press, 2011).

Lewis, Aneirin, 'Edward Richard a Ieuan Fardd', *Ysgrifau Beirniadol*, 10 (1977).

Lewis, Samuel, *A Topographical Dictionary of Wales ... Volume Two* (London: S. Lewis & Co., 1833).

Lewis, Saunders, *Williams Pantycelyn* (Llundain: Foyle's, 1927).

Lewis, Saunders, *Williams Pantycelyn*, ed. D. Densil Morgan (Cardiff: University of Wales Press, 2016).

Lloyd, Euros, 'Datblygiad Undodiaeth yn Ardal y Smotyn Du', *Ceredigion*, 15/4 (2008).

Lloyd, J. E. (ed.), *A History of Carmarthenshire, II: From the Act of Union (1536) to 1900* (Cardiff: William Lewis, 1939).

Lloyd, Jennifer, M., *Women and the Shaping of British Methodism: Persistent Preachers 1807–1907* (Manchester: Manchester University Press, 2009).

Lloyd, Thomas, Julian Orbach, Robert Scourfield and Richard Avent, *The Buildings of Wales: Carmarthenshire and Ceredigion* (London: Yale University Press, 2006).

Lloyd, Thomas, Julian Orbach and Robert Scourfield, *The Buildings of Wales: Pembrokeshire* (London: Yale University Press, 2004).

Lloyd-Jones, H. J., 'The Glanareth Murder', *Transactions of the Honourable Society of Cymmrodorion 1948* (London, 1949).

Lodwick, Malcolm and Edith, *The Story of Carmarthen* (Carmarthen: Malcolm and Edith Lodwick, 1954).

Mack, Phyllis, *Heart Religion in the British Enlightenment* (Cambridge: Cambridge University Press, 2008).

Mack, Phyllis, *Visionary Women: Estatic Prophecy in Seventeenth-Century England* (London: University of California Press, 1992).

Maddox, Randy L., *Responsible Grace: John Wesley and Practical Theology* (Nashville.: Kingswood Books, 1994).

Maddox, R. L. and J. E. Vickers (eds), *The Cambridge Companion to John Wesley* (Cambridge: Cambridge University Press, 2010).

Malmgreen, G. (ed.), *Religion in the Lives of English Women, 1760–1930* (London: Croom Helm, 1986).

Moore-Colyer, R., *Roads and Trackways of Wales* (Ashbourne: Landmark Publishing, 2001).

Morgan, D. Densil, *Theologia Cambrensis: Protestant Religion and Theology in Wales, 1: From Reformation to Revival 1588–1760* (Cardiff: University of Wales Press, 2018).

Morgan, D. Densil, *Wales and the Word: Historical Perspectives on Religion and Welsh Identity* (Cardiff: University of Wales Press, 2008).

Morgan, Derec Llwyd, 'Daniel Rowland (?1711–1790): Pregethwr Diwygiadol', *Ceredigion*, XI/3 (1991).

Morgan, Derec Llwyd, *Y Diwygiad Mawr* (Llandysul: Gwasg Gomer, 1981); trans. Dyfnallt Morgan as *The Great Awakening in Wales* (London: Epworth Press, 1988).
Morgan, Derec Llwyd, *Pobl Pantycelyn* (Llandysul: Gomer, 1986).
Morgan, Derec Llwyd, *Williams Pantycelyn* (Caernarfon: Gwasg Pantycelyn, 1983).
Morgan, Gerald, *Ieuan Fardd* (Llandysul: Gwasg Gomer, 1988).
Morgan, Sue, *Women, Religion and Feminism in Britain 1750–1900* (Basingstoke: Palgrave Macmillan, 2002).
Morgan, Walter T., 'Cases of Subtraction of Church Rate Before the Consistory Courts of St Davids', *Journal of the Historical Society of the Church in Wales*, 19 (1959).
Morgan, Walter T., 'William Williams, Pantycelyn, Before the Bishop's Court', *Cylchgrawn Cymdeithas Hanes y Methodistiaid Calfinaidd/ Journal of the Historical Society of the Presbyterian Church of Wales*, 33 (1948).
Morris, James, *Hanes Methodistiaeth Sir Gaerfyrddin* (Dolgellau: E. W. Evans, 1911).
Muir, Angela, 'Illegitimacy in Eighteenth-century Wales', *Welsh History Review*, 26/3 (2013).
Noll, Mark A., *God and Mammon: Protestants, Money and the Market 1790–1860* (Oxford: Oxford University Press, 2001).
Noll, Mark A., *The Rise of Evangelicalism: The Age of Edwards, Whitefield and the Wesleys* (Downers Grove, Illinois: InterVarsity Press, 2003).
Nuttall, Geoffrey, *Howel Harris: The Last Enthusiast* (Cardiff: University of Wales Press, 1965).
Obelkevich, Jim, Lyndal Roper and R. Samuel (eds), *Disciplines of Faith: Studies in Religion, Politics and Patriarchy* (London: Routledge and Kegan Paul, 1987).
O'Leary, Paul, *Claiming the Streets: Procession and Urban Culture in South Wales, c.1830–1880* (Cardiff: University of Wales Press, 2012),
Owen, Goronwy Prys, *Atgofion John Evans y Bala* (Caernarfon: Gwasg Pantycelyn, 1997).
Owen, Goronwy Prys, (ed.), *Canu Cynnar y Diwygiad Methodistaidd: Agweddau ar emynau Llawysgrif Llangeitho* (Caernarfon: Ymddiriedolwyr y Ddarlith Davies, 2016).

Owen, John, *Coffhad am y Parch. Daniel Rowlands* (Caerlleon: Edward Parry, 1839).
Parry, Glyn, 'Autobiography of a Smuggler', *National Library of Wales Journal*, 24 (1985).
Peate, Iorwerth C., *Clock and Watch Makers in Wales* (second edn, Cardiff: National Museum of Wales, 1960).
Phillips, Bethan, *Peterwell: The History of a Mansion and its Infamous Squire* (Llandysul: Gomer, 1981).
Podmore, Colin, *The Moravian Church in England 1728–1760* (Oxford: Clarendon Press, 1998).
Pryce, Huw, *J. E. Lloyd and the Creation of Welsh History: Renewing a Nation's Past* (Cardiff: University of Wales Press, 2011).
Rack, Henry D. 'Doctors, Demons and Early Methodist Healing', in W. Sheils (ed.), *The Church and Healing*, Studies in Church History, 19 (Oxford: Basil Blackwell, 1982).
Rack, Henry D., *Reasonable Enthusiast: John Wesley and the Rise of Methodism* (London: Epworth Press, 1980).
Rees, Eiluned, 'Bookbinding in Eighteenth-century Wales', *Journal of the Welsh Bibliographical Society*, 12 (1984).
Rees, Eiluned, 'An Introductory Survey of 18th Century Welsh Libraries', *Journal of Welsh Bibiographical Studies*, X/4 (1971).
Rees, Eiluned, 'Pre-1830 Welsh Subscription Lists', *Journal of the Welsh Bibliographical Society*, 11 (1974).
Rees, Thomas, *A History of Protestant Nonconformity in Wales, from its Rise to the Present Time* (London: John Snow, 1861).
Rivers, Isabel and David L. Wykes (eds), *Dissenting Praise: Religious Dissent and the Hymn in England and Wales* (Oxford: Oxford University Press, 2011).
Robbins, Keith (ed.), *Protestant Evangelicalism: Britain, Ireland, Germany and America, c. 1750–c. 1950: Essay in Honour of W. R. Ward*, Studies in Church History, Subsidia, 7 (Oxford: Blackwell, 1990).
Roberts, Dyfed Wyn (ed.), *Revival, Renewal and the Holy Spirit* (Milton Keynes: Paternoster, 2009).
Roberts, Gomer M., *Bywyd a Gwaith Peter Williams* (Caerdydd: Gwasg Prifysgol Cymru, 1943).
Roberts, Gomer M., 'Capten John Evans, Pen-y-Wenallt', *Cylchgrawn*

Cymdeithas Hanes y Methodistiaid Calfinaidd/Journal of the Historical Society of the Presbyterian Church of Wales, 41 (1956).
Roberts, Gomer M., *Hanes Plwyf Llandybïe* (Caerdydd: Gwasg Prifysgol Cymru, 1939).
Roberts, Gomer M., 'John Richard, Llansamlet', *Cylchgrawn Cymdeithas Hanes y Methodistiaid Calfinaidd/Journal of the Historical Society of the Presbyterian Church of Wales*, 27 (1942).
Roberts, Gomer M., *Methodistiaeth fy Mro: sef ymchwil i ddechreuad Methodistiaeth yn Nwyrain Myrddin* (Treforus: yr awdur, 1938).
Roberts, Gomer M., 'Y Methodistiaid a Chapeli Anwes yn Sir Gaerfyrddin', *Carmarthenshire Antiquary*, 2/1-2 (1945-6).
Roberts, Gomer M., *Morgan Rhys, Llanfynydd* (Caernarfon: Llyfrfa'r Methodistiaid Calfinaidd, 1951).
Roberts, Gomer M., 'Pa bryd y codwyd Capel Soar, Cil-y-cwm?', *Cylchgrawn Cymdeithas Hanes y Methodistiaid Calfinaidd/Journal of the Historical Society of the Presbyterian Church of Wales*, 27 (1942).
Roberts, Gomer M., *Y Pêr Ganiedydd: (Pantycelyn), Cyfrol I: Trem ar ei Fywyd* (Aberystwyth: Gwasg Aberystwyth, 1949).
Roberts, Gomer M., *Y Pêr Ganiedydd: (Pantycelyn), Cyfrol II: Arweiniad i'w Waith* (Llandysul: Gwasg Gomer, 1958).
Roberts, Gomer M., *Portread o Ddiwygiwr* (Caernarfon: Bwrdd Ymddiriedolwyr y Ddarlith Davies, 1969).
Roberts, Gomer M., 'Y Tair Sasiwn Gyntaf, 1742: Dugoedydd, Llwynyberllan a Glanyrafonddu Ganol', *Cylchgrawn Cymdeithas Hanes y Methodistiaid Calfinaidd/Journal of the Historical Society of the Presbyterian Church of Wales*, 26/4 (1941).
Roberts, Gomer M., 'Tanysgrifwyr Pregethau Cymraeg Daniel Rowland', *Cylchgrawn Cymdeithas Hanes y Methodistiaid Calfinaidd/Journal of the Historical Society of the Presbyterian Church of Wales*, 45 (1960).
Roberts, Gomer M., 'William John, Glancothi', *Cylchgrawn Cymdeithas Hanes y Methodistiaid Calfinaidd/Journal of the Historical Society of the Presbyterian Church of Wales*, 36 (1951).
Roberts, Gomer M. (ed.), *Hanes Methodistiaeth Galfinaidd Cymru: Cyfrol I: Y Deffroad Mawr* (Caernarfon: Llyfrfa'r Methodistiaid Calfinaidd, 1973).

Roberts, Gomer M. (ed.), *Hanes Methodistiaeth Galfinaidd Cymru, Cyfrol II: Cynnydd y Corff* (Caernarfon: Llyfrfa'r Methodistiaid Calfinaidd, 1978).

Roberts, H. P. 'Nonconformist Academies in Wales, 1662–1862', *Transactions of the Honourable Society of Cymmrodorion*, 111 (1928–9).

Roberts, John, *Hanes Methodistiaeth Galfinaidd Cymru* (Llundain: Foyle, 1931).

Royle, Edward, *Revolutionary Britannia? Reflections on the Threat of Revolution in Britain, 1789–1848* (Manchester: Manchester University Press, 2000).

Schlenther, Boyd S. and Eryn M. White, *Calendar of the Trevecka Letters* (Aberystwyth: Llyfrgell Genedlaethol Cymru/National Library of Wales, 2003).

Sell, Alan P. F. (ed.), *The Great Ejectment of 1662: Its Antecedents, Aftermath and Ecumenical Significance* (Eugene, Oregon: Pickwick Publications, 2012).

Sheils, W. (ed.), *The Church and Healing*, Studies in Church History, 19 (Oxford: Basil Blackwell, 1982).

Sirota, Brent S., *Christian Monitors: The Church of England and the Age of Benevolence, 1680–1730* (New Haven: Yale University Press, 2014).

Smith, Woodruff D., *Consumption and the Making of Respectability, 1600–1800* (London: Routledge, 2002).

Smout, T. C., 'Born Again at Cambuslang: New Evidence on Popular Religion and Literacy in Eighteenth-century Scotland', *Past and Present*, 97 (1982).

Spufford, Margaret, *Contrasting Communities: English Villagers in the Sixteenth and Seventeenth Centuries* (Stroud: Sutton Publishing, 2000).

Stevenson, John, *Popular Disturbances in England, 1700–1832* (second edn, Harlow, Longman, 1992).

Suggett, Richard, *A History of Magic and Witchcraft in Wales* (Stroud: History Press, 2008).

Swift, Wesley F., 'The Women Itinerant Preachers of Early Methodism', *Proceedings of the Wesley Historical Society*, 28/5 (1952), 29/4 (1953).

Thomas, Keith, 'Women and the Civil War Sects', *Past and Present*, 13 (1958).

Thomas, Owen, *Cofiant y Parchedig John Jones Talsarn* (Wrexham: Hughes and Son, 1874).

Thompson, A. C. (ed.), *The Oxford History of Dissenting Traditions, Volume II: The Long Eighteenth Century, c.1689–1828* (Oxford: Oxford University Press, 2018).

Thompson, E. P., *The Making of the English Working Class* (Harmondsworth: Penguin, 1970).

Tudur, Geraint, 'Gwir Ffrewyll y Methodisitiaid', *Y Cofiadur*, 46 (1981).

Tudur, Geraint, *Howell Harris: From Conversion to Separation 1735–1750* (Cardiff: University of Wales Press, 2000).

Tudur, Geraint, 'Papurau Howell Harris', in *Cof Cenedl*, XVI, ed. Geraint H. Jenkins (Llandysul: Gwasg Gomer, 2001).

Valenze, D. M., *Prophetic Sons and Daughters: Female Preaching and Popular Religion in Industrial England* (Princeton: Princeton University Press, 1985).

Walker, David (ed.), *A History of the Church in Wales* (Penarth: Historical Society of the Church in Wales, 1976).

Ward, W. R., *Early Evangelicalism: A Global Intellectual History, 1670–1789* (Cambridge: Cambridge University Press, 2006).

Ward, W. R., *The Protestant Evangelical Awakening* (Cambridge: Cambridge University Press, 1992).

Watson, David L., *The Early Methodist Class Meeting* (Eugene, Oregon: Wipf and Stock, 2002).

Watson, Kevin M., *Pursuing Social Holiness: The Band Meeting in Wesley's Thought and Popular Methodist Practice* (Oxford: Oxford University Press, 2014).

White, Eryn M., '"Gwnaeth ei Farwnad yn ei Fywyd": Cofio Daniel Rowland Llangeitho (1711?–1790)', *Y Traethodydd* (2011).

White, Eryn M., 'The Material World, Moderation and Methodism in Eighteenth-century Wales', *Welsh History Review*, 23/3 (2007).

White, Eryn M., '"Myrdd o Wragedd": Merched a'r Diwygiad Methodistaidd', *Llên Cymru*, 20 (1997).

White, Eryn M., *'Praidd Bach y Bugail Mawr': Seiadau Methodistaidd De-orllewin Cymru, 1737–50* (Llandysul: Gwasg Gomer, 1995).

White, Eryn M., *The Welsh Bible* (Stroud: Tempus, 2007).

White, Eryn M., 'Women in the Early Methodist Societies in Wales', *Journal of Welsh Religious History*, 7 (1999).

White, Eryn M., '"Yr Ysbryd Canu": Diwygiad Llangeitho, Williams Pantycelyn a'r Emyn', *Y Traethodydd*, CLXVIII (2013).
Williams, D. 'Cilcarw Uchaf Farm in the Hamlet of Cilcarw in the Ecclesiastical Parish of Llangyndeyrn', *Carmarthenshire Antiquary*, 47 (2011).
Williams, D. Emrys, 'Rice Williams: The Contact between Thomas Percy and Evan Evans', *Journal of the National Library of Wales*, 7 (1972).
Williams, Glanmor, *Grym Tafodau Tân: Ysgrifau Hanesyddol ar Grefydd a Diwylliant* (Llandysul: Gwasg Gomer, 1984).
Williams, Glanmor, *Religion, Language and Nationality in Wales* (Cardiff: University of Wales Press, 1979).
Williams, Glanmor, 'Stephen Hughes (1622–1688): "Apostol Sir Gâr", "the Apostle of Carmarthenshire"', *Carmarthenshire Antiquary*, 37 (2001).
Williams, Glanmor, *Wales and the Reformation* (Cardiff: University of Wales Press, 1997).
Williams, Glanmor, *The Welsh and their Religion: Historical Essays* (Cardiff: University of Wales Press, 1991).
Williams, Glanmor, *Welsh Reformation Essays* (Cardiff: University of Wales Press, 1967).
Williams, Glanmor, William Jacob, Nigel Yates and Frances Knight, *The Welsh Church from Reformation to Disestablishment, 1603–1920* (Cardiff: University of Wales Press, 2007).
Williams, Gwyn A., *When Was Wales? A History of the Welsh* (Harmondsworth: Penguin, 1985).
Wilson, L., *Constrained by Zeal: Female Spirituality among Nonconformists 1823–1875* (Carlisle: Paternoster Press, 2000).
Wolffe, John (ed.), *Evangelical Faith and Public Zeal: Evangelicalism and Society in Britain 1780–1820* (London: SPCK, 1995).
Wrightson, Keith, *Earthly Necessities: Economic Lives in Early Modern Britain, 1470–1750* (London: Penguin, 2002).
Wrightson, Keith, *English Society 1580–1680* (London: Hutchinson, 1988 edn).
Yates, Nigel (ed.), *Bishop Burgess and his World: Culture, Religion and Society in Britain, Europe and North America in the Eighteenth and Nineteenth Centuries* (Cardiff: University of Wales Press, 2007).

Unpublished Theses

Brueton, Anna, 'Illegitimacy in south Wales 1660–1870' (unpublished PhD thesis, University of Leicester, 2015).

Coward, Adam, 'Magic and the supernatural in eighteenth-century Wales: the world of the Rev. Edmund Jones (1702–1793)' (unpublished PhD thesis, University of Wales, Newport, 2012).

Hughes-Edwards, W. G., 'The development and organisation of the Methodist society in Wales, 1735–1750' (unpublished MA thesis, University of Wales, 1966).

Lewis, A. H. T., 'The development and administration of roads in Carmarthenshire, 1763–1860' (unpublished MA thesis, University of Wales, 1968.

Thomas, S. R., 'The diocese of St David's in the eighteenth century' (unpublished MA thesis, University of Wales, 1983).

Websites

Coflein, Royal Commission of Historical and Ancient Monuments in Wales, *http://www.coflein.gov.uk*

Dissenting Academies Online: Database and Encyclopedia, *https://dissacad.english.qmul.ac.uk/*

Oxford Dictionary of National Biography, *https://www.oxforddnb.com/*

Index

Aberaeron, Cardiganshire, 27
Aberglasney (Llangathen), Carmarthenshire, 160, 283
Abergorlech chapel (Llanybydder), Carmarthenshire, 121, 123, 124, 133, 310
Abergwili, Carmarthenshire, 31, 33, 40, 53, 74, 83, 115, 119, 150, 151, 167, 290, 310
   site of Bishop's Palace, 21, 27, 64
Aber-nant, Carmarthenshire, 33, 45, 47, 50, 310
Aberporth, Cardiganshire, 2, 5, 83, 212, 253
   society of, 145, 146, 148, 234, 236, 240, 309
Aberystwyth, Cardiganshire, 5, 7, 30, 32, 125, 313
Account of the Religious Societies in the City of London (1697), *An*, by Josiah Woodward, 189–90
Act for the Translating of the Bible and the Divine Service (1563), 29, 30
Adams, Thomas, 73
Aleluja, neu, casgljad o hymnau ar amryw ystyriaethau (1744), by William Williams, 271
Anglesey, 29, 65, 290
Anglicanism, Anglicans. *See* Church of England
Antinomianism, 255, 293
   defined, 102, 255
   Howel Harris accused of, 97, 102
Arianism, 54, 98
Arminianism, 3, 16, 53, 54, 96, 270, 290

Association
   and George Whitefield, 3, 9, 68, 74
   origins and authority, 67–9, 76, 79, 81, 85–6, 87, 115, 303
   meetings of, 23, 71, 73, 74, 75, 76, 77, 89, 93, 95, 102, 114, 121, 124, 132, 133, 158, 164, 232, 233, 254, 270, 285
   records of, 6, 8, 9
Atteb Philo-Evangelius (1763), by William Williams, 10, 94, 256, 276
Aurora Borealis (1774), by William Williams, 198

Bala, Calvinistic Methodist College, 7, 13
Bala, Merionethshire, 11
   and Thomas Charles, as major Calvinistic Methodist centre, 12 305
Bangor, 13, 129
Bangor diocese, 21, 28, 29, 30, 40, 46, 277, 278
Bangor Teifi, Cardiganshire, 135
Baptists, 51, 52, 53, 66, 125, 192, 272
Bateman, Richard Thomas, 124
Beaumont, James, 73, 97, 102
Berllandywyll (Llangathen), Carmarthenshire, 154, 160, 182, 283
Bethesda orphanage, Georgia, 199
Bevan, Bridget
   and Welsh circulating schools, 127, 131, 132, 134
Bible, 29, 30, 102, 119, 125, 128, 129,

INDEX

130, 135, 136, 143, 171–2, 182, 190, 193, 210, 228, 269, 280, 281
   1588 Welsh translation by William Morgan, 14, 22, 24
   Welsh editions, 29, 70, 127, 133
   use of verses from, 119, 185, 193, 206, 217, 226, 232, 233, 239–40, 259, 269, 291
Bisse, Phillip, bishop of St Davids, 26, 29
Blaen-porth, Cardiganshire, 83, 88, 151, 166, 185, 191, 212, 223, 275
   society of, 83, 88, 91, 133, 211, 212, 281, 309
Blaenhownant (Penbryn), Cardiganshire, 145, 148, 152, 191, 234, 258, 309
Blaenhyfer, Pembrokeshire, 205, 267, 312
Bloom, Milbourne, 64, 74, 83, 88, 115, 119, 123, 150, 275, 309–10
'Blue Books', 12–13, *see also* Education Commission of 1846
Bolahaul (Llangynnwr), Carmarthenshire, 119, 133, 311
Bowen, Lewis Lloyd, 44
Bowen, Marmaduke, 43–4
Bowen family (of Llwyn-gwair), 286
Brechfa, Carmarthenshire, 133, 168, 182
Brecon, 24, 27, 117
   archdeaconry of, 46
Breconshire, 1, 7, 21, 38, 65, 66, 68, 69, 70, 73, 83, 89, 102, 114, 126, 157, 282
   societies in, 74, 76, 114, 115
   Welsh language in, 31
Bron-y-mwyn, Cardiganshire, 75, 78, 309
Bryniau Bychain (Llansawel), Carmarthenshire, 95, 115, 138, 163, 164, 311
Builth, Breconshire, 121, 187
Bull, George, bishop of St Davids, 26, 27, 29, 128
Bunyan, John, 54, 188, 307
Burgess, Thomas, bishop of St David's, 28

Caeo, Carmarthenshire, 39, 42, 81, 85, 126, 151, 153, 157, 161, 162, 167, 169, 182, 186, 201
   society of, 39, 40, 77, 133, 146, 168, 229, 240, 268, 274, 310, 311
Caernarfon, 29, 58, 117
Caernarfonshire, 12, 29, 99
Calendar of the Trevecka Letters (2003), 8
Calvinistic Methodist Archive, 5–8, 148
Calvinistic Methodist Church of Wales, 5, 10, 13 195
Cambuslang, Scotland, revival in, 10
Campbell, John (of Stackpole), 123
Caniadau (y Rhai sydd ar y Môr o Wydr yn gymmysgedig a than, ac wedi cael y maes ar y bwystfil) i Frenhin y Saint (1762), by William Williams, 271
Capel Gwynfil (Llangeitho), Cardiganshire, 269, 309
Capel Ifan (Llanelli), Carmarthenshire, 122, 123, 159, 310
Cardigan, 2, 27, 30, 72, 81, 91, 117, 119–20, 154, 185, 253, 283, 284
   archdeaconry of, 34, 46, 51
Cardiganshire, 9, 12, 21, 45, 53, 54, 66, 69, 71, 78, 88, 92, 93, 113, 120, 123, 128, 129, 153, 154, 155, 156, 157, 158, 160, 164, 185, 194, 203, 204, 253, 272, 282, 284, 286, 290
   Church of England in, 25, 30, 32, 35, 36, 45, 135
   circulating schools in, 131, 133–5, 152
   gentry in, 153, 154, 155, 156, 157, 173
   nature of, 1–2
   population of, 2, 185
   societies in, 5, 32, 74, 75, 76, 78, 104, 114, 115, 117, 133, 143, 145, 148, 152, 164, 191, 202, 204, 207, 211, 226, 230, 231, 234, 240, 245, 246, 248, 252, 256, 258, 309–10
Carmarthen, 30, 33, 37, 38, 40, 47, 53, 54, 66, 70, 72, 74, 88, 91, 114, 116, 117, 118, 125, 127, 128, 129, 131, 154, 185, 186–7, 251, 284, 305

archdeaconry of, 30, 31, 34, 36, 46, 51, 52, 126, 186
society of, 79, 85, 89, 115, 119, 227, 229, 245, 310
Carmarthen Dissenting Academy, 8, 53–4, 72, 89, 98, 100, 118, 126, 184
Carmarthenshire, 12, 21, 47, 54, 64, 65, 66, 67, 71, 86, 92, 93, 98, 103
  Church of England in, 30–1, 35, 36, 40, 46, 48
  circulating schools in, 125, 131, 133, 135
  Dissent in, 52–3, 273, 274
  gentry in, 154–5, 160, 163, 173, 282, 283
  nature of, 2, 113–14, 127, 128, 129, 153, 155, 160, 162, 163, 191, 195, 255, 284, 291, 305
  population of, 2, 185
  societies in, 5, 33, 39–40, 74, 76, 114–15, 117, 118, 121, 143, 146, 157, 168, 197, 233, 234, 246, 267, 310–1
Cefnamwlch, Caernarfonshire, 99, 288
Cefntelych (Myddfai), Carmarthenshire, 145, 158, 233, 310
Cellan, Cardiganshire, 69
Cennick, John, 73
Census of religion, 1851, 10, 12, 13, 305
chapels of ease, 40, 104, 122–5, 133, 135, 159–60, 164, 194, 195, 275, 277
Charles, Thomas, 11–12, 305
Christopher, William, 114
Church of England, 2, 13, 14–15, 22, 122, 126, 132, 168, 172, 189, 211, 227, 228, 275, 283
  and circulating schools, 134–6
  clergy of, 35–47
  criticisms of, 23–6, 28, 41–2, 55, 89
  evangelical wing of, 5
  relationship of Calvinistic Methodists to, 4–5, 22–3, 41, 55–6, 123, 194–5, 233, 265, 272, 273–4, 275–6, 277–80, 286, 290
  and Welsh language, 22, 24, 25, 28–35, 55

Cilcarw (Llangyndeyrn), Carmarthenshire, 77, 121, 133, 164, 178, 196, 197, 213, 237, 240, 258, 310
Cilrhedyn, Pembrokeshire, 150, 167, 250, 310, 311
Cil-y-cwm, Carmarthenshire, 43, 68, 150, 151, 152, 157, 159, 161, 162, 166, 167, 172, 187
  societies of, 33, 116, 133, 152, 158, 268, 310
  society house at, 121–2, 133, 152, 164, 166, 168–9, 200
Claggett, Nicholas, bishop of St Davids, 23, 26, 27, 36, 57, 63–4, 73, 277,
Cleddau river, 2
Clyncoch (Llangrannog), Cardiganshire, 151
Colvill (unknown location), 116, 310
Come and Welcome to Jesus Christ (1719), by John Bunyan, 54, 188, 307
Communion
  in chapels of ease, 104, 122–5, 194–5
  at Llangeitho, 66, 185
  Methodists to receive at parish churches, 194, 275
  tensions regarding, 89, 96, 243, 274–5
Compton Census (1676), 22, 51
Congregationalists. *See* Independents
conversion experience
  of Methodists, 54, 63–4, 88, 145, 152, 183, 184, 227–8, 256–7, 307
  nature of, 182, 188–9, 197, 214
Cornwall, 253
Cornwallis, Mrs Jane (of Abermarlais), 36
Cothi river, 74, 76, 113
Countess of Huntingdon. *See* Hastings, Selina
Crowther, William, 33–4, 41
Crug Ifan (Cilrhedyn), 149, 150, 167, 206, 310
Cwm-ann, Carmarthenshire, 183, 295
  society of, 49, 146, 196, 310
Cwm-y-dŵr (Llandwrda), Carmarthenshire, 66
Cwmcynon (Llandysiliogogo), Cardiganshire, 149, 151, 156–7, 167, 172, 186, 206

INDEX

Cwmhowni (Blaenporth), Cardiganshire, 83, 88, 133, 166, 211, 212
Cwrtycadno, Carmarthenshire, 49, 133, 310
Cyfarwyddwr Priodas (1777), by William Williams, 146, 247
Cyffig and Marros, Carmarthenshire, 36–7
Cynwyl Elfed, Carmarthenshire, 67, 151, 153, 228
  society of, 33, 310
Cynwyl Gaeo, Carmarthenshire, 33, 39–40, 46, 133, 168

Dafydd, Dafydd William, 108
Dafydd, Richard William, 85
Dafydd, Thomas, 82
Dalton, Edward, 127, 281
David, Jenkin, 149, 150, 167, 206
David, John (of Bryniau Bychain), 163, 164
David, John (of Llandyfaelog), 77
David, Thomas (of Dyffryn-saith), 164, 202, 206
Davies, Henry, 71
Davies, Howel, 69, 157, 159, 164, 170, 192, 198, 266, 287
  conversion and early career, 64, 188
  and discipline, 252
  and Griffith Jones, 132, 199
  and Howel Harris, 101, 102, 269
  influence, 3, 63, 76, 77, 81
  marriage, 83, 162, 291
  preaching, 72, 186, 289
  site of his New Chapel, 232
  uses chapels of ease, 123, 124, 156, 277
Davies (or Dafydd), Isaac, 150, 152, 164, 167
Davies, James, 272
Davies, John (of Llanddarog), 69
Davies, Pryce, 194
Davies, Rees, 272
Davies, Richard, bishop of St Asaph and St Davids, 26, 55
death
  importance of last words, 204–7
  Methodist attitude towards, 201–7

Defynnog, Breconshire, 68
Devil, the, 65, 78, 94, 99, 100, 119, 201, 226, 237, 240, 241, 242, 251, 271, 290, 294
Dinas, Pembrokeshire, 145, 147, 188, 312
discipline
  disagreement over, 96, 243–4
  of exhorters, 81
  of society members, 241–58
dissenters, 14, 31, 32, 40, 43, 49, 50, 90, 120, 123, 128, 162, 168, 186, 189, 195, 227, 281, 283
  and 1689 Toleration Act, 2, 274
  influence in south-west Wales, 13, 14, 22, 50–4, 56, 125–6, 148
  Methodist exhorters turning to Dissent, 64, 74, 88–9, 170, 275, 284, 285, 287
  relationship with Welsh Calvinistic Methodists, 53, 54, 68, 71, 183, 192, 212, 265, 270, 271–6, 288
  see also Independents; Baptists; Unitarians
dissenting academies, 125
Diwygiad Mawr (1981), *Y*, by Derec Llwyd Morgan, 14
Drummond, Robert Hay, bishop of St Asaph, 29
Drws y Society Profiad (1777), by William Williams, 190, 191–2, 228, 235, 241, 244
Drych y Prif Oesoedd (1716, 1740), by Theophilus Evans, 293
Drych yr Amseroedd (1820), 11
Dugoedydd (Cil-y-cwm), Carmarthenshire, 68, 121
Dyer, Robert Archer (of Aberglasney), 160, 172, 283
Dyffryn-saith (Penbryn), Cardiganshire, 133, 145, 164, 202, 206, 240, 256, 309
Dygoed (Clydau), Pembrokeshire, 312
Dygoed (Llanarthney), Carmarthenshire, 54, 120, 164, 188, 289, 310

Education Commission, 1846, 12–13, 306

INDEX

Edward, William, 77–8
Edwards, Jonathan, 270
Edwards, Lewis, 13
Edwards, Sir Owen M., 7
Eglwys Gymyn, Carmarthenshire, 30, 70, 132, 292
Eglwyswrw, Pembrokeshire, 146, 231, 256, 312
enthusiasm, 11, 94, 187–9, 191–2, 194, 231–2, 256–7, 293–4
The Enthusiasm of Methodists and Papists Compared (1749–51), by George Lavington, 280
Evan, David (of Cwm-y-dŵr), 66
Evan, Griffith (of Tŵr-gwyn), 150, 153, 164, 171
Evangelical Magazine, 11, 88
Evans, Captain John (of Pen-y-wenallt), 150, 153, 157, 288
Evans, Eifion, 278
Evans, Evan ('Ieuan Fardd'), 24–5, 46
Evans, John, bishop of Bangor, 28
Evans, John (of Bala), 11, 12
Evans, John (of Eglwys Gymyn), 70, 132, 292
Evans, Owen, 165, 288
Evans, Theophilus, 38, 40, 69, 97, 157, 288–9
Evans, William (of Pencader), 126
Everitt, Alan, 162
exhorters
  age of, 63–4, 144
  levels of education, 72, 77, 170, 279, 292–3
  and livelihood, 85–6
  public and private, 76, 77, 30
  responsibilities, 73, 78–81, 202, 233, 235, 304
  as teachers, 86, 133–4

Feasts and Fasts (1704), by Robert Nelson, 29
Ffair-rhos, Cardiganshire, 287
Ffos-y-ficer (Abercych), Pembrokeshire, 164, 312
Ffrewyll y Methodistiaid (1746), by William Roberts, 289, 292

Ffrwdwenith (Aberporth), Cardiganshire, 120, 164, 310
Fishguard, 31, 33
  society of, 67, 87, 144, 146, 150, 165, 166, 169, 226, 231, 233, 234, 237, 243, 312
Francis, Enoch, 272
Francis, Mary (Mali), 83

Galltybere, Carmarthenshire, 116, 151, 172, 198, 311
Gambold, George, 72, 77, 81, 85, 88
Gambold, John, 81
Gambold, William, 81, 85
Gelli Glyd (Abergwili), Carmarthenshire, 74, 83, 119, 150, 310
gentry, 32, 43, 83, 84, 117, 126, 147, 170, 198, 209
  and charity, 126–7
  opposition to Methodism, 118, 119, 154, 163, 229, 280, 284–6
  support for Methodism, 153–60, 162, 172–3, 235, 305
Gilfach-yr-heddwch (Llandingad), Carmarthenshire, 155
Glamorgan, 12, 22, 65, 66, 67, 69, 70, 74, 76, 85, 102, 114, 115, 272
Glancothi (Llanegwad), Carmarthenshire, 74, 76, 77, 84, 107–8, 115, 287
  society at, 289, 311
Glanyrafonddu-ganol (Talley) Carmarthenshire, 23, 68, 73, 89, 121, 145, 151, 152, 153, 163, 175, 187, 200, 233
Gower, 31
Griffith, Eaton, 150, 166, 167, 169
Griffith, Nicholas, 289
Griffith, Sidney, 93–4, 99–100, 102, 103, 210, 211, 292
Griffiths, Ann, 192, 213
Griffiths, Evan, 128
Griffiths, Jonathan, 135
Griffiths, Mary, 151, 152, 163, 168, 169
Griffiths, Nicholas, 39, 42–3, 44
Griffiths, Thomas, 151, 152, 153, 163, 169

INDEX

Griffiths, Vavasor, 126
Gwynne, Marmaduke, 91, 155, 282, 283, 288, 294
Gwynne, Roderick, 282, 288
Gwynne, Sarah. *See* Sarah Wesley
Gwynne family, of Gwempa, Carmarthenshire, 285

halsingod, 50, 164, 193
Harris, Anne (née Williams), 43, 83, 99–100, 123, 158, 161–2
Harris, Howel, 3, 10
  and 1750 division, 102–3, 304
  and Anne Harris, 99–100, 123, 161
  and Association, 67–8, 70–1
  and assurance, 270–1
  belief in providence, 114, 284, 294–5
  and Bridget Bevan, 131, 132
  character, 94, 95–6
  conversion, 23
  correspondence of, 6, 8, 9
  diaries of, 6–7, 8, 9, 10
  and discipline, 79, 81, 243–4, 253, 254, 255
  and Dissent, 53, 54, 272–3
  education, 126
  enthusiasm, 94, 102, 194
  financial situation, 86
  focus on in Methodist history, 8, 12, 15
  as general superintendent of societies, 73, 96, 98, 243, 247
  and gentry, 154–6, 160–2, 172, 182, 282–3, 285–6
  and George Whitefield, 100
  handwriting of, 6
  and Howel Davies, 101, 269
  and hymns, 192, 287
  links with other groups in revival, 4
  and Marmaduke Gwynne, 91, 282, 283, 294
  and Moravianism, 96–8, 269–70
  organisational skills, 70–1, 104
  and Patripassianism, 98, 102
  and persecution, 282, 285, 2878, 290, 292
  preaching, 71, 72, 95, 97, 100–1, 121, 144, 182–3, 184–7
  preserves records, 6–7
  reconciliation with Methodist movement, 304–5
  refused ordination, 22–3, 73, 95, 277, 278
  relationship with Church and clergy, 23, 41, 279
  relationship with Daniel Rowland, 64–5, 66, 93, 94–6, 101–2, 232, 243, 269, 270–1, 273
  relationship with Griffith Jones, 66, 96, 132, 134
  relationship with Sidney Griffith, 93–4, 99–100, 102, 288
  and Sabellianism, 102
  and societies, 116, 189, 200, 229, 230, 232–3, 239
  as source, 114–15, 208
  and south-west, 63, 66–7, 92–3, 100, 104, 269
  and towns, 118–20
  translates society reports, 8
  travel, 90–3, 114
  and William Williams, 103, 243, 269, 270
  and women, 160–2, 210–11, 211–12, 215
  use of Bible verses, 119, 185, 232
Harris, John (of St Kennox, Pembrokeshire), 74, 81
Harris, Joseph, 6, 83, 154, 285
Harry, John, 81, 87, 103, 251, 252, 266, 269, 275, 276, 296, 309, 312
Harry, William (of Caeo), 201
Harry, William (of Llanfynydd), 201
Hastings, Selina, countess of Huntingdon, 12, 98, 207
Havard, David, 40, 127, 134
Haverfordwest, Pembrokeshire, 41, 76, 88, 103, 117, 118, 124, 128, 202, 229, 280
  Moravians at, 81
heart religion, 16, 72, 294
Hempton, David, 16, 208, 271–2
Henllan, Cardiganshire, 45, 49, 135
Henllan Amgoed, Carmarthenshire, 33, 50, 83, 267, 272, 274, 311
History of Modern Enthusiasm (1752), *A*, by Theophilus Evans, 157, 293

Hodges, John, 69, 70
Horsley, Samuel, bishop of St Davids, 27
Howell, David, 117, 147
Howell, John, 134
Howells family of Penybeili, 157
Hughes, John, 12
Hughes, Morgan, 64, 74–5, 78, 83, 88, 95, 115, 151, 166, 170, 212, 283–4, 286–7, 294, 309–10
Hughes, Stephen, 50, 51, 52, 54, 128
Hughes-Edwards, W. G., 15, 211
Humphreys, Joseph, 73
hymn singing, 186, 187–8, 192–4, 213–14, 216, 231, 236, 271, 287, 306
Hymnau Duwiol Yw canu mewn cymdeithasau Crefyddol (1744), 192

Ifan, Gruffydd, 164
Ifan, Jeffrey Dafydd (of Rhiwiau), 144, 153
Independents, 8, 51–2, 53, 54, 97, 123, 126, 272, 273, 274, 294
  Milbourne Bloom joins, 74, 88, 115, 275
  Morgan Hughes and, 88
  Morgan John Lewis and, 89, 275
  Thomas Morgan as, 98
  Richard Tibbott joins, 8, 275
  John Thomas and, 8
  see also Dissenters
Ingram, James, 285
Ioan ap Hywel, 290
Ireland, 2, 28, 304

Jacobitism, 26, 129, 155, 231, 280, 281
James, Catherine (of Llwynyceiliog), 161
James, David (of Llwynyceiliog), 151, 153, 161, 166, 167, 169, 171
James, Elizabeth. *See* Whitefield, Elizabeth
James, Mary, 151, 158, 167
James, William (of Pwllpriddog), 158
James, William (of Tre-lech), 206, 256
Jenkins, David, 69–70, 183
Jenkins, Geraint H., 14
Jenkins, Herbert, 73

Jenkins, Jenkin, 53–4
Jenkins, R. T., 13, 19, 116
Jesus College, Oxford, 24, 28, 43, 153
John, Daniel, 79, 100
John, David, 163
John, William (of Glancothi), 5, 74, 76, 77, 79, 80, 86, 89, 103, 115, 116, 119, 144, 191, 205, 206, 207, 234, 245, 247, 256, 267, 274, 288, 304, 309–11
  death and elegy, 64, 82, 84, 277
  and persecution, 277, 279, 284, 287–8
John, William (of Llanwrda), 77
John, William (of Llewele Mawr), 152–3, 163, 171, 209
Jones, Basil, bishop of St Davids, 28
Jones, Betty Rees, 215
Jones, David (of Aberporth), 253
Jones, David (of Dygoed), 54, 188, 307
Jones, David (of Maesnonni), 151, 167, 169, 171
Jones, David, J. V., 1
Jones, Dorothy, 114, 213–14
Jones, Edmund, 51, 68, 207, 272, 294
Jones, Edward, chancellor of St Davids, 47, 278
Jones, Edward (of Henllan), 135
Jones, Evan, 39–40, 45
Jones, Griffith (of Llanddowror), 125, 199, 292
  and Church, 34, 37, 40, 42, 48–9, 56
  and circulating schools, 14, 130–1, 136, 152, 201
  as a preacher, 48, 50, 64, 66, 72, 73, 181
  relationship with Methodists, 66, 68, 69, 76, 86, 96, 104, 124, 131–2, 133, 136, 152, 186, 194, 255
  and SPCK, 127, 129
Jones, Griffith (of Pantyrhaidd), 67, 151, 153, 169
Jones, Ieuan Gwynedd, 23–4
Jones, John (dean of Bangor), 128
Jones, John (of Caeo), 85
Jones, John (of Llan-gain), 45
Jones, John (of Llandovery), 295
Jones, John (of Llowes), 278

Jones, John (of Llys-y-frân), 78
Jones, Leoline, 155
Jones, M. H., 7
Jones, Noah, 100
Jones, Robert (of Rhoslan), 11, 94, 131
Jones, Theophilus (of Blaenplwyf), 151, 204
Jones, Thomas (of Cwm-iou), 69
Jones, Thomas (of Denbigh), 11
justification by faith, 227, 228, 271, 293

Lampeter, Cardiganshire, 30, 32–3, 53, 69, 72, 117, 154, 155, 156, 172
society of, 76, 115, 118, 269, 285, 309
Laugharne, Carmarthenshire, 30, 31, 36, 38, 90, 127, 131, 187
Dissenting meeting house at, 89
and Griffith Jones, 48, 129
Moravians at, 89
society of, 89, 267, 279, 311
Letter... to the Religious Societies Lately Set on Foot in Several Parts of England and Wales (1740), *A*, by George Whitefield, 190
Letters
Howel Harris's correspondence, 6, 8, 66, 68, 99, 103, 187
significance of in Methodist movement, 9, 90, 196–7
Lewis, Catherine, 84, 212
Lewis, David (of Aber-nant), 47
Lewis, Jenkin, 212
Lewis, John, 151, 164, 167
Lewis, Lewis, 43–4
Lewis, Leyshon, 39
Lewis, Morgan John, 78, 100, 235
and Dissent, 89, 275
as superintendent of societies, 5, 74, 76, 115, 309, 311
Lewis, Saunders, 281
Literacy, 147, 148
amongst Methodists, 170–2, 197, 212
growth of, 9, 14, 16, 125–36, 216, 303, 305, 307
Llan-y-crwys, Carmarthenshire, 37, 39, 42–4, 46, 50, 165
Llanarthney, Carmarthenshire, 33, 120, 122

society of, 148, 164, 240, 267, 289, 310–11
Llanbadarn Fawr, Cardiganshire, 30, 83, 128
Llanbadarn Odwyn, Cardiganshire, 83
Llandafen, Carmarthenshire, 77, 86, 311
Llandaff diocese, 21, 27, 40, 46
Llanddarog, Carmarthenshire, 1, 69, 120, 123, 133, 215, 310
Llanddeusant, Carmarthenshire, 33, 37, 66, 91, 144, 182
society in, 5, 74, 76, 86, 89, 114, 115, 153, 229, 234, 235, 311
Llanddewi Abergwesyn, Breconshire, 38, 69, 279
Llanddewibrefi, Cardiganshire, 36, 48, 64, 74, 76, 83, 84, 135, 144, 151, 155, 166, 188, 203
society of, 196, 310
Llandeilo, Carmarthenshire, 33, 39, 43, 89, 286, 310, 311
Llandeilo, Pembrokeshire, 31, 41, 135
Llandeilo Abercywyn, Carmarthenshire, 37, 48, 77, 132
Llandinam, Montgomeryshire, 230, 279
Llandovery, Carmarthenshire, 66, 115, 155, 158, 285, 295
Llandybïe, Carmarthenshire, 41, 67, 133, 144, 151, 167, 170, 288
Llandyfaelog, Carmarthenshire, 77, 85, 122, 210, 311
Llandysilio, Pembrokeshire, 53
Llandysiliogogo, Cardiganshire, 133, 150, 151, 152, 156, 167, 186, 206, 310
Llandysul, Cardiganshire, 37, 53, 128, 134
Llanegwad, Carmarthenshire, 33, 74, 84, 115, 133, 139, 144, 279, 287
society of, 234, 247, 267, 274, 311
Llanelli, Carmarthenshire, 31, 33, 77, 90, 114, 122, 123, 127, 159, 311
Llanfair-ar-y-bryn, Carmarthenshire, 32, 38, 53, 114, 120, 122, 152, 167, 187, 311
Llanfair Clydogau, Cardiganshire, 78, 100

INDEX

Llanfair Nant-y-gof, Pembrokeshire, 32
Llanfairorllwyn, Cardiganshire, 310
Llanfihangel Aberbythych,
  Carmarthenshire, 33, 311
Llanfihangel Abercywyn,
  Carmarthenshire, 38
Llanfihangel Abergwesyn, Breconshire,
  38, 69
Llanfihangel Rhos-y-corn,
  Carmarthenshire, 40, 45, 49, 135
Llanfihangel-uwch-Gwili,
  Carmarthenshire, 60
Llanfihangel Ystrad, Cardiganshire,
  151, 194, 204
Llanfynydd, Carmarthenshire, 33, 133,
  134, 151, 152, 163, 168, 192, 201
  society of 152, 168, 172, 237, 268,
  311
Llan-gain, Carmarthenshire, 45, 49
Llangathen, Carmarthenshire, 139, 146,
  160, 241, 311
Llangeitho, Cardiganshire, 5, 64, 92, 93,
  144, 151, 168, 183, 290
  Daniel Rowland as curate of, 37
  as place of Methodist 'pilgrimage', 66,
  114, 184, 185
  revival at (1762), 10–11, 192, 214,
  256, 271, 307
  society of, 5, 76, 195, 196, 267, 269,
  309
Llangeitho Manuscript, 192, 226, 236
Llangeler, Carmarthenshire, 115, 227,
  311
Llangoedmor, Cardiganshire, 34, 49, 123
Llangwarren (Jordanston),
  Pembrokeshire, 155, 159, 161, 173
Llangyndeyrn, Carmarthenshire, 33,
  72, 197, 200, 285
  society of, 77, 114, 121, 133, 164,
  196, 213, 237, 310
Llangynheiddon chapel, Llandyfaelog,
  Carmarthenshire, 122
Llangynnwr, Carmarthenshire, 33, 119,
  133, 311
Llanidloes, Montgomeryshire, 65, 102
Llanlluan chapel, Llanarthney,
  Carmarthenshire, 122, 123, 124,
  133, 135, 311

Llanllugan, Montgomeryshire, 230
Llanllwch, Carmarthenshire, 72
Llanllwni, Carmarthenshire, 33, 45, 49,
  151, 167, 169, 274, 294, 311
Llan-non, Carmarthenshire, 33, 45, 49,
  50
  society of, 86, 239, 240, 243, 311
Llanpennal, Cardiganshire, 230, 310
Llanpumsaint, Carmarthenshire, 33,
  191, 250, 267, 311
Llansadwrn, Carmarthenshire, 33, 77,
  168, 311
Llansadwrnen, Carmarthenshire, 30,
  36, 37
Llansawel, Carmarthenshire, 33, 39, 42,
  95, 122, 151, 152, 153, 183, 209,
  289
  society house, 121, 164, 200
  society of, 72, 115, 133, 146, 163,164,
  168, 229, 267, 268, 311
Llansteffan, Carmarthenshire, 90–1,
  114, 117
Llanwinio, Carmarthenshire, 33, 65,
  135, 197, 206, 250, 311
Llanwrda, Carmarthenshire, 33, 66, 77,
  135, 311
Llanwrtyd, Breconshire, 38, 69, 278
Llanybydder, Carmarthenshire, 33, 49,
  123, 310, 311
Llechryd, Cardiganshire, 119, 133, 185,
  204
  chapel at, 122, 123, 133, 156
  society at, 120, 133, 191, 229, 230,
  310, 312
Lledrod, Cardiganshire, 25, 191, 198,
  240, 247, 310
Lloyd, David (of Berllandywyll), 154,
  182, 283
Lloyd (or Llwyd), David (of
  Llwynrhydowen), 54, 160
Lloyd, Sir Herbert (of Peterwell),
  155–6, 172, 283
Lloyd, J. E., 13
Lloyd, Jennifer, 208, 213
Lloyd, John, bishop of St Davids, 28
Lloyd, John (of Narberth), 37, 124
Lloyd, John (of Peterwell), 154, 284
Lloyd, Sir Lucius, 154, 155, 172

INDEX

Lloyd, Marmaduke, 42
Lloyd, Philip, 122–3
Lloyd, Walter (of Peterwell), 284
Lloyd, William, 68
Llwyn-gwair, Pembrokeshire, 286
Llwyn-llwyd Dissenting Academy, 72, 126
Llwyndafydd, Cardiganshire, 146, 148, 150, 152, 156, 191, 196, 227, 234, 239, 245, 310
Llwynyberllan (Llandingad), Carmarthenshire, 66, 102, 121, 149, 150, 151, 152, 153, 158–9, 161, 167, 172, 210, 232
Llwynyceiliog (Cynwyl Gaeo), Carmarthenshire, 151, 153, 161, 167, 169
Llwynygorras, Pembrokeshire, 116, 146, 206, 230, 312
Llys-y-frân, Pembrokeshire, 78, 132,
Llyfr y Tri Aderyn (1653), by Morgan Llwyd, 54
Llythyr Martha Philopur (1762), by William Williams, 10, 214
London, 27, 64, 117, 124, 128, 212, 293
 evangelical revival in, 189, 230
 H. Harris in, 3, 68, 92, 96, 100, 104, 199, 210, 231
Longhouse (Mathry), Pembrokeshire
 family, 151, 159, 162, 166, 167, 199, 241
 society of, 87, 146, 147, 165, 187, 227, 229, 233, 312
love-feast, 232–3
Lucy, Robert, Registrar of St Davids, 26
Lucy, William, bishop of St Davids, 26

McCulloch, William, 10
Mack, Phyllis, 15, 210
Mackworth, Sir Humphrey, 127, 128
Maenclochog, Pembrokeshire, 31, 33, 41, 134
Malmgreen, Gail, 207
Mansel, Sir Edward, 285
Mathias family (Llangwarren, Pembrokeshire), 154, 159, 161, 173
Mathias, David, 154

Mathias, Elizabeth, 159, 161
Mathias, John, 154, 159
Mathias, Mary, 159, 161
Mathry, Pembrokeshire, 30, 151, 159, 162, 167, 187, 233, 312
Meidrim, Carmarthenshire, 33, 38, 45, 46–7, 52, 126, 151, 154
 society of, 49, 164, 167, 207, 244, 251, 268,
members of societies
 accepting new members, 226–7
 age, 144–5, 173
 charitable giving, 168–70, 199–200
 effect of 1750 division on, 104, 267, 269
 fellowship between, 195–201, 233, 240–1
 gender, 145–7, 173, 207–16
 language used by, 9
 and literacy, 170–2
 numbers of, 143, 267–9
 social status, 147–8, 153–65, 172–3
 use of chapels of ease by, 124
 wealth, 165–9
Mends, Christopher, 64, 78, 88–9, 119, 156–7, 267, 291, 309–11
Mends, William, 78, 88–9, 119, 156–7, 267, 291, 309–11
Merionethshire, 12, 29, 65, 200
Merthyr, Carmarthenshire, 33, 126, 165, 229, 288, 311
'Methodist', 265
Methodist view of history, 11, 14, 15
Methodistiaeth Cymru (1851–6), by John Hughes, 166, 171
Meurig, Edward, 85
Meurig, John, 77, 85
Meyrick, Edmund, 127, 128
Montgomeryshire, 12, 65, 74, 75, 102, 192, 230
Moravians, 4, 161
 and James Beaumont, 97
 in Laugharne, 89
 in Pembrokeshire, 81, 155
 influence on revival, 198, 232
 influence on Howel Harris, 96–8
Morgan, D. Densil, 14, 125, 183, 185
Morgan, David, 151

INDEX

Morgan, Derec Llwyd, 14, 94, 143, 248
Morgan, John (Cwm, Myddfai), 201
Morgan, Prys, 307
Morgan, Thomas (of Henllan
 Amgoed), 100
 diaries of, 8, 165, 209
 and Howel Harris, 98, 182, 184, 274
 and Methodism, 72, 74, 77, 118–19, 274
Morgan, William, 24
Morris, Lewis, 290–3
Morris, Samuel (of Llan-gan), 37
Morris, William, 25–6, 55
Mounton chapel, Narberth,
 Pembrokeshire, 77, 122, 123, 124, 195
Myddfai, Carmarthenshire, 33, 64, 144, 145, 158, 201, 310

Names
 of members, 144, 147–8, 165, 170, 278
 naming patterns, 148–9
 of societies, 115–16, 164
Nancwnlle, Cardiganshire, 37, 66
Nantgaredig, Carmarthenshire, 168
National Library of Wales,
 Aberystwyth, 5, 7
Nevern, Pembrokeshire, 34
'new birth'. *See* conversion experience
New Inn, Monmouthshire, 89, 274
New Quay, Cardiganshire, 5, 74, 76, 115, 309
New Weekly Miscellany (periodical),
 The, 57, 277
Newcastle Emlyn, Carmarthenshire, 54, 71, 115, 117, 118, 206, 272, 311
Newport, Pembrokeshire, 146, 147, 185, 188, 240, 286, 312
Nicholas, Mary, 206
Noll, Mark, 193, 216

Ottley, Adam, bishop of St Davids, 27–8, 29, 36, 38, 42, 48, 56, 117
Owen, Enos, 151
Owen, John, 65
Owen, John, chancellor of Bangor, 278
Owen, William (of Narberth), 253
Oxford, University of. *See* Jesus College

Palmer, Henry, 272, 274
Pant-teg Independent Church, 53, 273
Pantycelyn (Llanfair-ar-y-bryn), 83, 114
Parciau (Henllan Amgoed),
 Carmarthenshire, 83, 161–2
Parry, Elizabeth, 156, 206
Parry, Hester, 156–7
Parry, John (of Cwmcynon), 149, 151, 156, 157, 167, 172
Parry, John (of Talley), 202–3
Parry family (of Cwmcynon), 186
Patripassianism, 98, 102
Pember, John, 127, 129
Pembrey, Carmarthenshire, 33, 77, 86, 114, 146, 240, 285, 311
Pembroke, 116, 117
Pembrokeshire, 24, 30, 50, 65, 67, 71, 72, 78, 91, 92, 93, 113, 123, 132, 150, 151, 157, 167, 195, 197, 201, 232, 234, 240, 275, 286
 Church of England in, 21, 31–2, 33–5, 41
 circulating schools in, 131, 134–6
 Dissent in, 52
 exhorters in, 76, 77, 81, 87, 88, 103, 104, 134, 156, 291, 296
 gentry in, 155, 159, 161, 173
 nature of, 1–3
 language in, 3, 30, 31, 33, 186
 population of, 2, 185
 societies in, 5, 74, 76, 115, 116, 117, 146, 188, 206, 229, 230, 231, 251, 252–3, 266, 269, 310, 312
 SPCK's influence, 127–9
Pen-boyr, Carmarthenshire, 36–7, 40
Penbryn, Cardiganshire, 2, 151, 253
 societies of, 133, 163, 309
Pencarreg, Carmarthenshire, 45, 49, 83, 168
Pendine, Carmarthenshire, 30
Penry, John, 24
Persecution, 228, 232, 276–81, 295–6
 by gentry, 229, 284–6
 by JPs, 118, 281–3
 in north Wales, 70, 284
 in towns, 118, 285, 286
Philipps, Erasmus, 45

345

Phillips, James, 34
Philipps, John, 127
Philipps, Sir John, 36, 48, 127, 130
Philipps, Thomas, 36–7, 38, 127, 129, 279
Philipps family, Picton Castle (Pembrokeshire), 173
pietism, 281
Powell, John, 46, 69, 70
Powell, Samuel, 206
Powell, Vavasor, 50
Powell, William (of Glanareth), 44–5
Poyer, Catherine, 83, 159, 161–2
preaching
  appeal of, 65–6, 88, 184, 216, 225
  in Church of England, 34, 40, 42, 48, 129
  field preaching, 72–3, 95, 280
  itinerant preaching, 50, 52, 66–7, 70, 113, 282, 292–3
  message of Methodist preaching, 181–4, 185–6
  Methodist terms for, 71
  response to, 187–9, 253, 256, 286, 306
  by women, 207–8, 210, 211–13
Presbyterian Church of Wales, 5, 7, 10
Price, Grace (of Watford), 208
Price, Thomas (of Llandeilo Abercywyn), 77
Price, Thomas (of Watford), 95, 283, 284
Price, William (of Caeo), 39, 46
Price, William (of Llan-non), 45, 49
Pri Price family of Pigeonsford, Cardiganshire, 286–7
chard, Rees, 50, 193
print
  and the Calvinistic Methodist movement in Wales, 9, 10, 199, 216, 306
  and Dissent, 51, 54, 125
  growth of print culture in Wales, 14, 54, 129, 136
  importance of Carmarthen, 117, 305
  and Welsh Bible, 24, 29, 127, 133
Providence, 92, 114, 284, 294–5
Pugh, Catherine, 159, 209

Pugh, John, 151, 153
Pugh, Philip, 53, 54, 168, 183, 228, 272
Pum Pregeth (1772), by Daniel Rowland, 172
Puritans, 22, 52, 54, 128, 185, 280, 292, 305

Quakers. *See* Society of Friends

Radnorshire, 21, 73, 97, 102, 126, 160, 278
  Welsh language in, 31
Rebecca riots, 2
Rees, Anthony, 41, 67, 133–4, 151, 167, 170, 288
Rees, David, 151, 171–2
Rees, Thomas (19th-century historian), 13, 14
Rees, Thomas (of Llandybïe), 41
Rees, Thomas (of Meidrim), 38
Reformation, Protestant
  as slow process, 14, 16, 125
  in Wales, 10, 21, 22, 293
Revivals
  beginnings in Wales, 3, 53, 54, 125, 131, 216, 272, 305
  historiography of, 9, 10–16, 194
  international dimensions of, 16
  Llangeitho revival of 1762, 10–11, 192, 214, 256, 271, 307
  relationship with revival in England, 3–4, 15, 198–9
  in Scotland, 10
Reynold, Evan Rees, 251
Rhad Ras, by John Thomas, 8–9, 241
Rhiwiau (Llanddeusant), 66, 144, 153, 182
Rhydlewis, Cardiganshire, 310
Rhydwilym Baptist Church, 52, 53
Rhys, Dafydd William, 95
Rhys, Ifan Thomas, 290
Rhys, Morgan, 133, 151, 152, 168, 169, 171–2, 192, 202, 209
Richard, Evan, 151, 167
Richard, John, 5, 67, 74, 76, 77, 79, 82, 87, 88, 90, 115, 144, 240, 250–1, 266, 281, 304, 309–11
  as craftsman, 85, 86, 167–8, 289

death and will, 64, 85, 151, 167–8
and Howel Harris, 103, 269
and hymns, 295
and persecution, 89, 285
Richard, Thomas, 151, 166, 167, 172
Richard, William, 5, 74, 76, 81, 86, 88, 92, 115, 146, 148, 188, 191, 196, 202, 211, 227, 229, 230, 233, 234, 236, 237, 245, 251, 256, 266, 309–12
  death and elegy, 64, 84, 203, 204
  and persecution, 280, 284, 303
  sided with Daniel Rowland, 103, 104
Roberts, Revd Gomer M., 14, 84, 171
Roberts, John, 10
Roberts, William, 289, 292
Roman Catholicism, 134, 150, 231, 282
  Methodists likened to, 280–1
  numbers of, 22, 51
Rowland, Daniel, 15, 69, 70, 204, 206, 256, 307
  and chapels of ease, 122–4, 164
  character, 101
  and Church, 23, 37–8, 277–8
  and communion, 66, 122, 123, 124, 198
  and discipline, 243–4
  and division, 304
  and doctrine of assurance, 270–1
  and enthusiasm, 194
  financial status, 83, 169
  and Griffith Jones, 132
  and Harris, 64, 93–6, 101–2, 243, 269, 271, 273
  influence of, 5, 63, 64–6, 100, 103–4, 114–15, 123, 155
  as leader of Welsh Calvinistic Methodism, 101–2, 305
  limited sources relating to, 8, 12
  and marriage, 83
  and opposition, 210, 276, 284, 286, 290
  ordination and early ministry, 63–4, 65
  sermon and preaching, 3, 65–6, 72, 132, 152, 155, 166, 171, 172, 183–5, 276
  and societies, 78, 114–15, 197
  and travel, 65–6, 114, 116
  will, 151
  and William Williams, 70, 93, 102, 278
  writes hymns, 192
Rowland, Nathaniel, 65, 158, 159, 169

Sabellianism, 102
Sail, Dibenion a Rheolau,'r Societies (1742), 226, 228, 231
St Asaph diocese, 21, 26, 28, 29, 40, 46, 55
St Davids diocese, 3, 21, 22, 24, 113, 12, 149, 150, 160, 162, 277–8
  bishops, 24–9, 55–6, 71, 95, 277
  clergy, 35–50
  Dissent in 50–5
  libraries, 127–8
  Welsh language in, 29–35
St David's, Pembrokeshire, 21, 31
  society of, 74, 76, 77, 87, 115, 146, 165, 227, 284, 312
St Kennox (Llawhaden), Pembrokeshire, 41, 81
Samuel, Christmas, 53, 273
Saunders, Erasmus, 24, 35, 36, 38, 50, 113, 122, 181
schools, 39, 72
  Carmarthen Grammar School, 40, 70, 125, 126
  charity, 29, 126, 168, 169
  dancing, 39, 251
  Griffith Jones's circulating, 13, 40, 56, 122, 125, 130–6, 152, 170, 171, 197, 201, 305
  SPCK, 126–7, 128–9
  Sunday, 306
  Welsh Trust, 128
Scotland, 10, 15, 304
Sermons. *See* preaching
Seward, William, 72
  death of, 286
smuggling, 252–3
Society for Promoting Christian Knowledge (SPCK), 126–9, 281
  Bibles, 29, 133
society houses, 72, 121–2, 124, 133, 152, 164
Society of Friends, 47, 246

Society of Sea Sergeants, 281
Smallbrooke, Richard, bishop of St Davids, 26, 29
south-west Wales
  nature of area and people, 1–3, 5, 30, 40, 50, 113–14, 117–18, 147, 181, 187, 193, 198, 201, 252–3, 305
Sparks, John, 72, 81, 103, 202
Spufford, Margaret, 149
Stedman, Anne, 155
Stedman, Richard, 283, 284, 287
Stepney, Sir Thomas, 124
stewards of societies, 63, 67, 152, 170, 197, 202, 225, 242, 245, 303
  duties, 73, 76, 233–9, 240, 243
  terminology used, 234
Strata Florida, Cardiganshire, 103, 158, 283
superintendents of societies, 5, 309
  circuits, 52, 73, 74, 76, 82, 87, 115, 230
  reports, 8, 116, 143, 195, 197, 204, 208, 239, 266
  responsibilities, 68, 76, 77, 79, 82–3, 143, 197, 199, 202, 225, 227, 234, 243, 245, 246–7, 255–6, 303
  social and economic status, 83–5
Swift, Wesley, 207
Sydall, Elias, bishop of St Davids, 26

Tadau Methodistaidd (1895), *Y*, by J. M. Jones and W. Morgan, 94
Taith y Pererin (*Pilgrim's Progress*, by John Bunyan), 54
Talgarth, Breconshire, 7, 64
Talley, Carmarthenshire, 33, 36, 39–40, 45, 121, 151, 152, 153, 163, 169, 202, 203
  society of, 39–40, 77, 146, 168, 169, 195, 229, 268, 311
Tan-yr-allt (Tregaron), society, 75, 78, 198, 207, 257, 310
Teifi
  river, 2, 53, 114, 115, 123, 183, 185, 312
  valley, 119, 179
Tenison, Edward, archdeacon of Carmarthen, 30, 33, 36, 37, 39, 40, 42, 46, 50, 52, 53, 126, 186

Tenison, Thomas, archbishop of Canterbury, 26
Theologia Cambrensis (2018), by D. Densil Morgan, 14
Theomemphus (1764), by William Williams, 235
Thirlwell, Connop, bishop of St Davids, 28
Thomas, Elizabeth (of Blaen-porth), 83, 211–13, 275, 303
Thomas, Elizabeth (of Longhouse), 159, 160
Thomas, Godfrey, 151, 171
Thomas, James, 40, 45, 49
Thomas, John (of Llandysul, Cardiganshire), 37
Thomas, John (of Longhouse, Pembrokeshire), 151, 162, 166, 167
Thomas, John (of Rhaeadr, Radnorshire), 8, 64, 144, 182, 183, 186, 192, 241
Thomas, John (of Tre-main, Cardiganshire), 9, 104, 134, 184, 191, 231, 251
Thomas, Joshua, 65, 66, 125
Thomas, Philip, 46, 69, 70
Thomas, Thomas, 127, 129
Thomas, William, 45, 50
Thomas, William (of Michaelston-super-Ely), 66, 102
Thomas, William, bishop of St Davids, 28, 36
Thomas family (Longhouse), 151, 159–60, 162, 166, 167, 199, 241
Thompson, E. P., 15, 251
Tibbott, Richard, 54, 64, 95, 101, 114, 121, 165, 183, 188, 194, 196, 200, 209, 210–11, 213, 215, 230, 233, 237, 246
  and Griffith Jones, 86, 133
  diaries of, 8, 70, 75, 191
  and persecution, 89, 285, 295–6
  turned to Dissent, 8, 275
Tilsley, John, 279
tithe, 21, 24, 36, 37, 47–8, 164
Toleration Act (1689), 22, 51, 55, 274, 283

Towns
  and persecution, 284, 285–6
  in south-west, 3, 30, 33, 53, 117–20, 147
Tre-lech (a'r Betws), Carmarthenshire, 33, 50, 151, 184, 251
  society of, 133, 206, 229, 256, 311
Tre-main, Cardiganshire, 9, 104, 134, 184, 191, 231, 251
Trefeca, Breconshire
  association meetings at, 74, 75, 98, 233
  college at, 7
  Howel Harris's home, 83, 91, 99, 100, 195, 285
  religious community at, 7, 103
  spelling of, 17
Trefin, Pembrokeshire, 229
Tregaron, Cardiganshire, 5, 32, 64, 78, 114, 135, 183, 198, 257, 309, 310
Trevecka group of manuscripts, 5–8, 17, 66
Trevor, Richard, bishop of St Davids, 26, 37, 124, 277, 278
Trinity, doctrine of, 70, 101, 102, 227
Trysorfa Ysprydol (periodical), 11, 12, 306
Tudur, Geraint, 94, 189, 270
Tŵr-gwyn, Rhydlewis, Cardiganshire, 150, 153, 200
  association meetings at, 132
  chapel at, 153, 164
  society of, 146, 234, 274, 310
Tywi
  river, 2, 74, 76, 91, 114, 162
  valley, 117

Unitarianism, 53–4

Valenze, Deborah M., 207–8
Vaughan, John (of Derllys, Carmarthenshire), 127, 131
Vaughan family (of Golden Grove, Carmarthenshire), 139, 173
Vaughan family (of Trecŵn, Pembrokeshire), 32
View of the State of Religion in the Diocese of St. Davids (1721), *A*, by Erasmus Saunders, 24

Ward, W. R., 16
Watford, Glamorgan, associations at, 68, 71, 73, 74, 114, 133
Watkins, Watkin, 151, 152, 156, 157, 166, 170, 172, 191, 234–5
Watson, Richard, bishop of Llandaff, 27
Watson, Thomas, bishop of St Davids, 26
Waun-y-groes, Carmarthenshire, 116–17, 311
Weekly History (periodical), *The*, 197, 199
Welch Piety, 130, 134
Welsh language, 13, 14
  and Anglican Church in Wales, 22, 24, 25, 28–35, 55
  and education, 128–30
  strength of, 2–3
  use by Welsh Methodism, 9, 186–7, 305
Welsh Trust, 128–9
Wernos, Y, Breconshire, 114
Wesley, Charles, 155, 161, 186
Wesley, John, 114, 158, 165, 253, 270, 280
Wesley, Sarah, 155, 160
Wesleyan Methodism, 3, 4, 15–16, 96, 207, 211, 225, 236, 265, 287
White, Elizabeth, 83
Whitefield, Elizabeth, 100, 210
Whitefield, George, 9, 16, 69, 72, 87, 90, 93, 104, 165, 194, 199, 230, 271, 278, 290, 292
  allied to Welsh Methodists, 3, 68, 74
  and Howel Harris, 95, 100, 210
  preaching in Wales, 70, 72, 88, 187
  works by, 91, 190, 226, 236
Whitgift, John, Archbishop of Canterbury, 24
Willes, Edward, bishop of St Davids, 26, 33
William, Thomas, 75, 88, 95, 101
Williams, Anne. *See* Anne Harris
Williams, Catherine, 163
Williams, David, (of Llanfynydd), 134
Williams, David (of Pwll-y-pant), 68, 272–3
Williams, Glanmor, 14, 16, 55, 125
Williams, Gwyn A., 9
Williams, James, 5, 64, 74, 76, 77, 79, 115, 122, 144, 146, 196, 198, 229,

230, 237, 239–40, 242, 246, 269–70, 274, 275, 294, 296, 304, 309–11
death and will, 84, 150, 166, 167
and persecution, 285
support for Daniel Rowland, 103
Williams, John (of Bwlchgwynt), 154
Williams, John (of Cilcarw), 164, 197
Williams, John, (the elder of Llwynyberllan), 149, 150, 151, 153–4, 157–8, 166, 167
Williams, John (the younger of Llwynyberllan and Henllys), 149, 152, 157–8, 159, 161, 167, 172
Wiliams, John Phillips (of Bwlchgwynt), 176
Williams, Moses, 34, 40
Williams, Nathaniel, 103, 158
Williams, Sir Nicholas, 163
Williams, Peter, 157, 164
  as author and editor, 70, 307
  early life and career in Church, 70, 125, 132
  expulsion for heresy, 70
  influence of, 3, 63
  and persecution, 284
  preaching by, 99, 122
Williams, Rice, 153–4
Williams, Samuel, 34, 40, 45
Williams, William ('Pantycelyn'), 3, 8, 12, 15, 69, 70, 145, 148, 153, 164, 231, 254, 292–3, 307
  as assistant to D. Rowland, 70, 73, 93, 278
  and chapels of ease, 123, 124, 277
  and church courts, 69, 278
  conversion and ordination, 64, 69, 278
  as curate, 38, 69, 157
  and discipline, 243–5, 247, 251
  and Dissent, 53
  and education, 72, 126
  elegies, 152–3, 171, 203–4, 208–9
  financial status, 83, 167, 168
  and Harris, 95, 103, 184, 269, 270, 273
  as historian of revival, 10–11, 14, 54, 94, 304

hymns, 192–3, 213, 214, 271
influence, 63, 93, 104, 269
and marriage, 83, 248
and opposition, 276, 282, 286
poetry, 235
prose works, 184, 188–9, 190, 191–2, 198, 214, 228, 235, 241, 246–50, 256–7, 273, 276
and Rowland, 65, 95, 102, 183, 270
and societies, 78, 114, 123, 184, 190, 191, 195–6, 198, 234, 235, 236–7, 238, 239, 240, 245–6, 257
as superintendent of societies, 5, 8, 75, 76, 196
and travel, 90
will, 83, 152, 167, 169
and women, 146, 207, 208–9, 214–15, 248
Williams family of Glangwenlais, Carmarthenshire, 166
Wilson, Linda, 208
Winckler, Johann Joseph, 287
Woman as Good as the Man, or the Equality of Both Sexes (1677), *The*, by Poulain de la Barre, 248
Women, 13, 149, 291–2
  and hymns, 187–8, 213–14
  and marriage, 247–51
  as members, 16, 145–7, 173, 206–17, 230, 257
  and preaching, 210, 211–13
Woodward, Josiah, 105, 189–90, 232
Word to a Smuggler (1767), by John Wesley, 253
Wynne family of Foelas, Denbighshire, 99
Wynne, John, bishop of St Asaph, 28

Ymddiddan rhwng Methodist uniawngred ac un camsyniol (1750), by Daniel Rowland, 102
Ystrad-ffin, Carmarthenshire, 65, 114, 144, 152, 183, 196, 230, 282
  chapel of ease, 43, 123, 133, 195
  society, 116, 118, 120, 198, 311